SPEAKING SPANISH

in the U.S.A.

Variations in Vocabulary Usage

Alberto Barugel, Ph.D.

BARRON'S

DEDICATION

I dedicate this book to my wonderful wife, Julia,
whose boundless patience, understanding, and sense of humor
helped to make this task the enjoyable adventure that it was.

© Copyright 2005 by Barron's Educational Series, Inc.

All inquiries should be addressed to:
Barron's Educational Series, Inc.
250 Wireless Boulevard
Hauppauge, New York 11788
http://www.barronseduc.com

Library of Congress Catalog Card No. 2004050247

International Standard Book No. 0-7641-2953-8

Library of Congress Cataloging-in-Publication Data
Barugel, Alberto, 1951–
    Speaking Spanish in the USA. Variations in vocabulary usage / Alberto Barugel.
        p. cm.
    ISBN 0-7641-2953-8 (alk. paper)
    1. Spanish language—Errors of usage. I. Title.

PC4460.B293   2005
468.2'421—dc22   2004050247

PRINTED IN THE UNITED STATES OF AMERICA
9 8 7 6 5 4 3 2 1

CONTENTS

INTRODUCTION / iv

ENTRIES / 1

EXERCISES / 292

ENGLISH-SPANISH GLOSSARY AND INDEX / 314

INTRODUCTION

The influence of English in the Spanish we speak everyday is inescapable. I don't know of one bilingual Spanish speaker living in the United States who does not occasionally use an English cognate or anglicism in conversation, in place of a more "traditional" or "universal" Spanish term. While the debate rages among scholars and linguists as to what is and what is not appropriate usage, U.S. Spanish speakers have been creating and utilizing their own manner of expression for at least a hundred years.

A bit of history
The tendency to sprinkle the Spanish language with words borrowed or adapted from English began to gain momentum in the United States around the mid-nineteenth century, with the seizure of the southwestern territories from Mexico. In the century and a half that followed, successive waves of migration from all corners of Latin America were instrumental in shaping what many consider to be a developing U.S. Spanish dialect. While some celebrate a new language called Spanglish, others warn of the impending deterioration of traditional Spanish. Whichever perspective one espouses, the unrelenting influence of English on the Spanish spoken and written in the United States is real and unlikely to fade.

The impact of English
United States Spanish results from the persistent contact of traditional Spanish with American English, a language replete with multiple meanings and connotations of the same word. One of the effects of this collision of languages has been a lexical reduction in U.S. Spanish. Let us take, for example, the verb "to hear," commonly translated as **oír**. Its primary meaning both in English and standard Spanish is "to perceive a sound or voice." However, this verb also occurs routinely in English to mean "discover," "receive news," and "understand." As might be expected, U.S. Spanish imitates secondary as well as primary English usage and applies all four connotations to the verb **oír**. Standard academic Spanish, on the other hand, tends to distinguish according to context, and produces four different verbs:

American English	U.S. Spanish	Standard Spanish
1. Did you **hear** a scream?	¿**Oíste** un grito?	¿**Oíste** un grito?
2. I **heard** he arrived late.	**Oí** que llegó tarde.	**Me enteré de** que llegó tarde.
3. Have you **heard** from Ana?	¿**Has oído** de Ana?	¿**Tienes noticias** de Ana?
4. I **hear** what you're saying.	**Oigo** lo que dices.	**Entiendo** lo que dices.

Aside from lexical imitation and reduction, U.S. Spanish is characterized by word-for-word translations and extensive use of false cognates (**déjame saber** for "let me know," **tocar base** for "to touch base," **librería** for "library," **sensitivo** for "sensitive," and so on).

Another growing trend, perhaps more universal, is the adoption of English words, often but not always rendered phonetically: **esprey, estrés, suéter, tique, tránsfer, weekend, zum,** just to name a few. Many of these borrowed words are subsequently adapted to Spanish morphology: **accesar, estresado, chequear, parquear.**

Research base

For about fifteen years now, I have been documenting the use of anglicisms in the writing of my English-Spanish bilingual students. The entries in this book represent 650 of the most frequently used words and expressions among the thousands I have collected.

As I compiled and organized the data before me, I observed the following patterns:

- Despite my best efforts to teach and promote the use of a traditional form of Spanish, the percentage of anglicisms in my students' writing had increased over the years.
- Spanish-dominant speakers were only slightly less inclined to use anglicisms than English-dominant bilingual speakers.
- My attitude toward anglicized Spanish had evolved to become more liberal over time.

In short, what had been increasingly apparent to me in my daily interactions with Spanish speakers of many different backgrounds was clearly supported by my findings: the progressive and persistent anglicization of Spanish—and my eventual acceptance of it.

A series of surveys and questionnaires, administered to college-level students over a two-year period provided me with some additional facts, not entirely unexpected:

- The occurrence of anglicisms among native speakers of Spanish increased in tandem with the number of years spent in the United States.
- Older informants were more resistant to adopting anglicisms than younger informants.
- 90% of those surveyed were surprised *and* unhappy to discover the degree to which English was impacting on their Spanish.

Content and purpose

The principal objective of this book is to list and illustrate over 2000 uses of 650 words and expressions commonly used by Spanish-English bilingual speakers in the United States. Each entry is translated and explained within the context of U.S. Spanish, as spoken and written in our northeastern states, and contrasted with its more traditional variants in standard academic Spanish, as upheld by institutions such as the *Real Academia Española de la Lengua* (RAE).

The debate about what is correct and incorrect Spanish will not be settled here, as that is not the purpose of this book. My intention is to reflect actual Spanish usage in the United States by placing it within the larger context of traditional Spanish. This comprehensive approach allows the user to become familiar with Spanish on two separate tracks: one, authorized and sanctioned by tradition and history, widely regarded as "mainstream Spanish"; the other, flowing and evolving within the United States, and gradually gaining acceptance as a legitimate dialect. For the sake of conciseness, I refer to the former as "Standard Spanish" and to the latter as "U.S. Spanish."

Because its purpose is not to confirm or deny the validity of a particular form of expression, this book will be seen through a variety of lenses. Some will consider much of what I call "US usage" simply as "incorrect Spanish." Others might rejoice in seeing their way of speaking reflected and reinforced. Some will be interested to learn new words and expressions that are typical of United States Spanish. Others will use the book as a tool for strengthening their knowledge of academic Spanish.

Format

This book focuses on lexical rather than grammatical usage, and is written in the form of a dictionary. It lists, in alphabetical order, 650 Spanish words and expressions influenced by English to a greater or lesser degree. Based on my research, they are among the most common anglicisms occurring in U.S. Spanish.

Next to each entry, two sets of English definitions are generally provided. The first set represents standard Spanish usage. The second denotes U.S. usage that either deviates from or complements standard usage. In the case of loanwords and lexical adaptations sanctioned by the Real Academia, we provide their year of introduction into the lexicon of the *Diccionario de la Real Academia Española* (DRAE).

Many entries are followed by an explanation and/or clarification of usage in the form of a brief paragraph. This explanation may contain, as needed, some of the most current DRAE definitions. For each entry definition, I provide sample phrases and sentences in both English and Spanish to illustrate standard usage, where it exists, followed by extended usage documented in the United States. Illustrations of U.S. usage are followed by one or more examples of "standard variants," i.e., academic Spanish counterparts of U.S. Spanish phrases. On certain occasions, when a standard variant is itself a term borrowed from English, one or more traditional variants are also presented.

Finally, it should be noted that adjectives such as "academic," "conventional," "historical," and "traditional" are used throughout the book to refer alternately to what I call "standard" Spanish.

Words included

This is not a prescriptive manual of standard Spanish, nor is it a manual about Spanglish, which is a hybridization of English and Spanish, and can be a language unto itself. It is, on the other hand, a descriptive guide that reflects how Spanish is spoken and written in the United States. The words and expressions contained herein do not represent marginal usage but rather a vocabulary increasingly common among native and bilingual speakers of Spanish. The fact remains that many terms once regarded as Spanglish have become mainstream in U.S. Spanish even among proficient and highly-educated speakers.

For the most part, U.S. Spanish does not create new words as much as it extends or expands the meaning of traditional words and expressions. Thus, "Extended US usage" refers to the innovative use of cognates, loanwords, and loan translations that is such an integral part of this form of expression.

The entries in this book fall into one or more of the following categories:

(1) *False cognates*—Traditional Spanish words that look like English words but have different meanings in standard usage. <u>Ex</u>: **actual, aviso, carpeta, constipado, embarazada, machear**.
    Many of these false cognates have essentially become "true cognates" in U.S. Spanish.
(2) *Extended cognates*—Spanish words that resemble English words, and often have similar primary meanings, but whose usage in the United States extends beyond the traditional norm. <u>Ex</u>: **admitir, aplicación, atender, audiencia, balance, carácter, correcto, posición**.
(3) *Loanwords*—Spanish words borrowed directly from English and usually pronounced as in English. <u>Ex</u>: **baby-sitter, barbecue, day care, full time, hobby, manager, parking**.

(4) **Adapted words**—Spanish words created or adapted from English, and rendered phonetically in Spanish. _Ex_: **beicon, bisnes, chequear, esnob, estrés, marqueta, mitin**.

(5) **Loan translations**—Spanish words and expressions that do **not** resemble their English counterparts but are in common use as a result of word-for-word translations. _Ex_: **cercano** (close), **dejar saber** (to let someone know), **ganar peso** (to gain weight), **perro caliente** (hot dog), **ratón** (computer mouse), **tocar base** (to touch base), **tomar efecto** (to take effect).

Words not included

Certain popular anglicisms have been excluded from this book for a variety of reasons, including broad universal usage, technical nature, and colloquial usage. They generally fall under the following categories:

(1) English loanwords that are native to the culture of the United States and have no equivalent in traditional Spanish. These expressions tend to be used internationally. _Ex_: **béisbol, blues, jazz, jet set, rock and roll**.

(2) American brand names commonly used to refer to the products they are associated with: _Ex_: **band-aid, coca-cola, frigider, jello, klínex, pámper**.

(3) Technical terms used exclusively in the context of sports: _Ex_: **básquet, bateador, jonrón, pítcher, straik**.

(4) Words and constructions generally associated with slang or informal speech: _Ex_: **el rufo está liqueando** (the roof is leaking).

Features

Perhaps the most important feature of this book is that it is based on actual usage observed and recorded over many years. In that sense, it is an accurate reflection of the Spanish practiced in our region, and a reasonable representation of the Spanish spoken in the United States.

This is a multi-purpose text. It could serve as a supplement in a Spanish language curriculum at the intermediate and advanced levels, particularly in courses that involve speaking, writing, translation, and bilingualism. It also has all the elements of a self-help manual, including 20 pages of exercises for self-testing.

Another feature of this book is its nonjudgmental approach. Without condemning the use of "Spanglish" as a means of expression, the explanations and examples point out the principal differences between standard Spanish terms and popular U.S. Spanish equivalents.

The entries take into account regional variants from Spain and Latin America and are up-to-date. The distinction between "anglicisms" and "americanisms" is made clear, either in the explanation sections or within the examples themselves. Where there is a fine line between the two, traditional options are provided. This kind of versatility is a reflection of the _Real Academia Española_'s mounting tendency in recent years to sanction and incorporate anglicisms into its own lexicon.

The dilemma of standardization

One of the challenges faced by language students, not to mention linguists and lexicographers, is in dealing with the inconsistencies that arise when words are borrowed and adapted from one language to another, and the multiple forms that result. Spanish is no exception.

If we accept the premise that a language evolves continually, we may begin to understand the struggle that language educators and students face as they strive to somehow regulate or fix an "appropriate" form of expression. This struggle could not be more clearly illustrated than by examining some of the discrepancies that exist within the *Real Academia Española* itself.

As the guardian of the Spanish language, the RAE has been historically late in sanctioning new words. For example, whereas the Spanish philologist Joan Corominas documents the use of **champú** as early as 1908, this term does not appear in the DRAE until 1927. The same occurs with **eslogan**—documented by Corominas in 1940, but not listed in the DRAE until 1984. The RAE has also been known to reverse itself. Dozens, if not hundreds, of anglicisms appeared in the 1985 and 1989 editions of its dictionary—words such as **status**, **tipear**, **twist**, **weekend**, **yanqui**—only to be removed from the 1992 edition. Some re-surfaced in 2001 in different forms: **starter**, for example, became **estárter**. In effect, the issue of anglicized versus hispanicized forms is far from settled, as illustrated by the following lists of loanwords, all currently listed in the DRAE:

Hispanicized spelling	Spelled as in English
básquetbol	airbag
bisnes	baby-sitter
champú	best-seller
escáner	ketchup
esnob	full time
estándar	hardware
estrés	look
líder	lunch
magacín	manager
mitin	output
interviú	spray
póquer	stock

Oftentimes, the issue is never resolved, and two or more forms are allowed: **nailon** and **nilón**, **bacón** and **beicon**, **güisqui** and **whisky**. Interestingly, there are occasions when the extremes somehow converge and academic Spanish coincides with Spanglish. For example, whereas the Moliner and Vox dictionaries list **status**, both Spanglish proponent Ilan Stavans and the DRAE prefer **estatus**.

In light of these unresolved issues, no attempt has been made to standardize spelling in this book. For standard Spanish terms sanctioned by the RAE, the most current form is given. With respect to words that are unique to U.S. Spanish, the spelling used is that found to be most prevalent among bilingual speakers in the United States, according to the author's findings.

Who can benefit from this book

- **Bilingual speakers of Spanish and English** who live, work, and study in the United States, particularly those who are English-dominant. Their Spanish tends to be heavily influenced by English. Many are looking to formalize their skills so as to improve their chances in the international job market.

- **Bilingual Spanish-speaking professionals** engaged in areas such as business and industry, government, education, social services, health care, law enforcement, military service, translation and interpretation.
- **Spanish teachers** may use this text as a reference tool to determine the status of a particular anglicism: its present usage within standard academic Spanish as opposed to U.S. Spanish; its inclusion or exclusion in major dictionaries; and its current standing vis-à-vis the *Real Academia.*
- **Spanish language learners**. Because its entries tend to be common words and expressions, and because the explanations are in English, this book could be beneficial to those who study Spanish as a second language. Spanish learners are primarily taught academic Spanish, and are rarely exposed to dialectal U.S. Spanish, which is what they are most likely to hear outside of the classroom.
- **Spanish-dominant bilingual speakers**. Finally, this book can help Spanish-dominant speakers as well. As they gain proficiency in English, these individuals inevitably experience the same interlinguistic challenges as their English-dominant counterparts.

Self-help manual and course supplement

It is difficult to establish a difficulty level for this text since most of its entries can occur at any stage of language learning. In terms of classroom text, it would be a useful supplement in intermediate and advanced level classes, ranging from middle school grades through high school and college. It could serve as a primary or secondary text in college-level courses that focus on Spanish grammar, translation, or composition, as well as career-oriented courses such as Business Spanish and Spanish for the Service Professions. It would certainly be an essential component in a course for bilingual or native speakers of Spanish. Equally important is its usefulness as a reference text or self-help manual.

References used

Every effort has been made to integrate authentic cultural content into sample phrases and expressions. Linguistic variants, including regionalisms, are taken into account to a great extent. A number of highly regarded dictionaries have been consulted, including the *Diccionario de la Real Academia Española* (2001), Joan Corominas's *Diccionario etimológico de la lengua castellana* (2000), the *Larousse Gran Diccionario Usual de la Lengua Española* (2003), María Moliner's *Diccionario de uso del español* (2000), the *Vox Diccionario de uso del español de América y España* (2004), the *HarperCollins Unabridged Spanish-English Dictionary* (2000), the *New Oxford American Dictionary* (2001), and *Webster's New Universal Unabridged Dictionary* (2003). Finally, Ilan Stavan's latest book, *Spanglish: The Making of a New American Language* (2003) proved to be extremely useful as a comprehensive and up-to-date reference of U.S. Spanish usage.

Abbreviations used

adj	adjective
adv	adverb
comp	computer term
Corom	*Diccionario etimológico de la lengua castellana* (2000)
DRAE	*Diccionario de la Real Academia Española,* 21st ed. (2001)
excl	exclamation
fem	feminine
Harper	*HarperCollins Unabridged Spanish-English Dictionary* (2000)
intrans	intransitive verb
Lat Am	Term or expression used predominantly in Latin America
ling	linguistics
masc	masculine
med	medical term
Moliner	*Diccionario de uso del español* (2001)
prep	preposition
RAE	*Real Academia Española de la Lengua*
Sp	Term or expression used predominantly in Spain
Stavans	*Spanglish: The Making of a New American Language* (2003)
trans	transitive verb
US	Term or expression used predominantly in the United States
Vox	*Vox—Diccionario de uso del español de América y España* (2004)

ABIERTO (adj) = **open; open-minded; outgoing**
  = **vacant; available [US]**

- Abierto expresses "available, vacant" in U.S. Spanish when "open" is translated literally.
- In standard Spanish, disponible and vacante are more viable options.

Standard usage

1. open (=ajar):	*The door is open.*	La puerta está abierta.
2. open for business:	*The museum is open.*	El museo está abierto.
3. open to participants:	*an open contest*	un concurso abierto
4. open (=outgoing):	*an outgoing person*	una persona abierta
5. open-minded:	*an open mentality*	una mentalidad abierta
6. open (=direct):	*It was a direct attack.*	Fue un ataque abierto.

Extended US usage

7. open (=available, vacant):	*The position for vice president remains open.*	El puesto de vicepresidente queda **abierto**.
	Standard variants →	El puesto de vicepresidente queda **vacante** / **disponible**.

ACCESAR (verb) = **adapted from "to access" [US]**

- Used increasingly in the context of technology, accesar responds to the need for a Spanish verb meaning "to access."
- One of many loanwords categorized by Ilan Stavans[1] as "cyber-Spanglish."
- Both Moliner[2] and the DRAE[3] list acceso and accesible but not accesar.

US usage

1. to access (on computer):	*I was not able to access my file.*	No he podido **accesar** mi archivo.
	Standard variant →	No he podido **conseguir acceso** a mi archivo.

---

[1]Ilan Stavans, *Spanglish: The Making of a New American Language,* HarperCollins, 2003.
[2]Maria Moliner, *Diccionario de uso del español* (2nd edition), Gredos, 2000.
[3]*Diccionario de la Real Academia Española* (22nd edition), 2001.

ACTUAL (adj) = **current, present; topical; modern**
= **actual [US]**

ACTUALMENTE (adv) = **currently, at present; nowadays**
= **actually [US]**

actual. adj. Dicho del tiempo en que está alguien: presente. *[=current, presentl]* [DRAE]
adj. De ahora, moderno, lo que está de moda. *[=current, modern]* [Moliner]

actualmente. adv. En el tiempo presente. *[=currently, at present]* [DRAE]
adv. En el tiempo en que se está viviendo mientras se habla. [Moliner]

- A common false cognate, **actual** traditionally means "current," not "actual."
- "Actually" is expressed in standard Spanish with **en realidad, realmente, es que**.

Standard usage		
1. *current, present:*	*the current political situation*	la situación política actual
2. *topical, contemporary:*	*We discussed topical themes.*	Discutimos temas actuales.
3. *modern, fashionable:*	*It's a very modern style.*	Es una moda muy actual.
4. *currently, at present:*	*Presently I'm not working.*	Actualmente no trabajo.
5. *nowadays:*	*Nowadays people live better.*	Actualmente se vive mejor.

Extended US usage		
6. *actual, real:*	*That man is the actual father.*	Aquél es el padre **actual**.
	Standard variant →	Aquél es el **verdadero** padre.
7. *actually, in reality:*	*Actually I don't understand.*	**Actualmente** no entiendo.
	Standard variants →	**Realmente** no entiendo.
		En realidad no entiendo.
		Es que no entiendo.

ACTUAR (verb) = **to act: perform a function**
= **to act: behave**
= **to act: work, affect, take effect**
= **to act (in a particular film or play)**
= **to act: perform in general**
= **to act: pretend, make believe [US]**
= **to act: take action [US]**
= **to act the part [US]**
= **to act as, take the place of [US]**

- **Actuar** turns up in U.S. Spanish well beyond its traditional meaning, influenced by the multiple uses of the English verb "to act."

Standard usage

1. *to act (=perform a particular function):*	*I will act as representative.*	Actuaré como representante.
2. *to act (=behave):*	*He acted very strangely.*	Actuó de manera muy rara.
3. *to act (=work, affect):*	*This medicine acts on the nervous system.*	Esta medicina actúa sobre el sistema nervioso.
4. *to act (in a film or play):*	*She acted well in her last movie.*	Actuó bien en la última película que hizo.

Extended US usage

5. *to act (=perform in general):*	*I did some theatre acting many years ago.*	**Actué en el** teatro hace muchos años.
	Standard variant →	**Hice** teatro hace muchos años.
6. *to act the part (=play the role):*	*He acted the part of the son.*	**Actuó la parte** del hijo.
	Standard variant →	**Hizo el papel** del hijo.
7. *to act (=pretend):*	*He acted sick in order to stay home from school.*	**Actuó** enfermo para no ir a la escuela.
	Standard variant →	**Se fingió** enfermo ...
8. *to act (=take action):*	*We will act to help the needy.*	**Actuaremos** para ayudar a los necesitados.
	Standard variants →	**Obraremos / tomaremos medidas** para ayudar ...
9. *to act as (=take the place of):*	*She was acting as president.*	**Actuaba** de presidenta.
	Standard variant →	**Hacía** de presidenta.

ADICIONAL (adj)	=	**additional (cost, expense, task)**
	=	**additional (people) [US]**
	=	**additional: supplementary [US]**

- Extended cognate in U.S. Spanish by influence of "additional" in English.
- In standard Spanish, **adicional** suggests "added" rather than "another" or "more."
- Traditional variants include **más**, **suplementario**, **extra**.

Standard usage

1. *additional cost:*	*There will be an additional cost.*	Habrá un gasto adicional.
2. *additional task, duty:*	*He took on an additional task.*	Asumió un cargo adicional.

Extended US usage		
3. *additional people:*	*I have one additional student.*	Tengo un alumno **adicional**.
	Standard variants →	Tengo un alumno **más** *(more)*. ... un alumno **de más** *(extra)*.
4. *additional (=supplementary):*	*I received an additional book.*	Recibí un libro **adicional**.
	Standard variants →	Recibí un libro **de más / extra**. Recibí un libro **suplementario**.

ADMISIÓN (fem noun) = **admission: acceptance, recognition**
                  = **admission: entry [US]**
                  = **admission: confession [US]**

ADMITIR (verb) = **to admit; let in**
             = **to accept; recognize**
             = **to allow, permit, tolerate**
             = **to admit (to a program, an institution, etc.) [US]**

- Generally speaking, **admisión** and **admitir** are cognates of their English counterparts.
- In U.S. Spanish, their use is expanded to include "entry" and "confession."

Standard usage		
1. *to admit (=let in):*	*This club only admits singles.*	Este club sólo admite solteros.
2. *to accept, take:*	*They take credit cards.*	Se admiten tarjetas de crédito.
3. *to admit (=recognize):*	*He admitted his error.*	Admitió su error.

4. *to allow, tolerate:*	*That kind of behavior cannot be
	   allowed.*
		Esa clase de comportamiento
		   no se puede admitir.

Extended US usage		
5. *to admit to a program, school, institution, etc.:*	*The university admitted her.*	La universidad la **admitió**.
	Standard variant →	La universidad la **aceptó**.
6. *to be admitted to a school, institution, etc:*	*I was admitted to the hospital.*	**Fui admitido** al hospital.
	Standard variant →	**Ingresé en** el hospital.
7. *admission (=entry):*	*Admission to the club is free.*	La **admisión** al club es gratis.
	Standard variant →	La **entrada** al club es gratis.
8. *admission (=confession):*	*admission of guilt*	**admisión** de culpabilidad
	Standard variant →	**confesión** de culpabilidad

AFECCIÓN (fem noun)
= **inclination, penchant**
= **disease, trouble, complaint**
= **affection: esteem; fondness, love [US]**

- In U.S. usage, **afección** is an extended cognate of "affection," meaning "love, fondness."
- In that instance, standard Spanish prefers **afecto**, **amor**, **cariño**.

Standard usage		
1. *inclination, penchant:*	*He has a penchant for languages.*	Tiene afección a los idiomas.
2. *disease, trouble (med):*	*lung disease / heart trouble*	afección pulmonar / cardíaca

Extended US usage		
3. *affection (=esteem):*	*I feel great affection for my professor.*	Siento gran **afección** por mi profesor.
	Standard variant →	Siento gran **afecto** por mi profesor.
4. *affection (=fondness, love, tenderness):*	*He shows a lot of affection to his children.*	Les demuestra mucha **afección** a sus hijos.
	Standard variants →	Les demuestra mucho **cariño** / **amor** a sus hijos.

AFLUENTE (adj)
= **flowing, swelling (water, liquid)**
= **fluent, eloquent, fluid**
= **affluent, rich [US]**

- In standard usage, **afluente** means "flowing," referring to liquid or speech.
- In U.S. Spanish it occurs as a cognate of "affluent" meaning "wealthy."

Standard usage		
1. *flowing, swelling (liquid):*	*majestic mountains and flowing rivers*	montes majestuosos y ríos afluentes
2. *fluent, eloquent:*	*eloquent words*	afluentes palabras

Extended US usage		
3. *affluent, rich:*	*She is from an affluent family.*	Es de una familia **afluente**.
	Standard variants →	Es de una familia **adinerada** / **rica** / **acaudalada**.

AIRBAG (masc noun)   =   **loanword for "(automobile) air bag"** [DRAE 2001]

- Recently sanctioned by the RAE, **airbag** has come to be an international term in Spanish.
- The more traditional **bolsa de aire** is still in force in many places.

Standard/US usage		
1. *airbag:*	*Thanks to the airbag he suffered only minor injuries.*	Gracias al **airbag** sólo sufrió leves heridas.
	Traditional variant →	Gracias a la **bolsa de aire** ...

ALREDEDOR (DE) (adv & prep)   =   **around: surrounding**
  =   **around: approximately**
  =   **around: near; through** [US]
  =   **around: everywhere** [US]

- In standard Spanish, **alrededor (de)** denotes "surrounding" or "approximate quantity."
- In U.S. Spanish, it can also refer to physical approximation or a nonspecific area, influenced by similar usage of "around" in English.

Standard usage		
1. *around (=surrounding):*	*They formed a circle around the candidate.*	Formaron un círculo alrededor del candidato.
2. *around (=approximately):*	*I have around 80 CDs.*	Tengo alrededor de 80 discos.

Extended US usage		
3. *around (=near, next to):*	*Do you live around here?*	¿Vives **alrededor de** aquí?
	Standard variants →	¿Vives **cerca de** aquí? ¿Vives **por** aquí?
4. *around (=through):*	*I walked around the museum.*	Caminé **alrededor** del museo.
	Standard variant →	Caminé **por** el museo.
5. *around (=everywhere):*	*Look around before you go in.*	Mira **alrededor** antes de entrar.
	Standard variant →	Mira **por todas partes** antes de entrar.

AMBICIÓN (fem noun)   =   **ambition: greed, ruthlessness**
                           =   **ambition: longing, desire, aspiration [US]**

AMBICIOSO (adj)   =   **ambitious: greedy, ruthless**
                       =   **ambitious: eager, industrious [US]**

- Because **ambición** tends to have a negative connotation in standard Spanish, the more traditional rendering of "ambition" is **aspiración**, **deseo**, or **anhelo**.
- U.S Spanish mirrors English in that **ambición** can have a positive or negative intent.

Standard usage		
1. ambition (=greed):	*Napoleon's ambition was to conquer all of Europe.*	La **ambición** de Napoleón era conquistar toda Europa.
2. ambitious (=greedy):	*Don't be so ambitious!*	¡No seas tan ambicioso!

Extended US usage		
3. ambition (=longing, desire, aspiration):	*Her lifelong ambition was to become a lawyer.*	La **ambición** de su vida era hacerse abogada.
	Standard variants →	La **aspiración** / el **anhelo** / el **deseo** de su vida ...
4. ambitious (=eager, industrious):	*Because he is very ambitious, he'll complete the project.*	Por ser muy **ambicioso**, completará el proyecto.
	Standard variants →	Por ser muy **trabajador** / muy **ávido**, completará el proyecto.

ANCIANO (adj & noun)   =   **old, aged; elderly person**
                            =   **ancient [US]**

> anciano, -a. adj. y n. Aplicado sólo a personas, viejo. [Moliner]

- Regarded as a false cognate, **anciano** refers to an elderly person in standard usage.
- In U.S. Spanish, it also occurs as an adjective for "ancient."

Standard usage		
1. old, aged (adj):	*My grandfather is a very old man.*	Mi abuelo es un señor muy anciano.
2. elderly person (noun):	*The elderly need our help.*	Los ancianos necesitan nuestra ayuda.

Extended US usage		
3. ancient (=old, classical):	*He doesn't like ancient history.*	No le gusta la historia **anciana**.
	Standard variant →	No le gusta la historia **antigua**.
4. ancient (object):	*They discovered an ancient artifact.*	Descubrieron un artefacto **anciano**.
	Standard variants →	Descubrieron un artefacto **muy antiguo** / **antiquísimo**.

AÑADIR (verb) = **to add: join, increase, attach**
= **to add: say further**
= **to add: calculate numbers [US]**

- **Añadir** is employed in standard Spanish to mean "add" or "increase" in general terms.
- When adding numbers, the traditional choices are **sumar** and, less commonly, **adicionar**.

Standard usage		
1. to add (=join, increase):	*You can add sugar to it.*	Le puedes añadir azúcar.
	We added a name to the list.	Añadimos un nombre a la lista.
2. to add (=say further):	*I have a lot to add to what you just said.*	Tengo mucho que añadir a lo que acabas de decir.

Extended US usage		
3. to add (=calculate):	*My son is learning to add (in math).*	Mi hijo está aprendiendo a **añadir** (en matemáticas).
	Standard variants →	Mi hijo está aprendiendo a **sumar** / **adicionar** ...

APARECER (verb) = **to appear: arrive, present oneself**
= **to appear: be found, turn up**
= **to appear on TV, on stage, in public [US]**
= **to appear in court [US]**
= **to appear: be published [US]**
= **to appear: seem [US]**

- U.S. Spanish usage of **aparecer** generally coincides with English usage of "to appear."
- In the context of "public appearance" (TV, stage, marketplace, etc.), the traditional choice is **salir**, which conveys the idea of "going out to the public."
- As synonym of "to seem," "appear" is rendered as **parecer** in standard practice.

Standard usage

1. to appear (=arrive):	*He would appear in class from time to time.*	Aparecía en clase de vez en cuando.
2. to appear (=be found):	*My wallet has not appeared anywhere.*	Mi cartera no ha aparecido en ninguna parte.

Extended US usage

3. to appear (on TV, on stage, in public):	*She appeared on television last night.*	**Apareció** en la televisión anoche.
	Standard variants →	**Salió** en la televisión anoche. **Salió por** televisión anoche.
4. to appear (in court):	*You will have to appear before the judge.*	Tendrás que **aparecer** ante el juez.
	Standard variant →	Tendrás que **comparecer** ante el juez.
5. to appear (=be published):	*The first part of* Don Quixote *appeared in 1605.*	La primera parte del *Quijote* **apareció** en 1605.
	Standard variants →	La primera parte del *Quijote* **salió / se publicó** en 1605.
6. to appear (=seem):	*They appear very happy.*	**Aparecen** muy felices.
	Standard variant →	**Parecen** muy felices.

APARIENCIA (fem noun) = **appearance: look, countenance**
 = **appearance: aspect, demeanor [US]**
 = **appearance: coming into view [US]**

- **Apariencia** and **aspecto** are synonyms when concerned with "external look / demeanor."
- In standard Spanish, **aspecto** is more telling of the character or essence of a person or object, whereas **apariencia** refers mainly to that which is observed superficially.
- In the United States, by influence of English, **apariencia** covers a multitude of meanings.

Standard usage

1. appearance (=look):	*This fruit has the appearance of a small orange.*	Esta fruta tiene la apariencia de una pequeña naranja.
2. appearances (external):	*Don't be fooled by appearances.*	No te dejes engañar por las apariencias.

Extended US usage

3. appearance (=coming into view, showing oneself):	His appearance at the meeting surprised us all.	Su **apariencia** en la reunión nos sorprendió a todos.
	Standard variants →	Su **aparición** / su **presencia** en la reunión nos sorprendió ...
4. appearance (on TV, in film, theater):	It will be her first appearance on stage.	Será su primera **apariencia** en el escenario.
	Standard variants →	Será su primera **actuación** / **aparición** en el escenario.
5. appearance (in court):	I made several appearances before the judge.	Hice varias **apariencias** ante la justicia.
	Standard variant →	Hice varias **comparecencias** ante la justicia.
6. appearance (=aspect, look):	He was saved by his innocent appearance.	Lo que lo salvó fue su **apariencia** de inocente.
	Standard variant →	... su **aspecto** de inocente.

APLICACIÓN (fem noun)

= **application: use**
= **application: implementation**
= **request, application form [US]**

- One of the most frequently used cognates among U.S. Spanish speakers, **aplicación** is not sanctioned by the RAE nor by Moliner to refer to "request" or "form."
- Some traditional alternatives for "application form" are **solicitud**, **formulario**, **planilla**.

Standard usage

1. application (=use):	application of an ointment	aplicación de una crema
2. implementation:	application of an ancient law	la aplicación de una antigua ley
3. application (computers):	application program	programa de aplicaciones

Extended US usage

4. application (=request):	an application for funds	una **aplicación para** fondos
	Standard variant →	una **solicitud de** fondos
5. application form:	to fill out an application	llenar una **aplicación**
	Standard variants →	llenar una **solicitud** llenar un **formulario**

APLICAR (verb)

= **to apply: administer**
= **to apply: put into practice**
= **to apply for (a job, etc.); apply to [US]**
= **to apply: be relevant [US]**

- In standard usage, you may **aplicar** an ointment on your skin or **aplicar** the rules of grammar, but you may not **aplicar** for a job. That would be **solicitar**.
- In U.S. Spanish **aplicar para un trabajo** is quite common and increasingly frequent.

Standard usage		
1. *to apply (=administer):*	*to apply on the skin*	aplicar sobre la piel
2. *to apply (=put to use):*	*I applied everything I learned.*	Apliqué todo lo que aprendí.

Extended US usage		
3. *to apply for (=request):*	*I'm going to apply for the job.*	Voy a **aplicar para** el puesto.
	Standard variants →	Voy a **solicitar** / **pedir** el puesto.
4. *to apply to someone:*	*You should apply to the director.*	Debes **aplicar** al director.
	Standard variants →	Debes **presentarte** / **dirigirte** al director.
5. *to apply (=be relevant):*	*This law doesn't apply to me.*	Esta ley no **(se) aplica** a mí.
	Standard variants →	Esta ley no **me afecta** / no **tiene que ver conmigo**.

APOLOGÍA (fem noun)

= **justification, defense; praise, eulogy**
= **apology, regret [US]**

- In standard usage, **apología** is not an expression of regret, but rather an official or legal statement in defense of an individual or an idea and, by extension, a declaration of praise.

Standard usage		
1. *justification, defense:*	*an apology for terrorism*	una apología del terrorismo
2. *praise; eulogy:*	*an apology of his achievements*	una apología de sus logros

Extended US usage		
3. *expression of regret:*	*a letter of apology*	una carta de **apología**
	Standard variant →	una carta de **disculpa**
4. *admission of error:*	*They didn't accept his apology.*	No aceptaron su **apología**.
	Standard variant →	No aceptaron su **excusa**.

APRECIAR (verb)

= **to appreciate: be fond of, value**
= **to appreciate: notice, perceive**
= **to appreciate: give thanks for [US]**
= **to appreciate: understand [US]**

- In standard Spanish there are slight but significant differences in meaning between **apreciar** and **agradecer** (see examples below).
- In U.S. Spanish, these verbs are often interchangeable.
- **Apreciar** also occurs in the United States as a synonym of **entender**.

Standard usage		
1. *to appreciate (=be fond of):*	*She appreciates her mother.*	Ella aprecia a su mamá.
2. *to appreciate (=value):*	*I appreciate your friendship.*	Aprecio tu amistad.
3. *to notice, perceive:*	*He can appreciate a good wine.*	Sabe apreciar un buen vino.

Extended US usage		
4. *to give thanks for:*	*We appreciated her help.*	Le **apreciamos** su ayuda.
	Standard variant →	Le **agradecimos** su ayuda.
5. *to understand:*	*I appreciate what you're saying.*	**Aprecio** lo que dices.
	Standard variant →	**Entiendo** lo que dices.

ARGUMENTO (masc noun)

= **plot, storyline**
= **argument: reasoning**
= **argument: disagreement, quarrel [US]**

- **Argumento** primarily means "plot, storyline" in standard usage.
- It is extended in U.S. Spanish to refer to "quarrel" or "disagreement."

Standard usage		
1. *plot, storyline:*	*the plot of a novel*	el argumento de una novela
2. *argument (=reasoning):*	*a very rational argument.*	un argumento muy racional

Extended US usage		
3. *argument (=disagreement):*	*There is no room for argument.*	No hay lugar para **argumentos**.
	Standard variant →	No hay lugar para **discusiones**.
4. *argument (=debate):*	*the argument about abortion*	el **argumento** sobre el aborto
	Standard variant →	la **polémica** sobre el aborto
5. *argument (=quarrel):*	*They had a terrible argument.*	Tuvieron un **argumento** terrible.
	Standard variants →	Tuvieron una **discusión** terrible. **Se pelearon / se disputaron**.

ASISTENTA (fem noun) = **maid, housekeeper; servant (in religious order)**
                          = **worker (in service profession)**
                          = **assistant (fem) [US]**

ASISTENTE (masc noun) = **servant, aide (military, religious order)**
                            = **assistant (masc) [US]**

- Historically, both terms have a religious and/or military connotation.
- In more modern contexts, they simply translate as "worker" (e.g., **asistente social**).
- In U.S. Spanish, both are synonymous with "assistant," as used in English in various situations.

Standard usage

1. maid, housekeeper:	The housekeeper takes care of the children.	La asistenta se ocupa de los niños.
2. military aide:	The general consulted with his aides.	El general consultó con sus asistentes.
3. worker (service prof):	My sister is a social worker.	Mi hermana es asistenta social.

Extended US usage

4. assistant, helper:	Do you need an assistant?	¿Te hace falta un **asistente**?
	Standard variant →	¿Te hace falta un **ayudante**?
5. assistant (= deputy, associate, subordinate):	assistant director	director **asistente**
	assistant professor	profesor **asistente**
	Standard variants →	**sub**director
		profesor agregado

ASISTIR (verb) = **to attend, go**
                   = **to assist: help people**
                   = **to witness, be present at**
                   = **to help to do something [US]**

- The most common meaning of **asistir** is "to attend, be present."
- Of the nine denotations listed in the DRAE, five are related to the English cognate "to assist" (= to accompany, help, serve, care for).
- In U.S. Spanish, **asistir** is often confused with **atender** [see **atender**].

Standard usage

1. to attend, go:	I didn't attend class yesterday.	No asistí a clase ayer.
2. to assist, help people:	She helps the immigrants.	Ella asiste a los inmigrantes.
3. to witness:	We witnessed an accident.	Asistimos a un accidente.

Extended US usage		
4. to help to do something:	*Can you help me lift this?*	¿Me **asistes** a levantar esto?
	Standard variant →	¿Me **ayudas** a levantar esto?

ATACHMEN (masc noun) = **adapted from "attachment" [US]**

• Another expression classified by Ilan Stavans as "cyber-Spanglish," it seems to be preferred by bilingual speakers in the United States to the more traditional **adjunto**.

US usage		
1. attachment (computers):	*I sent you an attachment.*	Te envié un **atachmen**.
	Standard variant →	Te envié un **archivo adjunto**.

ATENDENCIA (fem noun) = **adapted from attendance [US]**

• Used very selectively in standard Spanish to mean "attention."
• U.S. Spanish equates **atendencia** with "attendance."

US usage		
1. attendance (=presence):	*We appreciate your attendance at this important event.*	Agradecemos su **atendencia** en este evento tan importante.
	Standard variant →	Agradecemos su **presencia** ...
2. attendance (=number of people present):	*The attendance at yesterday's game was more than 50,000.*	La **atendencia** en el partido de ayer fue más de 50.000.
	Standard variant →	**Asistieron** más de 50.000 personas al partido de ayer.

ATENDER (verb) = **to attend to: serve**
= **to look after, care for, take care of**
= **to attend: be present [US]**

• The dominance of cognates is evident in U.S. Spanish, where **asistir** is more likely to mean "to assist" (= to help), and **atender**, "to attend" (= to be present).
• In standard practice, the exact opposite would normally hold true.

Standard usage		
1. to attend to (=serve):	*Please attend to the customer.*	Favor de atender al cliente.
2. to look after, care for:	*Who will look after the children?*	¿Quién atenderá a los niños?

| **Extended US usage**
3. *to attend (=be present):* | *It's important to attend class.* | Es importante **atender** a clase. |
| | **Standard variant →** | Es importante **asistir** a clase. |

ATMÓSFERA (fem noun) = **atmosphere: air**
= **atmosphere: ambience, feeling [US]**

- **Atmósfera** refers primarily to the "air" that surrounds the earth and other planets.
- In U.S. Spanish, as in English, it is also used figuratively to mean "surroundings."
- Moliner allows it as a synonym of **ambiente**.

| **Standard usage**
1. *atmosphere (=air):* | *The space rocket crossed the atmosphere.* | El cohete espacial atravesó la atmósfera. |

| **Extended US usage**
2. *atmosphere (=feeling, ambience, surroundings):* | *I like the atmosphere in this restaurant.* | Me gusta la **atmósfera** en este restaurante. |
| | **Standard variant →** | Me gusta el **ambiente** en este restaurante. |

ATRÁS (adj & adv) = **behind; back, rear; backwards**
= **ago, back in time [Lat Am]**
= **back (n): reverse side [US]**
= **go back, come back, give back [US]**

- **Atrás** in U.S. Spanish often results from the literal translation of "back" (whether it be an adjective, adverb, or noun), as in **dar para atrás** ("to give back").

| **Standard usage**
1. *behind (adv):*
2. *back, rear (adj):*
3. *backwards (adv):* | *My mom remained behind.*
Did they check the rear brakes?
Please take a step backwards. | Mi mamá se quedó atrás.
¿Revisaron los frenos de atrás?
Favor de dar un paso atrás. |

| **Latin American usage**
4. *ago:* | *Twenty years ago …* | Veinte años **atrás** … |
| | **Traditional variant →** | **Hace** veinte años … |

Extended US usage		
5. *back (noun)* (=reverse side):	*You need to sign the back of the check.*	Tienes que firmar el **atrás** del cheque.
	Standard variants →	Tienes que firmar el **dorso** / el **revés** del cheque
6. *to go back, come back:*	*When are you coming back?*	¿Cuándo **vienes para atrás**?
	Standard variants →	¿Cuándo **regresas** / **vuelves**? ¿Cuándo **estarás de vuelta**?
7. *to give back:*	*Give it back to me.*	**Dámelo para atrás**.
	Standard variant →	**Devuélvemelo**.

"Back" expressions in standard Spanish		
	back and forth	de acá para allá
	back copy (of magazine, etc.)	número atrasado
	back cover (of book)	contraportada
	back door	puerta trasera
	back of chair	respaldo
	back of clothing (dress, coat)	espalda
	back of neck	nuca
	back of room (or large vehicle)	fondo
	back pay	atrasos
	back road	carretera secundaria
	back room	cuarto interior
	back seat	asiento trasero
	back tooth	muela
	backwards (back to front)	al revés

AUDIENCIA (fem noun) = **audience: interview; hearing**
= **audience of people, spectators, etc. [US]**

- Extended cognate of "audience" in U.S. Spanish.
- **Audiencia** does not typically refer to "spectators" or "listeners" in standard usage, although the Vox Dictionary[4] does list it as a primary definition.
- **Espectadores**, **oyentes**, **público** are more traditional alternatives for "audience."

Standard usage		
1. *audience (=interview):*	*an audience with the Pope*	una audiencia con el Papa
2. *hearing:*	*I attended a public hearing.*	Asistí a una audiencia pública.

[4]*Vox—Diccionario de uso del español de América y España*, McGraw-Hill, 2004.

Extended US usage		
3. audience (of people):	*The audience applauded.*	La **audiencia** aplaudió.
	Standard variants →	El **público** aplaudió.
	viewing audience:	Los **espectadores** aplaudieron.
	listening audience:	Los **oyentes** aplaudieron.

AVERAGE (adj & noun) = **loanword for "average" [US]**

- **Average** is borrowed directly from English but pronounced as in Spanish.
- It occurs in Latin American Spanish primarily in the context of sports.
- Traditional Spanish uses **medio** or **promedio** to express "average."

US usage		
1. average (noun):	*The average of my grades is B.*	El **average** de mis notas es B.
	Standard variant →	El **promedio** de mis notas...
2. average (adj):	*The average price is $100.*	El precio **average** es $100.
	Standard variant →	El precio **medio** es $100.

AVISAR (verb) = **to tell, inform, notify; call, send for**
  = **to warn, notify**
  = **to advise, counsel [US]**

- **Avisar** does not indicate "to advise" in standard Spanish but rather "to inform" or "notify."

Standard usage		
1. to tell, inform:	*Why didn't you tell me?*	¿Por qué no me avisaste?
2. to notify:	*Notify me when you arrive.*	Avísame cuando llegues.
3. to call, send for:	*You have to call the doctor.*	Tienes que avisar al médico.
4. to warn (=notify):	*I'm warning you that it's cold.*	Te aviso que hace frío.

Extended US usage		
5. to advise, counsel:	*What does your lawyer advise?*	¿Qué **avisa** tu abogado?
	Standard variant →	¿Qué **aconseja** tu abogado?

AVISO (masc noun) = **notice, notification; warning, alert**
= **advice, counsel [US]**

- **Aviso** is "advice" in academic Spanish only when it implies a warning of some kind.
- Otherwise, **consejo** is the traditional option.

Standard usage		
1. notice, notification:	*The notice mentions day and time.*	El aviso indica el día y la hora.
2. warning, alert:	*The alarm served as a warning.*	La alarma sirvió de aviso.

Extended US usage		
3. advice, counsel:	*My dad gave me good advice.*	Mi papá me dio buen **aviso**.
	Standard variant →	Mi papá me dio buen **consejo**.

BABY (noun) = **loanword for "baby, infant, newborn" [US]**

- Quite prevalent in U.S. Spanish, **baby** is pronounced exactly as in English.
- This word has not entered the RAE lexicon.

US usage		
1. baby: infant, newborn:	*What do you feed the baby?*	¿Qué le das de comer al **baby**?
	Standard variants →	¿Qué le das de comer al **bebé** / al **nene** / a la **criatura**?
2. baby (fig) (=creation):	*This project is my baby.*	Este proyecto es **mi baby**.
	Standard variant →	Este proyecto es **obra mía**.

"Baby" expressions in standard Spanish		
	baby boom	boom de natalidad
	baby boy / baby girl	nene / nena (niño / niña)
	baby carriage	cochecito de bebé
	baby face	cara de niño / de inocente
	baby food(s)	comida para bebés
	baby of the family	el benjamín / la benjamina
	baby talk	habla infantil
	baby tooth	diente de leche
	don't be such a baby!	¡No seas tan niño / niña!
	to have a baby (=give birth)	dar a luz

BABY-SITTER (noun)   =   **loanword for "babysitter"** [DRAE 2001]

• Interestingly, whereas baby is not listed in the DRAE (nor in Moliner), baby-sitter is:

baby-sitter. *(Voz inglesa).* Persona que atiende a los niños pequeños. [DRAE]

Standard/US usage		
1. babysitter:	*I need a babysitter for tonight.*	Necesito un baby-sitter para esta noche
	Traditional variants →	Necesito un canguro *(Spain)* / una niñera *(Lat Am)* / alguien que me cuide al niño.

BACKGROUND (masc noun)   =   **loanword for "background"** [US]

• Pronounced as in English, this term occurs increasingly in the United States despite the existence of a viable counterpart, trasfondo, in traditional Spanish.
• As currently used, background has broader applications than either fondo or trasfondo.

US usage		
1. background (spatial):	*yellow flowers on a blue background*	flores amarillas sobre un background azul
	Standard variant →	flores amarillas sobre un fondo azul
2. background (=away from the limelight):	*He prefers to remain in the background.*	Prefiere mantenerse en el background.
	Standard variant →	Prefiere mantenerse en segundo plano.
3. background (=previous experience, education, etc.):	*What is her intellectual background?*	¿Cúal es su background intelectual?
	Standard variant →	¿Cúal es su formación intelectual?
4. background (=preceding events):	*It's important to understand the historical background.*	Es importante entender el background histórico.
	Standard variants →	... el trasfondo histórico / los antecedentes históricos.

"Background" idioms in standard Spanish	background check	investigación personal
	background information	datos personales / históricos
	background music	música de fondo
	background noise	ruido de fondo
	background reading	lecturas preparatorias

BACKPACK (masc noun) = **loanword for "backpack" [US]**

backpack. (inglés) m. Mochila, bolsa que se lleva a la espalda. [Moliner]

• Used increasingly in U.S. Spanish, backpack is not listed in the DRAE.

U.S. usage

1. backpack:

	My son carries his books in a backpack.	Mi hijo lleva sus libros en un backpack.
	Traditional variant →	Mi hijo lleva sus libros en una mochila.

BACÓN (masc noun) See **BEICON**

BAGAJE (masc noun)
 = **baggage: military equipment & supplies**
 = **background, knowledge, experience**
 = **luggage [US]**

• A synonym of equipaje, the more figurative bagaje occurs in standard Spanish primarily in a military context, or as a figure of speech for "background" or "experience."
• In U.S. Spanish, equipaje and bagaje are used interchangeably to mean "luggage."

Standard usage

1. equipment (military): They stored the equipment in a safe place. — Almacenaron el bagaje en un lugar seguro.

2. background, experience: The artist's cultural background is reflected in his paintings. — El bagaje cultural del artista se refleja en sus cuadros.

Extended US usage

3. baggage, luggage: How much baggage do you need for the trip? — ¿Cuánto bagaje necesitas para el viaje?

Standard variant → ¿Cuánto equipaje necesitas para el viaje?

"Baggage" expressions in standard Spanish	baggage allowance	límite de equipaje
	baggage car	furgón de equipaje
	baggage check	registro de equipaje
	baggage claim	recogida de equipaje
	baggage handler	despachador de equipaje

BAGEL (masc noun) = **loanword for "bagel" [US]**

• Pronounced as in English, bagel has no conclusive translation in traditional Spanish.

US usage

1. bagel:	I would like a toasted bagel with cream cheese.	Me gustaría un bagel tostado con queso crema.
	Standard variants →	Me gustaría un bollo / un rosco tostado con queso crema.

BALANCE (masc noun)
= **balance (commercial); toll, result**
= **assessment, evaluation (with hacer)**
= **balance: equilibrium; scale [US]**
= **balance: remainder [US]**

• Balance occurs in U.S. Spanish with the same variety of usage as it does in English.
• In standard Spanish, "physical balance" is more likely expressed with equilibrio.

Standard usage

1. balance (commercial):	the balance of payments	el balance de pagos
2. toll, result:	the death toll	el balance de víctimas
3. assessment, evaluation:	We evaluated his talent.	Hicimos balance de su talento.

Extended US usage

4. balance (=equilibrium):	She lost her balance and fell.	Perdió el balance y se cayó.
	Standard variant →	Perdió el equilibrio y se cayó.
5. balance (=harmony):	There needs to be a balance between work and play.	Hace falta un balance entre trabajo y diversión.
	Standard variant →	Hace falta un equilibrio entre trabajo y diversión.
6. balance (=scale):	The balance indicates 500 lbs.	El balance indica 500 libras.
	Standard variant →	La balanza indica 500 libras.
7. balance (=remainder):	You have a balance of $1000.	Tienes un balance de $1000.
	Standard variant →	Tienes un saldo de $1000.

BALANCEADO / BALANCEAR(SE)

"Balance" expressions in standard Spanish	balance beam	barra de equilibrio
	balance control (for sound)	control de balance
	balance of power	equilibrio de poder
	balance sheet	hoja de balance
	balance weight	contrapeso
	on balance	teniendo todo en cuenta
	out of balance (mechanism)	desequilibrado
	outstanding balance	saldo pendiente
	to hang in the balance	estar pendiente de un hilo

BALANCEADO (adj) = **balanced (meal, viewpoint, etc.) [US]**

BALANCEAR(SE) (verb) = **to swing, rock, roll**
= **to balance, balance oneself [US]**

- The only officially recognized form of **balancear** in standard Spanish is the reflexive **balancearse**, meaning "to rock" or "swing back and forth."
- In the U.S., **balancear** is common as a transitive verb (e.g., "to balance a checkbook").
- The adjective **balanceado**, adapted from "balanced," occurs mainly in U.S. Spanish.
- Depending on the context, traditional alternatives are **equilibrado**, **nivelado**, **cuadrado**.

Standard usage		
1. to swing, rock, roll:	He's swinging back and forth.	Se balancea de acá para allá.
Extended US usage		
2. to balance (=place in equilibrium):	Look how he balances the ball.	Mira como **balancea** la pelota.
	Standard variant →	Mira como **pone / mantiene** la pelota **en equilibrio**.
3. to balance oneself:	You can use the cane to balance yourself.	Puedes usar el bastón para **balancearte**.
	Standard variant →	...para **equilibrarte**.
4. to balance (=compare):	balance one thing with another	**balancear** una cosa con otra
	Standard variants →	**comparar / compensar** una cosa con otra
5. to balance (commercial):	to balance an account to balance the budget	**balancear** una cuenta **balancear** el presupuesto
	Standard variants →	**hacer cuadrar** una cuenta **nivelar** el presupuesto
6. balanced (meal, view...):	I follow a balanced diet.	Sigo una dieta **balanceada**.
	Standard variant →	Sigo una dieta **equilibrada**.

BANDA (fem noun)
= **gang, organized group**
= **band, strip, sash**
= **waveband, soundtrack**
= **sideline (in sport)**
= **musical band [US]**

- The DRAE gives two sets of meanings for banda, based on its double origin: "band" or "strip," stemming from old French; and "gang" or "group," of Germanic derivation.
- In U.S. Spanish, banda refers primarily to "music band."

Standard usage
1. *gang:*	*gang of thieves*	banda de ladrones
2. *organized group:*	*terrorist group*	banda terrorista
3. *band, strip, sash:*	*magnetic strip*	banda magnética
4. *waveband, soundtrack:*	*broad-band radio*	radio de banda ancha
5. *sideline (in sports):*	*out of play*	fuera de banda

Extended US usage
6. *music band* (=*orchestra*):	*My son plays in the university band.*	Mi hijo toca en la **banda** de la universidad.
	Standard variant →	Mi hijo toca en la **orquesta** de la universidad.
7. *music band* (=*small group*):	*They formed a small jazz band.*	Formaron una pequeña **banda** de jazz.
	Standard variants →	Formaron un pequeño **grupo** / **conjunto** de jazz.

BARBECUE (masc noun)
= **loanword for "barbecue" [US]**

- Seems to have gained preference in U.S. Spanish over the more conventional **barbacoa**, which has been part of the RAE lexicon since 1884.

US usage
1. *barbecue* (=*grill*):	*Put the meat on the barbecue.*	Pon la carne en el **barbecue**.
	Standard variant →	Pon la carne en la **parrilla**.
2. *barbecue* (=*food*):	*I prepared a shrimp barbecue.*	Preparé un **barbecue** de camarones.
	Standard variant →	Preparé una **parillada** de camarones.
3. *barbecue* (=*party*):	*We were invited to a barbecue.*	Nos invitaron a un **barbecue**.
	Standard variants →	Nos invitaron a una **barbacoa** / a una **parrillada**.

BARTENDER (masc noun) = **loanword for "bartender" [US]**

- Academic Spanish has adopted **barman** from English (DRAE 1983) but not **bartender**:

  barman. (inglés). m. Hombre que sirve en un bar de copas y, particularmente, el que prepara las combinaciones de bebidas. [Moliner]

US usage		
1. bartender:	*He works as a bartender on weekends.*	Trabaja de **bartender** los fines de semana.
	Standard variants →	Trabaja de **camarero** / **barman** los fines de semana.

BASE (fem noun)
= **base: bottom part; foundation**
= **base: background, grounding**
= **base: main ingredient**
= **basis, reason, justification**
= **military base**
= **base (in baseball) [US]**

- Aside from its many standard uses, **base** means "base" in the context of baseball. As such, it is also used figuratively in verbal idioms such as **tocar base** ("to touch base").

US usage		
1. to get to first base (fig):	*We didn't even get to first base.*	No llegamos ni siquiera a la primera **base**.
	Standard variant →	No cumplimos ni siquiera la primera **meta**.
2. to touch base (idiom):	*I need to touch base with him.*	Tengo que **tocar base** con él.
	Standard variant →	Tengo que **ponerme en contacto** con él.
3. to cover all bases (fig):	*It's impossible to cover all bases.*	Es imposible cubrir todas las **bases**.
	Standard variant →	Es imposible **abarcarlo todo**.
4. to be off base (idiom):	*His figures are completely off base.*	Sus datos están totalmente **fuera de base**.
	Standard variant →	Sus datos están totalmente **equivocados**.

BASEMENT (masc noun)   See BÉISMENT

BÁSQUETBOL (masc noun)   =   loanword for "basketball" [DRAE 1992]

- The RAE classifies básquetbol and its shortened form, básquet, as americanisms for baloncesto, the more traditional term in Spanish.

US usage

1. *basketball (=sport):*	*Do you like to watch basketball?*	¿Te gusta mirar el básquetbol?
	Standard variant →	¿Te gusta mirar el baloncesto?
2. *basketball (=ball):*	*We will buy a basketball.*	Compraremos un basketball.
	Standard variant →	Compraremos una pelota de baloncesto.
3. *basket (=score):*	*Did you score a basket?*	¿Metiste un básquet?
	Standard variant →	¿Metiste una canasta?

BATERÍA (fem noun)
=   **battery: artillery**
=   **battery: drums**
=   **battery (electrical): wet cell, auto**
=   **battery (electrical): dry cell [US]**
=   **battery: series [US]**
=   **battery: violent assault [US]**

- Of the 15 denotations in the DRAE for batería, the first five are associated with "artillery."
- Only one definition refers to a certain type of "wet cell," such as a "car battery."
- In U.S. Spanish, batería means any kind of battery, and can also indicate "assault."

Standard usage

1. *battery (=artillery):*	*battery fire*	fuego de batería
2. *battery (=drums):*	*Who plays drums?*	¿Quién toca batería?
3. *battery (wet cell):*	*I replaced the battery in my car.*	Le cambié la batería a mi carro.

Extended US usage

4. *battery (dry cell):*	*This radio takes AA batteries.*	Este radio lleva baterías de AA.
	Standard variant →	Este radio lleva pilas de AA.
5. *battery (=series):*	*a battery of questions*	una batería de preguntas
	Standard variant →	una serie de preguntas
6. *battery (=assault):*	*He was accused of battery.*	Lo acusaron de batería.
	Standard variants →	Lo acusaron de violencia / agresión / asalto.

BEICON (masc noun) = **adapted from "bacon"** [DRAE 1992]

- Whereas **bacón** is the more standard form, **beicon** is preferred in the United States.
- Both are listed in the DRAE and defined as **panceta ahumada**.

Standard/US usage		
1. *bacon:*	*I had bacon and eggs for breakfast this morning.*	Desayuné huevos con **beicon** / **bacón** esta mañana.
	Traditional variants →	Desayuné huevos con **tocino** / **panceta ahumada**...

BÉIGOL (masc noun)   see **BAGEL**

BÉISMENT (masc noun) = **adapted from "basement"** [US]

- The widespread use of this term to refer to a "living space underneath a family home" stems largely from its unique nature and function in the United States.
- U.S. Spanish tends to distinguish **béisment** from the traditional **sótano**, which denotes an underground area or passage not normally suited for habitation.

    sótano. (Del latín *subtulus*, de *subtus*, debajo). m. Pieza subterránea, a veces abovedada, entre los cimientos de un edificio. [DRAE]

- Alternate forms of **béisment** in U.S. Spanish include **beisman** and **beismen** [Stavans].
- None of these forms are approved by the RAE.

US usage		
1. *basement:*	*We put a pool table in the basement.*	Pusimos una mesa de billar en el **béisment**.
	Standard variant →	Pusimos una mesa de billar en el **sótano**.

BEST SELLER (masc noun) = **loanword for "best-seller"** [DRAE 2001]

- Now sanctioned by the RAE, this term is widely used in the Spanish-speaking world.

Standard/US usage		
1. *best-seller:*	*Her first novel became a best-seller.*	Su primera novela llegó a ser un **best seller**.
	Standard variant →	Su primera novela llegó a ser un **éxito de ventas**.

BICIAR (masc noun)   see **VCR**

BIPEAR (verb)   =   **adapted from "to beep" [US]**

- Nonexistent in academic Spanish, the emergence and popularity of this term in the United States and parts of Latin America is a result of the technology boom.

US usage		
1. to beep [trans] (=make a sound):	*The microwave just beeped.*	El microondas acaba de **bipear**.
	Standard variant →	El microondas acaba de **sonar**.
2. to beep [intrans] (=make a sound):	*to beep the horn*	**bipear** la bocina / el claxon
	Standard variant →	**tocar** la bocina / el claxon
3. to beep [trans] (=call on a beeper):	*You can beep me at any time of the day.*	Me puedes **bipear** a cualquier hora del día.
	Standard variants →	Me puedes **llamar** / **localizar** a cualquier hora del día.

BÍPER (masc noun)   =   **adapted from "beeper" [US]**

- Prevalent in U.S. Spanish, **bíper** is a universal term for the popular electronic device.

US usage		
1. beeper:	*Do you use a beeper or a cell phone?*	¿Utilizas un **bíper** o un teléfono celular?
	Standard variant →	¿Utilizas un **localizador** ...?

BISNES (masc noun)   =   **adapted from "business"** [DRAE 2001]

> **bisnes.** (Del inglés *business*). m. Negocio, actividad comercial, dinero. En América, u. t. en plural con el mismo significado que en singular. [DRAE]

- Not listed in the Moliner dictionary but recently approved by the RAE, **bisnes** occurs in the United States beyond its accepted usage, and is often used figuratively.
- The prevalence of this term in U.S. Spanish stems from its many applications in English.

Standard/US usage

1. business (=field): — *He decided to study business.* — Decidió estudiar **bisnes**.

Traditional variant → — Decidió estudiar **comercio**.

2. business (=enterprise): — *They just set up a business.* — Acaban de montar un **bisnes**.

Traditional variant → — Acaban de montar un **negocio**.

3. business (=profit, clients): — *The shop is losing business.* — La tienda va perdiendo **bisnes**.

Traditional variants → — La tienda va perdiendo **dinero** / **clientela**.

4. business (=firm): — *He owns a family business.* — Es dueño de un **bisnes** familiar.

Traditional variant → — Es dueño de una **empresa** ...

Extended US usage

5. business (=occupation): — *What business are you in?* — ¿En qué **bisnes** estás?

Standard variants → — ¿Cuál es tu **oficio** / **profesión**? ¿**A qué te dedicas**?

6. business (=task, duty, responsibility): — *It is my business to help you.* — **Es mi bisnes** ayudarte.

Standard variants → — **Me corresponde** ayudarte. **Tengo la responsabilidad** de ayudarte.

7. business (=affair, matter, issue): — *They're discussing the business about the budget.* — Están discutiendo el **bisnes** del presupuesto.

Standard variants → — Están discutiendo el **asunto** / el **tema** / la **cuestión** del ...

8. business (=right): — *You have no business going to his house.* — No tienes ningún **bisnes** de ir a su casa.

Standard variant → — No tienes ningún **derecho** a ir a su casa.

"Business" expressions in standard Spanish
Used as an adjective:

business administration	administración de empresas
business address	dirección profesional
business agent	agente de negocios
business associate	socio / asociado
business card	tarjeta de visita
business center	centro financiero / de negocios
business class (airline)	clase preferente
business consultant	asesor(a) de empresas
business deal	trato comercial
business district	zona comercial
business hours	horas de oficina / de negocio
business language	lenguaje comercial

	businessman / woman	hombre / mujer de negocios
	business manager	director de empresa / gerente
	business plan	plan de empresa / de negocios
	business suit	traje de oficina
	business trip	viaje de negocios
Used as a noun:	*business as usual*	sigue igual / no pasa nada
	it's my business (fig)	es cosa mía / asunto mío
	it's none of your business	no te importa / no te metas
	it's not my business	no tengo que ver con eso
	to be in the business of	tener por costumbre
	to do business with	negociar / hacer negocio con
	to get down to business	ir al grano
	to go out of business	quebrar / arruinarse
	to make it one's business to	encargarse de / ocuparse de
	to mean business	hablar en serio
	to mind one's business	no meterse

BIZARRO (adj) = **gallant, valiant, brave**
　　　　　　　　　= **bizarre [US]**

bizarro, rra. (Del italiano *bizzarro*, iracundo). 1. *adj.* valiente (esforzado). 2. *adj.* generoso, lucido, espléndido. [DRAE]

- By influence of English, "bizarre" is expressed in some circles with **bizar** or **bizarro**.
- Moliner justifies this use as of French influence.

Standard usage		
1. *valiant, brave:*	*The brave boy was not scared.*	El niño bizarro no sintió miedo.
Extended US usage **2.** *bizarre (=strange):*	*bizarre behavior*	comportamiento **bizarro** / **bizar**
	Standard variant →	comportamiento **extraño**

BLÍSTER (masc noun) = **loanword for "blister" [US]**

blíster. (Del inglés *blisterpack*). m. Tecnol. Envase para manufacturados pequeños que consiste en un soporte de cartón o cartulina sobre el que va pegada una lámina de plástico transparente con cavidades en las que se alojan los distintos artículos. [DRAE]

- **Blíster** received sanction by the RAE in 1992 as an abbreviation for "blisterpack."
- In U.S. Spanish it is used primarily to refer to a "blister" on the skin.

US usage		
1. *blister (on skin):*	*The burn caused a blister on my finger.*	La quemadura me produjo un **blíster** en el dedo.
	Standard variant →	La quemadura me produjo una **ampolla** en el dedo.
2. *blister (on paintwork):*	*This wall is covered with blisters.*	Esta pared está cubierta de **blísters**.
	Standard variant →	Esta pared está cubierta de **burbujas**.

BLOFEAR (verb) = loanword for "to bluff" [US]

- Non-existent in standard usage, **blofear** combines the notions of "deceive" and "pretend."
- In parts of Latin American, however, its more conventional meaning is "to boast."

Latin American usage		
1. *to boast, brag:*	*She likes to brag about her son.*	Le gusta **blofear** de su hijo.
	Traditional variant →	Le gusta **jactarse** de su hijo.

Extended US usage		
2. *to bluff (=deceive by pretending):*	*He made me think he had three aces but he was bluffing.*	Me hizo creer que tenía tres ases pero estaba **blofeando**.
	Standard variant →	... pero estaba **engañando**.
3. *to bluff (=pretend, make believe):*	*He bluffed that he was angry.*	**Blofeó** que estaba enojado.
	Standard variant →	**Hizo creer** que estaba enojado.

BLOQUE (masc noun)
= block (of stone)
= bloc: political group
= city block [US]
= block: series, section [US]

BLOQUEO (masc noun) = blockage, obstruction

- There are numerous regional variants in standard Spanish for "city block," but **cuadra** [Lat Am] and **manzana** [Spain] are the most popular.
- In the United States, however, **bloque** is more common.
- **Bloqueo** refers to "blockage" in both traditional and U.S. Spanish.

Standard usage

1. block *(of stone):*	*a beautiful block of marble*	un bonito bloque de mármol
2. bloc *(=political group):*	*the communist bloc*	el bloque comunista
3. blockage *(=obstruction):*	*There's a blockage at the exit.*	Hay un bloqueo en la salida.

Extended US usage

4. block *(group of buildings):*	*The house is two blocks away.*	La casa queda a dos **bloques**.
	Standard variants →	La casa queda a dos **cuadras** / a dos **manzanas**.
5. block *(=series, section):*	*a block of seats*	un **bloque** de asientos
	Standard variants →	un **grupo** de asientos una **sección** de asientos

BLUYINS (masc plural) = **loanword for "jeans" or "bluejeans" [US]**

- Rendered as **blue jeans** in Moliner and Vox, and often shortened to **jeans**, this loanword is not approved by the RAE, nor is it listed in most Spanish-English dictionaries.
- It is more prevalent in the United States than the traditional **vaqueros**.

US usage

1. jeans, denims:	*I like to wear jeans when I go out with friends.*	Me gusta llevar **bluyins** cuando salgo con amigos.
	Standard variant →	Me gusta llevar **vaqueros** ...

BOICOT (masc noun) = **loanword for "boycott" [DRAE 1927]**

BOICOTEAR (verb) = **adapted from "to boycott" [DRAE 1927]**

- Both terms are fully incorporated into academic Spanish, along with the variant **boicoteo**.

Standard/US usage

1. boycott:	*The union organized a boycott.*	El sindicato organizó un boicot / un boicoteo.
2. to boycott:	*They decided to boycott certain products.*	Decidieron boicotear ciertos productos.

BÓILER (masc noun) = **loanword for "boiler" [US]**

- Unrecognized in standard Spanish, **bóiler** is mentioned in the Vox Dictionary.
- Categorized by Stavans as a New York expression, he spells it **boila**, which reflects more accurately the regional English pronunciation.
- The closest traditional equivalent is **caldera**.

US usage		
1. boiler (for heating):	*We have had problems with the boiler.*	Hemos tenido problemas con el **bóiler**.
	Standard variant →	Hemos tenido problemas con la **caldera**.
2. boiler room:	*The repairman is down in the boiler room.*	El reparador está abajo en el **bóiler**.
	Standard variant →	El reparador está abajo en la **sala de calderas**.

BOOM (masc noun) = **loanword for "boom"** [DRAE 1983]

> **boom**. (Voz inglesa). m. Éxito o auge repentino de algo, especialmente de un libro. [DRAE]

- As a synonym for "sudden rise" or "success," **boom** became popular in the 1950s.
- In the United States, it often has additional applications, reflecting English usage.

Standard usage		
1. boom (=sudden success):	*the boom of the modern novel*	el boom de la novela moderna
2. boom (=rise, expansion):	*the tourist boom*	el boom turístico

Extended US usage		
3. boom (=noise):	*We heard a loud boom.*	Oímos un fuerte **boom**.
	Standard variants →	Oímos un fuerte **retumbo** / **estruendo** / **ruido**.
4. boom (of microphone):	*The boom should reach the podium.*	El **boom** debe alcanzar el podio.
	Standard variant →	La **jirafa** debe alcanzar el podio.

"Boom" expressions in standard Spanish	*boom conditions*	condiciones de prosperidad
	boom economy	economía de alza
	boom market	mercado de alza

BOSS (masc / fem noun) = **loanword for "boss" [US]**

- Used in U.S. Spanish to refer to an authority figure, usually an employer.
- Unsanctioned in standard Spanish, the closest traditional variants are **jefe** and **patrón**.
- A related verb form, **bosear** ("to boss around"), has become increasingly common.

US usage		
1. *boss (=employer):*	*The boss gave me the day off.*	El **boss** me dio el día libre.
	Standard variants →	El **jefe** (la **jefa**) / el **patrón** (la **patrona**) me dio el día libre.
2. *boss (=owner, manager):*	*He is the boss of a small company.*	Él es **boss** de una pequeña empresa.
	Standard variants →	Él es **dueño** / **gerente** ...
3. *boss (=authority, one who decides):*	*From now on, I'm the boss.*	De ahora en adelante, yo soy **el boss**.
	Standard variants →	De ahora en adelante, yo soy **quien manda** / **quien decide**.
4. *to boss around:*	*He constantly bosses me around.*	Me **bosea** constantemente.
	Standard variant →	Me **da órdenes** constantemente.

BREAK (masc noun) = **loanword for "break" [US]**

- Accepted by the RAE in 1927 to refer to a nineteenth-century four-wheel coach.
- Listed by Moliner in the context of "break point" (tennis) or "break dance."
- **Break** (pronounced as in English) occurs in U.S. Spanish mainly as a synonym of **descanso** ("rest period"), but also to express "chance, opportunity."

US usage		
1. *break (=pause, rest, vacation):*	*We always take a break at ten o'clock.*	Siempre tomamos un **break** a las diez.
	Standard variant →	Siempre tomamos un **descanso** a las diez.
2. *break (=chance, opportunity):*	*She got her first break at the age of ten.*	Tuvo su primer **break** a la edad de diez años.
	Standard variant →	Tuvo su primera **oportunidad** ...
3. *break (=discount):*	*They'll give us a break on the price if we buy two.*	Nos darán un **break** en el precio si compramos dos.
	Standard variant →	Nos harán un **descuento** ...

BUDGET (masc noun) = **loanword for "budget" [US]**

• Also spelled **buget** (Stavans), and pronounced either "bo-jet" or "boo-jet," this loanword occurs frequently in U.S. Spanish as an alternative to the traditional **presupuesto**.

US usage		
1. *budget:*	*The state budget has been reduced.*	Han reducido el **budget** estatal.
	Standard variant →	Han reducido el **presupuesto** ...

BYTE (masc noun) = **loanword for "byte"** [DRAE 2001]

> **byte.** (Voz inglesa). m. Inform. octeto (unidad de información). [DRAE]

• Pronounced as in English and classified by Stavans as "cyber-Spanglish," this term was incorporated very recently into academic Spanish as an alternative to **octeto**.

Standard/US usage		
1. *byte:*	*millions of bytes of information*	millones de **bytes** de información
	Standard variant →	millones de **octetos** de ...

CACHOP (masc noun) See **KETCHUP**

CALIENTE (adj)
= **hot, warm (to the touch & taste)**
= **turbulent, explosive**
= **hot: sexually stimulated**
= **hot, warm (weather, climate) [US]**
= **spicy hot; affectionate [US]**

• The most prevalent non-standard use of **caliente** in U.S. Spanish involves loan translations of "weather" idioms (e.g., **está caliente** for "it is hot"—rather than **hace calor**).
• It also occurs as a synonym of **picante** ("spicy").

Standard usage		
1. *hot (to the touch / taste):*	*The soup is very hot.*	La sopa está muy caliente.
2. *warm (touch / taste):*	*I like warm bread.*	Me gusta el pan caliente.
3. *turbulent, explosive:*	*The situation is very explosive.*	La situación está muy caliente.
4. *hot (sexually):*	*to be / become hot (horny)*	estar / ponerse caliente

Extended US usage

5. *hot, warm (weather):*	*It was a hot summer day.*	Era un **caliente** día de verano.
	The weather was very warm.	El tiempo **estaba muy caliente.**
	Don't you feel warm?	¿No **te sientes caliente?**
	Standard variants →	Era un día de verano **caluroso.**
		Hacía mucho calor.
		¿No **tienes calor?**
6. *hot, warm (climate):*	*Cuba has a warm climate.*	Cuba tiene un clima **caliente.**
	Standard variant →	Cuba tiene un clima **cálido.**
7. *hot (=spicy):*	*This is a hot (spicy) sauce.*	Esta salsa es **caliente.**
	Standard variant →	Esta salsa es **picante.**
8. *warm (=affectionate):*	*She's a very warm person.*	Es una persona muy **caliente.**
	Standard variant →	Es una persona muy **cariñosa.**

CALIFICACIÓN (fem noun)

= **grade, mark; rating**
= **description**
= **qualification: requisite, ability [US]**
= **qualification: diploma, title [US]**

- In standard usage, **calificación** is the action or result of **calificar** ("to describe; to grade").
- It has little to do with "ability" or "credentials," as it does in U.S. Spanish.

Standard usage

1. *grade, mark:*	*Your final grade is a B+.*	Tu calificación final es una B+.
2. *rating, standing:*	*a movie with an R rating*	una película de calificación R
3. *description:*	*He gave a brief description.*	Dio una calificación concisa.

Extended US usage

4. *qualification (=requisite):*	*qualifications for a job*	**calificaciones** para un puesto
	Standard variant →	**requisitos** para un puesto
5. *qualification (=ability):*	*qualifications to teach*	**calificaciones** para enseñar
	Standard variants →	**capacidades / aptitud** para enseñar
6. *qualification (=diploma):*	*a teaching qualification*	una **calificación** de profesor
	Standard variant →	un **título** de profesor

CALIFICADO (adj)   =   **qualified: competent**
                  =   **described; graded**

CALIFICAR (verb)   =   **to describe as, to label**
                  =   **to grade, to score (an exam, etc.)**
                  =   **to qualify: meet requirements [US]**
                  =   **to qualify: have the ability, possess title [US]**

Standard usage

1. to describe as, to label:	*They labeled him a racist.*	Lo calificaron de racista.
2. to grade, mark:	*The teacher graded the test.*	La maestra calificó el examen.
3. qualified (=competent):	*He's a very qualified doctor.*	Es un médico muy calificado.
4. graded, scored:	*The essays are graded.*	Los ensayos están calificados.

Extended US usage

5. to qualify (meet requirements):	*Do you qualify for the diploma?*	¿**Calificas** para el diploma?
	Standard variant →	¿**Satisfaces los requisitos** para el diploma?
6. to qualify (=possess ability):	*He qualifies for goalie.*	**Califica** para portero.
	Standard variant →	**Tiene capacidades** para...
7. to qualify (on paper):	*She qualifies as a lawyer.*	**Califica** de abogada.
	Standard variant →	**Tiene título** de abogada.

CAMPING (masc noun)   =   **loanword for "camping" [DRAE 1983]**

> **camping**. (Voz inglesa). 1. m. campamento (lugar al aire libre). 2. m. Actividad que consiste en ir de acampada a este tipo de lugares. [DRAE]

• Borrowed directly from English, this term is used internationally.

Standard/US usage

1. camping (activity):	*We went camping in Arizona.*	Fuimos de **camping** en Arizona.
	Traditional variant →	Fuimos de **acampada** ...
2. camping (site):	*Where is the campsite?*	¿Dónde se encuentra el **camping**?
	Traditional variant →	¿Dónde se encuentra el **campamento**?

CAMPO (masc noun) = **countryside; field; sports ground**
= **camp, campground [US]**

- Contrary to standard practice, **campo** is used to mean "camp" in the U.S.
- The traditional equivalent of "summer camp" is **colonia de vacaciones**.

Standard usage

1. *country, countryside:*	*They live in the countryside.*	Viven en el campo.
2. *field (=farm land):*	*We saw a wheat field.*	Vimos un campo de trigo.
3. *field (=sports ground):*	*The playing field is dry.*	El campo de juego está seco.
4. *field (=defined area):*	*This used to be a battlefield.*	Esto era un campo de batalla.
5. *field (academic):*	*the field of science*	el campo de las ciencias

Extended US usage

6. *camp, campground:*	*They set up tents in the camp.*	Fijaron tiendas en el **campo**.
	Standard variant →	... en el **campamento**.
7. *camp (=activity, site):*	*My daughter will be going to a summer camp.*	Mi hija irá a un **campo** de verano.
	Standard variant →	Mi hija irá a una **colonia de vacaciones** este verano.
8. *camp (political):*	*They're from the liberal camp.*	Son del **campo** liberal.
	Standard variant →	Son del **bando** liberal.

CANCELAR (verb) = **to cancel, close (account, investment, etc.)**
= **to pay off a debt**
= **to erase from memory**
= **to cancel: annul (contract, reservation, etc.) [US]**
= **to cancel: suspend (game, performance, etc.) [US]**
= **to cancel a flight, a trip [US]**

- In many cases, **cancelar** is not a loanword but a true cognate of "to cancel."
- In U.S. Spanish, however, its use extends beyond the boundaries of the official definition.
- Two traditional alternatives are: **suspender**, when the occasion is the cancellation of an event; and **anular**, when the intent is more specifically "to render null and void."

Standard usage

1. *to close (an account):*	*I had to close the account.*	Tuve que cancelar la cuenta.
2. *to cancel (investment):*	*The bonds have been cancelled.*	Se cancelaron las obligaciones.
3. *to pay off (a debt, etc.):*	*She paid off the loan in 2003.*	Canceló el préstamo en 2003.
4. *to erase from memory:*	*There is no way to erase childhood traumas.*	No hay manera de cancelar los traumas de la niñez.

Extended US usage

5. to cancel (subscription, contract, reservation):	*They cancelled the contract.* *I have to cancel my reservation.*	**Cancelaron** el contrato. Tengo que **cancelar** la reserva.
	Standard variants →	**Anularon** el contrato. Tengo que **anular** la reserva.
6. to cancel (game, party, plans, performance):	*The game has been cancelled.* *They will cancel the concert.*	Se ha **cancelado** el partido. Van a **cancelar** el concierto.
	Standard variants →	Se ha **suspendido** el partido. Van a **suspender** el concierto.
7. to cancel (flight, trip):	*All flights were cancelled.*	**Cancelaron** todos los vuelos.
	Standard variant →	**Suspendieron** todos los vuelos.

CARÁCTER (masc noun)

= **character: personality; style**
= **character: nature**
= **character: letter, symbol**
= **character: role (in a film or story) [US]**
= **character: person, individual [US]**

- **Carácter** is not a person in academic Spanish, but rather a set of personal qualities.
- Referring to an individual, "character" is traditionally expressed with **tipo** or **personaje**.

Standard usage

1. character (=personality):	*He has a strong personality.*	Tiene un carácter bien fuerte.
2. character (=style):	*His house has a lot of character.*	Su casa tiene mucho carácter.
3. character (=nature):	*of a political nature*	de carácter político
4. character (=letter):	*written with Arabic characters*	escrito con caracteres árabes

Extended US usage

5. character (in film, story):	*the characters in the novel*	los **caracteres** en la novela
	Standard variant →	los **personajes** en la novela
6. character (=role):	*I play the character of Hamlet.*	Juego el **carácter** de Hamlet.
	Standard variant →	Hago el **papel** de Hamlet.
7. character (=individual):	*He is quite a strange character.*	Es un **carácter** bien raro.
	Standard variant →	Es un **tipo** bien raro.

CARPETA (fem noun)

= **folder, file; briefcase**
= **carpet, rug [US]**

- Traditionally considered a false cognate of "carpet," the primary meaning of **carpeta** in standard Spanish is "file folder" or "briefcase."

Standard usage

1. *folder, file:*	*the documents in the folder*	los documentos en la carpeta
2. *briefcase:*	*I bought a leather briefcase.*	Compré una carpeta de cuero.

Extended US usage

3. *carpet, rug:*	*The rug needs to be cleaned.*	Hay que limpiar la **carpeta**.
	Standard variant ➔	Hay que limpiar la **alfombra**.
4. *small carpet, area rug:*	*We put down an area rug.*	Pusimos una **carpeta**.
	Standard variants ➔	Pusimos un **tapete** / una **moquera**.

CARTA (fem noun) = **letter; playing card**
                = **menu; chart; charter**
                = **card (ID, credit, membership, etc.) [US]**
                = **greeting card; index card [US]**

- According to both the DRAE and Moliner, **carta** is primarily a "letter" (a piece of correspondence) and secondarily a "menu" or a "playing card."
- In U.S. Spanish, **carta** encompasses all sorts of cards (greeting, credit, business, ID, etc.).

Standard usage

1. *letter (correspondence):*	*I just received your letter.*	Acabo de recibir tu carta.
2. *playing card:*	*Do you want to play cards?*	¿Quieres jugar a las cartas?
3. *menu, list:*	*Have you seen the wine list?*	¿Has visto la carta de vinos?
4. *chart, map:*	*Look at the navigation chart.*	Mira la carta de navegación.
5. *charter:*	*United Nations Charter*	Carta de las Naciones Unidas

Extended US usage

6. *card (ID, credit, etc.):*	*I pay with a credit card.*	Pago con **carta** de crédito.
	Standard variant ➔	Pago con **tarjeta** de crédito.
7. *greeting card:*	*a birthday card*	una **carta** de cumpleaños
	Standard variant ➔	una **tarjeta** de cumpleaños
8. *index card:*	*Write it on an index card.*	Escríbelo en una **cartita**.
	Standard variant ➔	Escríbelo en una **ficha**.
9. *membership card:*	*Here's my press card.*	Aquí está mi **carta** de prensa.
	Standard variant ➔	Aquí está mi **carné** de prensa.
10. *business card:*	*Do you have my business card?*	¿Tienes mi **carta** de negocio?
	Standard variants ➔	¿Tienes mi **tarjeta** de negocio / mi **tarjeta de visita**?

CARTOON (masc noun) see **CARTÚN**

CARTÚN (masc noun) = **loanword for "cartoon" [US]**

• Despite its widespread use, **cartún** is not part of the standard Spanish lexicon.

US usage		
1. cartoon (=animated film):	*My daughter loves to watch cartoons on TV.*	A mi hija le encanta mirar los **cartunes** en la tele.
	Standard variant →	A mi hija le encanta mirar los **dibujos animados** ...
2. cartoon (=comic strip):	*My favorite cartoon in Spanish is Mafalda.*	Mi **cartún** preferido en español es Mafalda.
	Standard variants →	Mi **historieta / viñeta** preferida en español es Mafalda.

CASETE (masc & fem noun) = **adapted from "cassette" [DRAE 1983]**

• Occurs in both U.S. and standard Spanish to mean "cassette tape" or "tape recorder."
• Ilan Stavans accounts for the shortened form, **caset**, more prevalent in the United States.

Standard/US usage		
1. cassette tape:	*I bought a dozen cassettes at a very good price.*	Compré una docena de **casetes** a muy buen precio.
2. cassette player/recorder:	*I'll take a cassette recorder to tape the lectures.*	Llevaré un **casete** para grabar las conferencias.
	Traditional variant →	Llevaré un **magnetófono** para grabar las conferencias.

CASH (masc noun) = **loanword for "cash" [US]**

• Primarily refers to "cash" as a means of payment" in U.S. Spanish.
• Moliner accounts for compound expressions such as **cash-flow**, but not **cash**.

US usage		
1. cash (=means of payment):	*Whenever we buy a car, we pay cash.*	Siempre que compramos un carro, pagamos **cash**.
	Standard variant →	Siempre que compramos un carro, pagamos **al contado**.
2. cash (=bills & coins):	*I had 100 dollars cash in my wallet.*	Tenía cien dólares **cash** en mi cartera.
	Standard variant →	Tenía cien dólares **en efectivo** en mi cartera.

CASUAL (adj)   =   **chance, coincidental, accidental**
               =   **casual [US]**

CASUALMENTE (adv)   =   **by chance, accidentally**
                       =   **casually [US]**

• Standard Spanish tends to use **informal** for "casual," and **casual** to mean "accidental."

Standard usage

1. *chance, coincidental:*	*It was a chance encounter.*	Fue un encuentro casual.
2. *accidental:*	*Many inventions have been accidental.*	Muchas invenciones han sido casuales.
3. *accidentally, happen to, by chance:*	*We happened to be on the same flight.*	Casualmente nos encontramos en el mismo vuelo.

Extended US usage

4. *casual (=offhand, nonchalant):*	*He has a casual attitude.*	Tiene una actitud **casual**.
	Standard variant →	... una actitud **despreocupada**.
5. *casual (=informal):*	*I need casual clothing.*	Me hace falta ropa **casual**.
	Standard variants →	...ropa **informal** / **de sport**.
6. *casually (=occasionally):*	*He calls me very casually.*	Me llama muy **casualmente**.
	Standard variants →	Me llama **de vez en cuando** / **esporádicamente**.
7. *casually (=informally):*	*Do you dress casually to go to work?*	¿Vistes **casualmente** para ir al trabajo?
	Standard variant →	¿Vistes **informalmente** ...?

CD (masc noun)   =   **loanword for "CD" (compact disc)** [DRAE 2001]

CD-ROM (masc noun)   =   **loanword for "CD-ROM"** [DRAE 2001]

• Both terms gained recent acceptance in standard Spanish (RAE and Moliner).
• They tend to be vocalized as in Spanish, although the English pronunciation is just as prevalent in the United States.

Standard/US usage

1. *CD (=compact disc):*	*How many CDs did you buy?*	¿Cuántos **CDs** compraste?
	Traditional variant →	¿Cuántos **discos (compactos)** compraste?
2. *CD-ROM:*	*We have the Encyclopaedia Britannica on CD-ROM.*	Tenemos la Enciclopedia Británica en **CD-ROM**.

CERCA (DE) (adv & prep) = **near, nearby; close up, closely**
= **nearly, almost, first-hand**
= **close (emotionally) [US]**

- **Cerca** and **cerca de** occur in U.S. Spanish in the context of emotional as well as physical closeness, whereas in academic Spanish only the latter is deemed appropriate.

Standard usage		
1. *near, nearby:*	*There's a hospital nearby.*	Hay un hospital cerca.
2. *close (physically):*	*I like living close to you.*	Me gusta vivir cerca de ti.
3. *closely, close up:*	*We followed him closely.*	Lo seguimos de cerca.
4. *nearly, almost:*	*It's nearly twelve o'clock.*	Son cerca de las doce.
5. *in person, first-hand:*	*I saw the accident in person.*	Vi el accidente de cerca.

Extended US usage		
6. *close (emotionally):*	*I'm very close to my mother.*	Estoy muy **cerca** a mi madre.
	Standard variant →	Estoy muy **unida** a mi madre.

CERCANO (adj) = **close: near, nearby, linked, related**
= **close: intimate [US]**

- In standard practice, **cercano** denotes physical closeness in terms of time, space, and family connection. Emotional closeness is more likely expressed with **íntimo**.

Standard usage		
1. *nearby, close to:*	*They live in a nearby town.*	Viven en un pueblo cercano.
2. *close (=linked, related):*	*He is a close relative.*	Es un pariente cercano.
3. *near (in time):*	*in the very near future*	en el futuro muy cercano

Extended US usage		
4. *close (=intimate):*	*She's a close friend.*	Es una amiga **cercana**.
	Standard variant →	Es una amiga **íntima**.

CHAMPÚ (masc noun) = **adapted from "shampoo" [DRAE 1927]**

- With no traditional equivalent, **champú** has been part of standard Spanish since 1908 (Corominas). Interestingly, it was not sanctioned by the RAE until 1927.

Standard/US usage		
1. *shampoo:*	*Do you wash your hair with shampoo?*	¿Te lavas el pelo con **champú**?

CHANCE (masc / fem noun) = **loanword for "chance" [US]**

- Cited in the DRAE (2001) as meaning "opportunity" or "possibility," chance is more prevalent in the United States and Latin America than it is in Spain.
- Traditional Spanish variants are: **oportunidad, posibilidad, esperanza, casualidad.**
- U.S. Spanish tends to mirror the multiple connotations of this term in English.

US usage

1. *chance (=hazard, fate):*	*Leave nothing to chance.*	No deje nada al chance.
	Standard variant →	No deje nada al azar.
2. *chance (=coincidence):*	*We found each other by pure chance.*	Nos encontramos por pura chance.
	Standard variant →	... por pura casualidad.
3. *chance (=opportunity):*	*I had a chance to speak.*	Tuve la chance de hablar.
	Standard variant →	Tuve la oportunidad de hablar.
4. *chance (=possibility):*	*There is little chance of rain.*	Hay poca chance de lluvia.
	Standard variant →	Hay poca posibilidad de lluvia.
5. *chance (=risk):*	*You shouldn't take that chance.*	No debieras tomar esa chance.
	Standard variants →	No debieras correr ese riesgo. No debieras arriesgarte.
6. *chance (=hope):*	*There is still a chance that we can buy the house.*	Todavía hay chance de que podamos comprar la casa.
	Standard variant →	Todavía hay esperanza ...

CHATEAR (verb) = **loanword for "to chat (online)"**

- Chatear is used increasingly in U.S. Spanish to refer to "online chat," as opposed to conversar, charlar, and platicar, commonly associated with traditional forms of conversation (face-to-face, on the phone, etc.).
- The only definition of chatear currently sanctioned by the RAE is "tomar chatos de vino" (to have a few glasses of wine).

Standard usage

1. *to have a few drinks:*	*He was having drinks with friends.*	Estaba chateando con amigos.

Extended US usage

2. *to chat (online):*	*I spent the entire day chatting on the Internet.*	Me pasé todo el día chateando en el internet.
	Traditional variants →	Me pasé todo el día charlando / platicando en el internet.

CHEQUEAR (verb) = **to check: examine** [DRAE 1989]
= **to check: look over, verify [Lat Am]**
= **to check: check in, register [Lat Am]**
= **to check with: consult [US]**
= **to check: look at, look around [US]**
= **to check: test, taste [US]**
= **to check: hold back, stop, contain [US]**
= **to check: check off, flag, mark [US]**
= **to check into a hotel [US]**
= **to check on someone [US]**

chequear. (Del inglés *to check*, comprobar). 1. tr. Examinar, controlar, cotejar.
2. prnl. Hacerse un chequeo. [DRAE]

chequear. 1. tr. Examinar algo para comprobar su calidad o buen funcionamiento.
2. refl. Someterse a un chequeo médico. [Moliner]

- The many uses of the verb "to check" can produce as many as 30 translations in Spanish.
- Hence, the rapidly growing use of **chequear** in the United States and Latin America.
- The controversy over the acceptance of this term in standard Spanish was only partially settled when it became sanctioned in 1989 within certain constraints.
- Going well beyond the RAE definition, U.S. Spanish uses **chequear** as a substitute for **mirar, consultar, probar, señalar**, and other secondary meanings of the English verb.

Latin American usage		
1. *to check (=examine):*	*I had my lungs checked.*	Me **chequearon** los pulmones.
	Traditional variant →	Me **examinaron** los pulmones.
2. *to check (=look over):*	*I didn't check the documents.*	No **chequeé** los documentos.
	Traditional variant →	No **revisé** los documentos.
3. *to check (=verify):*	*Did you check the price?*	¿**Chequeaste** el precio?
	Traditional variants →	¿**Comprobaste** el precio? ¿**Te aseguraste** del precio?
4. *to check in (=register):*	*to check (in) the luggage*	**chequear** el equipaje
	Traditional variant →	**facturar** el equipaje

Extended US usage

5. *to check (=consult):*
I will check with the doctor.
Voy a **chequear** con el médico.
Standard variant →
Voy a **consultar** con el médico.

6. *to check (=look at):*
Did you check the motorcycle?
¿**Chequeaste** la moto?
Standard variants →
¿**Miraste** / **viste** la moto?
¿**Te fijaste** en la moto?

7. *to check (=look around):*
Did you check in the bedroom?
¿**Chequeaste** en el dormitorio?
Traditional variant →
¿**Buscaste** en el dormitorio?

8. *to check (=test, taste):*
Check to see if it's sweet.
Chequea a ver si está dulce.
Standard variant →
Prueba a ver si está dulce.

9. *to check (=hold back, step, contain):*
We must check the spread of the virus.
Hay que **chequear** la propagación del virus.
Standard variants →
Hay que **detener** / **frenar** la propagación del virus.

10. *to check, check off (=flag, mark):*
I checked off the names of those who arrived.
Chequeé los nombres de los que llegaron.
Standard variants →
Señalé / **marqué** los nombres de los que llegaron.

11. *to check into (a hotel, etc.):*
We checked into the hotel last night.
Nos **chequeamos** en el hotel anoche.
Standard variant →
Nos **registramos** en el hotel...

12. *to check on someone (=investigate):*
We'll need to check his past employment.
Tendremos que **chequear** su historial de empleo.
Standard variants →
Tendremos que **investigar** / **averiguar sobre** su historial de empleo.

CHEQUEO (masc noun) =
- **checkup (medical)** [DRAE 1983]
- **checkup (mechanical)** [US]
- **check: restraint, control** [US]
- **security check** [US]
- **check: mark, symbol** [US]
- **check: bill, charge** [US]

chequeo. (Del inglés *checkup*, reconocimiento médico). 1. m. Examen, control, cotejo. 2. m. Reconocimiento médico general. [DRAE]

- Usage of **chequeo** has limited sanction in standard Spanish, as does the verb **chequear**.
- U.S. Spanish extends its applications to reflect common English usage.

Latin American usage		
1. *checkup (medical):*	She had a complete checkup at the hospital.	Le hicieron un **chequeo** general en el hospital.
	Traditional variants➜	Le hicieron un **reconocimiento médico** / un **examen** general.

Extended US usage		
2. *checkup (mechanical):*	My car needs a checkup.	Mi carro necesita un **chequeo**.
	Standard variants ➜	Mi carro necesita una **revisión** / una **inspección**.
3. *check (=restraint, control):*	Corruption must be held in check.	La corrupción se tiene que mantener en **chequeo**.
	Standard variant ➜	La corrupción se tiene que mantener **bajo control**.
4. *security check (documents, ID, etc.):*	passport check security check	**chequeo** de pasaporte **chequeo** de seguridad
	Standard variants ➜	**control** de pasaporte **control** de seguridad
5. *check (=mark, symbol):*	Put a check next to his name.	Pon un **chequeo** junto a su nombre.
	Standard variants ➜	Pon una **marca** / una **señal** junto a su nombre.

CHIP (masc noun)   =   **loanword for "chip"** [DRAE 1989]

> **chip**. (Del inglés *chip*). m. Inform. Pequeño circuito integrado que realiza numerosas funciones en ordenadores y dispositivos electrónicos. [DRAE]

• Integrated into standard Spanish worldwide to indicate "computer chip," it also occurs in U.S. Spanish to refer to snacks ("potato chips, corn chips, etc.").

Standard usage		
1. *chip (=small circuit):*	The electronic boom began with the invention of the chip.	El boom electrónico comenzó con la invención del chip.

Extended US usage		
2. *chips (=snack):*	They served soda and chips.	Sirvieron refrescos y **chips**.
	Standard variant ➜	Sirvieron refrescos y **fritas de bolsa**.

CHOQUE (masc noun) =   **crash, collision**
=   **clash; emotional shock**
=   **shock: surprise, moment of fear [US]**
=   **shock: strong impression [US]**
=   **shock: medical condition [US]**
=   **electrical shock [US]**

• U.S. Spanish has extended the usage of **choque** well beyond its standard definition ("crash" or "clash"), imitating the numerous applications in English.
• The loanword **shock** also occurs in the United States with the same meanings.

Standard usage		
1. *crash, collision:*	*head-on collision*	choque frontal
2. *clash, conflict:*	*a personality clash*	un choque de personalidades
3. *emotional shock:*	*Her death was a terrible shock for all of us.*	Su muerte fue un choque terrible para nosotros.

Extended US usage		
4. *shock (=surprise):*	*It was a shock to her that she won the contest.*	Fue un **choque** para ella el que ganara el concurso.
	Standard variant ➔	Fue una **sorpresa** para ella ...
5. *shock (=scare, fright):*	*What a shock you gave me!*	¡Qué **choque** me diste!
	Standard variant ➔	¡Qué **susto** me diste!
6. *shock (=strong impression):*	*The shock was just too much for him.*	El **choque** fue demasiado para él.
	Standard variant ➔	La **impresión** fue demasiado ...
7. *shock (=medical condition):*	*to suffer from shock*	sufrir un **choque** / un **shock**
	Standard variant ➔	sufrir una **postración nerviosa**
8. *electrical shock:*	*I felt a shock when I touched the toaster.*	Sentí un **choque** / un **shock** al tocar el tostador.
	Standard variants ➔	Sentí un **calambre** / una **descarga** al tocar el tostador.

CLIP (masc noun)   =   **loanword for "clip"** [DRAE 1992]

• **Clip** is an accepted term in academic Spanish to indicate both "paper clip" and "video clip." It occurs in the same way in the United States.

Standard/US usage		
1. *paper clip:*	*Please use clips to keep the documents together.*	Favor de usar **clips** para juntar los documentos.
	Traditional variants →	Favor de usar **presillas** / **grapas** / **sujetapapeles** ...
2. *film / video clip:*	*We watched a clip about yesterday's incident.*	Miramos un **clip** sobre el incidente de ayer.
	Traditional variant →	Miramos una **secuencia** sobre el incidente de ayer.

CLÓSET (masc noun) = **loanword for "closet"** [DRAE 1992]

> **clóset**. (Del inglés *closet*). m. Am. Armario empotrado. [DRAE, Moliner]

- Considered an americanism, **clóset** is used to designate a "built-in closet," as opposed to the more traditional free-standing closet known as **armario**.
- Either type may also be referred to as **ropero** in standard Spanish.

Lat Am / US usage		
1. *closet:*	*How many blouses fit in this closet?*	¿Cuántas blusas caben en este **clóset**?
	Traditional variants →	¿Cuántas blusas caben en este **armario** / **ropero** / **placard**?

CLOWN (masc noun) = **loanword for "clown"** [DRAE 1927]

- Pronounced "clon" in Spain, **clown** tends to keep its English inflexion in U.S. Spanish.
- Moliner accounts for **clon** as well as **clown**, and validates its figurative use.

Standard/US usage		
1. *circus clown:*	*The clown made the children laugh.*	El **clown** hizo reír a los niños.
	Traditional variant →	El **payaso** hizo reír a los niños.
2. *clown (fig.):*	*Don't be such a clown.*	No hagas de **clown** / de **clon**.
	Traditional variants →	No hagas de **payaso** / No hagas **el ridículo**.

CLUB (masc noun) = **loanword for "club"** [DRAE 1837]

- Originally borrowed from English to refer to a "youth organization" or "political group," it was expanded to include "sports club" (1914) and, more recently, "night club" (1992).
- Nowadays, **club** has the same range of applications in Spanish as it does in English.

Standard/US usage

1. club (=association):	*I am a member of a youth club.*	Soy miembro de un **club** juvenil.
	Traditional variant →	Soy miembro de una **sociedad** juvenil.
2. club (=building):	*Let's meet at the club.*	Nos encontramos en el **club**.
	Traditional variant →	Nos encontramos en el **centro**.
3. club (=nightclub):	*She spent the night dancing in a club.*	Se pasó la noche bailando en un **club**.
	Traditional variant →	Se pasó la noche bailando en una **discoteca**.

COLECTAR (verb) = **adapted from "to collect"** [US]

- Although **colectar** is a valid term in standard Spanish, its historical contexts have been "taxes" and "charity." For the latter, **hacer una colecta** is a more common expression.
- Influenced by the many uses of "to collect," **colectar** is more widespread in U.S. Spanish.

US usage

1. to collect (as a hobby):	*My son collects stamps.*	Mi hijo **colecta** estampillas.
	Standard variant →	Mi hijo **colecciona** estampillas.
2. to collect (=pick up):	*We just collected firewood.*	Acabamos de **colectar** leña.
	Standard variant →	Acabamos de **recoger** leña.
3. to collect (=gather):	*This is going to collect dust.*	Esto va a **colectar** polvo.
	Standard variant →	Esto va a **acumular** polvo.
4. to collect (=get):	*Did they collect the mail?*	¿**Colectaron** el correo?
	Standard variant →	¿**Vinieron por** el correo?
5. to collect (money):	*to collect for the poor*	**colectar** para los pobres
	Standard variant →	**hacer una colecta** …
6. to collect (=get paid):	*When will you collect?*	¿Cuándo vas a **colectar**?
	Standard variant →	¿Cuándo **te pagan**?

COLEGIO (masc noun) = **school; group, association**
= **college [US]**

- In standard Spanish, colegio refers primarily to "grade school" (elementary, middle, or high school), but can also indicate a school or program within a university.
- In the U.S., it is frequently used to mean "college" or "university."

Standard usage		
1. *school (general):*	*I have two children in school.*	Tengo dos hijos en el colegio.
2. *professional group:*	*medical association*	colegio de médicos
	College of Cardinals	Colegio de Cardenales

Extended US usage		
3. *college (=university):*	*He studies art in college.*	Estudia arte en el colegio.
	Standard variant →	Estudia arte en la universidad.

COMPETICIÓN (fem noun) = **competition (sport)**
= **competition: rivalry; contest [US]**

- The RAE equates competición with competencia, with one notable difference: the latter is more appropriate in the world of business, while the former is applicable only to sports.
- U.S. Spanish favors the use of competición in either case.

Standard usage		
1. *competition (sport):*	*It's a competitive sport.*	Es un deporte de competición.

Extended US usage		
2. *competition (=rivalry):*	*There's a lot of competition.*	Hay mucha competición.
	Standard variant →	Hay mucha competencia.
3. *competition (=contest):*	*a talent competition*	una competición de talento
	Standard variant →	un concurso de talento
4. *competition (=rival):*	*Do you know your competition?*	¿Conoces a tu competición?
	Standard variants →	¿Conoces a tu competidor / competencia / rival?

COMPLEXIÓN (fem noun) = **build, constitution**
= **complexion: skin [US]**
= **complexion: facet, aspect [US]**

- A traditional false cognate, complexión refers to a person's "build" or "physical form" in standard Spanish and has little to do with skin tone or quality, as it does in U.S. Spanish.

Standard usage		
1. *build, constitution:*	*a well-built man*	un hombre de complexión fuerte

Extended US usage		
2. *complexion (=skin tone):*	*She has a dark complexion.*	Tiene la **complexión** morena.
	Standard variants →	Tiene la **piel** / la **tez** morena.
3. *complexion (=skin texture):*	*a very soft complexion*	una **complexión** muy suave
	Standard variant →	un **cutis** muy suave
4. *complexion (=facet):*	*issue with many complexions*	asunto de varias **complexiones**
	Standard variants →	asunto de varios **aspectos** / de varias **facetas**

COMPROMISO (masc noun) = **commitment; obligation**
= **compromise [US]**

- The RAE presents one situation where **compromiso** can mean "settlement:"

  compromiso. ... 6. *Der.* Convenio entre litigantes, por el cual someten su litigio a árbitros o amigables componedores. [DRAE]

- This definition, intimating a legal agreement between two or more parties, has limited use.
- **Compromiso** is more likely to mean "commitment" or "engagement" in standard Spanish.
- In U.S. Spanish, it is also used to suggest "compromise" or "agreement."

Standard usage		
1. *commitment:*	*He honored his commitment.*	Cumplió con su compromiso.
2. *obligation:*	*I felt obliged to go to the party.*	Fui a la fiesta por compromiso.
3. *engagement (appt):*	*I have an engagement at one.*	Tengo un compromiso a la una.
4. *marriage engagement:*	*an engagement party*	una fiesta de compromiso

Extended US usage		
5. *compromise (=agreement, settlement):*	*Despite their disagreements, they reached a compromise.*	A pesar de sus desacuerdos, llegaron a un **compromiso**.
	Standard variant →	... llegaron a un **arreglo**.
6. *compromise (=giving in):*	*It was an unfair compromise.*	Fue un **compromiso** injusto.
	Standard variant →	Fue una **transigencia** injusta.

CONDUCTOR (noun)

= **driver, motorist**
= **electrical conductor**
= **paid driver, chauffeur [US]**
= **music conductor [US]**

- Whereas U.S. Spanish is faithful to the corresponding English cognate, standard Spanish limits the use of **conductor** to "one who drives" and "that which transmits."

Standard usage

1. *driver, motorist:*	*driver and passenger*	conductor y pasajero
2. *conductor (of heat, electrical):*	*Copper is a good conductor.*	El cobre es buen conductor.

Extended US usage

3. *paid driver (public and private transportation):*	*taxi driver*	**conductor de taxi**
	truck driver	**conductor de camión**
	limousine driver	**conductor de limusina**
	Standard variants →	**taxista, camionero, chófer**
4. *conductor (music):*	*He is an orchestra conductor.*	Es **conductor** de orquesta.
	Standard variant →	Es **director** de orquesta.

CONEXIÓN (fem noun)

= **connection (electrical/mechanical/technological; logical)**
= **connection: afiliation, association**
= **connection (train, plane, etc.) [US]**

- Usage of this term in the United States does not differ significantly from that of standard Spanish, with the exception of idioms such as "train connection" or "bad connection."

Standard usage

1. *connection (electrical/mechanical):*	*There was no connection when I plugged in the TV.*	No había conexión cuando enchufé el televisor.
2. *connection (logical):*	*There is no connection between your idea and mine.*	No hay conexión ninguna entre tu idea y la mía.
3. *connection (=affiliation):*	*I have good connections in this company.*	Tengo buenas conexiones en esta empresa.

Extended US usage

4. *train connection:*	*We missed our connection.*	Perdimos nuestra **conexión**.
	Standard variants →	Perdimos nuestro **enlace** / nuestra **correspondencia**.

"Connection" idioms in standard Spanish	good / bad connection (tele) loose connection (elec) in connection with	se oye bien / no se oye bien un hilo suelto en relación a / con respecto a

CONFERENCIA (fem noun)
= **lecture; meeting; telephone call**
= **conference: assembly, convention [US]**

- Whereas in English, "conference" suggests "gathering" or "convention," the cognate **conferencia** is essentially a "lecture" in standard Spanish.
- In U.S. Spanish, "conference" is routinely translated as **conferencia**.

Standard usage		
1. lecture:	*My professor gave a lecture.*	Mi profesor dio una conferencia.
2. meeting (=discussion):	*press conference*	conferencia de prensa
3. telephone call:	*collect phone call*	conferencia a cobro revertido

Extended US usage		
4. conference, convention (=assembly, gathering):	*a national conference*	una **conferencia** nacional
	Standard variants →	un **congreso** nacional una **asamblea** nacional
5. in conference (at a meeting):	*The vice president is in conference.*	El vicepresidente está en **conferencia**.
	Standard variant →	... está en **una reunión**.

CONFIDENCIA (fem noun)
= **confidence: secret, revelation**
= **confidence: trust [US]**

CONFIDENTE (adj & noun)
= **confidant(e); informer**
= **secure, self-assured, certain [US]**

- Influenced by its English cognate, **confidencia** often replaces **confianza** in the U.S.

Standard usage		
1. confidence (=secret):	*They exchanged confidences.*	Se hicieron confidencias.
2. confidant (trusted friend):	*He has been a loyal confidant.*	Ha sido un confidente leal.
3. informer:	*police informer*	confidente policial

Extended US usage

4. *confidence (=trust):*	*Don't you have confidence in me?*	¿No tienes **confidencia** en mí?
	Standard variant →	¿No tienes **confianza** en mí?
5. *in confidence (=secretly):*	*I tell you this in confidence.*	Te lo digo en **confidencia**.
	Standard variant →	Te lo digo en **confianza**.
6. *confident (=secure):*	*He is a confident young man.*	Es un joven muy **confidente**.
	Standard variant →	... joven **seguro de sí mismo**.
7. *confident (=certain):*	*I feel confident that things will work out.*	Me siento **confidente** de que todo va a salir bien.
	Standard variant →	Me siento **segura** de que ...

CONFORT (masc noun) = **loanword for "comfort"** [DRAE 1927]

- Prevalent in the United States by influence of English.
- Borrowed from the French, **confort** is a substitute for **comodidad** in standard Spanish.

Standard/US usage

1. *comfort (=well-being):*	*The comfort of our customers is very important.*	El **confort** de nuestros clientes es muy importante.
	Traditional variant →	El **bienestar** de nuestros ...
2. *comfort (=convenience):*	*He lives surrounded by every comfort.*	Vive rodeado de todo **confort**.
	Traditional variant →	Vive rodeado de toda **comodidad**.
3. *comfort (=solace):*	*Her presence was a great comfort to me.*	Su presencia fue un gran **confort** para mí.
	Traditional variant →	Su presencia fue un gran **consuelo** para mí.

"Comfort" expressions in standard Spanish

comfort food	comida de terapia
comfort zone	terreno conocido
if it's any comfort to you	si te sirve de consuelo
to give comfort to the enemy	dar aliento al enemigo
to live in comfort	vivir cómodamente
to take comfort from something	consolarse con algo
too close for comfort	demasiado cerca para sentirse tranquilo

CONFORTABLE (adj)
= **comfortable (home, hotel, room...)**
= **comfortable (furniture, clothes, position) [US]**
= **comfortable (emotionally, financially) [US]**

- Used extensively in U.S. Spanish to refer to both physical and emotional comfort.
- In standard Spanish, its use is most appropriate when it refers to living quarters, i.e., the comforts of a home, a hotel, or other lodging.

Standard usage

1. comfortable (lodging):	*It's a very comfortable hotel.*	Es un hotel muy confortable.

Extended US usage

2. comfortable (furniture):	*Is the chair comfortable?*	¿Está confortable la silla?
	Standard variant →	¿Está cómoda la silla?
3. comfortable (clothing):	*These shoes are comfortable.*	Estos zapatos son confortables.
	Standard variant →	Estos zapatos son cómodos.
4. comfortable (position):	*Make yourself comfortable.*	Ponte confortable.
	Standard variants →	Ponte cómodo / Acomódate.
5. comfortable (emotionally):	*I don't feel comfortable in this situation.*	No me siento confortable en esta situación.
	Standard variants →	No me siento cómodo / a gusto en esta situación.
6. comfortable (financially):	*He earns a comfortable income.*	Gana un sueldo confortable.
	Standard variants →	Gana un sueldo adecuado / un buen sueldo.

CONSERVATIVO (adj & noun)
= **preservative**
= **conservative [US]**

- In academic Spanish, conservativo is first and foremost a noun meaning "preservative."
- As an adjective, it does not apply to a point of view or ideology, as it often does in English.
- The equivalent of "conservative" (i.e., traditional) in standard Spanish is conservador.

Standard usage

1. preservative	*This ice cream doesn't contain preservatives.*	Este helado no contiene conservativos.

Extended US usage		
2. *conservative (traditional):*	*conservative point of view*	punto de vista **conservativo**
	Standard variants →	punto de vista **tradicional** / **conservador**
3. *conservative (=classic):*	*He wears conservative suits.*	Lleva trajes **conservativos**.
	Standard variants →	Lleva trajes **conservadores** / **clásicos** / **elegantes**.
4. *conservative (=cautious):*	*a conservative estimate*	un cálculo **conservativo**
	Standard variants →	un cálculo **prudente** / **cauteloso**
5. *conservative (political group, ideology):*	*the Conservative Party*	el partido **conservativo**
	Standard variant →	el partido **conservador**

CONSTIPADO (adj)
= **congested, sick with a cold**
= **constipated [US]**

- Frequently used by U.S. Spanish speakers and learners to mean "constipated," **constipado** indicates respiratory rather than digestive problems in standard usage.

Standard usage		
1. *cold (illness):*	*I have a bad cold.*	Estoy muy constipado.
2. *congested (respiratory):*	*He has a congested lung.*	Tiene un pulmón constipado.

Extended US usage		
3. *constipated:*	*Have you been constipated?*	¿Has estado **constipado**?
	Standard variant →	¿Has estado **estreñido**?

CONTACTAR (verb)
= **adapted from "to contact" [DRAE 1983]**

- Somewhat eclipsed by traditional expressions such as **comunicarse** and **ponerse en contacto**, the cognate **contactar** has limited usage in standard Spanish.
- Its prevalence in U.S. Spanish reflects the popularity of "to contact" in English.

US usage		
1. *to contact (=get in touch with):*	*How will we contact her?*	¿Cómo la vamos a **contactar**?
	Standard variant →	¿Cómo nos vamos a **poner en contacto** con ella?

2. *to contact by phone:*	*I will contact you tomorrow.*	Te **contacto** mañana.
	Standard variant →	**Me comunico** contigo mañana.
3. *to contact (=find):*	*Where could I contact you?*	¿Dónde te podría **contactar**?
	Standard variant →	¿Dónde te podría **encontrar**?

CONTESTAR (verb)
- = **to answer, respond, reply**
- = **to answer back, talk back**
- = **to contest, protest [US]**

• In standard usage, **contestar** is "to answer," although the RAE allows for this definition:

> **contestar**. ... 6. intr. Adoptar actitud polémica y a veces de oposición o protesta violenta contra lo establecido, ya sean las autoridades y sus actos, ya formas de vida, posiciones ideológicas, etc. [DRAE]

• This use of **contestar** to mean "to contest" or "to protest" is sporadic in academic Spanish and largely dependent on circumstance and context.

Standard usage		
1. *to answer, respond:*	*I answered all the questions.*	Contesté todas las preguntas.
2. *to talk back:*	*Don't talk back to me.*	No me contestes así.

Extended US usage		
3. *to contest (=protest):*	*They contested the decision.*	**Contestaron** la decisión.
	Standard variants →	**Rebatieron / rechazaron** la decisión.
4. *to contest (=compete):*	*They are contesting for the World Cup.*	**Están contestando para** la Copa Mundial.
	Standard variant →	**Se están disputando** la Copa Mundial.

CONTROVERSIA (fem noun)   =   **controversy**

CONTROVERSIAL (adj)   =   **loanword for "controversial"** [DRAE 1970]

• Whereas **controversia** is a traditional term in standard Spanish, the RAE considers the adjective **controversial** an americanism for the more traditional **polémico**.

Standard/US usage
1. controversy: | *There is a lot of controversy about capital punishment.* | Hay mucha controversia acerca de la pena capital.

Extended US usage
2. controversial (=antagonistic): | *It was a controversial speech.* | Fue un discurso **controversial**.
Standard variant → | Fue un discurso **controvertido**.

3. controversial (=much debated): | *Abortion is a very controversial subject.* | El aborto es un tema muy **controversial**.
Standard variants → | El aborto es un tema muy **discutido / polémico**.

CORRECTO (adj)
= **correct (statement, response)**
= **proper (behavior)**
= **correct: exact [US]**
= **be correct: be right, do the right thing [US]**

- **Correcto** is the standard term for "correct" when it suggests "accurate" or "proper."
- A major discrepancy arises in negotiating verbal phrases such as "to be correct," in which case academic Spanish rejects **estar correcto** and upholds **tener razón** or **hacer bien**.

Standard usage
1. correct (=accurate): | *Your answer is correct.* | Tu contestación es correcta.
2. proper (behavior): | *It wouldn't be proper to yell.* | No sería correcto gritar.

Extended US usage
3. correct (=exact): | *Do you have the correct change?* | ¿Tienes la moneda **correcta**?
Standard variant → | ¿Tienes la moneda **exacta**?

4. to be correct (=be right): | *I believe you are correct.* | Creo que estás **correcto**.
Standard variants → | Creo que **estás en lo cierto**. Creo que **tienes razón**.

5. to be correct (=do the right thing): | *You were correct to fire him.* | **Estuviste / Fuiste correcto** de despedirlo.
Standard variant → | **Hiciste bien** de despedirlo.

CORRIENTE (adj) = **common, frequent; usual, customary**
 = **ordinary, run-of-the-mill; running**
 = **current: present [US]**

• As a feminine noun, **corriente** can mean "current," as in "electric current."
• As an adjective, however, **corriente** primarily means "common" or "customary."
• "Current" in the sense of "present" is rendered in standard Spanish as **actual**.

Standard usage

1. common, frequent:	The flu is very common in the winter.	La gripe es muy corriente en invierno.
2. usual, customary:	It's customary to leave a tip.	Es corriente dejar propina.
3. ordinary, run-of-the-mill:	They ordered an ordinary wine.	Pidieron un vino corriente.
4. running, circulating:	There is no running water.	No hay agua corriente.

Extended US usage

5. current (=present):	What is the current situation of the economy?	¿Cuál es la situación corriente de la economía?
	Standard variants →	¿Cuál es la situación actual / presente de la economía?

CORTE (fem noun) = **royal court; court of law; parliament**
 = **sports court; courtyard; open court [US]**

• Aside from conventional expressions such as **Corte Suprema**, the customary term for "court of law" in standard Spanish is **tribunal**.
• In U.S. Spanish, **corte** occurs extensively to refer to many types of "courts."

Standard usage

1. royal court:	the court of Louis XIV	la corte de Luis XIV
2. court of law:	Supreme Court decision	decisión de la Corte Suprema
3. Spanish parliament	Parliament met yesterday.	Las Cortes se reunieron ayer.

Extended US usage

4. court (sports):	The hotel has a tennis court.	El hotel tiene corte de tenis.
	Standard variant →	El hotel tiene cancha de tenis.
5. courtyard:	They're playing in the courtyard.	Están jugando en la corte.
	Standard variant →	Están jugando en el patio.
6. law court (idioms):	in open court	en plena corte
	Standard variant →	en pleno tribunal

CORTO (adj) = **short (in length, distance, duration)**
= **short (in height, quantity, memory) [US]**

- Confusion with respect to **corto** stems from the many connotations of "short" in English.
- Contrary to standard usage, **corto** often occurs in U.S. Spanish to refer to height, quantity, or memory, as does the English adjective.

Standard usage		
1. short (in length):	*She likes to wear her hair short.*	Le gusta llevar el pelo corto.
2. short (distance):	*This is the shortest path.*	Éste es el camino más corto.
3. short (duration):	*Winter days are short.*	Los días de invierno son cortos.

Extended US usage		
4. short (height):	*My father is shorter than I am.*	Mi padre es más **corto** que yo.
	Standard variant ➜	Mi padre es más **bajo** que yo.
5. short (quantity):	*I'm short of money.*	Estoy **corto** de dinero.
	Standard variants ➜	Ando **falto / escaso** de dinero.
6. short (memory):	*You have a short memory.*	Tienes la memoria **corta**.
	Standard variant ➜	Tienes **mala** memoria.
7. short for (=abbrev.):	*Pat is short for Patricia.*	Pat **es corto para** Patricia.
	Standard variant ➜	Patricia **se abrevia en** Pat.

COWBOY (masc noun) = **loanword for "cowboy' [US]**

- Listed by Moliner but not sanctioned by the RAE, the term **cowboy** is as common as the traditional **vaquero** in the United States and parts of Latin America.

US usage		
1. cowboy (=profession):	*There are many cowboys in the state of Montana.*	Hay muchos **cowboys** en el estado de Montana.
	Standard variant ➜	Hay muchos **vaqueros** ...
2. cowboy (in the movies):	*Cowboys and Indians*	indios y **cowboys**
	Standard variant ➜	indios y **americanos**

CRECER (verb) = **to grow, increase** (intrans)
= **to grow, cultivate** (trans) **[US]**

- Standard academic Spanish differentiates between transitive ("we grow tomatoes") and intransitive usage ("tomatoes grow").
- The variance produces two distinct verbs: **cultivar** (trans) and **crecer** (intrans).
- For "letting grow" (hair or beard, for example), there is a third option: **dejar crecer**.
- These distinctions are blurred in U.S. Spanish, where the use of **crecer** predominates.

Standard usage
1. to grow [intrans]: — *You have grown four inches.* — Has crecido cuatro pulgadas.
2. to increase: — *The wind increased and reached 100 mph.* — El viento creció y alcanzó cien millas por hora.

Extended US usage
3. to grow [trans] (=cultivate): — *I would like to grow vegetables in my garden.* — Quisiera **crecer** legumbres en mi huerta.

Standard variant → — Quisiera **cultivar** legumbres ...

4. to grow (hair, beard): — *He decided to grow a beard.* — Decidió **crecer** la barba.

Standard variant → — Decidió **dejarse crecer** la barba.

CUALIDAD (fem noun) = **quality: virtue; characteristic**
= **quality: worth, merit; condition [US]**

- When **quality** expresses "worth, merit, condition," the standard choice is **calidad**.
- In U.S. Spanish, **calidad** and **cualidad** are often interchanged.

Standard usage
1. quality (=virtue): — *Sincerity is an important quality.* — La sinceridad es una cualidad importante.
2. quality (=characteristic): — *He has the qualities to be a good father.* — Tiene las cualidades para buen padre de familia.

Extended US usage
3. quality (=of high merit or worth): — *This is a quality wine.* — Esto es un vino de **cualidad**.

Standard variant → — Esto es un vino de **calidad**.

4. quality (=condition, standard): — *We ended up in a low-quality hotel.* — Terminamos en un hotel de baja **cualidad**.

Standard variant → — ... un hotel de baja **calidad**.

CUALIFICAR (intrans verb) = adapted from "to qualify" [US]

- Although **cualificar** is valid in standard Spanish, it can only be a transitive verb.
- In U.S. Spanish, as in English, it occurs predominantly as an intransitive.

Extended US usage

1. *to qualify (=meet established criteria):*	*He didn't qualify for the army.*	No **cualificó** para el ejército.
	Standard variant →	No **cumplió con los requisitos** para el ejército.
2. *to qualify (=count as, be considered):*	*It qualifies as a medical expense.*	**Cualifica** como gasto médico.
	Standard variants →	**Cuenta** como gasto médico. **Se considera** gasto médico.
3. *to qualify (=be eligible, be entitled to):*	*Do I qualify for a scholarship?*	¿**Cualifico** para una beca?
	Standard variant →	¿**Tengo derecho** a una beca?
4. *to qualify (=have the credentials, be certified):*	*When will you qualify as a teacher?*	¿Cuándo **cualificarás** de maestra?
	Standard variants →	¿Cuándo **terminarás la carrera** de maestra / **conseguirás la licencia** de maestra?

CUESTIÓN (fem noun) = question: matter, issue
= question: inquiry, doubt [US]

- Although the multiple meanings of "question" in English have impacted on the usage of **cuestión**, U.S. Spanish and bilingual speakers are still most likely to use **pregunta**.

Standard usage

1. *question, matter, issue:*	*We'll have to discuss the matter.* *It's all a question of time.*	Habrá que discutir la cuestión. Todo es cuestión de tiempo.

Extended US usage

2. *question (=doubt):*	*There is no question that she passed the test.*	No **hay cuestión** de que aprobó el examen.
	Standard variant →	No **cabe duda** de que aprobó el examen.
3. *question (=inquiry):*	*I have a question (to ask).*	Tengo una **cuestión**.
	Standard variant →	Tengo una **pregunta**.

CUIDAR(SE) (verb) = **to take care of: look after, watch out for**
= **to take care of: mind, occupy oneself [US]**
= **to care for: like, love [US]**

• By extension, **cuidar** occurs in the U.S. in many verbal idioms that express "care."

Standard usage		
1. to take care of (=look after, watch):	She takes good care of her kids. Take care of yourself!	Ella cuida bien a sus hijos. ¡Cuídate! / ¡Cuídese!

Extended US usage		
2. to take care of (=mind):	Take care of your own business.	**Cuídate** de lo tuyo.
	Standard variant →	**Ocúpate** de lo tuyo.
3. to care for (=like, love):	He cares for you a great deal.	Él **cuida** mucho de ti.
	Standard variant →	Él te **quiere** mucho.

CURSOR (masc noun) = **loanword for "cursor" [DRAE 1989]**

> **cursor.** (Del latín *cursor, -oris,* corredor). 1. m. Electr. Marca movible, por lo común luminosa, en forma de circulito, flecha o signo semejante, que sirve como indicador en la pantalla de diversos aparatos, p. ej., de un computador. [DRAE]

• Although the origin of **cursor** is Latin, its use to refer to an "indicator on a computer screen" is borrowed from English.

Standard/US usage		
1. cursor:	Sometimes the cursor is shaped like an arrow.	A veces el **cursor** tiene forma de flecha.

DAYCARE (masc noun) = **loanword for "day care" [US]**

• Pronounced as in English, this term occurs in U.S. Spanish to refer to both the service and the center.

US usage		
1. day care (service):	Are there day care services at the university?	¿Hay servicios de **daycare** en la universidad?
	Standard variant →	¿Hay servicios de **guardería** en la universidad?
2. day care (center):	I need to take my son to day care.	Tengo que llevar a mi hijo al **daycare**.
	Standard variant →	Tengo que llevar a mi hijo a la **guardería**.

DECEPCIÓN (fem noun) = **disappointment**
= **deception [US]**

DECEPCIONADO (adj) = **disappointed**
= **deceived [US]**

- In standard usage, decepción means "disappointment" rather than "deception."
- U.S. Spanish is less restrictive and accepts both denotations.

Standard usage

1. *disappointment:*	*It was a great disappointment.*	Fue una tremenda decepción.
2. *disappointed:*	*I'm disappointed with the results.*	Estoy decepcionado con los resultados.

Extended US usage

3. *deception:*	*It's all deception and lies.*	Todo es **decepción** y mentiras.
	Standard variant →	Todo es **engaño** y mentiras.
4. *deceived:*	*She felt deceived by him.*	Se sintió **decepcionada** por él.
	Standard variant →	Se sintió **engañada** por él.

DECIR (verb) = **to say: state**
= **to tell: inform; order**
= **to say: represent, indicate, show [US]**
= **to tell: distinguish [US]**
= **to tell: know for sure, be certain [US]**
= **to tell a story, narrate; tell secrets [US]**

- The use of decir, limited in standard practice to "state, inform, order," is extended in U.S Spanish to include "represent, distinguish, narrate" and other uses more typical of English.

Standard usage

1. *to say (=state):*	*He says he doesn't know.*	Dice que no sabe.
2. *to tell (=inform):*	*Who told you that?*	¿Quién te dijo eso?
3. *to tell (=order, ask):*	*He told her not to leave.*	Le dijo que no se fuera.

Extended US usage

4. *to say (=represent, indicate, show):*	*What does the traffic light say?*	¿Qué **dice** el semáforo?
	Standard variant →	¿Qué **indica** el semáforo?
5. *to tell (=distinguish):*	*I can't tell the difference.*	No **puedo decir** la diferencia.
	Standard variants →	No **veo** la diferencia.
		No **llego a distinguir**.

6. *to tell (=know for sure, be certain):*	*I can tell that she is sad.* *Who can tell? (=Who knows?)*	Yo **puedo decir** que está triste. ¿Quién **puede decir**?
	Standard variants →	Yo **he notado** que está triste. ¿Quién **sabe**?
7. *to tell (a story), narrate:*	*I'll tell you what happened.*	Te voy a **decir** lo que pasó.
	Standard variant →	Te voy a **contar** lo que pasó.
8. *to tell (secrets):*	*She goes around telling secrets.*	Ella anda **diciendo** secretos.
	Standard variant →	Ella anda **contando** secretos.

DEFINITIVO (adj)
= **definitive, final**
= **definite: fixed**
= **definite: certain, sure [US]**
= **definite: clear; firm [US]**

- In U.S. Spanish, **definitivo** indicates "definite, certain."
- In standard usage, it primarily means "definitive, final, conclusive."

Standard usage

1. *definitive, final:*	*Her decision is final.*	Su decisión es definitiva.
2. *definite (=fixed):*	*I don't have a definite plan.*	No tengo plan definitivo.

Extended US usage

3. *definite (=certain, sure):*	*It's definite that he's coming.*	Es **definitivo** que viene.
	Standard variant →	Es **seguro** que viene.
4. *definite (=clear):*	*a definite possibility*	una posibilidad **definitiva**
	Standard variant →	una posibilidad **clara**
5. *definite (=firm):*	*Do you have a definite opinion?*	¿Tienes una opinión **definitiva**?
	Standard variant →	¿Tienes una opinión **firme**?

DEJAR (verb)
= **to leave a person / an object**
= **to let, allow**
= **to leave a place [US]**
= **to leave for good [US]**

Standard usage

1. *to leave (a person):*	*I'll leave you at the entrance.*	Te dejo en la entrada.
2. *to leave (an object):*	*He left his wallet on the table.*	Dejó la cartera en la mesa.
3. *to let (=allow):*	*Let him sleep!*	¡Déjalo que duerma!

Extended US usage		
4. *to leave (a place):*	*I left my house at six o'clock.*	**Dejé** mi casa a las seis.
	Standard variant →	**Salí de** mi casa a las seis.
5. *to leave (for good):*	*He decided to leave his wife.*	Decidió **dejar** a su mujer.
	Standard variants →	Decidió **abandonar a /** **separarse de** su mujer.

DEJAR SABER (verb) = adapted from "to let (someone) know" [US]

- The result of a loan translation, **dejar saber** is widespread in U.S. Spanish.
- Traditional alternatives are **avisar**, **hacer saber**, or simply **decir**.

US usage		
1. *to let (someone) know:*	*I'll let you know tomorrow.*	Te **dejo saber** mañana.
	Standard variants →	Te **lo digo** / Te **aviso** mañana.
	Let me know when he arrives.	**Déjame saber** cuando llegue.
	Standard variant →	**Avísame** cuando llegue.
	She'll let you know by mail.	Te lo **dejará saber** por correo.
	Standard variant →	Te lo **hará saber** por correo.

DEMANDANTE (noun) = **plaintiff**
(adj) = **demanding [US]**

DEMANDAR (verb) = **to sue, file a lawsuit**
= **to demand: insist, request, require, claim [US]**

- In U.S. usage, **demandar** tends to remain faithful to the many English applications of "to demand," despite their classification as false cognates in standard Spanish.

Standard usage		
1. *to sue, file a lawsuit:*	*He sued his company.*	Demandó a su empresa.
2. *plaintiff:*	*The lawsuit was settled in favor of the plaintiff.*	El pleito se resolvió a favor del demandante.

Extended US usage

3. *to demand (=insist on):* | I demand that you leave. | **Demando** que te marches.
| **Standard variant →** | **Insisto en** que te marches.

4. *to demand (=request):* | He demanded an explanation. | **Demandó** una explicación.
| **Standard variant →** | **Exigió** una explicación.

5. *to demand (=require):* | The situation demands that we call the police. | La situación **demanda** que llamemos a la policía.
| **Standard variant →** | La situación **requiere** que ...

6. *to demand (=claim):* | I demand my rights. | **Demando** mis derechos.
| **Standard variant →** | **Reclamo** mis derechos.

7. *demanding:* | My son is very demanding. | Mi hijo es muy **demandante**.
| **Standard variant →** | Mi hijo es muy **exigente**.

DEMOSTRACIÓN (fem noun)
= **demonstration: illustration**
= **demonstration: protest [US]**
= **model, demo [US]**

• Translated literally from English, **demostración** occurs frequently in U.S. Spanish to mean "protest," in contrast to the more conventional **manifestación**.

Standard usage

1. *demonstration (=illustration):* | He gave us a demonstration of how it works. | Nos dio una demostración de cómo funciona.

Extended US usage

2. *demonstration (=protest):* | an anti-war demonstration | una **demostración** antiguerra
| **Standard variant →** | una **manifestación** antiguerra

3. *model (=demo):* | a demonstration model | un modelo de **demostración**
| **Standard variant →** | un modelo de **muestra**

DEMOSTRAR (verb)
= **to demonstrate: illustrate, prove**
= **to demonstrate: protest; display emotion [US]**

• Like **demostración**, the verb **demostrar** occurs in U.S. Spanish to denote "protest."

Standard usage

1. *to demonstrate (=prove, illustrate):* | You must demonstrate that you can do it. | Tienes que demostrar que lo puedes hacer.

Extended US usage

2. *to demonstrate (=protest):*	*The workers demonstrated in favor of better wages.*	Los obreros **demostraron** a favor de mejores sueldos.
	Standard variant →	Los obreros se **manifestaron** ...
3. *to demonstrate (=display):*	*He demonstrated fear and anxiety.*	**Demostró** miedo y ansiedad.
	Standard variants →	**Manifestó** miedo y ansiedad. **Expresó** miedo y ansiedad.

DEPENDIENDO DE (prep) = adapted from "depending on" [US]

- In standard Spanish, **dependiendo** exists only as the gerund of **depender**.
- In U.S. Spanish it occurs with **en** or **de** in place of the more conventional **según**.

US usage

1. *depending on:*	*Depending on the situation...*	**Dependiendo** de la situación...
	Standard variants →	**De acuerdo a** la situación... **Según** la situación...

DEPENDIENTE, A (noun) = store clerk, assistant; subordinate
  = dependent (child, etc.) [US]

- Although **dependiente** is generally defined as "el que depende de otro," it does not suggest "dependent," as the term is employed in the United States.
- Traditionally, it refers to a subordinate or employee such as a "store clerk."

Standard usage

1. *store clerk, assistant:*	*Why don't you ask the store clerk for help?*	¿Por qué no le pides ayuda al dependiente?
2. *subordinate:*	*The president of the company met with his subordinates.*	El presidente de la empresa se reunió con sus dependientes.

Extended US usage

3. *dependent (child, etc.):*	*I don't have any dependents.*	No tengo **dependientes**.
	Standard variants →	No tengo **personas a mi cargo**. No tengo **hijos**.

DESGRACIA (fem noun)   =   **misfortune, bad luck**
=   **disgrace, shame [US]**

> **desgracia.** (De *des-* y *gracia*). 1. f. Suerte adversa. 2. f. Suceso adverso o funesto. 3. f. Motivo de aflicción debido a un acontecimiento contrario a lo que se deseaba. [DRAE]

- In standard usage, **desgracia** has little to do with the English term "disgrace."

Standard usage		
1. *misfortune, bad luck:*	*I had the misfortune of missing my flight.*	Tuve la desgracia de perder el vuelo.

Extended US usage		
2. *disgrace (=shame):*	*What he did was a disgrace.*	Lo que hizo fue una **desgracia**.
	Standard variants →	Lo que hizo fue una **deshonra** / una **vergüenza**.

DESGRACIADO (adj & noun)   =   **unlucky, unhappy; wretched**
=   **disgraced [US]**

- The conventional meaning of **desgraciado** is "unfortunate" rather than "disgraced."

Standard usage		
1. *unlucky, unhappy:*	*In matters of health, he was an unlucky soul.*	En cuestión de salud, era un desgraciado.
2. *wretched:*	*They lived a wretched life.*	Tuvieron una vida desgraciada.

Extended US usage		
3. *disgraced:*	*She felt disgraced by what she had done.*	Se sintió **desgraciada** por lo que había hecho.
	Standard variants →	Se sintió **deshonrada** / **avergonzada** por lo que ...

DESHABILITADO, A (adj & noun)   =   **adapted from "disabled" [US]**

- The RAE and Moliner both sanction **discapacitado** as a calque of the English "disabled" along with the more traditional **minusválido**, but neither one accounts for **deshabilitado**.
- A fourth variant, more prevalent in Latin America, is **incapacitado**.

US usage		
1. *handicapped, disabled (adj):*	*She has a handicapped child.*	Tiene un hijo **deshabilitado**.
	Standard variants →	Tiene un hijo **discapacitado** / **minusválido** / **incapacitado**.
2. *handicapped, disabled (noun):*	*Who will help the disabled?*	¿Quién va a ayudar a los **deshabilitados**?
	Standard variant →	¿Quién va a ayudar a los **incapacitados**?

DEVOTAR (verb) = **adapted from "to devote" [US]**

- **Devoto** (adj & noun), standard for "devout," has no corresponding verb form in Spanish.
- **Devotar** is patterned after the English verb in form and usage.

US usage		
1. *to devote (=dedicate):*	*She devoted her life to helping the needy.*	**Devotó** su vida a ayudar a los necesitados.
	Standard variant →	**Dedicó** su vida a ayudar ...
2. *to devote (=assign, earmark):*	*They devoted thousands of dollars to scientific research.*	**Devotaron** miles de dólares a la investigación científica.
	Standard variant →	**Asignaron** miles de dólares ...

DIFERENTE (adj) = **different: distinct**
  = **different: various [US]**
  = **different: changed [US]**
  = **different: another [US]**

- The many nuances of "different" in English ("distinct, various, new, another," etc.) are reflected in the widespread use of **diferente** in U.S. Spanish.
- Even when the connotation is "distinct" or "dissimilar," traditional Spanish prefers **distinto**.

Standard usage		
1. *different (=distinct):*	*These are very different cases.*	Estos son casos muy diferentes.
	Traditional variant →	Estos son casos muy distintos.

Extended US usage

2. *different (=various):*

I like different types of music. — Me gustan **diferentes** tipos de música.

Standard variant → — Me gustan **varios** tipos ...

3. *different (=changed):*

Something is different about her. — Algo **es diferente** en ella.

Standard variant → — Algo **ha cambiado** en ella.

4. *different (=another):*

She wants a different desk. — Quiere un escritorio **diferente**.

Standard variant → — Quiere **otro** escritorio.

DIRECCIÓN (fem noun) =
- **address**
- **direction (course, destination)**
- **management, leadership**
- **directions, instructions [US]**
- **sense of direction [US]**

• Usage of **dirección** in the United States coincides with standard practice, with one notable exception: U.S. Spanish applies **direcciones** to "directions / instructions."

Standard usage

1. *address:* — What is your address? — ¿Cuál es tu dirección?

2. *direction (=destination):* — We are going in the direction of the airport. — Vamos en dirección al aeropuerto.

3. *direction (of play, film):* — This film won the award for best direction. — Esta película ganó el premio de dirección.

4. *management, leadership:* — The company is under new management. — La empresa está bajo nueva dirección.

Extended US usage

5. *directions (for use):* — Before using the phone, you should read the directions. — Antes de usar el teléfono, debes leer las **direcciones**.

Standard variants → — ... debes leer las **instrucciones de uso** / el **modo de empleo**.

6. *directions (to a place):* — Can you give me directions to the university? — ¿Me podrías dar **direcciones** a la universidad?

Standard variant → — ¿Me podrías dar **las señas** ...?

7. *sense of direction:* — good sense of direction — buen sentido de **dirección**

Standard variant → — buen sentido de **orientación**

71

DISGUSTAR(SE) (verb)
- = **to displease, upset**
- = **to become angry; argue**
- = **to disgust, be disgusted [US]**

- In standard usage, **disgustar** does not have the intensity of the English cognate "disgust."

Standard usage

1. to displease, upset:	*I'm upset about having to wait.*	Me disgusta tener que esperar.
2. to become angry, upset:	*He got angry and left.*	Se disgustó y se marchó.
3. to argue:	*She started to argue with him.*	Empezó a disgustarse con él.

Extended US usage

4. to disgust (=be repulsive, be repugnant):	*That food disgusted me.*	Esa comida me **disgustó**.
	Standard variants →	Esa comida me **repugnó** / me **dio asco**.
5. to disgust (=offend):	*We were disgusted by his racist ideas.*	Sus ideas racistas nos **disgustaron**.
	Standard variants →	Sus ideas racistas nos **ofendieron** / **indignaron**.

DISGUSTO (masc noun)
- = **displeasure, upset, annoyance**
- = **quarrel, argument**
- = **disgust, repugnance [US]**

- Much the same as the corresponding verb form, **disgusto** can express "bad taste" in standard practice, but not to the point of "repugnance," as it can in U.S. Spanish.

Standard usage

1. displeasure, upset:	*He really upset me when he ordered me to leave.*	Me dio un verdadero disgusto cuando me mandó salir.
2. quarrel, argument:	*They had a big argument.*	Tuvieron un gran disgusto.

Extended US usage

3. disgust (=repugnance):	*I felt disgust when he told me what he had eaten.*	Sentí **disgusto** cuando me dijo lo que había comido.
	Standard variant →	Sentí **repugnancia** cuando …
4. disgust (=anger):	*She left the party in disgust.*	Se fue de la fiesta **en disgusto**.
	Standard variants →	Se fue de la fiesta **indignada** / **ofendida**.

DISKET, DISQUETE (masc noun)   =   **adapted from "diskette"** [DRAE 1992]

disquete. (Del inglés *diskette*). m. Inform. Disco magnético portátil de poca capacidad, que se introduce en el ordenador para grabar o reproducir información. [Moliner]

- Made current by the use of computers, U.S. Spanish speakers tend to prefer the shortened form **disket**, more faithful to the English pronunciation.

Standard/US usage		
1. diskette (computer):	*I left my diskette in the computer.*	Me dejé el **disquete** / **disket** en la computadora.

DOMÉSTICO (adj)   =   **domestic: household**
=   **domestic: national, internal [US]**
=   **domestic: homebody [US]**

- In standard Spanish, the adjective **doméstico** concerns itself primarily with the home.
- It may be used, secondarily, in opposition to "wild" or "untamed."
- U.S. Spanish adapts the use of **doméstico** to common English practice.

Standard usage		
1. domestic (=household):	*domestic chores*	tareas domésticas
	household expenses	gastos domésticos
2. domestic (=not wild):	*The cat is a domestic animal.*	El gato es un animal doméstico.

Extended US usage		
3. domestic (=national):	*schedule of domestic flights*	horario de vuelos **domésticos**
	Standard variant →	horario de vuelos **nacionales**
4. domestic (=internal):	*serious domestic problems*	graves problemas **domésticos**
	Standard variant →	graves problemas **internos**
5. domestic (=homebody):	*my sister is very domestic*	mi hermana es muy **doméstica**
	Standard variants →	mi hermana es muy **casera** / muy **hogareña**.

DONA (fem), DÓNUT (masc noun)   =   **adapted from "doughnut"** [US]

- With no exact equivalent in academic Spanish, there are many variants in use in the United States. Ilan Stavans prefers **dona** (fem) whereas most dictionaries list **dónut** (masc) as first or only option. The Vox Dictionary lists both.

US usage		
1. *doughnut:*	*I had a doughnut with my coffee.*	Me comí una **dona** con el café.
	Standard variant →	Me comí un **buñuelo** ...

DORMITORIO (masc noun) = **bedroom; bedroom set**
= **dormitory, student residence [US]**

• Traditionally classified as a false cognate, **dormitorio** bears no relation to "student dormitory" in standard practice.

Standard usage		
1. *bedroom:*	*a three-bedroom house*	una casa de tres dormitorios
2. *bedroom set:*	*We bought a nice bedroom set.*	Compramos un lindo dormitorio.

Extended US usage		
3. *dormitory (=student residence):*	*The student dormitories are near the university.*	Los **dormitorios** estudiantiles están cerca de la universidad.
	Standard variant →	Las **residencias** estudiantiles ...

DOWNLOAD (noun) = **loanword for "download" [US]**

• This term, pronounced as in English, can occur in U.S. Spanish as part of a verb phrase.

US usage		
1. *download (noun):*	*Each download takes one minute.*	Cada **download** dura un minuto.
	Standard variant →	Cada **descarga** dura un minuto.
2. *to download:*	*I downloaded twenty songs on the internet.*	**Hice download de** veinte canciones en el internet.
	Standard variant →	**Descargué** veinte canciones ...

DROGUERÍA (fem noun) = **adapted from "drugstore" [US]**

• In Spain, **droguería** refers primarily to a store that sells household goods such as paint and cleaning products (DRAE 1989).
• In the United States, it commonly refers to a drugstore or convenience store.

Standard usage		
1. *household supply store:*	*They sell paint at the supply store.*	Venden pintura en la droguería.

Extended US usage

2. *drugstore (=pharmacy):*	*I'm going to the drugstore to buy aspirin.*	Voy a la **droguería** a comprar aspirina.
	Standard variant →	Voy a la **farmacia** a comprar …
3. *convenience store:*	*CVS is a popular convenience store.*	CVS es una **droguería** popular.
	Standard variant →	CVS es una **tienda de comestibles y medicamentos** popular.

DROGUISTA (masc / fem noun) = **adapted from "druggist" [US]**

- Historically, this term conveys the notion of "liar" or "cheater."
- Since 1989, **droguista** and **droguero** refer to a seller in a household supply store.
- In U.S. Spanish, it is used in lieu of **farmacéutico** to indicate "druggist" or "pharmacist."

Standard usage

1. *household supplier:*	*I ordered some brooms from the supplier.*	Le encargué unas escobas al droguista.

Extended US usage

2. *druggist, pharmacist:*	*The druggist recommended these lozenges.*	El **droguista** me recomendó estas pastillas.
	Standard variant →	El **farmacéutico** me recomendó estas pastillas.

DUMPING (masc noun) = **loanword for "dumping"** [DRAE 1989]

dumping. (Voz inglesa). m. Econ. Práctica comercial de vender a precios inferiores al costo, para adueñarse del mercado, con grave perjuicio de este. [DRAE]

- Sanctioned by the RAE and listed in Moliner in connection with the commercial practice of selling goods or securities at a price below market value.
- In the United States, it is used increasingly to refer to the illegal "dumping" of garbage, wastes, chemicals, etc.

Standard usage

1. *dumping (commercial):*	*Excessive dumping can have an impact on the market.*	El dumping excesivo puede afectar la bolsa de valores.

Extended US usage

2. *dumping (=spillage of wastes, chemicals, etc.):*	*The dumping of nuclear wastes is a serious problem.*	El **dumping** de residuos nucleares es un grave problema.
	Standard variant →	El **vertido** de residuos …

EDITOR, RA (noun) = **publisher**
= **newspaper editor [Lat Am]**
= **editor, text editor [US]**

- In traditional Spanish, **editor** refers mainly to "someone who publishes or prints."
- In U.S. Spanish, it can also mean "someone who edits or corrects a text."

Standard usage
1. *publisher:* — *publisher of books and articles* — editor de libros y artículos

Extended US usage

2. *chief editor (Spain):* — *We spoke with the chief editor of "El País."* — Hablamos con el **editor** de "El País."

Standard variant → — Hablamos con el **director** de "El País."

3. *text editor:* — *An editor corrected the text.* — Un **editor** corrigió el texto.

Standard variant → — Un **redactor** corrigió el texto.

4. *editor's note:* — *Did you read the editor's note?* — ¿Leíste la nota del **editor**?

Standard variant → — ¿Leíste la nota de **redacción**?

EDITORIAL (fem noun) = **publishing house**
(masc noun) = **lead article**
(adjective) = **text editing [US]**

Standard usage
1. *publishing house:* — *Gredos is a well-known Spanish publishing house.* — Gredos es una editorial española muy conocida.

2. *lead article:* — *Have you read the lead article?* — ¿Has leído el editorial?

Extended US usage
3. *text editing:* — *The editing of the text took two months.* — La **tarea editorial** duró dos meses.

Standard variant → — La **redacción** duró dos meses.

EDUCACIÓN (fem noun) = **manners; education (in general)**
                              = **education: schooling, culture, training [US]**
                              = **education: teaching, pedagogy [US]**

- Depending on the intended connotation in English, "education" may or may not be translated as **educación** in standard practice.
- Generally speaking, **educación** (**buena** or **mala**) refers to overall "breeding," including manners, courtesy, and other social refinements, rather than "schooling" or "training."
- U.S. Spanish goes well beyond this traditional definition and imitates English usage.

Standard usage		
1. education (general):	*the education of children*	la educación de los niños
2. education (central body):	*the education department*	el departamento de educación
3. manners, breeding:	*poor manners*	falta de educación

Extended US usage		
4. education (=schooling):	*Who paid for her education?*	¿Quién le pagó la **educación**?
	Standard variant →	¿Quién le pagó los **estudios**?
5. education (=knowledge):	*people of little education*	gente de poca **educación**
	Standard variant →	gente de pocos **conocimientos**
6. education (=training):	*a good musical education*	una buena **educación** musical
	Standard variant →	una buena **formación** musical
7. education (=teaching):	*She works in education.*	Trabaja en la **educación**.
	Standard variant →	Trabaja en la **enseñanza**.
8. education (=pedagogy):	*I took an education course.*	Tomé un curso de **educación**.
	Standard variant →	Tomé un curso de **pedagogía**.

EDUCACIONAL (adj) = **educational: in general, instructive**
                          = **educational: for school use [US]**
                          = **educational: related to teaching [US]**
                          = **educational: pedagogical; academic [US]**

- To express "educational," academic Spanish offers a variety of context-specific terms, such as **instructivo**, **docente**, **pedagógico**, etc.
- U.S. Spanish tends to apply **educacional** very broadly, as does American English.

Standard usage		
1. educational (in general):	*an educational film*	una película educacional
	Traditional variants →	una película instructiva / educativa

Extended US usage

2. *educational (=for school use):*	*We have educational textbooks.*	Tenemos libros **educacionales**.
	Standard variant →	Tenemos libros **escolares**.
3. *related to teaching:*	*the educational standards*	los estándares **educacionales**
	Standard variants →	los estándares **de educación / de enseñanza**
4. *educational (role, function):*	*the educational role of television*	el papel **educacional** de la televisión
	Standard variant →	el papel **docente** de la televisión
5. *educational theory:*	*I study educational psychology.*	Estudio sicología **educacional**.
	Standard variant →	Estudio sicología **pedagógica**.
6. *educational (=academic):*	*educational success*	éxito **educacional**
	Standard variant →	éxito **académico**

EDUCADO (adj) = **well-mannered, polite**
= **educated, trained [US]**

- Just as **educación** refers primarily to "manners" and "breeding" in academic Spanish, **educado** generally implies "well-mannered."
- U.S. Spanish, which takes its cue from English, broadens the meaning of **educado** to include "educated, knowledgeable, cultured."

Standard usage

1. *well-mannered, polite:*	*a well-mannered young man*	un joven bien educado
2. *ill-mannered, rude:*	*an ill-mannered young man*	un joven mal educado

Extended US usage

3. *educated (=well-trained, cultured, knowledgeable):*	*a well-educated person*	una persona **bien educada**
	Standard variants →	una persona **culta / instruida**
4. *uneducated (=unschooled, uncultured):*	*an uneducated person*	una persona **mal educada**
	Standard variant →	una persona **inculta**
5. *educated (=prepared academically):*	*I was educated at the University of Puerto Rico.*	**Fui educada** en la universidad de Puerto Rico.
	Standard variant →	**Cursé mis estudios** en ...

EDUCAR (verb)

= **to bring up, raise**
= **to educate: train, develop, teach**

- Interestingly, the RAE has relegated what is perhaps the most traditional definition of **educar** ("to teach good manners") to last position, while Moliner places it at the top.
- Unquestionably, contemporary usage of **educar** has become more consistent with formal education and schooling, both in standard and U.S. Spanish.

Standard/US usage		
1. *to bring up, raise:*	*My parents raised me well.*	Mis padres me **educaron** bien.
	Traditional variant →	Mis padres me **criaron** bien.
2. *to train, develop:*	*One needs to train the mind.*	Hace falta **educar** el intelecto.
	Traditional variant →	Hace falta **desarrollar** el intelecto.
3. *to educate (=teach, provide instruction):*	*Who is going to educate our children?*	¿Quién va a **educar** a nuestros hijos?
	Traditional variants →	¿Quién va a **enseñar** / a **instruir** a nuestros hijos?

EFECTIVO (adj)

= **effective: in force**
= **effective: useful, potent [US]**
= **effective: capable, competent [US]**
= **effective: striking, impressive [US]**

- **Eficiente**, **efectivo**, and **eficaz** are often used interchangeably in U.S. Spanish.

Standard usage		
1. *effective (=in force):*	*The law took effect yesterday.*	La ley se hizo efectiva ayer.
	Traditional variant →	La ley entró en vigor ayer.

Extended US usage		
2. *effective (=useful, yields good results):*	*What is the most effective remedy for a headache?*	¿Cuál es el remedio más **efectivo** para el dolor de cabeza?
	Standard variant →	¿Cuál es el remedio más **eficaz** para el dolor de cabeza?
3. *effective (=competent):*	*My secretary is very effective.*	Mi secretaria es muy **efectiva**.
	Standard variants →	Mi secretaria es muy **capaz** / **eficiente** / **competente**.
4. *effective (=striking):*	*That color combination is quite effective.*	Esa combinación de colores es muy **efectiva**.
	Standard variants →	Esa combinación ... es muy **lograda** / **causa buen efecto**.

ELABORAR (verb)

= **to produce, make; work, shape (a material)**
= **to draw up, prepare, devise**
= **to elaborate: develop, explain further [US]**

- **Elaborar** has two standard meanings in Spanish: (1) "to make a product" and (2) "to prepare, devise" (a plan, for example).
- The use of **elaborar** in the United States for "to develop" or "explain further" results from the influence of its English cognate.

Standard usage

1. to produce, make:	*Spain produces some excellent wines.*	En España se elaboran vinos excelentes.
2. to work, shape (material):	*We work various kinds of metals.*	Elaboramos varios tipos de metal.
3. to draw up, devise:	*You need to draw up a plan.*	Tienes que elaborar un plan.

Extended US usage

4. to elaborate (=develop):	*It is essential to elaborate the main idea.*	Es imprescindible **elaborar** la idea principal.
	Standard variant →	Es imprescindible **desarrollar** ...
5. to elaborate (=provide details):	*He refused to elaborate.*	Se negó a **elaborar**.
	Standard variant →	Se negó a **dar detalles**.
6. to elaborate on (=explain):	*Could you elaborate on your strategy?*	¿Podrías **elaborar** acerca de tu estrategia?
	Standard variants →	¿Podrías **explicar** tu estrategia?

ELECTIVO (adj)

= **elective: related to "political election"**
= **elective: optional [US]**

Standard usage

1. elective (=related to political election):	*He is not familiar with our elective process.*	No conoce bien nuestro proceso electivo.

Extended US usage

2. elective (=optional):	*These are elective courses.*	Éstos son cursos **electivos**.
	Standard variants →	Éstos son cursos **facultativos** / **optativos** / **opcionales**.
3. elective (medical procedure):	*elective surgery*	cirugía **electiva**
	Standard variant →	cirugía **optativa**

ELEVADOR (masc noun)

= **elevator (of products & merchandise)**
= **electrical booster**
= **passenger elevator** [DRAE 1984]

- The standard term for "elevator" in Spanish is **ascensor**.
- **Elevador**, used extensively in the United States and much of Latin America, is fully sanctioned by the RAE as an American variant.

Standard usage		
1. *elevator (of products):*	*We placed the sacks on the grain elevator.*	Colocamos los sacos en el elevador de granos.
2. *booster:*	*energy booster*	elevador de energía

US usage		
3. *passenger elevator:*	*The elevator is not working.*	El **elevador** no funciona.
	Standard variant →	El **ascensor** no funciona.
4. *freight elevator:*	*freight elevator*	**elevador** de mercancías
	Standard variants →	**ascensor** de mercancías / **montacargas**

E-MAIL (masc noun) = **loanword for "e-mail" [US]**

- Used widely in modern Spanish, **e-mail** (pronounced as in English) appears in major dictionaries (Moliner, Vox, Larousse, etc.), but is not approved by the RAE.
- The need for a short version of the standard **correo electrónico** has produced a growing number of variants for "e-mail message" in the United States: **emilio**, **imalito**, **manuelito**.

US usage		
1. *e-mail (system):*	*Everyone uses e-mail.*	Todo el mundo usa **e-mail**.
	Standard variant →	Todo el mundo usa **el correo electrónico**.
2. *e-mail message:*	*Send him an e-mail.*	Envíale un **e-mail** / un **emilio**.
	Standard variant →	Envíale un **correo electrónico**.

EMBARAZADA (adj) = **pregnant**
= **embarrassed, embarrassing [US]**

EMBARAZAR (verb) = **to make pregnant; hamper, hinder**
= **to embarrass [US]**

- Moliner allows for **embarazar** to mean "to embarrass" or "intimidate," a common secondary application in U.S. Spanish.

Standard usage		
1. to make pregnant:	*He made her pregnant.*	La embarazó.
2. to hamper, hinder:	*Don't get in his way.*	No le embaraces el paso.
3. pregnant:	*She is six months pregnant.*	Está embarazada de seis meses.

Extended US usage		
4. to embarrass:	*My mother embarrassed me in front of my friends.*	Mi madre me **embarazó** delante de mis amigos.
	Standard variants →	Mi madre me **avergonzó / me hizo pasar vergüenza** ...
5. embarrassed:	*She felt very embarrassed.*	Se sintió muy **embarazada**.
	Standard variants →	Se sintió muy **comprometida**. Sintió **mucha vergüenza**.
6. embarrassing:	*an embarrassing moment*	un momento **embarazado**
	Standard variant →	un momento **embarazoso**

ENFORZAR (verb) = **adapted from "to enforce" [US]**

- Current in the United States, this verb does not exist in academic Spanish.

US usage		
1. to enforce (=make effective):	*It is very difficult to enforce certain laws.*	Es muy difícil **enforzar** ciertas leyes.
	Standard variant →	Es muy difícil **hacer cumplir** ciertas leyes.
2. to enforce (=insist on):	*We must enforce mutual respect.*	Tenemos que **enforzar** el respeto mutuo.
	Standard variant →	Tenemos que **insistir en** el respeto mutuo.

3. *to enforce (=carry out):*	*The sentence was enforced.*	La sentencia fue **enforzada**.
	Standard variant →	**Se ejecutó** la sentencia.
4. *to enforce (=compel):*	*The school will need to enforce the rules of attendance.*	La escuela tendrá que **enforzar** las reglas de asistencia.
	Standard variant →	La escuela tendrá que **imponer** las reglas de asistencia.

EN LÍNEA   see **LÍNEA** and **ONLINE**

ENROLAR(SE) (verb)   =   **to enlist, sign up, join**
=   **to enroll (in school) [US]**

- Traditionally, **enrolar(se)** is "to enlist" (in the military, for ex.) or "to join" (an organization).
- In U.S. Spanish, it is the equivalent of "to enroll" (in school, in a course, etc.).

Standard usage		
1. *to enlist, sign up (trans):*	*We signed up 100 people for the march.*	Enrolamos a cien personas para la manifestación.
2. *to enlist, join (intrans):*	*My brother wants to join the army.*	Mi hermano quiere enrolarse en el ejército.

Extended US usage		
3. *to enroll (trans):*	*I enrolled fifteen students.*	**Enrolé** a quince estudiantes.
	Standard variant →	**Matriculé** a quince estudiantes.
4. *to enroll (intrans):*	*Did you enroll in the course?*	¿Te **enrolaste** en el curso?
	Standard variants →	¿Te **inscribiste / matriculaste** en el curso?

ÉNTER (masc noun)   =   **loanword for "enter button" [US]**

- Another cyber-Spanglish term cited by Ilan Stavans, the traditional term for "enter button" is **tecla de retorno**, a carryover from the "return key" on a typewriter.

US usage		
1. *enter button:*	*Don't forget to hit enter.*	Que no se te olvide apretar el **énter**.
	Standard variant →	... apretar la **tecla de retorno**.

ENTRAR (verb)
- = **to enter: go in**
- = **to bring in, take in**
- = **to fit**
- = **to start to feel** (idiomatic)
- = **to enter: be admitted, join [US]**
- = **to enter (school, contest, field) [US]**

• In standard English, "to enter" is often used figuratively as a synonym of "to join," "be admitted," "become involved," etc. U.S. Spanish extends the use of **entrar** accordingly.

Standard usage		
1. *to enter (=go in):*	*The student entered the office.*	El alumno entró en la oficina.
2. *to bring in:*	*Bring in the chair before it rains.*	Entra la silla antes que llueva.
3. *to fit:*	*This doesn't fit in the suitcase.*	Esto no entra en la maleta.
4. *to start to feel (idiom):*	*I'm starting to feel sleepy.*	Me está entrando sueño.

Extended US usage		
5. *to enter (=be admitted):*	*When did he enter the hospital?*	¿Cuándo **entró** en el hospital?
	Standard variant →	¿Cuándo **ingresó** en el hospital?
6. *to enter (=join):*	*I entered the company in 1994.*	**Entré** en la empresa en 1994.
	Standard variants →	**Me incorporé a** la empresa … **Entré a formar parte de** …
7. *to enter (into school):*	*I am entering him into school.*	Lo voy a **entrar** en la escuela.
	Standard variants →	Lo voy a **inscribir / matricular** en la escuela.
8. *to enter (a contest):*	*Did you enter the contest?*	¿**Entraste** en el concurso?
	Standard variants →	¿**Te inscribiste / participaste** en el concurso?
9. *to enter (a field, a profession):*	*He plans to enter politics.*	Piensa **entrar** en la política.
	Standard variant →	Piensa **meterse** en la política.

ENVOLVER (verb) = **to wrap, wrap up**
                 = **to surround, shroud**
                 = **to involve: concern; implicate [US]**
                 = **to involve: entail, imply [US]**
                 = **to involve: require [US]**

- Although **envolver** does not ordinarily mean "to involve" in standard Spanish, one of Moliner's definitions supports such usage:

    envolver ...7. Hacer intervenir a alguien en un enredo o asunto irregular. [Moliner]

- By influence of English, this usage is more typical of U.S. Spanish.

Standard usage		
1. *to wrap, wrap up:*	*Shall I wrap it up for you?*	¿Quieres que te lo **envuelva**?
2. *to surround, shroud:*	*A mist surrounded the castle.*	Una niebla **envolvía** el castillo.

Extended US usage		
3. *to involve (=concern):*	*That doesn't involve me.*	Eso no me **envuelve**.
	Standard variants →	Eso no me **concierne**. Eso no me **atañe**.
4. *to involve (=implicate):*	*Don't involve me in your issues.*	No me **envuelvas** en tus asuntos.
	Standard variants →	No me **impliques / metas / involucres** en tus asuntos.
5. *to involve (=entail, imply):*	*This involves a lot of work.*	Esto **envuelve** mucho trabajo.
	Standard variant →	Esto **supone** mucho trabajo.
6. *to involve (=require)*	*The project involves money.*	El proyecto **envuelve** dinero.
	Standard variant →	El proyecto **requiere** dinero.
7. *to get involved:*	*He doesn't want to get involved.*	No quiere **envolverse**.
	Standard variant →	No quiere **meterse**.

ENVUELTO (adj)

= **wrapped**
= **surrounded, shrouded**
= **involved: implicated [US]**
= **involved: absorbed [US]**
= **involved: complicated [US]**

Standard usage

1. wrapped:	*two boxes wrapped in paper*	dos cajas envueltas en papel
2. surrounded, shrouded:	*a death shrouded in mystery*	una muerte envuelta en misterio

Extended US usage

3. involved (=implicated):	*involved in the crime*	**envuelto** en el crimen
	Standard variant →	**implicado** en el crimen
4. involved (=absorbed):	*He's so involved he can't hear.*	Está tan **envuelto** que no oye.
	Standard variant →	Esta tan **absorto** que no oye.
5. involved (=complicated):	*This case is too involved.*	Este caso es muy **envuelto**.
	Standard variant →	Este caso es muy **complicado**.
6. people involved (idiom):	*Those involved will speak out.*	Los **envueltos** hablarán.
	Standard variants →	Los **interesados** / los **involucrados** hablarán.

EQUIVOCADO (adj)

= **wrong: mistaken (number, date, address, etc.)**
= **morally wrong [US]**
= **wrong (answer, response) [US]**

- **Equivocado** is appropriate in academic Spanish when "wrong" implies the misjudging or mistaking of one thing for another (such as a number, an address, a date, etc.).
- In many such cases, however, the verb form **equivocarse** is preferred.

Standard usage

1. wrong (mistaken info):	*You have the wrong date.*	Tienes la fecha equivocada.
	I dialed a wrong number.	Me equivoqué de número.
2. be wrong (=mistaken):	*You are wrong.*	Estás equivocado.
	You made a mistake.	Te equivocaste.

Extended US usage		
3. *wrong (morally)*:	*He was wrong to insult him.*	**Fue equivocado** en insultarlo.
	Standard variant →	**Hizo mal** en insultarlo.
4. *wrong, incorrect (answer, response)*:	*Your answer is wrong.*	Tu respuesta es **equivocada**.
	Standard variant →	Tu respuesta es **incorrecta**.
5. *do something wrong (idiomatic)*:	*You're doing it all wrong.*	Lo estás haciendo **equivocado**.
	Standard variants →	Lo estás haciendo **mal**. **Así no se hace**.

ESCANEAR (verb) = **adapted from "to scan"** [DRAE 2001]

ESCÁNER (masc noun) = **adapted from "scanner"** [DRAE 2001]

• Both terms have been incorporated into academic Spanish. In the United States, **escáner** refers primarily to a "document scanner" linked to a computer.

Standard/US usage		
1. *to scan*:	*Were you able to scan the documents?*	¿Llegaste a **escanear** los documentos?
2. *scanner (med / comp)*:	*I need to buy a scanner for my computer.*	Necesito comprar un **escáner** para mi computadora.

ESCÚTER (masc noun) = **adapted from "scooter"** [DRAE 2001]

• Newly sanctioned term, it is spelled **escúter** in Moliner, and **scooter** in the DRAE.

Standard/US usage		
1. *scooter*:	*My son spends all day riding on his scooter.*	Mi hijo se pasa todo el día montado en el **escúter**.

ESLOGAN (masc noun) = **adapted from "slogan"** [DRAE 1984]

• Sanctioned in 1984, **eslogan** made its way into the standard Spanish lexicon in 1940 as **slogan** (Corominas). The latter spelling is more common in the United States.

Standard/US usage		
1. *slogan*:	*Every product needs a slogan.*	Todo producto necesita un **eslogan**.

ESMOG (masc noun)   see **SMOG**

ESNAC (masc noun)   =   **loanword for "snack" [US]**

- The American concept of "snack" is not accurately conveyed with the traditional Spanish **merienda**. Hence, the popularity of **snack** or **esnac** in U.S. Spanish.
- This term is not mentioned in Moliner nor is it sanctioned by the RAE.

US usage		
1. *snack:*	*When you give up snacks, you'll start to lose weight.*	Cuando dejes **los esnacs**, empezarás a adelgazar.
	Standard variants →	Cuando dejes **la merienda** ... Cuando dejes **de picar** ...
2. *snack bar:*	*I went to the snack bar to have a sandwich.*	Fui al **snack** a comerme un sándwich.
	Standard variant →	Fui a la **cafetería** a comer ...

ESNOB (adj & noun)   =   **adapted from "snob" [DRAE 1927]**

- The incorporation of **snob** into Spanish took place in the early twentieth century.
- The RAE and Moliner prefer **esnob**, although both forms are equally common.

Standard/US usage		
1. *snob (noun):*	*That woman is a snob.*	Esa señora es una **esnob**.
	Traditional variant →	Esa señora es una **elitista**.
2. *snob (adj):*	*Don't be such a snob!*	¡No seas tan **esnob**!
	Traditional variant →	¡No seas tan **presumido**!

ESPÁNGLISH (masc noun)   =   **loanword for "Spanglish" [US]**

- Moliner and Vox call it **spanglish**; HarperCollins prefers **espánglish**; Stavans cites as many as seven variants, including **casteyanqui** and **inglanol**; and the DRAE makes no mention of it.

  Spanglish. (Inglés; pronunciado [espánglis]). m. Lengua española con gran influencia del inglés; se usa sobre todo para referirse a la lengua hablada por los puertorriqueños o por los hispanos que viven en los Estados Unidos. [Moliner]

ESPICH (masc noun)   see **SPEECH**

ESPÓNSOR (masc noun) = **adapted from "sponsor"** [DRAE 2001]

- **Espónsor** is fully embraced in standard Spanish as a synonym of **patrocinador**.
- The RAE sanctions **spónsor** while favoring the Spanish form of the verb (**esponsorizar**).

Standard US usage		
1. sponsor:	*The sponsor of the program is the Spanish Embassy.*	El **espónsor** del programa es la Embajada Española.
	Traditional variant →	El **patrocinador** del programa es la Embajada Española.

ESPONSORIZAR (verb) = **adapted from "to sponsor"** [DRAE 2001]

- Sanctioned by the RAE and Moliner, this verb is used increasingly in the United States along with the more traditional **patrocinar**.

Standard usage		
1. to sponsor (=fund):	*The university sponsors a variety of programs.*	La universidad esponsoriza diversos programas.

Extended US usage		
2. to sponsor (=support):	*Which countries sponsor terrorism?*	¿Qué países **esponsorizan** el terrorismo?
	Standard variants →	¿Qué países **respaldan** /**apoyan** el terrorismo?
3. to sponsor (a bill, law):	*Our congressman plans to sponsor a new bill.*	Nuestro congresista piensa **esponsorizar** una nueva ley.
	Standard variant →	... **proponer** una nueva ley.

ESPREY (masc noun) = **adapted from "spray"** [DRAE 1985]

ESPREYAR (verb) = **adapted from "to spray"** [US]

- Only the noun form **spray** is sanctioned by the RAE as a variant of **atomizador**.
- It appears in certain dictionaries as **espray** or **esprey**, along with the verb **espreyar**.

Standard usage		
1. spray:	*Put a little spray on your hair.*	Ponte un poquito de spray / de esprey en el pelo.

Extended US usage		
2. *to spray:*	*I have to spray the plants.*	Tengo que **espreyar** las flores.
	Standard variant →	Tengo que **rociar** las flores.

"Spray" expressions in standard Spanish	*spray can*	spray pulverizador
	spray gun	pistola rociadora
	spray paint	pintura spray

ESTADO DE ARTE (adj) = **adapted from "state-of-the-art" [US]**

• This unconventional expression borrowed from English has been gaining popularity in the United States, particularly in reference to modern technology.

US usage		
1. *state-of-the-art:*	*The technology we use is state-of-the-art.*	La tecnología que usamos es **estado de arte**.
	Standard variants →	La tecnología que usamos es **reciente / de vanguardia / de la más moderna**.

ESTÁNDAR (adj & masc noun) = **adapted from "standard"** [DRAE 1970]

> **estándar**. (Del inglés *standard*). 1. adj. Que sirve como tipo, modelo, norma, patrón o referencia. 2. m. Tipo, modelo, patrón, nivel. Estándar de vida. [DRAE]

• Also spelled **standard**, this loanword has wide acceptance in Spain and Latin America.
• It occurs in U.S. Spanish, as in English, in dozens of contexts, too many to mention here.
• As a noun, **estándar** can indicate "level, norm, perspective, quality, values," and so on.
• As an adjective it can imply "normal, normative, official, legal, habitual," etc.

Standard/US usage		
1. *standard (adj):*	*I bought the standard model.*	Compré el modelo standard.
2. *standard (noun):*	*standard of living*	estándar de vida

"Standard" expressions in traditional Spanish	*a good (high) standard*	un nivel alto
	a poor (low) standard	un nivel bajo
	above standard (quality)	de alta calidad
	below standard (quality)	de baja calidad
	by any standard	de cualquier punto de vista
	gold standard	el patrón oro

impossible standards	patrones / normas imposibles
moral standards	valores morales
standard class	clase turista
standard English	inglés estándar / normativo
standard (equipment)	de serie
standard grammar	gramática normativa
standard practice / procedure	una norma / la norma
standard price	precio oficial
standard quality	calidad normal
standard rate (of interest)	tasa de interés vigente
standard size / weight	tamaño / peso legal
standard time	hora oficial
standard treatment	tratamiento habitual
standard of conduct	norma de conducta
standard of excellence	nivel de excelencia
standard of medical care	calidad de atención médica
standard of service	nivel de servicio
to become standard	imponerse como norma

ESTÁRTER (masc noun)   =   **adapted from "starter (motor)"** [DRAE 1985]

estárter. (Del inglés *starter*). m. Dispositivo de los motores de explosión que facilita su arranque mediante el enriquecimiento de la mezcla de carburación. [DRAE]

- One of many automotive terms borrowed from English, **estárter** is prevalent in U.S. as well as standard Spanish along with the traditional **motor de arranque.**
- Originally approved as **starter** by the RAE in 1985, it was left out of the 1992 dictionary edition, and hispanicized to **estárter** in 2001.

Standard/US usage		
1. starter motor:	The starter in my new car was defective.	El **estárter** de mi nuevo auto tenía un defecto.
	Traditional variant →	El **motor de arranque** de mi nuevo auto tenía un defecto.

ESTATUS (masc noun)   =   **adapted from "status"** [DRAE 1985]

- First listed as **status**, the RAE changed it to **estatus** in its 2001 dictionary edition.
- Vox and Moliner prefer **status**. Stavans favors the hispanicized form.
- U.S. Spanish applies this term more broadly to reflect common English usage.

Standard usage

1. *status (social):*	*There is a connection between social status and well-being.*	Hay una relación entre estatus social y bienestar.
	Traditional variant →	... una relación entre posición social y bienestar.
2. *status (=place, link):*	*What is the status of the novel in our century?*	¿Cuál es el estatus de la novela en nuestro siglo?
	Traditional variant →	¿Cuál es la situación de la novela en nuestro siglo?

Extended US usage

3. *status (legal):*	*What is her legal status in this country?*	¿Cuál es su estatus legal en este país?
	Standard variant →	¿Cuál es su estado legal en este país?
4. *status (=rank, prestige):*	*His status in the organization is an important factor.*	Su estatus en la organización es un factor importante.
	Standard variant →	Su rango en la organización ...

"Status" expressions in standard Spanish		
	marital status	estado civil
	status inquiry	valoración crediticia
	status quo	statu quo
	status report	informe situacional
	status symbol	símbolo de rango

ESTIMADO (masc noun)   =   adapted from "estimate" [US]

- **Estimado** is a viable adjective in standard usage for "dear" or "esteemed," but not a noun.
- As a noun, **estimado** has become the counterpart of "estimate" in U.S. Spanish.

US usage

1. *estimate (=approx. cost):*	*They gave me an estimate for labor costs.*	Me dieron un estimado para la mano de obra.
	Standard variant →	Me dieron un presupuesto para la mano de obra.
2. *estimate (calculation):*	*Do you want the exact total or an estimate?*	¿Quieres el resultado exacto o un estimado?
	Standard variant →	¿Quieres el resultado exacto o un cálculo aproximativo?

ESTIMAR (verb)   =   **to esteem: appreciate; consider**
                       =   **to estimate: judge, calculate [US]**

• In the United States, **estimar** means not only "to esteem" but also "to estimate."

Standard usage		
1. to esteem (=respect):	*I respect my colleagues.*	Estimo a mis colegas
2. to consider:	*I don't consider it impossible.*	No estimo que sea imposible.

Extended US usage		
3. to estimate (=calculate):	*I estimate the cost at $5000.*	**Estimo** que va a costar $5000.
	Standard variant →	**Calculo** que va a costar $5000.
4. to estimate (cost for work to be done):	*We did not estimate for a new kitchen.*	No **estimamos** para una nueva cocina.
	Standard variant →	No **hicimos el presupuesto** para una nueva cocina.

ESTOC (masc noun)   see **STOCK**

ESTRÉS (masc noun)   =   **adapted from "stress" [DRAE 1984]**

ESTRESADO (adj)   =   **adapted from "stressed" [DRAE 2001]**

ESTRESANTE (adj)   =   **adapted from "stressful" [DRAE 1984]**

ESTRESAR (verb)   =   **adapted from "to stress" [DRAE 2001]**

estrés. (Del inglés *stress*). m. situación de tensión nerviosa prolongada, que puede alterar ciertas funciones del organismo. [Moliner]

• With no exact equivalent in traditional Spanish, all four terms are now sanctioned by the RAE and have become mainstream expressions throughout the Spanish-speaking world.

Standard/US usage		
1. stress:	*My aunt suffers from stress.*	Mi tía sufre del **estrés**.
	Traditional variant →	Mi tía sufre de **los nervios**.
2. stressed:	*At times I feel completely stressed out.*	A veces me siento totalmente **estresado**.
	Traditional variant →	... totalmente **agobiado**.

3. *stressful:*	*a very stressful situation*	una situación muy **estresante**
	Traditional variant →	una situación muy **agitada**
4. *to stress (out):*	*Exams always stress me out.*	Los exámenes siempre me **estresan**.
	Traditional variant →	... siempre me **ponen nervioso**.

ESTROC, ESTROQUE (masc noun) = **adapted from "stroke" [US]**

• Nonexistent in academic Spanish, this term occurs in the United States to refer primarily to the medical condition, and less frequently to the swing of a club, bat, or racket.

US usage

1. *stroke (medical):*	*The man suffered a stroke.*	El hombre sufrió un **estroc**.
	Standard variant →	El hombre sufrió un **derrame cerebral**.
2. *stroke (in a sport):*	*I gave the ball a good stroke.*	Le di un buen **estroque** a la pelota.
	Standard variant →	Le di un buen **golpe** a la pelota.

EVALUACIÓN (fem noun)
= **evaluation (of evidence)**
= **assessment (of effect, loss, damage, etc.)**
= **evaluation of performance**
= **examination, formal test**
= **evaluation: appraisal; calculation [US]**

• To express "exam," "assessment," or "evaluation of performance," both standard and U.S. Spanish would normally use **evaluación**.
• In regard to "monetary value," **valoración** and **cálculo** are more traditional alternatives.

Standard usage

1. *evaluation (of evidence):*	*The evaluation of the data has been completed.*	La evaluación de los datos se ha completado.
2. *assessment (of effect):*	*an assessment of the impact on the environment*	una evaluación del impacto ambiental
3. *evaluation (performance):*	*The students completed a course evaluation.*	Los estudiantes hicieron una evaluación del curso.
4. *exam, formal test:*	*formal school exam*	evaluación escolar

Extended US usage

5. *evaluation (=appraisal of value):*	*They did an evaluation of a Picasso painting.*	Hicieron una **evaluación** de un cuadro de Picasso.
	Standard variants →	Hicieron una **valoración** ... Hicieron una **valorización** ...
6. *evaluation (=calculation):*	*According to his evaluation, the price was very high.*	De acuerdo a su **evaluación**, el precio era muy alto.
	Standard variant →	De acuerdo a su **cálculo** ...

EVIDENCIA (fem noun)
= **evidence: presence**
= **evidence: proof; signs [US]**

- **Evidencia** in standard Spanish suggests "that which can be seen or felt," rather than "signs" or "proof" of past actions and events.

Standard usage

1. *evidence (=presence):*	*The evidence of death was all around us.*	La evidencia de la muerte nos rodeaba.

Extended US usage

2. *evidence (=proof):*	*There is no evidence against him.*	No hay **evidencia** contra él.
	Standard variant →	No hay **pruebas** contra él.
3. *evidence (=signs):*	*There is evidence that someone was in this room.*	Hay **evidencia** de que alguien estuvo en este cuarto.
	Standard variant →	Hay **indicios** de que alguien estuvo en este cuarto.
4. *evidence (idioms):*	*to give evidence* *to show evidence*	**dar evidencia** **mostrar evidencia**
	Standard variants →	**prestar declaración** **dar muestras**

EXCITADO (adj)
= **excited: hyperactive, worked up**
= **excited: sexually aroused**
= **excited: emotional, enthusiastic [US]**

Standard usage

1. *excited (=hyperactive):*	*The kids are overexcited.*	Los niños están muy excitados.
2. *excited (=worked up):*	*She is all worked up because she can't find her son.*	Está excitada porque no encuentra a su hijo.
3. *sexually excited:*	*to become sexually aroused*	ponerse excitado

Extended US usage

4. *excited (emotionally):*	*She was very excited to see her family.*	**Estuvo muy excitada** de ver a su familia.
	Standard variant →	**Se emocionó** de ver a su …
5. *excited (=enthusiastic):*	*I was excited about my grades.*	Quedé **excitado** con mis notas.
	Standard variants →	Quedé **entusiasmado / muy contento** con mis notas.
6. *excited (=looking forward):*	*I'm excited about your visit.*	**Estoy excitado** con tu visita.
	Standard variants →	**Espero con ansia** tu visita. **Espero con anticipación** …

EXCITANTE (adj) = **stimulating; sexually arousing**
= **exciting: emotional, passionate [US]**
= **exciting: fascinating, interesting [US]**

Standard usage

1. *stimulating:*	*Coffee has a stimulating effect.*	El café tiene efecto excitante.
2. *sexually arousing:*	*a sexually arousing dance*	una danza excitante (sensual)

Extended US usage

3. *exciting (emotionally):*	*His arrival was exciting.*	Su llegada fue **excitante**.
	Standard variant →	Su llegada fue **emocionante**.
4. *exciting (=passionate):*	*an exciting performance*	una actuación **excitante**
	Standard variant →	una actuación **apasionante**
5. *exciting (=fascinating):*	*She is an exciting person.*	Es una persona **excitante**.
	Standard variant →	Es una persona **fascinante**.

EXCITARSE (verb) = **to get excited: become hyper, stimulated**
= **to get excited: become sexually aroused**
= **to get excited: become emotional, nervous [US]**
= **to get excited: be happy, enthusiastic [US]**

• The many connotations of "excited" in English requires one to distinguish between emotional excitement (sentiment, enthusiasm) and more physical excitement (agitation, sexual arousal). In standard Spanish, only the latter calls for **excitarse**.

Standard usage

1. *to get excited (=hyper):*	*Calm down, you're getting too excited!*	¡Cálmate, te estás excitando demasiado!
2. *to get excited (sexually):*	*He became excited when he saw her nude.*	Se excitó cuando la vio desnuda.

Extended US usage

3. *to get excited (emotionally):*	*She got excited when she saw her son come off the plane.*	Se **excitó** cuando vio a su hijo bajar del avión.
	Standard variants →	Se **emocionó** / Se **entusiasmó** cuando vio a su hijo ...
4. *to get excited (=become nervous):*	*I get very excited when I have to take a test.*	Me **excito** mucho cuando tengo que hacer un examen.
	Standard variant →	Me **pongo muy nerviosa** ...
5. *to get excited (=be happy, enthusiastic):*	*She got excited about the gift.*	Se **excitó** con el regalo.
	Standard variants →	Se **entusiasmó** / Se **puso muy contenta** con el regalo.

EXCUSAR(SE) (verb) = **to ignore; exempt; apologize**
= **to excuse, forgive, excuse onseself [US]**

- The pervasiveness of **excusar** in U.S. Spanish is largely due to the widespread use of the verb "to excuse" in English.

Standard usage

1. *to ignore, forget about:*	*You should not ignore the things he says about you.*	No deberías excusar las cosas que dice de ti.
2. *to excuse (=exempt):*	*I was excused from military service.*	Me excusaron del servicio militar.
3. *to apologize:*	*He apologized for having yelled.*	Se excusó de haber gritado.

Extended US usage

4. *to excuse (=pardon):*	*Excuse me for interrupting.*	**Excúseme** por interrumpir.
	Standard variant →	**Discúlpeme** que interrumpa.
5. *to forgive, pardon:*	*He will never be forgiven.*	Nunca lo **excusarán**.
	Standard variant →	Nunca lo **perdonarán**.
6. *excuse me (to get someone's attention):*	*Excuse me, do you have the time?*	**Excúseme**, ¿tiene la hora?
	Standard variant →	**Por favor**, ¿tiene la hora?
7. *excuse me (when asking for permission):*	*Excuse me, I'd like to get through.*	**Excúseme**, quisiera pasar.
	Standard variant →	**Con permiso**, quisiera pasar.

ÉXITO (masc noun) = success; smash hit, best seller
= exit [US]

- Interestingly, the Latin root of éxito (exitus) is closer in meaning to "exit" in English.
- In modern Spanish, however, éxito and "exit" are considered false cognates.

Standard usage		
1. success:	He was successful in business.	Tuvo éxito en los negocios.
2. hit, best seller:	She will sing one of her hits.	Va a cantar uno de sus éxitos.

Extended US usage		
3. exit:	There is one exit on this floor.	Sólo hay un éxito en este piso.
	Standard variant →	Sólo hay una salida ...

EXPERIENCIAR (verb) = loanword for "to experience" [US]

EXPERIMENTAR (verb) = to test, try out
= to experience: show, indicate
= to conduct scientific experiments
= to experience difficulty or hardship [US]

- Experienciar, nonexistent in academic Spanish, occurs in U.S. Spanish along with experimentar, and conforms to the multiple connotations of "to experience" in English.

Standard usage		
1. to test, try out:	New drugs are being tested.	Se está experimentando con nuevas drogas.
2. to experience (=show):	Our population has experienced an increase.	Nuestra población ha experimentado un aumento.
3. to conduct experiments:	They have been experimenting with animals.	Han estado experimentando con animales.

Extended US usage		
4. to experience (problems/difficulties):	She has experienced a number of difficulties.	Ha experimentado muchas dificultades.
	Standard variants →	Ha tenido / pasado por muchas dificultades.
5. to experience (=suffer) (pain, loss, hardship):	I experienced terrible pain. Did you experience hunger?	Experimenté un dolor terrible. ¿Experimentaste hambre?
	Standard variants →	Sentí / Sufrí un dolor terrible. ¿Pasaste hambre?

EXPIRAR (verb) = **to expire: die**
                = **to expire: run out, conclude, lapse [US]**
                = **to exhale, breathe out [US]**

Standard usage		
1. to expire (=die):	*Our patient expired last night.*	Nuestro paciente expiró anoche.

Extended US usage		
2. to expire (=end, conclude):	*The fiscal year just expired.*	El año fiscal acaba de **expirar**.
	Standard variant →	El año fiscal acaba de **terminar**.
3. to expire (=lapse) (contract, license, etc.):	*My passport expired yesterday.* *The contract has expired.*	Mi pasaporte **expiró** ayer. El contrato se ha **expirado**.
	Standard variants →	Mi pasaporte **caducó** ayer. El contrato se ha **vencido**.
4. to exhale, breathe out:	*You need to exhale very slowly.*	Tienes que **expirar** muy lento.
	Standard variant →	Tienes que **espirar** muy lento.

EXPRÉS (adj & noun) = **adapted from "express" [DRAE 1927]**

EXPRESO (adj) = **clear, patent, explicit**
           = **express: special delivery**
           = **express: direct, non-stop**

• Both forms are standardized, although **exprés** is used more broadly in U.S. Spanish.

Standard usage		
1. clear, patent, explicit:	*We don't have explicit laws.*	No tenemos leyes expresas.
2. express, special delivery:	*Send it by express mail.*	Mándala por correo expreso.
3. express (=non-stop):	*I'll take the express (train).*	Tomaré el (tren) expreso.

Extended US usage		
4. express (=urgent):	*an express letter*	una carta **exprés**
	Standard variant →	una carta **urgente**
5. express (=fast):	*We have express service.*	Tenemos servicio **exprés**.
	Standard variant →	Tenemos servicio **rápido**.

EXTRANJERO (adj & noun)

- = **foreign; foreigner, alien**
- = **abroad**
- = **stranger [US]**

- The use of **extranjero** to refer to "stranger" is gaining popularity in U.S. Spanish.
- In standard usage, **extranjero** strictly means "foreigner" or "abroad."

Standard usage		
1. *foreign (adj):*	*She has a foreign accent.*	Tiene acento extranjero.
2. *foreigner, alien (noun):*	*a program for foreigners*	un programa para extranjeros
3. *abroad:*	*I spent a year abroad.*	Pasé un año en el extranjero.

Extended US usage		
4. *stranger (=unknown person):*	*Don't speak to strangers.*	No hables con **extranjeros**.
	Standard variants →	No hables con **desconocidos**. No hables con **extraños**.
5. *stranger (=person from another region):*	*There are many strangers here from other towns.*	Hay muchos **extranjeros** aquí de otros pueblos.
	Standard variant →	Hay muchos **forasteros** aquí ...
6. *foreign (=external, international):*	*He explained his country's foreign policy.*	Explicó la política **extranjera** de su país.
	Standard variant →	Explicó la política **exterior** ...

FÁBRICA (fem noun)

- = **factory, plant; manufacture**
- = **fabric: cloth [US]**

Standard usage		
1. *factory, plant:*	*a lamp factory*	una fábrica de lámparas
2. *manufacture:*	*The manufacture of diamonds is a complicated process.*	La fábrica del diamante es un proceso complicado.

Extended US usage		
3. *fabric (=cloth):*	*Silk is a delicate fabric.*	La seda es una **fábrica** delicada.
	Standard variants →	La seda es una **tela** delicada / un **tejido** delicado.

FACILIDAD (fem noun)
- = **easiness, facility**
- = **gift, talent, ease**
- = **facility: place, prison, center [US]**
- = **facility: equipment, services [US]**

- **Facilidad** to indicate "something that is built or established for a particular purpose" occurs in U.S. Spanish by influence of a secondary meaning of the English term "facility."

Standard usage

1. *easiness, simplicity:*	*I was surprised by the simplicity of the game.*	Me sorprendió la facilidad del juego.
2. *gift, talent, ease:*	*She has a gift for languages.*	Tiene facilidad para los idiomas.

Extended US usage

3. *facility (=place built for recreation):*	*recreational facilities* *sports facilities*	**facilidades** de recreación **facilidades** deportivas
	Standard variants →	**instalaciones** recreativas **instalaciones** deportivas
4. *facility (=prison):*	*The defendant will spend five years at a state facility.*	El acusado pasará cinco años en una **facilidad** estatal.
	Standard variant →	El acusado pasará cinco años en una **prisión** estatal.
5. *facility (=center, building complex):*	*a new medical facility* *nuclear facilities*	una nueva **facilidad** médica **facilidades** nucleares
	Standard variants →	un nuevo **centro** médico **centros** / **plantas** nucleares
6. *facility (=equipment):*	*Do you have cooking facilites?*	¿Tienes **facilidades** de cocina?
	Standard variant →	¿Tienes **equipo** de cocina?
7. *facilities (=services)*	*There are day-care facilities.*	Hay **facilidades** de day-care.
	Standard variant →	Hay **servicios** de guardería para los niños.

FACTORÍA (fem noun) = **adapted from "factory"** [DRAE 1970]

- **Factoría** is the equivalent of "factory" in the U.S., Mexico, and parts of the Caribbean.
- Historically, **factoría** referred to a "trading post" in standard Spanish (DRAE 1852).
- It received RAE approval as "manufacturing plant" and "industrial complex" in 1970.
- Still, the conventional term for a modern factory in academic Spanish is **fábrica**.

Standard usage		
1. *trading post:*	*In colonial times, there were trading posts near the coast.*	En la época colonial, habían factorías por la costa.
2. *factory (=large plant):*	*automobile factory*	factoría de carros

Extended US usage		
3. *factory, plant:*	*My father used to work in a lamp factory.*	Mi padre trabajaba en una **factoría** de lámparas.
	Standard variant ➔	... en una **fábrica** de lámparas.

FACULTAD (fem noun) = **faculty: power of mind and body**
= **authority, power**
= **university, college, school within university**
= **faculty: teaching staff [US]**

Standard usage		
1. *faculty (=body & mind):*	*He's losing his faculties.*	Va perdiendo sus facultades.
2. *authority, power:*	*He has the authority to fire him.*	Tiene la facultad de despedirlo.
3. *university, college:*	*We'll see you at the university.*	Te vemos en la facultad.
4. *school within university:*	*the School of Medicine*	la Facultad de Medicina

Extended US usage		
5. *faculty (=teaching staff):*	*members of the faculty*	miembros de la **facultad**
	Standard variant ➔	miembros del **profesorado**

FALLAR (verb) = **to fail: not function**
= **to fail: worsen**
= **to fail: let down**
= **to miss a target**
= **to fail: not pass, not succeed, fall apart [US]**
= **to fail to (do something, fulfill obligation) [US]**

• The many connotations of the verb "to fail" converge to become **fallar** in U.S. Spanish.

Standard usage		
1. *to fail (=not function):*	*His brakes failed.*	Le fallaron los frenos
2. *to fail (=worsen):*	*My memory is failing.*	Me falla la memoria.
3. *to fail (=let down):*	*Please don't let me down.*	Por favor no me falles.
4. *to miss (a target):*	*He took two shots and missed.*	Disparó dos veces y falló.

Extended US usage

5. *to fail (exam, course):*	*Did you fail the exam?*	¿**Fallaste** el examen?
	Standard variant →	¿**Suspendiste** el examen?
6. *to fail (=not succeed):*	*Our plan has failed.*	Ha **fallado** nuestro plan.
	Standard variant →	Ha **fracasado** nuestro plan.
7. *to fail (=fall apart):*	*The marriage fell apart.*	El matrimonio **falló**.
	Standard variant →	El matrimonio **fracasó**.
8. *to fail to (do something):*	*Don't fail to call the doctor.*	No **falles de** llamar al médico.
	Standard variant →	No **dejes de** llamar al médico.
9. *to fail to (fulfill obligation):*	*They failed in their duty.*	**Fallaron en** su deber.
	Standard variant →	**Faltaron a** su deber. **No cumplieron con** su deber.

FALTA (fem noun)

- = **lack, shortage, need**
- = **mistake, error**
- = **foul (in sport)**
- = **fault: weakness, defect [US]**
- = **fault: blame [US]**

Standard usage

1. *lack:*	*a lack of respect*	falta de respeto
2. *shortage:*	*a shortage of teachers*	falta de maestros
3. *need (idiom w.* hacer*):*	*I don't need anything.*	No me hace falta nada.
4. *mistake, error:*	*spelling mistakes*	faltas de ortografía
5. *foul (in sport):*	*to foul somebody*	cometer una falta contra

Extended US usage

6. *fault (=weakness):*	*We all have faults.*	Todos tenemos **faltas**.
	Standard variant →	Todos tenemos **defectos**.
7. *fault (=blame):*	*It's not my fault.*	No es mi **falta**.
	Standard variant →	No tengo **la culpa**.

FALTAR (verb)

= **to lack, be short, not have enough; need**
= **to be absent; be missing; remaining**
= **to default, fail to meet obligation**
= **to fault, blame, criticize [US]**
= **to be lost: be missing [US]**
= **to miss: feel the absence of [US]**

Standard usage

1. to lack:	*They lack running water.*	Les falta agua corriente.
2. to be short:	*We are two people short.*	Faltan dos personas.
3. to not have/be enough:	*There aren't enough doctors.*	Faltan médicos.
4. to need:	*Do you need money?*	¿Te falta dinero?
5. to miss (=be absent):	*I missed class three times.*	Falté a clase tres veces.
6. to be missing:	*The cashbox is missing $100.*	Faltan cien dólares de la caja.
7. remaining, to go:	*There are two weeks to go before summer.*	Faltan dos semanas para el verano.
8. to default:	*He defaulted on his payments.*	Faltó en los pagos.

Extended US usage

9. to fault, blame, criticize:	*They faulted him for not having fully explained.*	Lo **faltaron** por no haber bien explicado.
	Standard variants →	Lo **criticaron** por no haber ... **Le echaron la culpa** ...
10. to be lost (=be missing):	*One of the hikers is missing.*	Un excursionista está **faltando**.
	Standard variant →	Un excursionista está **perdido**.
11. to miss (=feel the absence of):	*I miss my parents.*	**Falto** a mis padres. **Me faltan** mis padres.
	Standard variants →	**Extraño / Echo de menos** a mis padres.

FAMILIAR (adj)

= **familiar: recognizable**
= **family-like, friendly, warm**
= **colloquial, informal**
= **familiar: well-known [US]**
= **familiar with people, places, facts [US]**

Standard usage

1. familiar (=recognizable):	*Her face looks familiar.*	Su cara me resulta familiar.
2. family, friendly, warm:	*I live in a family environment.*	Vivo en un ambiente familiar.
3. colloquial, informal:	*We use colloquial expressions.*	Usamos expresiones familiares.

Extended US usage		
4. *familiar (=well-known):*	*a familiar restaurant*	un restaurante **familiar**
	Standard variant →	un restaurante **conocido**
5. *be familiar with (=know):*	*I'm familiar with Salamanca.*	**Estoy familiar con** Salamanca.
	Standard variants →	**Conozco** Salamanca.
6. *familiar with facts:*	*I'm not familiar with his work.*	No estoy **familiar con** su obra.
	Standard variant →	No estoy **enterado de** su obra.

FAXEAR (verb)   =   **loanword for "to fax"** [DRAE 2001]

- The noun form (**fax**) first appeared in the DRAE in 1992 to refer to the means of communication and the machine, as well as the document.
- **Faxear** is a newly sanctioned term, increasingly used in lieu of **enviar por fax**.

Standard/US usage		
1. *to fax:*	*Could you fax me the review sheet?*	¿Me podrías **faxear** le hoja de repaso?
	Traditional variants →	¿Me podrías **enviar por fax** / **mandar por fax** la hoja ...?

FEEDBACK (masc noun)   =   **loanword for "feedback"** [US]

- Also spelled **fidbac**, this term is listed by Moliner but not sanctioned by the RAE.

US usage		
1. *feedback (=reaction):*	*What was the feedback from students?*	¿Cuál fue el **feedback** de los estudiantes?
	Standard variant →	¿Cuál fue la **reacción** de los estudiantes?
2. *feedback (=information):*	*They didn't give us feedback.*	No nos dieron **feedback**.
	Standard variants →	No nos dieron **información**. No nos **tuvieron informados**.

FERRY (masc noun)   =   **loanword for "ferry"** [DRAE 1984]

• Approved by Moliner and the RAE as an alternative to the traditional **transbordador**.

Standard/US usage		
1. *ferry, ferry boat:*	*We took a ferry to one of the islands.*	Tomamos un **ferry** a una de las islas.
	Traditional variant →	Tomamos un **transbordador** a una de las islas.

FIFTY- FIFTY (adj & adv)   =   **loanword for "uncertain" or "evenly split"** [US]

• Defined by Moliner as "**a partes iguales**," this colloquial expression seems to have more applications in U.S. Spanish than it does in English.

US usage		
1. *fifty-fifty (=50%):*	*The chances of success are fifty-fifty.*	Las posibilidades de éxito están a **fifty-fifty**.
	Standard variant →	Las posibilidades de éxito están a **cincuenta por ciento**.
2. *fifty-fifty (=shared, even, evenly split):*	*It's a fifty-fifty deal.*	Es un negocio a **fifty-fifty**.
	Standard variants →	Es un negocio a **medias**. Es un negocio **compartido**.
3. *doubtful, uncertain:*	*The situation is uncertain.*	La situación está **fifty-fifty**.
	Standard variants →	La situación está **incierta** / **insegura** / **inestable**.

FIGURA (fem noun)   =   **figure: person**
=   **figure: statue; silhouette**
=   **figure: shape, form**
=   **figure of speech**
=   **figure: number, statistic** [US]
=   **figure: physique** [US]

• The many connotations of "figure" in English lead to a wide array of Spanish translations, the most problematic of which is "body shape" or "physique."
• When emphasis is on shape, **figura** is the preferred term (as in **bonita figura**).
• When emphasis is on physique and health, standard Spanish prefers **tipo** or **físico**.

Standard usage

1. *figure (=person):*	*Beethoven is a key figure in the world of music.*	Beethoven es una figura clave en el mundo de la música.
2. *figure (=statue):*	*a porcelain figure*	una figura de porcelana
3. *figure (=silhouette):*	*A figure appeared at the door.*	Una figura apareció en el portal.
4. *figure (=shape):*	*star-shaped tray*	bandeja en figura de estrella
5. *figure (language):*	*a figure of speech*	una figura retórica

Extended US usage

6. *figure (=number):*	*These figures don't add up.*	Estas **figuras** no cuadran.
	Standard variant →	Estas **cifras** no cuadran.
7. *figure (=statistic):*	*The latest figures indicate …*	Las últimas **figuras** indican …
	Standard variants →	Los últimos **datos** indican …
		Las últimas **estadísticas** …
8. *figure (=physique):*	*He has a good (healthy) figure.*	Tiene buena **figura**.
	Standard variants →	Tiene buen **tipo** / buen **físico**.
9. *figure (expressions):*	*to watch one's figure*	cuidar la **figura**
	to keep / lose one's figure	guardar / perder la **figura**
	Standard variants →	cuidar la **línea**
		guardar / perder la **línea**

FILE (masc noun)   =   **loanword for "file" [US]**

- Listed by Moliner but not sanctioned by the RAE, both **file** (pronounced as in English) and **fólder** are used by Spanish speakers in the United States, particularly in business and technology—along with their more traditional variants: **archivo** and **carpeta**.
- Stavans renders it phonetically: **fail**.

US usage

1. *file (=folder):*	*I'm looking for the contract file.*	Busco el **file** de contratos.
	Standard variant →	Busco la **carpeta** de contratos.
2. *file (=dossier, records):*	*We keep a file on every client.*	Mantenemos un **file** para cada cliente.
	Standard variants →	Mantenemos un **expediente** / **archivo** para cada cliente.
3. *computer file:*	*I couldn't open the file.*	No pude abrir el **file**.
	Standard variants →	No pude abrir el **fichero** / el **archivo**.

FILMAR (verb)   =   **adapted from "to film"** [DRAE 1970]

FILME (masc noun)   =   **adapted from "film"** [DRAE 1970]

> **filmar**. (Del inglés "film"). tr. Tomar o fotografiar una escena en una película. [Moliner]
> **filme**. (Del inglés "film"). m. Película cinematográfica. [Moliner]

Standard/US usage		
1. *to shoot a film:*	*They filmed the movie in Australia.*	**Filmaron** la película en Australia.
	Traditional variant →	**Rodaron** la película en Australia.
2. *to film (=photograph):*	*Did you film the wedding?*	¿**Filmaste** la boda?
	Traditional variant →	¿**Fotografiaste** la boda?
3. *film (=movie):*	*I saw a film about the Civil War.*	Vi un **filme** de la Guerra Civil.
	Traditional variant →	Vi una **película** de la Guerra Civil.

FLASH (masc noun)   =   **loanword for "flash"** [DRAE 1984]

- Both Moliner and the RAE list three denotations of **flash** in academic Spanish, all of which correspond to common U.S. Spanish usage.

Standard/US usage		
1. *flash (camera feature):*	*The flash on my camera doesn't work well.*	El **flash** de mi cámara no funciona bien.
2. *flash (of light):*	*The flash almost blinded me.*	Por poco me ciega el **flash**.
	Traditional variant →	Por poco me ciega el **destello** de luz.
3. *news flash:*	*They interrupted the TV show with a news flash.*	Interrumpieron el programa con un **flash**.
	Traditional variant →	Interrumpieron el programa con una **noticia de última hora**.

FLASHBACK (masc noun)   =   **loanword for "flashback"** [DRAE 2001]

> **flashback**. (Inglés; pronunciado [flashbác]). m. Técnica cinematográfica y literaria que consiste en romper el desarrollo lineal de la acción para evocar el pasado. [Moliner]

- Borrowed from the English in the mid-twentieth century, the use of **flashback** in academic Spanish is limited to the context of literature and film.

Standard usage		
1. *flashback (in a film or narrative):*	*Juan Rulfo is a master of the flashback technique.*	Juan Rulfo es un maestro de la técnica del flashback.

Extended US usage		
2. *flashback (=memory):*	*I have been having flashbacks of the accident.*	He estado teniendo **flashbacks** del accidente.
	Standard variants →	... **recuerdos** / **memorias** del accidente.

FLASHLIGHT (masc noun) = **loanword for "flashlight" [US]**

- Commonly pronounced as in English, **flashlight** is an alternative to **linterna** in U.S. Spanish to refer to a "small battery-operated portable electric light," as opposed to the larger and more old-fashioned "lantern." Not approved in standard Spanish.

US usage		
1. *flashlight:*	*It's very dark in there; take a flashlight.*	Está muy oscuro ahí dentro; llévate un **flashlight**.
	Standard variant →	Está muy oscuro ahí dentro; llévate una **linterna**.

FLIPAR, FLIPEAR(SE) (verb) = **adapted from "to flip" [DRAE 2001]**

> **flipar.** (Del inglés americano *to flip*, agitar, sacudir). 1. intr. coloq. Estar bajo los efectos de una droga. 2. intr. coloq. Estar o quedar entusiasmado. 3. intr. coloq. Agradar o gustar mucho. [DRAE]

- Used colloquially in standard Spanish, these verbs have the same double connotation in the United States: (1) to flip for something or someone, meaning "to like" or "to be fond of" and (2) to flip out, meaning "to get high" or "to be under the effect of drugs."
- Other popular uses in U.S. Spanish are "to lose one's mind" and "to lose one's temper."
- Both forms are approved by the RAE. **Flipear** is more common in the U.S.

Standard usage		
1. *to flip for (=be fond of):*	*My kids flip for that kind of music.*	Mis hijos flipean con ese tipo de música.
2. *to flip out (on drugs):*	*They used to flip out (on drugs) every day.*	Se flipaban (flipeaban) todos los días.

Extended US usage		
3. *to flip out (=go crazy):*	*She flipped out and wound up in the asylum.*	**Se flipeó** y terminó en el asilo.
	Standard variants →	**Se volvió loca / perdió el juicio** y terminó en el asilo.
4. *to flip out (=get angry, lose one's temper):*	*When he saw the mess in his office, he flipped out.*	Cuando vio su despacho en desorden, **se flipeó**.
	Standard variant →	... **se puso furioso**.

FLIRTEAR (verb) = **adapted from "to flirt"** [DRAE 1927]

FLIRTEO (masc noun) = **adapted from "flirting" or "flirtation"** [DRAE 1927]

- Both forms have long been sanctioned by the RAE in the context of "amorous behavior."
- In U.S. Spanish, **flirtear** is also used figuratively (to flirt with danger, with an idea, etc.).

Standard usage		
1. *to flirt (=behave amorously):*	*You are always flirting with the girls in the neighborhood.*	Estás siempre flirteando con las niñas del barrio.
	Traditional variant →	Estás siempre coqueteando ...
2. *flirting, flirtation:*	*She has mastered the art of flirting.*	Ha dominado el arte del flirteo.
	Traditional variant →	... el arte del coqueteo.

Extended US usage		
3. *to flirt (=to challenge):*	*He likes to flirt with death.*	Le gusta **flirtear** con la muerte.
	Standard variant →	Le gusta **jugar** con la muerte.
4. *to flirt (=to consider, show some interest):*	*I am flirting with the idea of going to Mexico.*	Estoy **flirteando** con la idea de ir a México.
	Standard variants →	Estoy **acariciando / jugando con** la idea de ir a México.

FLOPPY (masc noun) = **loanword for "floppy disk"** [US]

- Another cyber-Spanglish term coined by Ilan Stavans (he spells it "flopi"), this variant seems to be less prevalent than **disquete** in U.S. Spanish.

US usage

1. floppy disk (computers):	*Did you put the floppy into the computer?*	¿Metiste el **floppy** en la computadora?
	Standard variants →	¿Metiste el **disquete** / **disco flexible** en la computadora?

FÓLDER (masc noun) = **loanword for "folder"** [DRAE 1992]

- Common in U.S. office lingo, along with **file**, as alternatives to **carpeta** and **archivo**.
- Interestingly, whereas **file** is not RAE-sanctioned, **fólder** is.

US usage

1. file folder:	*All the documents are in the folder.*	Todos los documentos están en el **fólder**.
	Standard variant →	Todos los documentos están en la **carpeta**.

FORMA (fem noun)

=	**form: shape, health**
=	**form: structure, syntax**
=	**form: way, manner**
=	**form: document; application form [US]**

- **Llenar la forma** for "to fill out the form" has become commonplace in U.S. Spanish.

Standard usage

1. form (=shape):	*It has the shape of a circle.*	Tiene forma circular.
2. form (=health):	*He's in good physical form.*	Está en buena forma.
3. form (=structure):	*content and form*	fondo y forma
4. way, manner:	*You shouldn't talk that way.*	No debes hablar de esa forma.

Extended US usage

5. form (=document):	*Did you bring the forms?*	¿Trajiste las **formas**?
	Standard variant →	¿Trajiste los **documentos**?
6. form (to fill out):	*You have to fill out this form.*	Tienes que llenar esta **forma**.
	Standard variants →	Tienes que llenar esta **hoja** / este **formulario** / **impreso**.

FORMAL (adj)

- = **serious; reliable, responsible**
- = **formal (style, language...)**
- = **formal: official, in writing [US]**
- = **formal: elegant, ceremonial [US]**

Standard usage		
1. *serious, thoughtful:*	*I wrote a very serious letter.*	Escribí una carta muy formal.
2. *reliable, responsible:*	*He's a reliable student.*	Es un estudiante formal.
3. *formal (=adhering to certain norms):*	*formal language / formal tone / formal style*	lenguaje formal / tono formal / estilo formal

Extended US usage		
4. *formal (=in writing):*	*I filed a formal complaint.*	Presenté una queja **formal**.
	Standard variant →	... una queja **por escrito**.
5. *formal dress:*	*Formal dress is advised.*	Se aconseja llevar ropa **formal**.
	Standard variant →	... llevar ropa **de etiqueta**.
6. *formal event:*	*We attended a formal dinner.*	Asistimos a una cena **formal**.
	Standard variant →	Asistimos a una cena **de gala**.

FORMATEAR (verb) = **loanword for "to format"** [DRAE 2001]

- Formato (noun for "format") has been listed in the DRAE since 1927.
- The verb variant, **formatear**, received limited sanction in 1992. Its definition was expanded in 2001 to encompass most current applications in English.

Standard/US usage		
1. *to format (a text):*	*After you write the essay, you'll need to format it.*	Después de escribir el ensayo, lo tendrás que **formatear**.
	Traditional variant →	Después de escribir el ensayo, tendrás que **darle forma**.
2. *to format (a disk):*	*The disks have already been formatted.*	Los disquetes ya se han formateado.

FRANKFURTER (fem noun) = **loanword for "frankfurter" [US]**

- With no exact equivalent in standard Spanish, the American frankfurter has a number of designations in the United States, including **hot dog**, **frankfurter** (pronounced "franfura") and **perro caliente**.
- The closest rendition in traditional Spanish is **salchicha de Frankfurt**.

US usage		
1. frankfurter:	*Would you like mustard with your frankfurter?*	¿Deseas mostaza con la **frankfurter**?
	Standard variant →	¿Deseas mostaza con la **salchicha**?

FRATERNIDAD (fem noun) = **fraternity: friendship, camaraderie**
  = **brotherhood: organization [US]**
  = **fraternity: association of students [US]**

- In academic Spanish, **fraternidad** does not refer to an "association of university students" but rather to "fraternity" or "brotherhood" as social concepts.

Standard usage		
1. friendship, camaraderie:	*There is great camaraderie among the soldiers.*	Hay mucha fraternidad entre los soldados.
2. fraternity (=social ideal):	*We fight for the ideals of liberty, equality, and fraternity.*	Luchamos por los ideales de libertad, igualdad, fraternidad.

Extended US usage		
3. brotherhood (=union, organization):	*The firemen of our town have formed a brotherhood.*	Los bomberos del pueblo han formado una **fraternidad**.
	Standard variant →	... formado una **hermandad**.
4. fraternity (=student association):	*My brother belongs to a college fraternity.*	Mi hermano es miembro de una **fraternidad**.
	Standard variant →	Mi hermano es miembro de un **círculo estudiantil**.

FRISAR(SE) (verb) = **adapted from "to freeze" [US]**

FRÍSER (masc noun) = **adapted from "freezer" [US]**

- Firmly considered Spanglish by most linguists, neither term is sanctioned by the RAE despite frequent usage by U.S. Spanish speakers.
- In standard practice, **frisar** means primarily "to frizz or curl one's hair."

US usage		
1. to freeze (trans):	*Did you freeze the vegetables?*	¿**Frisaste** los vegetales?
	Standard variant →	¿**Congelaste** los vegetales?
2. to freeze (intrans):	*I was freezing.*	Me estaba **frisando**.
	Standard variants →	Me estaba **congelando**. Me estaba **muriendo de frío**.
3. freezer:	*We need to put the meat in the freezer.*	Tenemos que meter la carne en el **fríser**.
	Standard variant →	Tenemos que meter la carne en el **congelador**.

FULL TIME (adj & adv) = **loanword for "full-time"** [DRAE 2001]

• Recently sanctioned by the RAE, this expression is quite common in U.S. Spanish along with its traditional counterpart **a tiempo completo**.

Standard/US usage		
1. full-time (adj):	*I got a full-time job.*	Conseguí un trabajo **full time**.
	Traditional variant →	Conseguí un trabajo a **tiempo completo**.
2. full-time (adv):	*Do you work full-time?*	¿Trabajas **full time**?
	Traditional variant →	¿Trabajas a **tiempo completo**?

FURNITURA (fem noun) = **adapted from "furniture"** [US]

• Also spelled **fornitura** (Stavans).

US usage		
1. piece of furniture:	*a nice piece of furniture*	una linda **pieza de furnitura**
	Standard variant →	un lindo **mueble**
2. furniture:	*nineteenth century furniture*	**furnitura** del siglo XIX
	Standard variants →	**mobiliario / muebles** del s. XIX

GANAR (verb) = **to win: be victorious**
= **to gain respect, support, approval**
= **to gain weight [US]**
= **to gain experience [US]**
= **to gain friends [US]**
= **to gain (intrans): increase [US]**
= **to gain (intrans): benefit [US]**

• **Ganar peso**, a common phrase in U.S. Spanish, is a loan translation of "to gain weight."

Standard usage
1. to win (=be victorious):	*They won the contest.*	Ganaron el concurso.
2. to gain (respect, support):	*to gain the respect of the public*	ganarse el respeto del público

Extended US usage
3. to gain (weight):	*I gained a lot of weight.*	**Gané** mucho **peso**.
	Standard variant →	**Engordé** mucho.
4. to gain (experience):	*He gained experience at work.*	**Ganó** experiencia en el trabajo.
	Standard variants →	**Obtuvo** / **adquirió** experiencia en el trabajo.
5. to gain (friends):	*a good way to gain friends*	buen modo de **ganar** amigos
	Standard variant →	buen modo de **hacerse** amigos
6. to gain (=increase):	*My shares gained 20%.*	Mis acciones **ganaron** un 20%.
	Standard variants →	Mis acciones **aumentaron** / **subieron** un 20%.
7. to gain (=benefit):	*I gained from his knowledge.*	**Gané** de sus conocimientos.
	Standard variants →	**Beneficié** / **saqué provecho** de sus conocimientos.

GANG (masc) = **loanword for "gang"** [DRAE 2001]

GANGA (fem) = **bargain, deal, gift**
= **gang [US]**

• To refer to a "band of people with unlawful intentions," The RAE approves of **gang** (masc) as the more generic term, and **ganga** (fem) as a variant in Puerto Rico.
• Aside from its primary definition ("bargain, deal"), **ganga** has a number of meanings specific to particular regions, including a type of bird, a sarcastic remark, a type of plow, and a mineral product. In the U.S., **ganga** is the preferred term for "gang."

Standard usage

1. bargain, deal, gift:	*It was a great bargain.*	Fue una verdadera ganga.

Extended US usage

2. gang of criminals:	*a gang of thieves*	una **ganga** de ladrones
	Standard variant →	una **banda** de ladrones
3. gang of youths:	*There are youth gangs in the inner cities.*	Hay **gangas** de jóvenes en los centros urbanos.
	Standard variants →	Hay **pandillas** / **grupos** de jóvenes en los centros ...
4. gang (=group of friends or colleagues):	*He's part of our gang.* *The gang is all here.*	Forma parte de nuestra **ganga**. Ya esta aquí toda la **ganga**.
	Standard variants →	Es uno de **los nuestros**. Ya **estamos todos**.

GAP (masc noun) = **loanword for "gap"** [DRAE 2001]

> **gap**. (Del inglés *gap*). m. Vacío o distancia excesiva entre dos términos que se contrastan. [DRAE]

- The use of **gap** among Spanish speakers worldwide is partly due to its versatility.
- There are multiple traditional variants for this term, depending on the precise context: **hueco**, **vacío**, **brecha**, **distancia**, **separación**, **espacio**, **intervalo**, **laguna**, etc.

Standard/US usage

1. gap (=distance or separation):	*There is a big gap between the rich and the poor.*	Hay un enorme **gap** entre el rico y el pobre.
	Traditional variant →	Hay una enorme **distancia** entre el rico y el pobre.
2. gap (=differences in attitude or perspective):	*the generation gap*	el **gap** generacional
3. gap (=vacuum):	*He left a gap that will be hard to fill.*	Dejó un **gap** difícil de llenar.
	Traditional variants →	Dejó un **hueco** / un **vacío** difícil de llenar.

GASETERÍA (fem noun) = adapted from "gas station" [US]

- **Gasolinera**, the standard equivalent of "gas station" has many regional variants: **bencinera** in Chile, **grifo** in Perú, etc., as well as the generic **estación de servicio**.
- U.S. and Caribbean Spanish add **gasetería** to the long list.

US usage

1. *gas station:*	*There is an Exxon gas station on the corner.*	Hay una **gasetería** Exxon en la esquina.
	Standard variant →	Hay una **gasolinera** Exxon en la esquina.

GASTAR (verb)

- = **to spend (money)**
- = **to use, consume; waste (energy)**
- = **to play (a practical joke)**
- = **to spend (time) [US]**
- = **to waste (money, time, food, talent) [US]**

- In denoting "to spend," traditional Spanish prescribes **gastar dinero** but **pasar tiempo**.
- These differences are often blurred in U.S. Spanish, where **gastar** can express "to spend," "to use," and "to waste" in varying contexts.

Standard usage

1. *to spend (money):*	*I spent 500 dollars today.*	Gasté quinientos dólares hoy.
2. *to use, consume:*	*This car uses very little gas.*	Este carro gasta poca gasolina.
3. *to waste (water, gas, electricity):*	*I don't want you to waste water.*	No quiero que gastes agua.
4. *to play (jokes or tricks):*	*This kid loves to play jokes on everyone.*	A este chico le encanta gastar bromas.

Extended US usage

5. *to spend (time):*	*I spent a year in Spain.*	**Gasté** un año en España.
	Standard variant →	**Pasé** un año en España.
6. *to waste (money):*	*You are wasting your money.*	Estás **gastando** tu dinero.
	Standard variants →	Estás **malgastando** / **derrochando** tu dinero.
7. *to waste (time):*	*We can't afford to waste time.*	No podemos **gastar** tiempo.
	Standard variant →	No podemos **perder** tiempo.
8. *to waste (food):*	*It is a pity to waste food.*	Es una pena **gastar** comida.
	Standard variant →	Es una pena **desperdiciar** ...
9. *to waste (talent, skill, opportunity):*	*She is wasting the talent she has.*	Está **gastando** el talento que tiene.
	Standard variant →	Está **desaprovechando** ...

GAY (masc noun & adj)   =   **loanword for "gay" (homosexual)** [DRAE 1984]

- The term **gay** entered the Spanish lexicon in the late seventies, both as an adjective and a noun. It is used interchangeably with **homosexual** (male, not female).

Standard/US usage		
1. *gay (adj):*	*the gay liberation movement*	el movimiento de liberación **gay**
	Traditional variant →	... de liberación **homosexual**
2. *gay (noun):*	*an organization of lesbians and gays*	una organización de lesbianas y **gays**

GOL (masc noun)   =   **goal: score (in sports)** [DRAE 1927]
                    =   **goal: aim, objective [US]**
                    =   **goal net (in sports) [US]**

- Borrowed from English, **gol** occurs in standard Spanish strictly in the context of sports.

Standard usage		
1. *goal (=score, in sports):*	*The team scored three goals.*	El equipo marcó tres goles.

Extended US usage		
2. *goal (=aim, objective):*	*My goal is to be a doctor one day.*	Mi **gol** es ser médico algún día.
	Standard variants →	Mi **meta** / **objetivo** es ser médico algún día.
3. *goal net (in sports):*	*The ball went over the goal.*	La pelota pasó por encima del **gol**
	Standard variant →	... por encima de la **portería**

GRADO (masc noun)   =   **degree: temperature; in mathematics**
                     =   **rank, level, category**
                     =   **grade: school class, mark, quality [US]**

Standard usage		
1. *degree (temperature):*	*The temperature is 50 degrees.*	La temperatura es 50 grados.
2. *degree (mathematics):*	*a 90-degree angle*	un ángulo de 90 grados
3. *rank, level, category:*	*He holds the rank of captain.*	Tiene el grado de capitán.
	a high-level position	un puesto de alto grado

Extended US usage

4. grade (=school class):	*My son is in the fifth grade.*	Mi hijo está en el quinto **grado**.
	Standard variants →	Mi hijo está en el quinto **año** / en el quinto **curso**.
5. grade (=mark):	*I got good grades this semester.*	Obtuve buenos **grados** este semestre.
	Standard variants →	Obtuve buenas **calificaciones** / buenas **notas** este semestre.
6. grade (=quality):	*high-grade material*	material de alto **grado**
	Standard variant →	material de alta **calidad**

GRADUACIÓN (fem noun) = **adjustment**
= **military ranking**
= **alcoholic strength / content**
= **graduation [US]**

graduación. 1. f. Acción y efecto de graduar. 2. f. Cantidad proporcional de alcohol que contienen las bebidas espiritosas. 3. f. Mil. Categoría de un militar en su carrera. [DRAE]

• The RAE definitions of **graduación** are relevant to "adjustment," "alcohol content," and "military rank," and have little to do with "school graduation," which is how the term is primarily used in the United States.

Standard usage

1. adjustment:	*temperature adjustment*	graduación de temperatura
2. military ranking:	*a high-ranking officer*	un oficial de alta graduación
3. alcoholic strength:	*This wine has a low alcohol content (low proof).*	Este vino es de baja graduación.

Extended US usage

4. graduation (=academic ceremony):	*We attended our daughter's graduation.*	Asistimos a la **graduación** de nuestra hija.
	Standard variant →	Asistimos a la **entrega de títulos** de nuestra hija.

GRADUAR(SE) (verb)
= **to adjust, regulate; calibrate, test**
= **to confer a military rank**
= **to graduate: receive a degree [US]**

• Out of eight standard denotations for graduar, two refer to "graduating from school:"

5. tr. En las enseñanzas media y superior, dar el título de bachiller, licenciado o doctor.
8. prnl. Recibir un título de bachiller, licenciado o doctor. [DRAE]

Standard/US usage		
1. to adjust, regulate:	*Could you adjust the volume?*	¿Podrías graduar el volumen?
2. to calibrate, test:	*The scale must be calibrated before it is used.*	Hay que graduar la balanza antes de usarla.
3. to confer a rank:	*They ranked him as captain.*	Lo graduaron de capitán.
4. to graduate (from school):	*I graduated last year.*	Me gradué el año pasado.
	Traditional variants →	Me dieron el título / el diploma el año pasado.

GRILL (masc noun) = **loanword for "grill"** [DRAE 1984]

grill. (Del inglés *grill*). 1. m. parrilla (utensilio de hierro). 2. m. parrilla (restaurante). 3. m. gratinador. [DRAE]

• Academic Spanish has adopted this term to indicate the cooking utensil as well as "an informal restaurant."
• In U.S. Spanish, grill (pronounced "gril") refers mainly to the utensil or appliance.

Standard/US usage		
1. grill (=utensil):	*I like to cook on the grill.*	Me gusta cocinar al grill.
	Traditional variant →	Me gusta cocinar a la parrilla.
2. grill (=restaurant):	*We're having lunch at the grill.*	Vamos al grill a almorzar.
	Traditional variant →	Vamos al restaurante ...

GROCERÍA (fem noun) = **adapted from "grocery"** [US]

GROSERÍA (fem noun) = **vulgar remark; rudeness, vulgarity**

• Depending on the country or region, there are many variants for "grocery" and "grocery store" in standard Spanish, but grocería is not among them. However, this term is quite common in U.S. Spanish, where it is distinguished from grosería, meaning vulgarity.

Standard usage
1. offensive/vulgar remark: | Don't make vulgar remarks. | No digas groserías.
2. rudeness, vulgarity: | There is plenty of rudeness in his behavior. | Hay mucha grosería en su comportamiento.

Extended US usage
3. grocery (=food): | She went to buy groceries. | Fue a comprar **grocerías**.

Standard variant → | Fue a comprar **comestibles**.

4. grocery store: | They opened a grocery store. | Abrieron una **grocería**.

Standard variants → | Abrieron una **tienda de comestibles / de abarrotes /** un **almacén** / una **bodega**.

GUAFLE (masc noun)   see **WAFFLE**

HÁBITO (masc noun)   = **habit: dress**
= **habit, trend (in certain expressions)**
= **habit: customary behavior [US]**

- In standard practice, **hábito** refers primarily to "religious dress."
- In U.S. Spanish, it also occurs as an alternative to **costumbre** ("custom").

Standard usage
1. habit (=religious dress): | a nun's habit / to become a priest / a nun / to leave the priesthood | hábito de monja / tomar el hábito / colgar los hábitos
2. habit (=trend): [in certain expressions] | a habit-forming drug / buying habits | una droga que crea hábito / hábitos de consumo

Extended US usage
3. habit (=customary behavior): | He has very strange habits. / I turn off the light out of habit. | Tiene **hábitos** muy raros. / Apago la luz por **hábito**.

Standard variants → | Tiene **costumbres** muy raras. / Apago la luz por **costumbre**.

4. habit (idioms): | to be in the habit of / to get into the habit | tener la **costumbre** de / **soler** **acostumbrarse**

HACER (verb) = **to do (in general)**
= **to make: prepare, create, build**
= **to make: carry out; cause to do**
= **to make (earn) money [US]**
= **to make trouble; to make a mistake [US]**
= **to make a decision; to make a difference [US]**

- The literal translation of "to make" has produced a number of verbal idioms unique to U.S. Spanish: **hacer dinero, hacer una decisión,** etc.
- These loan translations, as well as phrasal verbs such as "make up, make over, make out," etc. need to be studied individually.

Standard usage

1. *to do (general):*	*What are you doing?*	¿Qué estás haciendo?
2. *to make (=prepare):*	*I'm going to make a cake.*	Voy a hacer un pastel.
3. *to make (=create, build):*	*Let's make a pyramid.*	Hagamos una pirámide.
4. *to make (=carry out):*	*I need to make a phone call.*	Tengo que hacer una llamada.
5. *to make (=cause to do):*	*He always makes me laugh.*	Siempre me hace reír.
6. *Selected expressions:*	*to ask a question*	hacer una pregunta
	to become late	hacerse tarde
	to harm, damage	hacer daño a
	to notice, pay attention	hacer caso de
	to play the role of	hacer el papel de
	to take a trip	hacer un viaje
	to tear, smash, break to pieces	hacer pedazos

Extended US usage

7. *to earn money:*	*My boss makes a lot of money.*	Mi patrón **hace** mucho dinero.
	Standard variant →	Mi patrón **gana** mucho dinero.
8. *to make trouble:*	*He likes to make trouble.*	Le gusta **hacer** problemas.
	Standard variant →	Le gusta **causar** problemas.
9. *to make a mistake:*	*Did you make any mistakes?*	¿**Hiciste** alguna falta?
	Standard variants →	¿**Cometiste** alguna falta? ¿**Te equivocaste**?
10. *to make a decision:*	*Let's make a decision.*	**Hagamos** una decisión.
	Standard variant →	**Tomemos** una decisión.
11. *to make a difference:*	*She made a difference in the lives of many people.*	**Hizo una diferencia** en la vida de mucha gente.
	Standard variants →	**Tuvo un impacto / influyó** en la vida de mucha gente.

HALL (masc noun)   =   **loanword for "hallway" [US]**

> **hall**. (Voz inglesa). 1. m. Vestíbulo, recibidor. [DRAE]

- In standard usage, hall refers strictly to "the entrance area of a building" (DRAE 1927).
- Other denotations such as "corridor" or "passage" are more typical of U.S. Spanish.

Standard usage		
1. lobby, vestibule, foyer:	*We'll wait for you in the hotel lobby.*	Te esperamos en el hall del hotel.

Extended US usage		
2. hallway, corridor:	*The exit is located at the end of the hall.*	La salida se encuentra al extremo del hall.
	Standard variants →	... al extremo del pasillo /del corredor.

HAMBURGER (fem noun)   =   **loanword for "hamburger" [US]**

HAMBURGUESA (fem noun)   =   **loanword for "hamburger" [DRAE 1984]**

- Hamburguesa is sanctioned by the RAE and widely accepted as standard Spanish.
- Hamburger (pronounced as in English) is the more common form in the United States.

Standard usage		
1. hamburger (patty):	*Hamburgers are made with ground meat.*	Las hamburguesas se hacen con carne picada.
2. hamburger (sandwich):	*We ordered a hamburger and french fries.*	Pedimos una hamburguesa con papas fritas.

Extended US usage		
3. hamburger (patty or sandwich):	*He ate two hamburgers.*	Se comió dos hamburgers.
	Standard variant →	Se comió dos hamburguesas.

HÁNDICAP (masc noun) = **loanword for "handicap"** [DRAE 1927]

• Academic Spanish maintains **hándicap** largely within the context of sports, such as golf or horse racing. U.S. Spanish applies it to other situations.

Standard usage

1. *handicap (in sports):*	*He won the tournament thanks to a ten-point handicap.*	Ganó el torneo gracias a un hándicap de diez puntos.
2. *handicap (=drawback, disadvantage):*	*My only handicap is lack of experience.*	Mi único hándicap es la falta de experiencia.
	Traditional variant →	Mi única desventaja ...

Extended US usage

3. *handicap (=obstacle, impediment):*	*Bad weather was a handicap in yesterday's parade.*	El mal tiempo fue un **hándicap** en el desfile de ayer.
	Standard variants →	El mal tiempo fue un **estorbo** / un **obstáculo** ...
4. *handicap (=physical incapacity):*	*She couldn't participate due to a physical handicap.*	No pudo participar a causa de un **hándicap** físico.
	Standard variants →	... a causa de una **minusvalía** / una **discapacidad**

HARDWARE (masc noun) = **loanword for "hardware"** [DRAE 2001]

hardware. (Inglés; pronunciado [járguar]). m. Informática. Conjunto de elementos físicos de un ordenador. [Moliner]

• Sanctioned as a "computer" term, **hardware** has wider applications in U.S. Spanish.

Standard usage

1. *hardware (computer):*	*IBM makes the hardware for computers.*	IBM fabrica el hardware para las computadoras.

Extended US usage

2. *hardware (=tools and supplies):*	*Do you have the hardware to take it apart?*	¿Tienes el **hardware** para desarmarlo?
	Standard variant →	¿Tienes la **herramienta** para desarmarlo?
3. *hardware store:*	*I bought the materials in a hardware store.*	Compré los materiales en una **tienda de hardware**.
	Standard variant →	Compré los materiales en una **ferretería**.

HESITAR (verb) = **to hesitate [US]**

- Despite its Latin root, **hesitar** is rarely used in standard Spanish.
- **Dudar**, **vacilar**, and **pensar** are the traditional verbs for "to hesitate."

US usage		
1. *to hesitate (=doubt, be apprehensive):*	*Don't hesitate to ask.*	No **hesites** en preguntar.
	Standard variant →	No **vaciles** en preguntar.
2. *to hesitate (=think, ponder):*	*I hesitated before signing the contract.*	**Hesité** antes de firmar el contrato.
	Standard variant →	**Lo pensé** antes de firmar …
3. *to hesitate (=pause, stutter):*	*He hesitates when he speaks.*	**Hesita** cuando habla.
	Standard variant →	**Titubea** cuando habla.

HIT (masc noun) = **loanword for "hit" [US]**

- Defined by Moliner as "disco de gran éxito" but unlisted in the DRAE, **hit** (also spelled "**jit**") occurs in the U.S. in many contexts, including entertainment, business, and sports.

Standard/US usage		
1. *hit (=success):*	*That song became a big international hit.*	Esa canción llegó a ser un gran **hit** internacional.
	Standard variant →	… un gran **éxito** internacional.

Extended US usage		
2. *hit (=blow, stroke):*	*He gave the ball a good hit.*	Le dio un buen **jit** a la pelota.
	Standard variant →	Le dio un buen **golpe** …

HOBBY (masc noun) = **loanword for "hobby" [DRAE 1984]**

> **hobby.** (Voz inglesa). m. Pasatiempo, entretenimiento que se practica habitualmente en los ratos de ocio. [DRAE]

- **Hobby** is a succinct and more precise alternative in both U.S. and standard Spanish to the all-encompassing **pasatiempo favorito**.

Standard/US usage		
1. *hobby:*	*He began to paint as a hobby.*	Empezó a pintar como **hobby**.
	Traditional variants ➔	Empezó a pintar **por afición** / como **pasatiempo**.

HUMORÍSTICO (adj) = **humorous: containing elements of humor**
= **humorous (person, book, movie...) [US]**

- **Humorístico** has a more literary connotation in academic Spanish than does the English term "humorous," and is therefore less common than **cómico**, **gracioso**, **divertido**.
- This adjective is most appropriate when applied to forms of expression that contain elements of humor (article, story, saying, scene, etc.).

Standard usage		
1. *humorous (=containing elements of humor):*	*a humorous scene* *a humorous essay*	una escena humorística un ensayo humorístico

Extended US usage		
2. *humorous (person):*	*My uncle is very humorous.*	Mi tío es muy **humorístico**.
	Standard variants ➔	Mi tío es muy **gracioso** / **divertido** / **chistoso**.
3. *humorous (book/movie):*	*It was a humorous movie.*	Fue una película **humorística**.
	Standard variants ➔	Fue una película **cómica**. Fue una película **divertida**.

IDIOMA (masc noun) = **language**
= **idiom [US]**

- A traditional false cognate, **idioma** is used occasionally to mean "idiom" in U.S. Spanish.

Standard usage		
1. *language:*	*She speaks three languages.*	Ella habla tres idiomas.

Extended US usage		
2. *idiom (=phrase):*	*I'm learning English idioms.*	Estoy aprendiendo **idiomas** ingleses.
	Standard variants ➔	Estoy aprendiendo **giros** / **modismos** ingleses.
3. *idiom (=style of expression, lingo):*	*They speak the doctors' idiom.*	Hablan el **idioma** de los médicos.
	Standard variant ➔	... el **lenguaje** de los médicos.

IGNICIÓN (fem noun)

= **ignition: fire, explosion**
= **ignition (automobile) [US]**

- **Ignición** tends to have a scientific connotation in standard Spanish, and is not ordinarily used to refer to the mechanism of "starting a car," as it often is in the United States.

Standard usage		
1. *ignition (=lighting up, fire, explosion):*	*The ignition of certain gases is very dangerous.*	La ignición de ciertos gases es muy peligrosa.

Extended US usage		
2. *ignition (automobile):*	*I have had problems with the ignition.*	He tenido problemas con la **ignición**.
	Standard variants →	He tenido problemas con el **arranque** / el **encendido**.

"Ignition" expressions in standard Spanish:	*ignition coil*	bobina de encendido
	ignition key	llave de contacto
	ignition switch	interruptor de arranque
	to turn off the ignition	apagar el motor
	to turn on the ignition	arrancar el motor

IGNORAR (verb)

= **to not know; be ignorant of**
= **to ignore: disregard, omit, forget [US]**

- The use of **ignorar** to express "disregard" (usage # 3) is mentioned by Moliner ("no hacer caso") but is not sanctioned by the RAE.

Standard usage		
1. *to not know:*	*I don't know his address.*	Ignoro su dirección.
2. *to be ignorant of:*	*He is ignorant about the history of his country.*	Ignora la historia de su país.

Extended US usage		
3. *to ignore (=disregard):*	*Ignore him! (Don't listen to him!)*	**¡Ignóralo!**
	Standard variant →	**¡No le hagas caso!**
4. *to ignore (=omit, forget):*	*She ignored the accents.*	**Ignoró** los acentos.
	Standard variants →	**Omitió** / **olvidó** los acentos.

INCLUYENDO (adv) = loan translation for "including" [US]

- **Incluído**, **incluso**, and **inclusive** are all acceptable variants in standard Spanish.
- By influence of English, however, U.S. Spanish prefers the gerund **incluyendo**.

US usage		
1. *including (=together with):*	*The dinner cost us 60 dollars including service.*	La cena nos costó 60 dólares, **incluyendo** servicio.
	Standard variant →	La cena nos costó 60 dólares, servicio **incluido**.
2. *including (=even, as well as):*	*They made everybody pay, including my little brother.*	Nos hicieron pagar a todos, **incluyendo** a mi hermanito.
	Standard variant →	Nos hicieron pagar a todos, **incluso** a mi hermanito.
3. *including (=inclusive):*	*Read up to and including page twenty.*	Lea hasta e **incluyendo** la página veinte.
	Standard variant →	Lea hasta la página veinte **inclusive**.

INFANTE (masc noun) = prince; infantryman, marine
                     = infant, baby, small child [US]

- Although **infante** suggests any "young child" in academic Spanish, it tends to refer historically to the "son of a monarch."
- U.S. Spanish makes broader use of this term to correspond to "infant" in English.

Standard usage		
1. *prince, king's son:*	*Which of the king's children will ascend the throne?*	¿Cuál de los infantes subirá al trono?
2. *infantryman, marine:*	*Her son was a marine.*	Su hijo fue infante de marina.

Extended US usage		
3. *infant (=small child):*	*I was an infant when the war ended.*	Yo era **infante** cuando terminó la guerra.
	Standard variant →	Yo era **niño** cuando ...
4. *infant (=baby):*	*The infant wouldn't stop crying.*	El **infante** no paraba de llorar.
	Standard variants →	La **criatura** / El **bebé** no paraba de llorar.

5. *infant (=newborn):*	*Where is the newborn unit?*	¿Dónde queda la sección de **infantes**?
	Standard variant →	... de los **recién nacidos**?
6. *infant (adjective):*	*the infant mortality rate*	la mortalidad **de infantes**
	Standard variant →	la mortalidad **infantil**

INFLUENCIAR (verb)   =   **adapted from "to influence"** [DRAE 1927]

- **Influir** is the more conventional form in standard Spanish, although **influenciar** is used selectively to emphasize the influence of a person on another.

Standard usage		
1. *to exert influence on someone:*	*A profesor can influence his students.*	Un profesor puede influenciar a sus alumnos.
Extended US usage		
2. *to influence (an action, result, decision, etc.):*	*What influenced your decision?*	¿Qué **influenció** tu decisión?
	Standard variant →	¿Qué **influyó en** tu decisión?

INFORMAL (adj)   =   **unreliable, not serious**
=   **informal: without ceremony**
=   **informal: friendly; unofficial [US]**
=   **informal (expression): colloquial [US]**

- Just as **formal** means "reliable" in standard Spanish, **informal** suggests "unreliable."
- In U.S. Spanish, **informal** can also express "unofficial, friendly, relaxed."

Standard usage		
1. *unreliable, not serious:*	*I can't count on him; he is an unreliable person.*	Yo no puedo contar con él; es una persona muy informal.
2. *informal (=casual, without ceremony):*	*You can wear informal dress.*	Puedes llevar ropa informal.
	The atmosphere was informal.	El ambiente era informal.
Extended US usage		
3. *informal (=friendly):*	*an informal discussion*	una discusión **informal**
	Standard variant →	una discusión **de confianza**
4. *informal (=unofficial):*	*an informal meeting*	una reunión **informal**
	Standard variant →	una reunión **no oficial**
5. *informal (=colloquial):*	*She uses informal expressions.*	Usa expresiones **informales**.
	Standard variants →	Usa expresiones **coloquiales**.
		Usa expresiones **familiares**.

INICIALIZAR (verb) = **adapted from "to initialize"** [DRAE 2001]

> **inicializar.** (Del inglés *to initialize*).1. tr. Inform. Establecer los valores iniciales para la ejecución de un programa. [DRAE]

- This verb is used exclusively in the context of computer technology.

Standard/US usage		
1. to initialize:	*You must initialize the disk before using it.*	Hay que **inicializar** el disco antes de usarlo.

INJURIA (fem noun) = **insult, abuse, slander**
= **injury (physical or emotional) [US]**

- **Injuria** indicates "insult" rather than "injury" in standard usage.

Standard usage		
1. insult, abuse, slander:	*I will not tolerate your insults.* *They sued him for slander.*	No soportaré tus injurias. Lo demandaron por injurias.

Extended US usage		
2. injury (physical):	*He suffered a facial injury.*	Sufrió una **injuria** en la cara.
	Standard variant →	Sufrió una **herida** en la cara.
3. injury (emotional):	*injury to one's reputation* *injury to one's feelings*	una **injuria** a la reputación una **injuria** a los sentimientos
	Standard variants →	una **ofensa** a la reputación un **agravio** a los sentimientos

INPUT (masc) = **loanword for "input"** [DRAE 1984]

- The RAE accounts for three denotations of this term, but leaves out its most common application in U.S. Spanish: **input** meaning "advice, opinion, comment."

Standard usage		
1. input (=raw material):	*The type of input will determine the quality of the product.*	La clase de input determinará la calidad del producto.
2. input (=data):	*The input could not be processed.*	No se pudo procesar el input.

Extended US usage

3. *input (=advice, help, opinion, comment):*	*I need input from my colleagues before I can proceed.*	Necesito **input** de mis colegas antes de proceder.
	Standard variants →	Necesito **consejo** / **ayuda** de mis colegas ...
4. *input (electrical):*	*The TV set doesn't have an input.*	El televisor no tiene **input**.
	Standard variant →	El televisor no tiene **entrada**.

INSENSITIVO (adj) = adapted from "insensitive" (see SENSITIVO) [US]

- The RAE defines **sensitivo** as "related to the senses," but does not list **insensitivo**.
- Both are generally regarded as false cognates in standard Spanish.

US usage

1. *insensitive (person):*	*You are insensitive to my feelings.*	Eres **insensitivo** a mis sentimientos.
	Standard variant →	Eres **insensible** a mis sentimientos.
2. *insensitive (action, behavior):*	*He made an insensitive comment.*	Hizo un comentario **insensitivo**.
	Standard variant →	Hizo un comentario **falto de sensibilidad**.

INSPECTAR (verb) = adapted from "to inspect" [US]

- **Inspeccionar** is the appropriate equivalent in standard Spanish.
- U.S. Spanish borrows **inspectar** from English along with its many applications.

US usage

1. *to inspect (=examine):*	*The meat was inspected and found to be fresh.*	**Inspectaron** la carne y la encontraron fresca.
	Standard variant →	**Examinaron** la carne ...
2. *to inspect (building, vehicle, machinery):*	*Is this where cars are inspected?*	¿Es aquí donde **inspectan** los autos?
	Standard variant →	¿Es aquí donde **inspeccionan** los autos?
3. *to inspect (=look over, look through):*	*They inspect your luggage when you go through customs.*	Te **inspectan** el equipaje al pasar por la aduana.
	Standard variant →	Te **revisan** el equipaje al pasar por la aduana.

INSULADO (adj) = **adapted from "insulated" [US]**

- Standard Spanish accounts for **ínsula** and the adjective **insular**, but not **insulado**.
- In U.S. Spanish, it is used for "insulated" and, less frequently, to mean "isolated."

US usage		
1. insulated (=protected):	*Our house is well insulated from the cold.*	Nuestra casa está bien **insulada** del frío.
	Standard variant →	Nuestra casa está bien **protegida** del frío.
2. isolated:	*I feel very isolated in this community.*	Me siento muy **insulada** en esta comunidad.
	Standard variant →	Me siento muy **aislada** en esta comunidad.

INTENTAR (verb) = **to try, attempt**
= **to intend to: mean to, plan to [US]**

Standard usage		
1. to try to, attempt to:	*I tried to call you three times.*	Intenté llamarte tres veces.

Extended US usage		
2. to intend to (=mean to):	*He did not intend to hurt you.*	**No intentó** hacerte daño.
	Standard variants →	**No tenía la intención de / No quería** hacerte daño.
3. to intend to (=plan to):	*I intend to go to class tomorrow.*	**Intento** ir a clase mañana.
	Standard variant →	**Pienso** ir a clase mañana.
4. intended for:	*This is intended for you.*	Esto está **intentado** para ti.
	Standard variant →	Esto **es para ti.**

INTERFACE (masc) = **loanword for "interface" [US]**

INTERFAZ (fem) = **adapted from "interface"** [DRAE 1984]

INTERFACER (verb) = **adapted from "to interface" [US]**

- Moliner, DRAE, and most major dictionaries list only one form: **interfaz** (fem).
- U.S. Spanish favors **interface** (masc), and makes use of the corresponding verb form.

Standard usage		
1. interface (computers):	*connection by interface*	conexión mediante interfaz

Extended US usage		
2. interface (computers):	*serial interface*	**interface** de serie
	Standard variant →	**interfaz** de serie
3. to interface (computers):	*The computer interfaces with the printer.*	La computadora **interface** con la impresora.
	Standard variant →	La computadora **conecta** con la impresora.

INTERNET (masc noun) = **loanword for "internet" [US]**

- Entered in most dictionaries (incl. Moliner), the RAE does not list this widely used term.
- In the U.S., **el internet** is preferred over **la red** ("the web").

US usage		
1. internet:	*I found an interesting article on the internet.*	Encontré un artículo interesante en el **internet**.
	Standard variant →	Encontré un artículo interesante en la **red**.

INTERVIÚ (masc / fem noun) = **adapted from "interview"** [DRAE 1984]

INTERVIUVAR (verb) = **adapted from "to interview"** [DRAE 1984]

- These terms, borrowed from English, are both sanctioned in standard Spanish despite the existence of traditional alternatives such as **entrevista** and **entrevistar**.

Standard/US usage		
1. interview:	*How was your interview?*	¿Cómo te fue en el (la) **interviú**?
	Traditional variant →	¿Cómo te fue en la **entrevista**?
2. to interview:	*It looks like they are going to interview the president.*	Parece que van a **interviuvar** al presidente.
	Traditional variant →	Parece que van a **entrevistar** al presidente.

INTOXICADO (adj) = **poisoned; indoctrinated**
                     = **intoxicated: drunk, inebriated [US]**

- In standard practice, **intoxicado** means "poisoned" and, in a figurative sense, "indoctrinated" ("poisoned by ideas," so to speak). It does not suggest "intoxicated by alcohol consumption," which is traditionally expressed with **borracho** or **ebrio**.

Standard usage		
1. *poisoned:*	*It was discovered that the victim had been poisoned.*	Se descubrió que la víctima había sido intoxicada.
2. *indoctrinated:*	*He ended up indoctrinated with revolutionary ideas.*	Terminó intoxicado de ideas revolucionarias.

Extended US usage		
3. *intoxicated (=drunk, inebriated):*	*It was confirmed that the driver was intoxicated.*	Se confirmó que el conductor estaba **intoxicado**.
	Standard variants →	... estaba **borracho** / **ebrio**.

INTRODUCIR (verb) = **to put, place into**
                     = **to insert, get into**
                     = **to input, enter (information)**
                     = **to introduce: bring into, bring about**
                     = **to introduce one person to another [US]**

- Standard usage of **introducir** coincides with that of U.S. Spanish, with one notable exception: "to introduce one person to another," traditionally expressed as **presentar**.

Standard usage		
1. *to put, place...into:*	*He placed his feet in the water.*	Introdujo los pies en el agua.
2. *to insert, get...into:*	*I could not get the key into the lock.*	No pude introducir la llave en la cerradura.
3. *to input, enter (data):*	*I entered all the information you gave me.*	Introduje todos los datos que me diste.
4. *to introduce (=bring into):*	*Tobacco was brought into Europe in the seventeenth century.*	Se introdujo el tabaco en Europa en el siglo XVII.
5. *to introduce (=bring about):*	*Our congressman wants to introduce a new law.*	Nuestro congresista quiere introducir una nueva ley.

Extended US usage		
6. *to introduce (one person to another):*	*Let me introduce you to my boss.*	Te quiero **introducir** a mi jefe.
	Standard variant →	Te quiero **presentar** a mi jefe.
7. *to introduce oneself:*	*Please introduce yourself.*	Favor de **introducirse**.
	Standard variant →	Favor de **presentarse**.

IRRELEVANTE (adj)   =   **insignificant, unimportant**
   =   **irrelevant, unrelated [US]**

- Historically, **relevante** and **irrelevante** indicate "importance" rather than "relationship."
- **Irrelevante** meaning "unrelated" is more typical of U.S. Spanish.

Standard usage		
1. irrelevant (=unimportant):	*Those details are irrelevant.*	Esos detalles son irrelevantes.

Extended US usage		
2. irrelevant (=unrelated):	*What he said was irrelevant to the discussion.*	Lo que dijo **era irrelevante** a la discusión.
	Standard variants →	Lo que dijo **no tenía relación con** la discusión. Lo que dijo **no venía al caso.**

JANITOR (masc noun)   see **YANITOR**

JEANS (masc noun)   =   **loanword for "jeans" [US]**

- **Jeans** (also spelled **yins**) occurs in U.S. Spanish along with **bluejeans** and **vaqueros**.
- Moliner accounts for all three forms whereas the RAE only accepts **vaqueros**.

US usage		
1. jeans:	*I'll put on my jeans to go to the park.*	Me pondré los **jeans** para ir al parque.
	Standard variant →	Me pondré los **vaqueros** para ir al parque.

JEEP (masc noun)   =   **loanword for "jeep" [US]**

- Cited in many dictionaries, neither **jeep** nor **yip** are mentioned in the DRAE despite their widespread use in the United States and throughout the Spanish-speaking world.
- Moliner lists **yipi** as a variant used in Cuba and the Dominican Republic.

US usage		
1. jeep:	*We crossed the desert on a jeep.*	Atravesamos el desierto en un **jeep**.
	Standard variant →	Atravesamos el desierto en un **vehículo todo terreno**.

JERSEY (masc) = **loanword for "jersey" or "sweater"** [DRAE 1984]

- In standard usage, jersey (rendered phonetically in Spanish) is limited to a type of "light sweater" or "sweatshirt."
- In U.S. Spanish, as in English, it can also refer to a "jersey" worn by a sports team, in which case it is usually pronounced "**yersi**."

Standard usage *1. jersey (=light sweater):*	*Put on a jersey; it's cold today.*	Ponte un jersey; hace frío hoy.
Extended US usage *2. jersey (=team outfit):*	*Everyone is wearing a Yankees jersey.*	Todo el mundo lleva el **jersey** de los Yankees.
	Standard variant →	Todo el mundo lleva la **camisa** de los Yankees.

JET LAG (masc noun) = **loanword for "jet lag"** [US]

- Listed in Moliner but not approved by the RAE, **jet lag** (pronounced as in English) is more common in U.S. Spanish than the traditional equivalent, **desfase horario**.

US usage *1. jet lag:*	*I slept ten hours because of the jet lag.*	Dormí diez horas a causa del **jet lag**.
	Standard variant →	Dormí diez horas a causa del **desfase horario**.

JORNADA (fem noun) = **working day; special day**
= **expedition, trip**
= **act (in a traditional play)**
= **journey: trip, trajectory** [US]

Standard usage		
1. working day:	*an eight-hour workday*	una jornada de ocho horas
2. special day:	*open house day*	jornada informativa
	day of action, day of protest	jornada de movilización
3. expedition, long trip:	*I read about Marco Polo's expeditions to the Orient.*	Leí sobre las jornadas de Marco Polo al Oriente.
4. act (in a play):	*The plays of Calderón consist of three acts.*	Las obras de Calderón constan de tres jornadas.

Extended US usage

1. journey (=trip):	My journey through Thailand was unforgettable.	Mi **jornada** por Tailandia fue inolvidable.
	Standard variant →	Mi **viaje** por Tailandia ...
2. journey (=trajectory):	We watched the capsule's journey through space.	Observamos la **jornada** de la cápsula por el espacio.
	Standard variant →	Obervamos el **trayecto** de la cápsula ...

JUEGO (masc noun)
- = **game, contest (in general)**
- = **play (in sport)**
- = **game: scheme, joke**
- = **gambling**
- = **game: sport, match [US]**
- = **board / card game [US]**

• Whereas U.S. Spanish, in mimicking English, applies **juego** uniformly, standard academic Spanish prescribes separate terms for "game," "sport," and "match."

Standard usage

1. game (in general):	Chess is a difficult game.	El ajedrez es un juego difícil.
2. games (=contest):	the Olympic Games	los Juegos Olímpicos
3. play (in sport):	The ball is out of play.	La pelota está fuera de juego.
4. game (=scheme, joke):	I am fed up with his games.	Estoy harto de sus juegos.
5. gambling:	He got addicted to gambling.	Se envició con el juego.

Extended US usage

6. game (=sport):	Soccer is the national game of many countries.	El fútbol es el **juego** nacional de muchos países.
	Standard variant →	... es el **deporte** nacional ...
7. game (=match):	Did you see yesterday's game?	¿Viste el **juego** de ayer?
	Standard variant →	¿Viste el **partido** de ayer?
8. board game, card game, round:	Would you be interested in a game of cards?	¿Te interesaría un **juego** de cartas?
	Standard variant →	¿Te interesaría una **partida** de cartas?

JUGAR (verb)

= **to play (in general)**
= **to play sports & games**
= **to play a team / an opponent**
= **to play an instrument [US]**
= **to play a role; pretend to be [US]**
= **to play: show; sound [US]**

- The generic equivalent of "to play" is **jugar**. Depending on the context, however, standard Spanish also renders it as **tocar**, **hacer**, **pasar**, etc.
- By influence of English, U.S. Spanish makes very broad use of **jugar**.

Standard usage

1. *to play (in general):*	*Who wants to play?*	¿Quién quiere jugar?
2. *to play (sports & games):*	*Do you play baseball?*	¿Juegas al béisbol?
	We like to play chess.	Nos gusta jugar al ajedrez.
3. *to play (team, opponent):*	*I played him twice.*	Jugué contra él dos veces.

Extended US usage

4. *to play an instrument:*	*I love to play the piano.*	Me encanta **jugar** el piano.
	Standard variant →	Me encanta **tocar** el piano.
5. *to play a role:*	*She played the role of Ophelia.*	**Jugó el rol** de Ofelia.
	Standard variant →	**Hizo el papel** de Ofelia.
6. *to play (=pretend to be):*	*He likes to play dead.*	Le gusta **jugar** al muerto.
	Standard variant →	Le gusta **hacerse** el muerto.
7. *to play (=show):*	*What movie is playing?*	¿Qué película **está jugando**?
	Standard variants →	¿Qué película **se está dando / están pasando**?
8. *to play (=sound):*	*I like when the organ plays.*	Me gusta cuando **juega** el órgano.
	Standard variant →	Me gusta cuando **suena** el órgano.

JUNGLA (fem noun) = **adapted from "jungle"** [DRAE 1970]

jungla. (Del inglés *jungle*). 1. f. En la India y otros países de Asia y América, terreno de vegetación muy espesa. [DRAE]

- Despite the acceptance of **jungla** in standard Spanish, the tropical rainforest of South and Central America is traditionally referred to as **selva**.

Standard usage		
1. *jungle (African/Asian):*	*There are tigers in the jungles of Africa.*	Hay tigres en las junglas de África.
2. *jungle (figurative):*	*This city is a real jungle.*	Esta ciudad es una verdadera jungla.

Extended US usage		
3. *jungle (American):*	*We traveled through the Brazilian jungle.*	Viajamos por la **jungla** brasileña.
	Standard variant →	Viajamos por la **selva** brasileña.
4. *jungle (adj):*	*We saw jungle plants.*	Vimos plantas **de jungla**.
	Standard variant →	Vimos plantas **selváticas**.

"Jungle" expressions in standard Spanish:	*the law of the jungle*	la ley de la selva
	jungle warfare	guerra en la selva
	tropical rainforest	selva tropical

KETCHUP (masc noun) = **loanword for "ketchup"** [DRAE 2001]

ketchup. (Voz inglesa, y ésta del chino *k'e chap*, zumo de tomate). 1. m. Salsa de tomate condimentada con vinagre, azúcar y especias. [DRAE]

• The closest traditional variant, **salsa de tomate**, does not accurately describe this unique sauce. Hence its eventual entry into the standard Spanish lexicon.

Standard/US usage		
1. *ketchup:*	*Do you put ketchup on your hamburger?*	¿Le pones **ketchup** a la hamburguesa?
	Traditional variant →	¿Le pones **salsa de tomate** a la hamburguesa?

KIT (masc noun) = **loanword for "kit"** [DRAE 2001]

kit. (Del inglés *kit*, y éste del neerlandés *kit*). 1. m. Conjunto de productos y utensilios suficientes para conseguir un determinado fin, que se comercializan como una unidad. [DRAE]

• Popular term in the U.S., the use of **kit** in standard Spanish is increasingly common.

Standard/US usage		
1. kit (=case, kit):	*I left my make-up kit at home.*	Me dejé el **kit** de maquillaje en casa.
	Traditional variants →	Me dejé el **bolso** / la **bolsa** / el **juego** de maquillaje en casa.

"Kit" expressions in standard Spanish →		
	assembly kit	kit de montaje
	first-aid kit	botiquín
	game / toy kit	juego por piezas
	sewing kit	costurero
	tool kit	herramientas

LANDLORD (masc noun) = **loanword for "landlord" [US]**

• **Landlord** is widespread in the U.S. to designate the "owner" or "manager" of an apartment building. It is neither approved by the RAE nor listed in major dictionaries.

US usage		
1. landlord (=owner):	*The landlord increased our rent.*	El **landlord** nos aumentó el alquiler.
	Standard variants →	El **dueño** / **propietario** nos aumentó el alquiler.
2. landlord (=manager):	*We asked our landlord to turn on the heat.*	Le pedimos al **landlord** que nos pusiera la calefacción.
	Standard variants →	Le pedimos al **encargado** /al **jefe** que nos pusiera ...

LAPTOP (masc noun) = **loanword for "laptop computer" [US]**

• **Laptop** is not sanctioned by the RAE nor is it mentioned by Moliner despite its dissemination throughout the Spanish-speaking world.

US usage		
1. laptop computer:	*I'm going to buy myself a laptop.*	Me voy a comprar un **laptop**.
	Standard variants →	... un **ordenador portátil** / una **computadora portátil**.

LÁSER (masc noun) = **loanword for "laser"** [DRAE 1984]

láser. (Del inglés *laser*, acrónimo de *light amplification by stimulated emission of radiation*, amplificación de luz mediante emisión inducida de radiación). [DRAE]

Standard/US usage

1. laser (=technique):	*Laser is used to do eye surgery.*	Se usa el **láser** para la cirujía óptica.
2. laser (=beam):	*The machine produces a beam.*	La máquina produce un **láser**.
	Traditional variant →	La máquina produce un **rayo**.
3. Selected expressions:	*laser beam*	rayo láser
	laser gun	pistola de rayos láser
	laser printer	impresora láser
	laser surgery	cirugía con láser

LAYOFF (masc noun) = **loanword for "layoff" (from work)** [US]

• Generally pronounced "**leyó**" by Spanish speakers, this term is indigenous to the United States and seems to have no exact equivalent in standard Spanish.

US usage

1. layoff (=act):	*There have been many layoffs at work lately.*	Han habido muchos **layoffs** en el trabajo últimamente.
	Standard variant →	Han habido muchos **despidos** en el trabajo últimamente.
2. layoff (=period):	*What do you plan to do during your layoff?*	¿Qué piensas hacer durante el **layoff**?
	Standard variants →	¿Qué piensas hacer durante el **paro** / la **baja**?

LEASE (fem noun) = **loanword for "lease"** [US]

LEASING (masc noun) = **loanword for "leasing"** [DRAE 1984]

• Both terms occur in U.S. Spanish in lieu of the traditional **contrato de arrendamiento**.
• The DRAE accounts for a secondary use of **leasing** ("rent with option to buy"), but does not mention **lease** (pronounced as in English).

Standard usage		
1. *leasing (=option to buy):*	*Auto leasing is not as costly as you think.*	El leasing de autos no es tan costoso como piensas.
	Traditional variant →	El arrendamiento de autos ...

Extended US usage		
2. *lease:*	*I signed a two-year lease.*	Firmé una **lease** de dos años.
	Standard variant →	Firmé un **contrato de arrendamiento** de dos años.

LECTURA (fem noun) = **act of reading; reading material**
  = **lecture [US]**

• **Lectura** is generally classified as a false cognate of "lecture" in standard Spanish.

Standard usage		
1. *act of reading:*	*His reading of the poem was very moving.*	Su lectura del poema fue muy emocionante.
2. *reading material, literary work:*	*Does the book appear on your reading list?*	¿Aparece el libro en tu lista de lecturas?

Extended US usage		
3. *lecture (=class):*	*I attended every lecture.*	Asistí a todas las **lecturas**.
	Standard variant →	Asistí a todas las **clases**.
4. *formal lecture:*	*She gave a lecture about women's rights.*	Dio una **lectura** sobre los derechos de la mujer.
	Standard variant →	Dio una **conferencia** sobre ...
5. *informal lecture:*	*I attended an informal lecture on public safety.*	Asistí a una **lectura** sobre la seguridad pública.
	Standard variant →	Asistí a una **charla** sobre ...
6. *lecture (=sermon):*	*My dad gave us a lecture.*	Mi papá nos **dio una lectura**.
	Standard variant →	Mi papá nos **echó un sermón**.

LENGUAJE (masc noun) = **language (faculty)**
  = **style of speech**
  = **technical language, lingo**
  = **language of a country or region [US]**

• Used widely in the U.S. to refer to English, Spanish, and other national languages.
• Standard Spanish reserves **lenguaje** for particular types of "lingo" or styles of speech.

Standard usage		
1. *language (faculty):*	*language acquisition*	adquisición del lenguaje
2. *style of speech:*	*I use very simple language.*	Uso lenguaje muy sencillo.
	Don't use bad language.	No uses lenguaje grosero.
3. *technical language*	*business language*	lenguaje comercial
(=lingo):	*medical language*	lenguaje médico
	language of violence	lenguaje de violencia
	computer language	lenguaje de informática

Extended US usage		
4. *national language:*	*She speaks three languages.*	Ella habla tres **lenguajes**.
	Standard variants →	Ella habla tres **idiomas** / **lenguas**.

LIBRERÍA (fem noun) = **bookstore; bookcase**
= **library [US]**

• The use of this false cognate to mean "library" seems to be on the rise in U.S. Spanish.

Standard usage		
1. *bookstore:*	*I bought my textbooks at the university bookstore.*	Compré mis textos en la librería de la universidad.
2. *large bookcase:*	*We put the bookcase against the left wall.*	Pusimos la librería contra la pared de izquierda.

Extended US usage		
3. *library:*	*I visited the public library.*	Visité la **librería** pública.
	Standard variant →	Visité la **biblioteca** pública.

LÍDER (masc noun) = **adapted from "leader"** [DRAE 1970]

• Fully incorporated into standard Spanish, **líder** is used in politics, business, and sports.

Standard/US usage		
1. *leader (political):*	*There will be a summit of European leaders.*	Habrá una conferencia de **líderes** europeos.
	Traditional variant →	Habrá una conferencia de **jefes de estado** ...
2. *leader (in sports):*	*This team needs a leader.*	Este equipo necesita un **líder**.
	Traditional variant →	Este equipo necesita un **jefe**.
3. *leader (=first, best):*	*He is the leader in goals scored.*	Él es el **líder** en cuanto a goles marcados.
	Traditional variants →	Él es el **primero** / el **mejor** ...

LIGHT (adj)   =   **loanword for "light"** [DRAE 2001]

- The use of the adjective **light** (pronounced as in English) is sanctioned by the RAE to mean "low-calorie," "low-tar," and "toned-down." U.S. Spanish adds "soft" to the list.

Standard usage		
1. light (=low-calorie):	*One light beer, please.*	Una cerveza light, por favor.
	Traditional variant →	... cerveza baja en calorías ...
2. light (=low-tar):	*I only smoke light cigarrettes.*	Sólo fumo cigarrillos light.
	Traditional variant →	Sólo fumo cigarrillos de bajo contenido en alquitrán.

Extended US usage		
3. light (=soft):	*Do you prefer light music?*	¿Prefieres música light?
	Standard variants →	¿... música suave / ligera?

LÍNEA (fem noun)

=	**line (in general)**	
=	**line of writing**	
=	**line of communication**	
=	**cable (electrical)**	
=	**figure: body shape (idiomatic)**	
=	**drawn line, underline [US]**	
=	**row; line of people [US]**	
=	**family line; wrinkles [US]**	
=	**(on) line: on the internet [US]**	

- The multiple denotations of "line" in English give rise to many applications of **línea** in U.S. Spanish, including loan translations such as **en línea** for "online."

Standard usage		
1. line (in general):	*a straight line*	una línea recta
	assembly line	línea de montaje
2. line of writing:	*to read between the lines*	leer entre las líneas
3. communication line:	*telephone lines*	líneas telefónicas
4. cable:	*high-tension cable*	línea de alta tensión
5. figure (=body shape):	*to keep one's figure trim*	guardar la línea

Extended US usage

6. *drawn line, underline:*	*Put a line under the paragraph.*	Pon una **línea** debajo del párrafo.
	Standard variant →	Pon una **raya** debajo del ...
7. *line (=row of people or objects, queue):*	*There was a line of cars.* *Please make a line.*	Había una **línea** de carros. Favor de hacer una **línea**.
	Standard variants →	Había una **fila** de carros. Favor de **ponerse en fila**.
8. *to get / wait on line:*	*One has to wait on line.*	Hay que **esperar en (la) línea**.
	Standard variant →	Hay que **hacer (la) cola**.
9. *line (=family):*	*He comes from a long line of doctors.*	Proviene de una **línea** de médicos.
	Standard variants →	Proviene de una **familia** / un **linaje** de médicos.
10. *lines (=wrinkles):*	*I already have lines on my face.*	Ya tengo **líneas** en la cara.
	Standard variant →	Ya tengo **arrugas** en la cara.

LINK (masc noun)   =   **loanword for "link" [US]**

- This non-standardized term occurs in U.S. Spanish primarily in the context of computers and technology.

US usage

1. *link (computer):*	*This link connects to the National Library.*	Este **link** conecta con la Biblioteca Nacional.
	Standard variant →	Este **enlace** conecta con la Biblioteca Nacional.
2. *link (=association):*	*Our university has links with Mexico.*	Nuestra universidad tiene **links** con México.
	Standard variants →	... tiene **vínculos** / **lazos** con México.

LIPSTICK (masc noun) = **loanword for "lipstick" [US]**

• Very common in U.S. Spanish, lipstick is not part of the standard Spanish lexicon.

US usage

1. lipstick:	*That color lipstick looks very good on you.*	Ese color de lipstick te va muy bien.
	Standard variant →	Ese color de lápiz de labios …
2. to put on lipstick:	*I put on lipstick when I go to a party.*	Me pongo lipstick cuando voy a una fiesta.
	Standard variant →	Me pinto los labios cuando …

LIVING (masc noun) = **loanword for "living room"** [DRAE 2001]

• Living is defined as "cuarto de estar" by Moliner and the DRAE.
• U.S. Spanish prefers living room.

Standard usage

1. living room:	*I watch TV in the living room.*	Miro la tele en el living.
	Traditional variants →	Miro la tele en la sala / en la sala de estar.

Extended US usage

2. living room:	*We need a larger living room.*	Nos hace falta un living room más grande.
	Standard variants →	Nos hace falta un living / una sala más grande.

LLENO (DE) (adj)
= **full: filled, complete**
= **filled with emotion, fear, doubt, etc.**
= **full of, covered with**
= **full from eating; full attendance [US]**
= **full: entire (time period) [US]**

Standard usage

1. full (=filled):	*two full glasses*	dos vasos llenos
2. full (=complete):	*the moon is full*	la luna está llena
3. filled with (emotion):	*She was filled with hope.*	Estaba llena de esperanza.
4. full of, covered with:	*You are covered with dust.*	Estás lleno de polvo.

Extended US usage		
5. *full from eating:*	*No, thank you, I'm full.*	No, gracias, **estoy lleno**.
	Standard variants →	No, gracias, **no puedo más**. No, gracias, **estoy harto**.
6. *full house (=sold out):*	*The house (theater) is full.*	La casa está **llena**.
	Standard variant →	Estamos **completos**.
7. *entire time period:*	*I wasted a full day.*	Me perdí un día **lleno**.
	Standard variant →	Me perdí un día **entero**.

Expressions with "full" in standard Spanish	*full board*	pensión **completa**
	full brother / sister	hermano / hermana **carnal**
	in full color	a **todo** color
	in full daylight	en **pleno** día
	in full dress	vestido **de gala**
	full employment	**pleno** empleo
	full fare	tarifa **completa**
	full figure	de talla **grande**
	full-length	de cuerpo **entero**
	a full life	una vida **completa**
	full name	nombre y **apellido**
	full price	precio **total**, **íntegro**
	at full speed	a **toda** velocidad
	full-time	a tiempo **completo**

LOBBY (masc noun) = **loanword for "lobby"** [DRAE 1984]

• The multiple uses of this term in English give rise to similar applications in U.S. Spanish, two of which are sanctioned by the RAE ("pressure group" and "vestibule").

> **lobby.** (Voz inglesa). 1. m. Grupo de personas influyentes, organizado para presionar en favor de determinados intereses. 2. m. Vestíbulo de un hotel y de otros establecimientos como cines, teatros, restaurantes, etc., especialmente si es grande. [DRAE]

Standard usage		
1. *lobby* (=pressure group):	*the senior citizens lobby*	el lobby a favor de ancianos
2. *lobby* (=entrance hall):	*I will be in the hotel lobby.*	Estaré en el lobby del hotel.

Extended US usage		
3. *lobby* (=ground floor):	*This elevator will take us to the lobby.*	Este ascensor nos llevará al **lobby**.
	Standard variants →	... nos llevará al **primer piso** / a la **planta baja**.

LOCACIÓN (fem noun) = **loanword for "location" [US]**

- **Locación** appears in many standard Spanish dictionaries, not as an equivalent of "location" but rather as a legal term for "renting."

US usage

1. *location (=place, site):*	*They live in a good location.*	Viven en una buena **locación**.
	Standard variant →	Viven en un buen **lugar**.
2. *location (=placing):*	*The location of the new museum has not been decided.*	La **locación** del nuevo museo no se ha decidido.
	Standard variant →	La **ubicación** del nuevo museo no se ha decidido.
3. *locating (=act of finding):*	*Locating the accident was a difficult task.*	La **locación** del accidente fue una tarea difícil.
	Standard variant →	La **localización** del accidente fue una tarea difícil.
4. *location (=position):*	*We haven't been able to pinpoint the plane's location.*	No hemos podido precisar la **locación** del avión.
	Standard variant →	... la **posición** del avión.

LONCHAR (verb) = **adapted from "to eat lunch" [US]**

LONCHE (masc noun) = **adapted from "lunch" [US]**

LONCHERÍA (fem noun) = **adapted from "luncheonette" [US]**

- The RAE sanctions **lunch** in a limited context [see **LUNCH**], but has approved neither **lonchería** nor **lonchar**, both prevalent in U.S. Spanish. Moliner accounts for **lonchería**.
- Interestingly, **lonche** was once listed by the RAE as a Mexican variant for "lunch" (1927).

US usage

1. *lunch (food, meal):*	*She prepared a good lunch for the kids.*	Preparó un buen **lonche** para los niños.
	Standard variant →	Preparó un buen **almuerzo** ...
2. *to eat lunch:*	*At what time will you have lunch?*	¿A qué hora vas a **lonchar**?
	Standard variant →	¿A qué hora vas a **almorzar**?
3. *luncheonette, lunch counter, snack bar:*	*I bought a sandwich at the corner luncheonette.*	Me compré un sándwich en la **lonchería** de la esquina.
	Standard variants →	... en el **café** / el **mostrador** / la **cafetería** de la esquina.

LOOK (masc noun) = **loanword for "look" (appearance, style)** [DRAE 2001]

look. (Voz inglesa). 1. m. Imagen o aspecto de las personas o de las cosas, especialmente si responde a un propósito de distinción. [DRAE]

Standard/US usage

1. look (=appearance):	*He has an aristocratic look that is unmistakable.*	Tiene un **look** de aristocracia que es inconfundible.
Traditional variants →	Tiene un **aspecto** / un **aire** de aristocracia ...
2. look (=fashion, style):	*It's the new look in shoes.*	Es el nuevo **look** de zapatos.
Traditional variant →	Es la nueva **moda** de zapatos.

LUNCH (masc noun) = **loanword for "lunch"** [DRAE 1927]

lunch. (Voz inglesa). 1. m. Comida ligera que se sirve a los invitados en una celebración. [DRAE]

- In academic Spanish, **lunch** generally refers to a light midday meal or snack.
- U.S. Spanish alternates it with **almuerzo** to mean "lunch" in general terms [see **LONCHE**].

Standard usage

1. luncheon, light lunch, midday reception:	*The company organized a luncheon for the employees.*	La empresa organizó un lunch para los empleados.

Extended US usage

2. lunch (food, meal):	*What did you have for lunch?*	¿Qué comiste de **lunch**?
Standard variant →	¿Qué comiste de **almuerzo**?

LUZ (fem noun) = **light: brightness**
  = **light: lamp; electricity**
  = **lighting; traffic light; cigarette light [US]**

Standard usage

1. light (=brightness):	*This room needs more light.*	Este cuarto necesita más luz.
2. light (=lamp):	*Please turn off the light.*	Favor de apagar la luz.
3. electricity:	*I have no electricity at home.*	No tengo luz en casa.

Extended US usage		
4. lighting:	*a stage with good lighting*	un escenario con buena **luz**
	Standard variant →	... con buena **iluminación**
5. traffic light:	*Turn left at the (traffic) light.*	Doble a la izquierda cuando llegue a la **luz (de tráfico)**.
	Standard variant →	... cuando llegue al **semáforo**.
6. light (for cigarette):	*Do you have a light?*	¿Tienes **luz**?
	Standard variant →	¿Tienes **fuego**?

MACHEAR (verb) = **to impregnate; to produce male offspring**
                     = **to match [US]**

- Prevailing usage of this verb in U.S. Spanish has little to do with the standard definition.
- In the United States, **machear** (also spelled **matchear**) emulates the many applications of the English verb "to match."

US usage		
1. to match (=find pairs):	*You need to match each word with its synonym.*	Tienes que **machear** cada palabra con su sinónimo.
	Standard variant →	Tienes que **emparejar** cada palabra con su sinónimo.
2. to match (=equal):	*Let's see if you can match my score.*	A ver si puedes **machear** mi puntaje.
	Standard variant →	A ver si puedes **igualar** mi puntaje.
3. to match (=correspond):	*He doesn't match the description we have.*	No **machea** la descripción que tenemos.
	Standard variants →	No **corresponde a / coincide con** la descripción ...
4. to match (=go together):	*The tie doesn't match the shirt.*	La corbata no **machea** bien con la camisa.
	Standard variants →	La corbata no **hace juego** / no **combina bien** con ...

MACHO (adj & noun)

= **male**
= **macho: manly, brave**
= **macho: male chauvinist [US]**

• **Macho**, whose standard meaning is "male," gets its negative connotation from English.

Standard usage		
1. male:	*Is your cat male or female?*	¿Tu gato es macho o hembra?
2. macho (=manly, brave):	*I was told to be macho and not be afraid.*	Me dijeron que tenía que ser macho y no tener miedo.

Extended US usage		
3. macho (=male chauvinist):	*He has very macho concepts about women.*	Tiene conceptos muy **machos** acerca de la mujer.
	Standard variant →	... conceptos muy **machistas** acerca de la mujer.

MAGACÍN (masc noun)

= **adapted from "magazine"** [DRAE 1992]

• Although the traditional term for "magazine" is **revista**, Moliner and the RAE approve of **magacín** to refer to a periodic publication as well as the television program concept.

Standard/US usage		
1. magazine (publication):	*She is reading a magazine.*	Está leyendo un **magacín**.
	Traditional variant →	Está leyendo una **revista**.
2. magazine (TV format):	*Magazine style programs are popular in Spain.*	Los programas **tipo magacín** son populares en España.
	Traditional variant →	Los programas **de temas diversos** son populares ...

MAJOR (masc noun)

= **loanword for "major"** [US]

• **Major** (pronounced as in English) is used to indicate "course of study" in U.S. Spanish.
• It is combined with **hacer** to produce a verb phrase for "to major:" **hacer el major**.

US usage		
1. major (=subject, course of study):	*One must select a major in the second year.*	Hay que escoger un **major** en el segundo año.
	Traditional variants →	Hay que escoger una **concentración / especialización** ...

2. *major (=student):*	*She is a psychology major.*	Es **major** de psicología.
	Traditional variant →	Es **estudiante** de psicología.
3. *to major in a subject:*	*I'm majoring in Spanish.*	**Hago el major** en español.
	Traditional variant →	**Me especializo** en español.

MALL (masc noun) = **loanword for "shopping mall" [US]**

- Occurs frequently in U.S. Spanish in part because the generic **centro comercial** does not accurately evoke the complex of stores referred to as "mall" in the United States.
- Pronounced as in English (Stavans spells it "**mol**"), this term is not listed in the DRAE.

US usage		
1. *shopping mall (usually indoor):*	*They went to the mall to do some shopping.*	Fueron al **mall** a hacer compras.
	Standard variant →	Fueron al **centro comercial** a hacer compras.
2. *pedestrian mall (with stores):*	*a pedestrian mall lined with small shops*	un **mall** bordeado de tiendas pequeñas
	Standard variant →	una **calle peatonal** bordeada de tiendas …

MÁNAGER (noun) = **loanword for "manager" [DRAE 1984]**

- Most dictionaries list **mánager** (pronounced as in English) as an americanism used in the world of sports and entertainment. In the U.S., this term has broader applications.

Standard usage		
1. *manager (sports):*	*the manager of the Yankees*	el mánager de los Yankees

Extended US usage		
2. *manager (of firm, bank):*	*I wish to speak with the bank manager.*	Deseo hablar con el **mánager** del banco.
	Standard variant →	… con el **director** del banco.
3. *manager (of hotel, sales):*	*He is a sales manager.*	Es **mánager** de ventas.
	Standard variant →	Es **gerente** de ventas.
4. *manager (of finances):*	*She's a good money manager.*	Es buena **mánager** del dinero.
	Standard variant →	Es buena **administradora**.
5. *manager (of store, shop, restaurant):*	*Who is the manager of this store?*	¿Quién es el **mánager** de esta tienda?
	Standard variant →	¿Quién es el **encargado** …?

6. *manager, agent (of actor, singer...):*	*The actor's manager will negotiate his contract.*	El **mánager** del actor negociará su contrato.
	Standard variant →	El **representante** del actor ...

MANERA (fem noun)

= **way: mode, manner**
= **manners, conduct (Lat Am)**
= **way: aspect, respect [US]**
= **way: style [US]**
= **way: gift, skill [US]**
= **way: manners [US]**

Standard usage

1. *way (=manner):*	*I did it my way.*	Lo hice a mi manera.
2. *manners (Lat Am):*	*to have good manners*	tener buenas maneras

Extended US usage

3. *way (=aspect, respect):*	*They are alike in many ways.*	Son iguales en muchas **maneras**.
	Standard variant →	... en muchos **sentidos**.
4. *way (=style):*	*a different way of life*	una distinta **manera de vivir**
	Standard variant →	un distinto **estilo de vida**
5. *way (=gift, skill):*	*He has a way with kids.*	**Tiene manera** con los niños.
	Standard variants →	**Sabe manejar** a los niños. **Se lleva bien** con los niños.
6. *person's manners:*	*He has terrible manners.*	Tiene **maneras** muy feas.
	Standard variants →	Tiene **modales** muy feos. Es un **maleducado**.

MAPA (masc noun)

= **map (of country, world)**
= **street map, transportation map [US]**

Standard usage

1. *map (of country, continent, world):*	*the map of Europe*	el mapa de Europa

Extended US usage

2. *street map, city map:*	*I need a map of Madrid.*	Necesito un **mapa** de Madrid.
	Standard variant →	Necesito un **plano** de Madrid.
3. *transportation map:*	*Do you have a subway map?*	¿Tienes un **mapa** del metro?
	Standard variant →	¿Tienes un **plano** del metro?

MÁRKETING (masc noun) = **loanword for "marketing"** [DRAE 1984]

Standard/US usage

1. *marketing (=selling):*

The marketing of this product was not successful.	El **márketing** de este producto no resultó bien.
Traditional variant →	La **comercialización** de este producto no resultó bien.

2. *marketing (academic subject):*

He's going to study marketing.	Va a estudiar **márketing**.
Standard variant →	Va a estudiar **mercadotecnia**.

MARQUETA (fem noun) = **loanword for "market"** [US]

- Common in U.S. Latino communities, **marqueta** is generally regarded as Spanglish.
- Used primarily to mean "food market," it also occurs generically to refer to any "market."

US usage

1. *market (=food store):*

I bought milk at the market.	Compré leche en la **marqueta**.
Standard variant →	Compré leche en **el mercado**.

2. *supermarket:*

I spent 100 dollars at the supermarket.	Me gasté cien dólares en la **supermarqueta**.
Standard variant →	... en **el supermercado**.

3. *market (=demand):*

There is no market for this product.	No hay **marqueta** para este producto.
Standard variant →	No hay **demanda** para ...

4. *stock market:*

They have money in the market.	Tienen dinero en la **marqueta**.
Standard variants →	Tienen dinero en la **bolsa** / ... **bolsa de valores**.

MASCARA (fem noun) = **loanword for "mascara"** [US]

- In U.S. Spanish, **mascara** refers to "eye makeup" and is distinguished from **máscara** (standard for "mask"), notwithstanding the RAE's approval of **máscara de pestañas**.

US usage

1. *mascara:*

She puts on mascara every day.	Se pone **mascara** todos los días.
Standard variants →	Se pone **rímel** / **máscara de pestañas** todos los días.

MÁSTER (masc noun) = **loanword for "Master's program / degree"** [DRAE 1989]

- Despite the incorporation of **máster** into standard Spanish, a "Master's degree" or "program" continues to be known as **maestría** in most Spanish-speaking countries.
- In the U.S., **máster** can also refer to an "original recording."

Standard/US usage

1. *Master's program:*	*I'm going to apply for the Master's program.*	Voy a solicitar para el **máster**.
	Traditional variant →	Voy a solicitar para el **programa de maestría**.
2. *Master's degree:*	*I got my Master's five years ago.*	Conseguí el **máster** hace cinco años.
	Traditional variants →	Conseguí la **maestría** / el **título de maestría** ...
3. *master (original recording):*	*We made copies from the master.*	Hicimos copias del **máster**.
	Traditional variant →	Hicimos copias del **original**.

MATCHEAR (verb)   see **MACHEAR**

MATERIAL (noun)
= **material: substance**
= **material: tools, ideas**
= **materials: tools & supplies; equipment**
= **material: cloth [US]**
= **raw material [US]**
= **material: potential [US]**

- Inspired by "material" and "fabric" as English synonyms for "cloth," **material** and **fábrica** turn up in U.S. Spanish, despite their status as false cognates in standard usage.

Standard usage

1. *material (=substance):*	*a synthetic material*	un material sintético
2. *material (=tools, ideas):*	*Do you have enough material for the lesson?*	¿Tienes suficiente material para la lección?
3. *materials (=supplies):*	*I bought painting materials.*	Compré materiales de pintura.
4. *equipment, machinery:*	*military equipment*	material de guerra

Extended US usage

5. *material (=cloth):*	*material to make a shirt*	**material** para una camisa
	Standard variants →	**tela** / **tejido** para una camisa
6. *raw material:*	*Iron is a raw material.*	El hierro es un **material** crudo.
	Standard variant →	... es una **materia prima**.
7. *material (=potential):*	*He is not college material.*	No es **material** de universidad.
	Standard variant →	No tiene **madera** de universitario.

MAUS (masc noun)   see **MOUSE**

MAYOR (adj & noun)
- = **older person, adult**
- = **greater, larger; greatest, biggest**
- = **major** (adj), **mayor** (noun) **[US]**

- In U.S. Spanish, **mayor** is often used as an adjective for "major" and, less frequently, as a noun to mean "mayor," particularly in the Southwest.

Standard usage

1. *older, elderly, adult:*	*an older (elderly) person*	una persona mayor
2. *greater, larger:*	*of greater importance*	de mayor importancia
3. *greatest, biggest:*	*That's my biggest problem.*	Ése es mi mayor problema.

Extended US usage

4. *major (=important):*	*the major aspects*	los aspectos **mayores**
	Standard variants →	los aspectos **de mayor importancia** / **de mayor interés** / **fundamentales**
5. *major (=principal):*	*What is the major issue?*	¿Cuál es el asunto **mayor**?
	Standard variant →	¿Cuál es el asunto **principal**?
6. *major (in sports):*	*the major leagues*	las ligas **mayores**
	Standard variant →	las **grandes** ligas
7. *mayor (noun):*	*the mayor of Los Angeles*	el **mayor** de Los Angeles
	Standard variant →	el **alcalde** de Los Angeles

MENOR (adj & noun) = **smaller, smallest, slightest**
= **fewer, less, lesser**
= **younger, youngest**
= **minor, under-age**
= **minor: unimportant, not serious [US]**
= **minor: secondary specialization [US]**

• By influence of English, **menor** can mean "secondary" or "unimportant" in U.S. Spanish.

Standard usage

1. *smaller:*	*You need a smaller size.*	Necesitas un tamaño menor.
2. *smallest:*	*This is the smallest of the three.*	Éste es el menor de los tres.
3. *slightest:*	*The slightest noise bothers me.*	El menor ruido me molesta.
4. *fewer, less:*	*Six is less than seven.*	Seis es menor que siete.
5. *lesser:*	*to a lesser extent*	en menor grado
6. *younger:*	*I have a younger brother.*	Tengo un hermano menor.
7. *youngest:*	*This is my youngest daughter.*	Ésta es mi hija menor.
8. *minor (=underage):*	*This program is not suitable for minors.*	Este programa no es apto para menores (de edad).

Extended US usage

9. *minor (=unimportant):*	*a minor problem*	un problema **menor**
	Standard variants →	un problema **insignificante** / **de poca importancia**
10. *minor (=secondary):*	*She played a minor role.*	Hizo un papel **menor**.
	Standard variant →	Hizo un papel **secundario**.
11. *minor (=not serious):*	*It was a very minor injury.*	Fue una herida muy **menor**.
	Standard variants →	Fue una herida muy **leve**. Fue una herida **poco grave**.
12. *academic minor:*	*My minor is French.*	Mi **menor** es francés.
	Standard variant →	Mi **concentración secundaria** es francés.

MICROWAVE (masc noun) = **loanword for "microwave oven" [US]**

• The widespread use of **microwave** in U.S. Spanish (Stavans spells it "**maicrogüey**") is a good example of the tendency to prefer an English term over a viable Spanish equivalent (**microondas**).

US usage		
1. microwave oven:	*Ten minutes in the microwave and it's done.*	Diez minutos en el **microwave** y está hecho.
	Standard variant ➜	Diez minutos en el (**horno**) **microondas** y está hecho.

MINORIDAD (fem noun) = **loanword for "minority" [US]**

- **Minoría** is the conventional term for "minority."
- In U.S. Spanish, perhaps by influence of cognates such as **comunidad** and **sociedad**, the preferred variant is **minoridad**, particularly when referring to an ethnic group.

US usage		
1. minority (=ethnic group):	*Latinos represent the largest minority in the United States.*	Los latinos representan la **minoridad** más numerosa en Estados Unidos.
	Standard variant ➜	... la **minoría étnica** más numerosa ...
2. minority (=individual):	*Two of the five board members are minorities.*	Dos de los cinco miembros de la junta son **minoridades**.
	Standard variant ➜	... son **personas de minoría étnica**.
3. minority (=small portion):	*A minority of the students voted.*	Una **minoridad** de estudiantes votaron.
	Standard variant ➜	Una **minoría** de estudiantes ...

MISERABLE (adj)
= **stingy, miserly, cheap**
= **miserable: paltry, meager**
= **miserable: vile, mean, despicable**
= **miserable: sad, depressed; depressing [US]**
= **miserable: unpleasant [US]**
= **miserable: wretched, squalid [US]**
= **miserable (fig): complete [US]**

Standard usage		
1. stingy, miserly, cheap:	*Don't be so stingy (cheap).*	No seas tan miserable.
2. miserable (=meager):	*All I had left was a miserable piece of bread.*	Sólo me quedaba un miserable pedazo de pan.
3. miserable (=vile, mean):	*The young woman was afraid of the miserable old man.*	La jovencita tenía miedo del miserable viejo.

Extended US usage

4. *miserable (=very sad):*	*Your father looks miserable.*	Tu padre se ve **miserable**.
	Standard variants →	Tu padre se ve **muy triste** / **deprimido** / **abatido**.
5. *miserable (=difficult, depressing):*	*What miserable weather!* *He had a miserable childhood.*	¡Qué tiempo más **miserable**! Tuvo una infancia **miserable**.
	Standard variants →	¡Qué tiempo más **deprimente**! Tuvo una infancia **infeliz** / **desdichada**.
6. *miserable (=unpleasant):*	*We had a miserable time.*	Pasamos un rato **miserable**.
	Standard variants →	Pasamos un **mal** rato. Lo pasamos **muy mal** / **fatal**.
7. *miserable (=wretched, squalid):*	*She was living in miserable conditions.*	Vivía en condiciones **miserables**.
	Standard variants →	Vivía en condiciones **míseras**. Vivía en **la miseria**.
8. *miserable (=complete):*	*It was a miserable failure.*	Fue un **miserable** fracaso.
	Standard variants →	Fue un **rotundo** fracaso / un fracaso **total**.

MISS (fem noun) = **loanword for "miss"** [DRAE 1927]

miss. (Voz inglesa, acortada de *mistress*, señorita). 1. f. Ganadora de un concurso de belleza. [DRAE]

- Originally defined by the RAE as "**señorita en Inglaterra**," **miss** has since taken on additional meanings, the most recent of which is "beauty queen" (DRAE 1984).
- Moliner defines it as "unmarried woman," somewhat more consistent with U.S. usage.

Standard usage

1. *beauty queen:*	*He married a beauty queen.*	Se casó con una miss.
2. *beauty queen title:*	*She won the title of Miss Europe.*	Ganó el título de Miss Europa.

Extended US usage

3. *Miss (=title for a young woman):*	*You need to speak to Miss Taylor.*	Tienes que hablar con **miss** Taylor.
	Standard variant →	... con **la señorita** Taylor.

MITIN (masc noun) = **popular gathering, political rally** [DRAE 1914]
 = **meeting [US]**

• Borrowed from English almost a century ago, **mitin** is generally used in standard Spanish to mean "political rally" or "gathering" rather than "meeting."

Standard usage		
1. *gathering, rally:*	*There will be a rally tomorrow at the university.*	Habrá un **mitin** mañana en la universidad.

Extended US usage		
2. *business meeting:*	*The department meeting starts at three o'clock.*	El **mitin** del departamento comienza a las tres.
	Standard variant →	La **reunión** del departamento…
3. *arranged meeting:*	*We have a meeting with the attorney.*	Tenemos un **mitin** con el abogado.
	Standard variants →	Tenemos una **cita** / un **compromiso** con el abogado.
4. *accidental meeting:*	*It was a fortuitous meeting.*	Fue un **mitin** fortuito.
	Standard variant →	Fue un **encuentro** fortuito.
5. *meeting (in a series):*	*the third congressional meeting*	el tercer **mitin** del congreso
	Standard variant →	la tercera **sesión** del congreso

MÓDEM (masc noun) = **loanword for "modem"** [DRAE 1984]

• One of hundreds of computer terms borrowed from English, with no Spanish equivalent.

Standard/US usage		
1. *modem:*	*You will need a modem to gain access to the internet.*	Te hará falta un **módem** para tener acceso al internet.

MOFIN (fem noun) see **MUFFIN**

MOFLE (masc noun) see **MUFFLER**

MOL (masc noun) see **MALL**

MOLESTAR (verb)
= **to bother, annoy; disturb, interrupt**
= **to upset; hurt, give trouble**
= **to be in the way; mind, object**
= **to molest [US]**

- *Molestar* has no sexual connotation in standard usage, as does its English cognate.
- In U.S. Spanish, it is frequently used with and without **sexualmente** to mean "to molest."

Standard usage

1. *to bother, annoy:*	*Please don't bother me.*	Favor de no molestarme.
2. *to disturb, interrupt:*	*I'm very sorry to disturb you.*	Siento mucho molestarte.
3. *to upset:*	*That news item upset me.*	Esa noticia me molestó.
4. *to hurt, give trouble:*	*My back is giving me trouble.*	Me molesta la espalda.
5. *to be in the way:*	*Am I in your way?*	¿Estoy molestando?
6. *to mind, object:*	*Do you mind if I turn off the TV?*	¿Te molesta si apago la tele?

Extended US usage

7. *to molest (sexually):*	*He was accused of molesting a young girl.*	Lo acusaron de **molestar** (sexualmente) a una niña.
	Standard variant →	Lo acusaron de **abusar** (sexualmente) de una niña.

MONEDA (fem noun)
= **coin; small change; currency**
= **money [US]**

- *Moneda* is used colloquially in the United States to refer to "coins" as well as "money."

Standard usage

1. *coin:*	*a ten-cent coin*	una moneda de diez centavos
2. *small change:*	*Do you have change of a dollar?*	¿Tienes moneda de un dólar?
3. *currency:*	*What is the currency of Peru?*	¿Cuál es la moneda del Perú?

Extended US usage

4. *money:*	*Do you need money?*	¿Te hace falta **moneda**?
	Standard variant →	¿Te hace falta **dinero**?

MONEY ORDER (masc noun) = **loanword for "money order" [US]**

- Not sanctioned in standard Spanish, **money order** (pronounced as in English) is more prevalent in the United States than the traditional **giro bancario**.

US usage

1. *money order:*	*You can pay with check or money order.*	Se puede pagar con cheque o **money order**.
	Standard variant →	... cheque o **giro bancario**.
2. *postal money order:*	*A postal money order can be easily cashed.*	Un **money order** postal se cobra fácilmente.
	Standard variant →	Un **giro** postal se cobra ...

MOPA (fem noun) = **adapted from "mop"** [DRAE 2001]

MOPEAR (verb) = **adapted from "to mop"** [US]

mopa. (Del inglés *mop*). 1. f. Utensilio de limpieza compuesto por un palo largo y un conjunto de hilos o tiras en uno de sus extremos, que sirve para sacar brillo a los suelos. [DRAE]

- Moliner and the RAE sanction the noun **mopa** but not the verb form **mopear**.
- Both are quite common in the United States.

Standard usage

1. *mop:*	*Clean it with the mop.*	Límpialo con la mopa.
	Traditional variants →	Límpialo con la fregona / el trapeador (Lat Am).

Extended US usage

2. *to mop:*	*I just mopped the floor.*	Acabo de **mopear** el suelo.
	Standard variants →	Acabo de **fregar** / **trapear** (Lat Am) el suelo.

MOUSE (masc noun) = **loanword for "computer mouse"** [US]

- Popular alternative in U.S. Spanish to the standard translation from English: **ratón**.
- Stavans offers alternate spellings, including **maus**.

US usage

1. *computer mouse:*	*The mouse is used to control the cursor.*	El **maus** / **mouse** sirve para controlar el cursor.
	Standard variant →	El **ratón** sirve para controlar el cursor.

MOVER(SE) (verb) = **to move (object, body part)**
                     = **to move (oneself); budge, change position**
                     = **to stir, shake**
                     = **to incite, motivate**
                     = **to mix with, socialize**
                     = **to move: transport; relocate [US]**
                     = **to move: convince, sway; propose [US]**
                     = **to move emotionally, move to tears [US]**
                     = **to move: sell (merchandise) [US]**
                     = **to move: travel, flow [US]**
                     = **to move to: take steps to [US]**

- This common verb has many non-standard applications in the U.S., all stemming from literal translations of the English cognate "to move."

Standard usage

1. *to move (an object):*	*The desk will need to be moved.*	Habrá que mover el escritorio.
2. *to move (body part):*	*I can't move this finger.*	No puedo mover este dedo.
3. *to move oneself*	*It was impossible to move.*	Era imposible moverse.
4. *to move (=budge):*	*Please don't move.*	Por favor no te muevas.
5. *to stir, shake:*	*You don't need to stir the rice.*	No hace falta mover el arroz.
6. *to incite, motivate:*	*The good weather motivated me to fix the garden.*	El buen tiempo me movió a arreglar el jardín.
7. *to mix with, socialize:*	*He mixes with business people.*	Se mueve entre gente de negocios.

Extended US usage

8. *to move (=transport):*	*He moved his entire family.*	**Movió** a toda su familia.
	Standard variant →	**Trasladó** a toda su familia.
9. *to move (=relocate):*	*We are moving to Miami.*	Nos **movemos** a Miami.
	Standard variant →	Nos **mudamos** a Miami.
10. *to move (=convince):*	*He won't be moved (swayed).*	No lo podremos **mover**.
	Standard variant →	No **se dejará convencer**.
11. *to move (=propose):*	*I move that we start the discussion.*	**Muevo** que empecemos la discusión.
	Standard variant →	**Propongo** que empecemos …
12. *to move (emotionally):*	*She was moved by the public show of support.*	El apoyo del público la **movió**.
	Standard variants →	… la **conmovió** / la **emocionó**.
13. *to move to tears:*	*His story moved me to tears.*	Su historia me **movió a** llorar.
	Standard variant →	Su historia me **hizo** llorar.

14. *to move (merchandise):*	*These overcoats have to move.*	Hay que **mover** estos abrigos.
	Standard variant →	Hay que **vender** estos abrigos.
15. *to move (=travel, flow):*	*The car was moving at 80 mph.* *Traffic is starting to move.*	El carro **se movía** a 80 mph. El tráfico ya está **moviendo**.
	Standard variants →	El carro **iba** a 80 mph. El tráfico ya está **circulando**.
16. *to move (=take steps):*	*The mayor moved to resolve the* *issue.*	El alcalde **se movió** para resolver el problema.
	Standard variant →	El alcalde **tomó medidas** ...

"Move" expressions in standard Spanish	*to move ahead* *to move around* *to move away* *to move back* *to move backward* *to move closer* *to move down* *to move forward* *to move in* *to move off* *to move out* *to move over* *to move toward* *to move up*	adelantar(se), avanzar andar, circular apartar(se), alejar(se) atrasar, regresar retroceder, regresar acercar(se), arrimar(se) bajar(se), correr(se) aplazar, avanzar, adelantar meter, instalar(se) en quitar(se), bajar(se) sacar, mudar(se), trasladar(se) arrimar(se), correr(se) acercar(se) a subir, ascender

MOVIMIENTO (masc noun)

- = **physical movement; motion**
- = **movement of money, transactions**
- = **political / artistic movement**
- = **movement (in musical piece)**
- = **move (in a game) [US]**
- = **move: step, action, decision [US]**
- = **moving, move (from house or job) [US]**

Standard usage

1. *movement (physical):*	*the movement of planets*	el movimiento de los planetas
2. *motion, moving:*	*to set things in motion*	poner las cosas en movimiento
3. *movement of money,* *activity, transactions:*	*There is a lot of movement in the* *stock market.*	Hay mucho movimiento en la bolsa de valores.
4. *movement (=political* *or artistic tendency):*	*romantic movement / civil rights* *movement*	movimiento romántico / movi- miento de derechos civiles
5. *movement (in music):*	*three-movement symphony*	sinfonía de tres movimientos

Extended US usage

6. move (in a game):	*You made a good move.*	Hiciste un buen **movimiento**.
	Standard variant →	Hiciste una buena **jugada**.
7. move (=turn):	*Now it's your move.*	Ahora **mueves tú**.
	Standard variants →	Ahora **te toca a ti** / **es tu turno**.
8. move (=step, action):	*to make the first move*	**hacer** el primer **movimiento**
	Standard variant →	**dar** el primer **paso**
9. move (=decision):	*Telling him the truth was a bad move.*	El decirle la verdad fue un mal **movimiento**.
	Standard variant →	... fue una mala **decisión**.
10. move, moving (house):	*Today is moving day.*	Hoy es día de **movimiento**.
	Standard variant →	Hoy es día de **mudanza**.
11. move (=job change):	*The move to Chicago did not work out.*	El **movimiento** a Chicago no resultó bien.
	Standard variant →	El **traslado** a Chicago ...

MUFFIN (fem noun) = loanword for "muffin" [US]

- With no exact equivalent in the Hispanic world, the American / English style "muffin" has no corresponding term in standard Spanish, **magdalena** being the closest variant.
- Hence, the widespread use of **muffin** (also spelled **mofin**) in U.S. Spanish.

US usage

1. muffin:	*I had a corn muffin with my coffee.*	Me comí una **mofin** de maíz con el café.
	Standard variant →	Me comí una **magdalena** ...

MUFFLER (masc noun) = loanword for "automobile muffler" [US]

- Listed by Stavans as **mofle**, this term is not mentioned in any major dictionary.

US usage

1. muffler:	*My car needs a new muffler.*	Mi carro necesita un nuevo **mofle** / **muffler**.
	Standard variant →	Mi carro necesita un nuevo **silenciador**.

MULTIMEDIA (adj) = **loanword for "multimedia"** [DRAE 2001]

multimedia. (Del inglés *multimedia*).
1. adj. Que utiliza conjunta y simultáneamente diversos medios, como imágenes, sonidos y texto, en la transmisión de una información. [DRAE]

Standard/US usage		
1. multimedia:	*a multimedia presentation*	una presentación multimedia

NAILON (masc noun) = **loanword for "nylon"** [DRAE 1970]

• The RAE accepts two variants, **nailon** and **nilón**, both common in U.S. Spanish.

Standard/US usage		
1. nylon:	*I'm wearing a nylon shirt.*	Llevo camisa de **nailon** / de **nilón**.

NAITCLUB (masc noun)   see **NIGHTCLUB**

NATIVO (adj & noun) = **native: language, speaker, country**
  = **native of, native born [US]**
  = **indigenous (people, plants, animals) [US]**

• In the majority of cases, **nativo** is a suitable equivalent of "native" in standard usage.
• Influenced by English, U.S. Spanish favors it over traditional terms such as **indígena**.

Standard usage		
1. native (language):	*What is your native language?*	¿Cuál es tu lengua nativa?
	Traditional variants →	¿Cuál es tu lengua materna?
		¿Cuál es tu primer idioma?
2. native (speaker):	*a native speaker of Spanish*	un hablante nativo de español
3. native (country, soil):	*Portugal is my native country.*	Portugal es mi país nativo.
	Traditional variants →	Portugal es mi país natal.
		Portugal es mi patria.

Extended US usage

4. native of (=born in):	*I am a native of Madrid.*	Soy **nativo** de Madrid.
	Standard variants →	Soy **natural** de Madrid.
		Nací en Madrid.
5. native born:	*native-born Dominican*	dominicano **nativo**
	Standard variant →	dominicano **de nacimiento**
6. natives (=indigenous peoples):	*the natives of Yucatan*	los **nativos** del Yucatán
	Standard variant →	los **indígenas** del Yucatán
7. native (plant / animal):	*The plant is native to Brazil.*	La planta es **nativa** del Brasil.
	Standard variants →	La planta es **autóctona** / **originaria** del Brasil.

NIGHTCLUB (masc noun)   =   **loanword for "nightclub" [US]**

- **Nightclub** (pronounced as in English) occurs in the U.S. and, oftentimes, in standard Spanish as an alternative to the more conventional **club nocturno**.
- Whereas **club** is sanctioned by the RAE, **nightclub** is not. VOX and Moliner list both.

US usage

1. nightclub:	*We danced all night at the nightclub.*	Bailamos toda la noche en el **nightclub**.
	Standard variants →	Bailamos ... en la **discoteca** / en el **club nocturno**.

NILÓN (masc noun)   see **NAILON**

NOMBRE (masc noun)   =   **name (in general), first name**
                           =   **noun**
                           =   **name: reputation**
                           =   **last name; title [US]**

- The multiple applications of "name" in English have contributed to unconventional uses of **nombre** in U.S. Spanish, the most conspicuous of which is **último nombre**, a loan translation of "last name," in lieu of the more universally accepted **apellido**.

Standard usage

1. *name (general):*	*The name of the company is...*	El nombre de la empresa es...
2. *to give a name:*	*What are you going to name your son?*	¿Qué nombre le vas a poner a tu hijo?
3. *first name:*	*My first name is Adrian.*	Mi nombre (de pila) es Adrián.
4. *by name (idiom):*	*I only know her by name.*	Sólo la conozco de nombre.
5. *noun:*	*"People" is a collective noun.*	*Gente* es un nombre colectivo.
6. *name (=reputation):*	*a product with a good name*	un producto de buen nombre
7. *Selected expressions:*	*addressed to (a person)*	a nombre de
	be despicable, outrageous	no tener nombre
	by (in) name only	sólo de nombre
	full name	nombre y apellido
	in the name of	en nombre de
	nameless	sin nombre
	pen name	nombre de pluma

Extended US usage

8. *last name:*	*Her last name is López.*	Su **último nombre** es López.
	Standard variant →	Su **apellido** es López.
9. *my name is, etc:*	*What is your name?*	**¿Cuál es tu nombre?**
	My name is ...	**Mi nombre es ...**
	Standard variants →	**¿Cómo te llamas?**
		Me llamo ...
10. *name (=title):*	*What is the name of the book?*	¿Cuál es el **nombre** del libro?
	Standard variant →	¿Cuál es el **título** del libro?

"Name" expressions in standard Spanish	*a big name (=important figure)*	gran personaje / gran figura
	by the name of	llamado, -a
	maiden name	apellido de soltera
	married name	apellido de casada
	nickname	apodo
	to call someone a name	insultar a alguien

NOQUEAR (verb) = adapted from "to knock out" [DRAE 1984]

noquear. (Del inglés *to knock out*). 1. tr. Dep. En el boxeo, dejar al adversario fuera de combate. 2. tr. Dejar sin sentido a alguien con un golpe. 3. tr. Derrotar, imponerse sobre alguien rápida o notablemente. [DRAE]

• To the three uses of **noquear** listed by Moliner and standardized by the RAE, U.S. Spanish adds at least one: "to knock out with anesthesia."

Standard/US usage

1. to knock out (in boxing):	He was knocked out in the first round.	Quedó noqueado en el primer asalto.
	Traditional variant →	Quedó fuera de combate en el primer asalto.
2. to knock out (=render unconscious):	The force of the blow knocked me out completely.	La fuerza del golpe me noqueó por completo.
	Traditional variants →	... me dejó sin sentido / me hizo perder el conocimiento.
3. to defeat decisively:	Chicago defeated Boston 12–1.	Chicago noqueó a Boston 12 a 1.
	Traditional variant →	Chicago derrotó a Boston ...

Extended US usage

4. to knock out (=put to sleep, anesthetize):	They'll knock you out and you won't feel anything.	Te van a **noquear** y no vas a sentir nada.
	Standard variants →	Te van a **anestesiar** / **drogar** / **dormir** y no vas a sentir ...

NORSA (fem noun) = **loanword for "nurse" [US]**

- Cited by Moliner but not the DRAE, **norsa** occurs in the U.S. and parts of Latin America not only as a substitute for **enfermera** but also to mean a child's "escort" or "governess."

US usage

1. nurse:	The nurse gave me an injection.	La **norsa** me puso una inyección.
	Standard variant →	La **enfermera** me puso una inyección.
2. governess:	A governess takes care of the children.	Una **norsa** se ocupa de los niños.
	Standard variant →	Una **institutriz** se ocupa ...

NOTA (fem noun) = **mark, grade**
= **musical note: sound produced**
= **note: brief message**
= **note: text commentary, annotation**
= **note: expression, tone**
= **notes: written information [US]**
= **banknote: currency [US]**
= **musical note: key on instrument [US]**

- More often than not, "to take notes" is rendered as **tomar notas** in the United States, rather than the traditional **tomar apuntes**.

Standard usage

1. *mark, grade:*	*A and A- are excellent grades.*	A y A- son notas excelentes.
2. *musical note (=sound):*	*The dominant note is C.*	La nota dominante es C.
3. *note (=message):*	*You should write him a note.*	Deberías escribirle una nota.
4. *note (=commentary):*	*a text with notes in the margin*	un texto con notas al margen
5. *note (=expression, tone):*	*a note of optimism*	una nota de optimismo

Extended US usage

6. *notes (=written info):*	*I always take notes in class.*	Siempre tomo **notas** en clase.
	Standard variant →	Siempre tomo **apuntes** ...
7. *banknote (=currency):*	*a thousand-dollar note*	una **nota** de mil dólares
	Standard variant →	un **billete** de mil dólares
8. *musical note (=key):*	*I hit the wrong note.*	Me equivoqué de **nota**.
	Standard variant →	Me equivoqué de **tecla**.

NOTICIA (fem noun)
= **news item, news (pl.)**
= **news: knowledge, information about someone**
= **notice: warning [US]**
= **notice: announcement, sign, poster [US]**
= **notice: intent to quit work, to dismiss [US]**

- In English, "notice" has a variety of connotations depending on context.
- By extension, **noticia** can mean more than just "news" or "information" in U.S. Spanish.

Standard usage

1. *news item:*	*the best news of the day*	la mejor noticia del día
2. *news (pl):*	*Did you listen to the news?*	¿Escuchaste las noticias?
3. *news (about someone):*	*Any news from your son?*	¿Alguna noticia de tu hijo?
	I haven't heard from her.	No tengo noticias de ella.

Extended US usage

4. *notice (=warning):*	*I received a notice from the landlord.*	Recibí una **noticia** del dueño.
	Standard variant →	Recibí un **aviso** del dueño.
5. *notice (=announcement):*	*a notice about a clearance sale*	una **noticia** de liquidación
	Standard variant →	un **anuncio** de liquidación

6. notice (=sign, poster):	*The notice says "No Smoking."*	La **noticia** dice "Prohibido Fumar."
	Standard variants →	El **letrero** / El **cartel** dice ...
7. notice (of intent to quit):	*I gave my boss notice yesterday.*	Le **di noticia** a mi jefe ayer.
	Standard variant →	Le **dije que renunciaba** ...
8. notice (intent to dismiss):	*They gave notice to seven employees.*	**Dieron noticia** a siete empleados.
	Standard variant →	**Despidieron** a siete empleados.

"Notice" expressions in standard Spanish	*a day's notice*	un día de anticipación
	a week's notice	una semana de anticipación
	on short notice	con poco tiempo de aviso
	to give notice (=notify)	dar aviso, notificar
	to serve notice	dar noticia / hacer saber
	to take notice	hacer caso / prestar atención
	until further notice	hasta nuevo aviso
	without previous notice	sin aviso previo

NULIFICAR (verb) = **loanword for "to nullify" [US]**

- Non-existent in standard Spanish, this verb form occurs in the U.S. as an alternative to **anular** and **invalidar**.

US usage		
1. to nullify:	*We're going to have to nullify the contract.*	Vamos a tener que **nulificar** el contrato.
	Standard variants →	Vamos a tener que **anular** / **invalidar** el contrato.

OBNOXIO (adj) = **harmful, noxious**
= **obnoxious [US]**

> **obnoxio, xia.** (Del latín *obnoxius*, obligado, sujeto a algo). 1. adj. ant. Expuesto a contingencia o peligro. [DRAE]

- The only authorized definition of **obnoxio** suggests "noxious" or "dangerous," and has little to do with the prevailing use of "obnoxious" in modern English.
- With no precise equivalent in standard Spanish, there are many variants depending on the intended connotation: **desagradable**, **odioso**, **ofensivo**, **repugnante**, and so on.

US usage

1. *obnoxious (=annoying, unpleasant):*	*What an obnoxious guy!*	¡Qué tipo más **obnoxio**!
	Standard variant →	¡Qué tipo más **desagradable**!
2. *obnoxious (=offensive):*	*He made obnoxious comments about my country.*	Hizo comentarios **obnoxios** acerca de mi país.
	Standard variant →	Hizo comentarios **ofensivos** ...
3. *obnoxious (=repulsive):*	*There is an obnoxious smell in your room.*	Hay un olor **obnoxio** en tu cuarto.
	Standard variant →	Hay un olor **repugnante** ...

OCULTO (adj & noun) = **hidden, concealed; mysterious (adj)**
= **occult (noun) [US]**

- In standard practice, **oculto** is an adjective for "hidden" or "concealed."
- It also occurs in U.S. Spanish as a noun to refer to "the science of the occult."

Standard usage

1. *hidden, concealed:*	*He remained hidden for two hours.*	Permaneció oculto por dos horas.
2. *mysterious, inner:*	*She never did reveal her inner thoughts.*	Nunca llegó a revelar sus pensamientos ocultos.

Extended US usage

3. *occult (noun):*	*My professor wrote a book about the occult.*	Mi profesor escribió un libro sobre el **oculto**.
	Standard variant →	... sobre el **ocultismo**.

OFENSA (fem noun) = **offense: insult, affront**
= **offense: crime, transgression [US]**

- The applications of this term in U.S. Spanish reflect the double meaning of "offense" in English: "insult" and "transgression." Only "insult" is approved by the RAE.

Standard usage

1. *offense (=insult):*	*It's an offense to those who died for our country.*	Es una ofensa a los que murieron por nuestra patria.

Extended US usage

2. *offense (=crime):*	*He committed his first offense when he was fifteen.*	Cometió su primera **ofensa** a los quince años de edad.
	Standard variant →	Cometió su primer **delito** ...
3. *offense (in sports):*	*It was the second offense of the game.*	Fue la segunda **ofensa** del partido.
	Standard variant →	Fue la segunda **falta** del partido.

OÍR (verb) = **to hear: perceive sound**
= **to hear: heed, consider**
= **to hear mass**
= **to hear: discover, find out [US]**
= **to hear about someone or something [US]**
= **to hear from: receive news [US]**
= **to hear: understand [US]**

- In principle, **oír** has a more literal meaning in Spanish than it does in English.
- When the intended meaning is "to discover" or "to hear about," **oír** is accompanied by **decir** or **hablar** so as to indicate that the information is from a second-hand source.
- U.S. Spanish, which reflects English custom, tends to do without helping verbs.

Standard usage

1. *to hear (voice, sound):*	*I hear a very strange noise.*	Oigo un ruido muy extraño.
2. *to hear, heed, consider:*	*Who will hear our prayers?*	¿Quién oirá nuestras súplicas?
3. *to hear mass:*	*We're going to hear mass.*	Vamos a oír misa.

Extended US usage

4. *to hear (=discover, find out):*	*I heard you were sick.*	**Oí** que estabas enfermo.
	Standard variants →	**Oí decir / Me enteré de** que estabas enfermo.
5. *to hear of / about (someone or something):*	*They heard a lot about her.* *We heard about your trip.*	**Oyeron** mucho de ella. **Oímos** de tu viaje.
	Standard variants →	**Oyeron hablar** mucho de ella. **Nos enteramos** de tu viaje.
6. *to hear from (=receive news):*	*Do you hear from your brother?*	¿**Oyes** de tu hermano?
	Standard variants →	¿**Sabes algo / Tienes noticias** de tu hermano?
7. *to hear (=understand):*	*I hear what you're saying.*	**Oigo** lo que dices.
	Standard variant →	**Entiendo** lo que dices.

OKEY (adj & excl) = **OK** (excl): **fine, all right, yes [US]**
 = **OK** (excl): **well; stop, that's enough [US]**
 = **OK** (adj): **in good health, in good condition [US]**
 = **OK** (adj): **fine, all right, agreed, not an issue [US]**
 = **OK** (adj): **acceptable, not bad [US]**
 = **OK** (adj): **no problem, no harm done [US]**

- Although the DRAE does not mention this universal expression, it has been assimilated into standard Spanish, particularly as an exclamation meaning "all right, fine."
- Its use as an adjective is less conventional and more typical of U.S. Spanish.

US usage		
1. *OK (=fine, all right, yes):*	*"Shall we leave?" "OK."*	—¿Nos vamos?—**Okey**.
	Traditional variants →	—¿Nos vamos?—**Vale / Sí / Está bien**.
2. *OK, exclam. (=well):*	*OK, what do we do now?*	**Okey**, ¿qué hacemos ahora?
	Standard variants →	**Bueno**, ¿qué hacemos ahora? **Pues**, ¿qué hacemos ahora?
3. *OK, exclam. (=stop, that's enough):*	*OK, OK, I don't want any more.*	**Okey, okey**, no quiero más.
	Standard variants →	**Basta, basta / Ya, ya / Ya está bien**, no quiero más.
4. *OK, adj. (=in good health, good condition):*	*Are you feeling OK?*	¿Te sientes **okey**?
	Standard variant →	¿Te sientes **bien**?
5. *OK, adj. (=fine, all right, not an issue, agreed):*	*It's OK with me.*	**Está okey conmigo**.
	Standard variants →	**Está bien / No me molesta**.
6. *OK, adj. (=not bad, acceptable):*	*The food was OK (not bad).*	La comida estaba **okey**.
	Standard variants →	La comida estaba **regular / no** estaba **mal**.
7. *OK, adj. (=no problem, no harm done):*	*"I'm so sorry!" "That's OK."*	—¡Ay, lo siento!—**Es okey**.
	Standard variants →	—¡Ay, lo siento!—**Tranquilo / Ningún problema / No se preocupe**.

ONLINE (adj & adv) = **loanword for "online" [US]**

- **Online** (pronounced as in English) is common in U.S. Spanish along with its loan translation, **en línea**. Moliner favors **online**. Neither term is sanctioned by the RAE.

US usage		
1. *online (adj):*	*This semester we offer three online courses.*	Este semestre ofrecemos tres cursos **online**.
	Standard variant →	... tres cursos **a distancia**
2. *online (adv):*	*I do my shopping online.*	Hago mis compras **online**.
	Standard variant →	Hago mis compras **por la red**.
3. *online (=connected):*	*Are you going to be online the entire day?*	¿Vas a estar **online** el día entero?
	Standard variant →	¿Vas a estar **conectado** ...?

OPÓSITO (adj) = **loanword for "opposite" [US]**

- **Opósito** is strictly a noun in standard Spanish. It occurs as an adjective in the U.S. in lieu of the more conventional **opuesto** or **contrario**.

Extended US usage		
1. *opposite (=contrary):*	*in the opposite direction*	en sentido **opósito**
	Standard variant →	en sentido **contrario**
2. *opposite (=opposing):*	*He plays for the opposite team.*	Juega con el equipo **opósito**.
	Standard variant →	Juega con el equipo **opuesto**.
3. *opposite (=facing):*	*She sat down opposite me.*	Se sentó **opuesto** a mí.
	Standard variant →	Se sentó **enfrente de** mí.
4. *the opposite:*	*I said just the opposite.*	Dije exactamente lo **opósito**.
	Standard variant →	Dije exactamente lo **contrario**.

ORDENAR (verb)

- = **to put in order, arrange, tidy up**
- = **to order: command**
- = **to ordain**
- = **to order: request, ask for [US]**

• In standard usage, **ordenar** means primarily "to put in order."

Standard usage		
1. *to put in order (=arrange):*	*Did you put the checks in order?*	¿Ordenaste los cheques?
2. *to put in order, tidy up:*	*I have to tidy up my things.*	Tengo que ordenar mis cosas.
3. *to order (=command):*	*The captain ordered the soldiers to fire their guns.*	El capitán ordenó a los soldados que dispararan.
4. *to ordain:*	*He was ordained as a priest.*	Fue ordenado sacerdote.

Extended US usage		
5. *to order (=request)*	*Did you order the books?*	¿**Ordenaste** los libros?
	Standard variants →	¿**Encargaste / Pediste** los libros?
6. *to order (at a restaurant):*	*I ordered a seafood paella.*	**Ordené** una paella marinera.
	Standard variant →	**Pedí** una paella marinera.
7. *to order (to have made):*	*She ordered a wedding dress.*	**Ordenó** un traje de boda.
	Standard variant →	**Mandó hacer** un traje de boda.

ORDINARIO (adj)

- = **vulgar, low-class; coarse, crude**
- = **ordinary: usual, normal, average [US]**

Standard usage		
1. *vulgar, low-class:*	*She is a low-class individual.*	Es una persona ordinaria.
2. *coarse, crude:*	*very crude language*	lenguaje muy ordinario

Extended US usage		
3. *ordinary (=usual, normal, regular):*	*I'll have ordinary milk.*	Tomaré leche **ordinaria**.
	Standard variants →	Tomaré leche **corriente**. Tomaré leche **normal**.
4. *ordinary (=average, unremarkable):*	*an ordinary interview*	una entrevista **ordinaria**
	Standard variants →	una entrevista **cualquiera / normal / común y corriente**.

OUTPUT (masc noun) = **loanword for "output"** [DRAE 2001]

output. (Voz inglesa). 1. m. Econ. Producto resultante de un proceso de producción. 2. m. Inform. Información que sale procesada por un sistema informático o por una computadora. [DRAE]

Standard/US usage		
1. *output (=production):*	*The steel output increased by twenty percent.*	El **output** de acero aumentó un veinte por ciento.
	Traditional variant →	La **producción** de acero …
2. *output (=processed information):*	*The computer sends the output to the printer.*	La computadora manda el **output** a la impresora.
	Traditional variant →	La computadora manda la **información** a la impresora.

OVERBOOKING (masc noun) = **loanword for "overbooking"** [DRAE 1984]

• This has become a standardized term in many languages, including Spanish.

Standard/US usage		
1. *overbooking:*	*Because of overbooking, I had to cancel the trip.*	A causa del **overbooking** tuve que cancelar el viaje.
	Traditional variant →	A causa del **exceso de reservas** tuve que cancelar …

PANCAKE (masc noun)   see **PANQUEQUE**

PANIQUEAR(SE) (verb) = **adapted from "to panic"** [US]

• There is a perfectly sound cognate for the noun form in Spanish (**pánico**), but <u>no</u> verb.
• The need for **paniquear** in the U.S. reflects the widespread use of "to panic" in English.
• The intransitive form is expressed as a reflexive (**paniquearse**).

US usage		
1. *to panic (intrans):*	*Don't panic if the alarm sounds.*	No te **paniquees** si suena la alarma.
	Standard variants →	No te **dejes llevar por el pánico** / No te **asustes** …
2. *to panic (trans):*	*The smoke on the stage panicked the audience.*	El humo en el escenario **paniqueó** al público.
	Standard variant →	El humo … **provocó el pánico** entre el público.

PANQUEQUE (masc noun) = **loanword for "pancake" [US]**

- **Panqueque** has become part of the U.S. Spanish lexicon along with other popular food items, such as **dona** and **mofin**, unique to the culture of the United States.
- The closest equivalent for "pancake" in Spain and Latin America is **tortita** or **crepa**.
- Stavans prefers **pancake** and spells it as pronounced by Spanish speakers: **panquei**.

US usage		
1. pancake:	*I ate three pancakes for breakfast this morning.*	Desayuné tres **panqueques** / **panqueis** esta mañana.
	Standard variant →	Desayuné tres **tortitas** ...

PANTI(S) (masc noun) = **loanword for "panties" [DRAE 1984]**

- **Panty** (sing or plural) means "tights" or "pantyhose" in standard usage.
- In the United States, it is usually spelled **panti** and is more likely to refer to a woman's undergarment.

Standard usage		
1. pantyhose:	*There is a run in your pantyhose.*	Se te hizo una carrera en los pantys.

Extended US usage		
2. panty, panties:	*I only wear cotton panties.*	Sólo uso **pantis** de algodón.
	Standard variants →	Sólo uso **calzones** (Lat Am) / **bragas** (Spain) de algodón.

PAPEL (masc noun)
- = **paper: material; piece of paper**
- = **papers: documents**
- = **role, part**
- = **paper: newspaper [US]**
- = **essay, scholarly paper, term paper [US]**

Standard usage		
1. paper (=material):	*He sells paper products.*	Vende productos de papel.
2. piece of paper:	*Write it on a piece of paper.*	Escríbelo en un papel.
3. papers, documents:	*Are your papers in order?*	¿Tienes tus papeles en regla?
4. role, part:	*She played her role very well.*	Hizo muy bien su papel.

Extended US usage

5. *paper (=newspaper):*	*Did you read today's paper?*	¿Leíste el **papel** de hoy?
	Standard variants →	¿Leíste el **periódico** / **diario** de hoy?
6. *paper (=essay):*	*I wrote a paper about capital punishment.*	Escribí un **papel** sobre la pena capital.
	Standard variant →	Escribí un **ensayo** sobre ...
7. *paper, scholarly article:*	*She hopes her paper will be published.*	Espera que se publique su **papel**.
	Standard variant →	... que se publique su **artículo**.
8. *term paper:*	*I have three (term) papers to do.*	Tengo tres **papeles** que hacer.
	Standard variants →	Tengo tres **monografías** / **trabajos escritos** ...

PAPERBACK (masc noun) = **loanword for "paperback" [US]**

• Not sanctioned by the RAE nor listed in Moliner, **paperback** (pronounced as in English) has no exact equivalent in standard Spanish.

US usage

1. *paperback:*	*The paperback edition is less expensive than the hardcover.*	La edición **paperback** es más barata que la encuadernada.
	Standard variant →	La edición **rústica** es más barata que la encuadernada.

PARIENTE (masc noun) = **relative, relation**
= **parent [US]**

Standard usage

1. *relative, family relation:*	*He has more than 100 relatives.*	Tiene más de cien parientes.

Extended US usage

2. *parent (mother or father):*	*One of the parents needs to sign.*	Uno de los **parientes** tiene que firmar.
	Standard variant →	**El padre o la madre** tiene que firmar.
3. *parent (=central):*	*parent company*	compañía **pariente**
	Standard variants →	casa **matriz** / casa **central**

PÁRKING (masc noun) = **loanword for "parking" [US]**

PARQUEO (masc noun) = **action of parking** [DRAE 1985]
= **parking lot [US]**
= **parking space [US]**

- The RAE sanctions **parqueo** as an americanism but makes no mention of **párking**.
- Moliner does just the opposite. These terms are used interchangeably in U.S. Spanish.

US usage		
1. parking:	*Parking is restricted to residents.*	El **párking** / El **parqueo** se limita a los residentes.
	Traditional variants →	El **estacionamiento** / El **aparcamiento** (Sp) se limita a ...
2. parking lot:	*The parking lot is full.*	El **párking** / El **parqueo** está lleno.
	Traditional variants →	El **aparcamiento** / La **playa de estacionamiento** está ...
3. parking space:	*I found a parking space on this street.*	Encontré un **párking** / un **parqueo** en esta calle.
	Traditional variants →	Encontré un **aparcamiento** / un **estacionamiento** en ...
"Parking" expressions in standard Spanish:	*parking attendant*	guardacoches, guardacarros
	parking lights	luces de estacionamiento
	parking meter	parquímetro
	parking permit	permiso de estacionamiento
	parking ticket	multa por estacionamiento indebido

PARQUEAR (verb) = **to park a vehicle** [DRAE 1970]
= **to park: to put [US]**

- Aside from the RAE approved usage, U.S. Spanish gives **parquear** a secondary meaning, common in colloquial English: "to put" an object or person in a particular place.

Standard/US usage		
1. to park (vehicle):	*Where did you park your car?*	¿Dónde **parqueaste** el carro?
	Traditional variants →	¿Dónde **estacionaste** / **aparcaste** (Sp) el carro?

Extended US usage

2. *to park (=put, place):*

He parked himself on the chair. Se **parqueó** en la silla.

Standard variants → Se **colocó** / **instaló** en la silla.

PARQUEO (masc noun) see **PÁRKING**

PARTE (fem noun) = **part: portion, section**
= **part: area, region, place**
= **part: share of responsibility**
= **fraction, segment**
= **side, perspective**
= **party (in contract)**
= **part: aspect [US]**
= **mechanical part [US]**
= **part: role, character [US]**
= **part (in hair) [US]**

Standard usage

1. *part (=portion, section):* the first part of the movie la primera parte de la película
2. *part (=area, region):* What part of Spain is he from? ¿De qué parte de España es?
3. *place, (any)where, etc:* I don't see her anywhere. No la veo en ninguna parte.
4. *part (=share):* You have to do your part. Tienes que poner de tu parte.
5. *[fraction, segment]:* He ate a quarter of it. Se comió la cuarta parte.
6. *side (=family line):* on my father's side por parte de mi padre
7. *side (=perspective):* It looks the same from all sides. Se ve igual de cualquier parte.
8. *party (in contract):* Both parties must sign. Ambas partes deben firmar.
9. *Selected expressions:* back and forth de una parte a otra
be a part of, be a member of formar parte de
for the most part en su mayor parte
from, on behalf of de parte de
in part, partly en parte
most, the majority of la mayor parte de
on the other hand por otra parte
on the part of por parte de
the back la parte de atrás
the bottom la parte de abajo
the front la parte delantera
the top la parte de arriba
to a large extent en gran parte
to take part tomar parte

Extended US usage

10. *part (=aspect):* | *The best part is that we don't have to pay.* | **La mejor parte** es que no tenemos que pagar.
| **Standard variant →** | **Lo mejor** es que ...

11. *mechanical part:* | *The engine is missing a part.* | Le falta una **parte** al motor.
| **Standard variant →** | Le falta una **pieza** al motor.

12. *part (=role):* | *He played the part of the king.* | **Jugó la parte** del rey.
| **Standard variant →** | **Hizo el papel** del rey.

13. *part (in hair):* | *I part my hair on the right.* | Llevo la **parte** a la derecha.
| **Standard variant →** | Llevo la **raya** a la derecha.

PARTIR (verb) = **to cut, split, break**
= **to leave, depart, set out**
= **to part: separate, open [US]**
= **to part with [US]**

Standard usage

1. *to cut, split:* | *I cut the watermelon in half.* | Partí la sandía por la mitad.
2. *to break:* | *He broke a tooth.* | Se le partió un diente.
3. *to leave, depart, set out:* | *My sister left yesterday for California.* | Mi hermana partió ayer para California.

Extended US usage

4. *to part (=separate):* | *After twenty years of marriage, they decided to part.* | Después de veinte años de casados, decidieron **partir**.
| **Standard variant →** | ... decidieron **separarse**.

5. *to part (=open):* | *The curtains parted and the show began.* | Se **partieron** las cortinas y el espectáculo comenzó.
| **Standard variant →** | Se **abrieron** las cortinas ...

6. *to part with (=let go of):* | *The little girl doesn't want to part with the toy.* | La niñita no quiere **partir con** el juguete.
| **Standard variants →** | ... no quiere **soltar** el juguete.
 ... **desprenderse del** juguete.

PART-TIME (adj & adv)   =   **loanword for "part-time" [US]**

- Whereas **full-time** is listed in most dictionaries (incl. DRAE), **part-time** is not.
- Both are used frequently in U.S. Spanish, as adjectives and adverbs.

US usage

1. *part-time (adj):*	*I found a part-time job.*	Encontré un trabajo **part-time**.
	Standard variants →	... trabajo **a tiempo parcial** / **de jornada reducida** (Sp) / **de medio tiempo** (Lat Am).
2. *part-time (adv):*	*How long have you been working part-time?*	¿Cuánto hace que trabajas **part-time**?
	Standard variants →	¿Cuánto hace que trabajas **a tiempo parcial** / **medio tiempo**?

PARTY (masc / fem noun)   =   **loanword for "party" (celebration) [US]**

- **Party** is popular in U.S. Spanish as a more specific variant of **fiesta**, which can have multiple connotations (celebration, holiday, feast, vacation, festival).
- Occurring as a masculine or feminine noun, Moliner defines **party** as "fiesta privada."

US usage

1. *party (=celebration):*	*We went to a party and had a lot of fun.*	Fuimos a un(a) **party** y nos divertimos mucho.
	Standard variant →	Fuimos a una **fiesta** y nos divertimos mucho.

PASAR (verb)   =   **to pass: go past**
=   **to pass: go by, elapse**
=   **to pass: go away, disappear**
=   **to pass: give, transfer**
=   **to spend time**
=   **to pass an exam, a course [US]**
=   **to pass a law, a bill [US]**

- **Pasar un examen**, a common U.S. Spanish idiom, is the result of a loan translation.

Standard usage

1. *to pass (=go past):*	*They did not let us pass.*	No nos dejaron pasar.
2. *to pass (=go by, elapse):*	*How time passes!*	¡Cómo pasa el tiempo!
3. *to pass (=disappear):*	*All your problems will pass.*	Todos tus problemas pasarán.
4. *to pass (=give, transfer):*	*Could you pass me the salt?*	¿Me pasas la sal, por favor?
5. *to spend time:*	*I spent a month in Seville.*	Pasé un mes en Sevilla.

Extended US usage

6. *to pass (an exam, a course, etc.):*	*If you don't pass the exam, you won't pass the course.*	Si no **pasas** el examen, no **pasarás** el curso.
	Standard variant →	Si no **apruebas** el examen, no **aprobarás** el curso.
7. *to pass (a bill, a law):*	*The state passed a new law.*	El estado **pasó** una nueva ley.
	Standard variant →	… **aprobó** una nueva ley.

PATRÓN (masc noun)

- = **boss, employer, owner, landlord**
- = **protector, patron saint**
- = **pattern, standard, norm**
- = **patron: supporter, sponsor [US]**
- = **patron: customer [US]**

Standard usage

1. *boss, employer, owner:*	*My boss gave me the day off.*	Mi patrón me dio el día libre.
2. *landlord:*	*The landlord increased the rent.*	El patrón aumentó el alquiler.
3. *patron saint (=protector):*	*Santiago is the patron saint of Spain.*	Santiago es el santo patrón de España.
4. *pattern, standard:*	*I bought the pattern to make a dress.*	Compré el patrón para hacer un vestido.

Extended US usage

5. *patron (=benefactor, sponsor, supporter):*	*patron of the arts*	**patrón** de las artes
	Standard variant →	**patrocinador** de las artes
6. *patron (=customer):*	*This store has many new patrons.*	Esta tienda tiene muchos **patrones** nuevos.
	Standard variant →	… muchos **clientes** nuevos.

PENALTI (masc noun)   =   **loanword for "penalty"** [DRAE 1985]

- Fully sanctioned as a soccer term, **penalti** (spelled **penalty** in the DRAE until 1992) can also occur in U.S. Spanish in connection with a "monetary fine" or "surcharge."

Standard usage

1. *penalty:*	*Our team lost because of the penalties.*	Nuestro equipo perdió a causa de los penaltis.

Extended US usage

2. *penalty (=additional charge):*	*There will be a penalty if you don't pay on time.*	Habrá un **penalti** si no pagas a tiempo.
	Standard variant →	Habrá un **recargo** si no pagas a tiempo.
3. *penalty (=fine):*	*The penalty for speeding is 200 dollars.*	El **penalti** por exceso de velocidad es 200 dólares.
	Standard variant →	La **multa** por exceso de …

PERDER (verb)

= **to lose: fail to find**
= **to lose: fail to keep**
= **to lose: fail to win**
= **to lose: waste**
= **to lose: confuse [US]**
= **to lose weight [US]**

Standard usage

1. *to lose (=fail to find):*	*I have lost my keys.*	He perdido las llaves.
2. *to lose (=fail to keep):*	*He often loses control.*	Pierde el control a menudo.
3. *to lose (=fail to win):*	*How many games did they lose?*	¿Cuántos partidos perdieron?
4. *to lose (=waste):*	*I lost an hour waiting on line.*	Perdí una hora haciendo cola.

Extended US usage

5. *to lose (=confuse):*	*When he explained the rules, he lost me completely.*	Cuando explicó las reglas, me **perdió** por completo.
	Standard variant →	Cuando explicó las reglas, me **confundió** por completo.
6. *to lose weight:*	*I have to lose weight.*	Tengo que **perder peso**.
	Standard variants →	Tengo que **bajar de peso** / **adelgazar**.

PERFORMANCE (fem noun) = **loanword for "performance" [US]**

- Unlisted in the DRAE, this term is defined by Moliner as a type of avant-garde theatre.

    performance. (Inglés). amb. Espectáculo teatral de carácter vanguardista en que se mezclan elementos de artes y campos diversos. [Moliner]

- In Latin America, **performance** is primarily applied to machines and vehicles, by influence of standard English commercial phrases.
- U.S. Spanish applies it more broadly, reflecting the many uses of its English cognate.

Latin American usage

1. *performance (of vehicle):*	*a high-performance car*	un carro de alta **performance**
	Traditional variant →	un carro de alto **rendimiento**

Extended US usage

2. *performance (=show, session):*	*The next performance begins at eight o'clock.*	La próxima **performance** comienza a las ocho.
	Standard variant →	La próxima **función** comienza a las ocho.
3. *performance (=presentation):*	*We saw two performances of the same play.*	Vimos dos **performances** de la misma obra.
	Standard variant →	Vimos dos **representaciones** de la misma obra.
4. *performance (=acting, singing, playing, etc.):*	*Her performance in the movie was superb.*	Su **performance** en la película fue estupenda.
	Standard variants →	Su **actuación** / **interpretación** en la película fue estupenda.
5. *performance (=outcome, result):*	*I am not happy with my performance on the test.*	No estoy contenta con mi **performance** en el examen.
	Standard variant →	No estoy contenta con mis **resultados** en el examen.

"Performance" phrases in standard Spanish	*the performance of a task*	la **realización** de una tarea
	the performance of a duty	el **ejercicio** de un cargo
	the performance of investments	el **rendimiento** de inversiones

PERFORMAR (verb) = **loanword for "to perform" [US]**

• Non-existent in standard usage, **performar** is indigenous to U.S. Spanish.

US usage

1. *to perform (=put on a play):*	*What play are they performing?*	¿Qué obra van a **performar**?
	Standard variant →	¿Qué obra van a **representar**?
2. *to perform (=act in a play or movie):*	*My daughter just performed in her first play.*	Mi hija acaba de **performar** en su primera obra.
	Standard variant →	Mi hija acaba de **actuar** en su primera obra.

3. to perform (=sing, dance, play, etc.):	*They're going to perform the music of the Beatles.*	Van a **performar** la música de los Beatles.
	Standard variant →	Van a **interpretar** ...
4. to perform (=carry out):	*The experiment was performed in a lab.*	El experimento se **performó** en un laboratorio.
	Standard variants →	El experimento **se realizó** / **se llevó a cabo** ...
"Perform" expressions in standard Spanish	*The appliance performs well.*	El aparato **funciona bien**.
	The car is performing poorly.	El carro **responde** mal.
	The company performed well.	La empresa **dio resultados**.
	The investments did not perform.	Las inversiones no **rindieron**.
	to perform a ceremony	**celebrar** una ceremonia
	to perform a dance	**interpretar** una danza
	to perform a duty	**ejercer** un cargo
	to perform one's duty	**cumplir con** un deber
	to perform a function	**desempeñar** una función
	to perform on an instrument	**tocar** un instrumento
	to perform a miracle	**hacer** / **realizar** un milagro
	to perform an operation	**hacer** una operación / **operar**
	to perform a service	**prestar** servicio
	to perform a song	**cantar** / **interpretar** una canción
	to perform a task	**realizar** / **llevar a cabo** una tarea
	to perform a trick	**hacer** / **realizar** un truco
	to perform poorly in school	**rendir** malos **resultados**
	to perform poorly on an exam	**salir mal** en un examen
	to perform well in school	**rendir** buenos **resultados**
	to perform well on an exam	**salir bien** en un examen

PERMISIÓN (fem noun) = **loanword for "permission" [US]**

- **Permisión** occurs in U.S. Spanish by influence of "permission" in English.
- Although listed in the DRAE, the more conventional term in Spanish is **permiso**.

US usage		
1. permission:	*They gave me permission to leave early.*	Me dieron **permisión** a salir temprano.
	Standard variant →	Me dieron **permiso** a salir temprano.

PERRO CALIENTE (masc noun) = **hot dog** [DRAE 1992]

- **Perrito caliente** is one of the few loan translations to gain acceptance by the RAE.

> **perrito caliente**. m. Salchicha que se sirve dentro de un pan blando y alargado, generalmente con mostaza o ketchup. [Moliner]

- U.S. Spanish favors **perro caliente** but also employs **hot dog** and **frankfurter**.

Standard/US usage		
1. hot dog:	*I ate two hot dogs with mustard.*	Me comí dos **perros / perritos calientes** con mostaza.
	Traditional variants →	Me comí dos **salchichas / panchos** (parts of Lat Am) …

PESO (masc noun)
= **weight (physical)**
= **weight: worry, responsibility**
= **weight: importance**
= **scale**
= **peso (currency)**
= **U.S. dollar [US]**

- Spanish speakers in the U.S. often translate "dollar" as **peso**, the unit of currency in many Latin American countries (Argentina, Colombia, Cuba, Mexico, etc.).

Standard usage		
1. weight (physical):	*The weight of the books brought down the shelf.*	El peso de los libros hizo caer el estante.
2. weight (fig.):	*That certainly took a weight off my mind.*	Eso sí que me quitó un peso de encima.
3. weight (=importance):	*The weight of the issue calls for immediate action.*	El peso del asunto requiere acción inmediata.
4. scale:	*The bathroom scale doesn't work.*	El peso del baño no funciona.
5. peso (=currency):	*the Mexican peso*	el peso mexicano

Extended US usage		
6. U.S. dollar:	*Can you lend me ten dollars?*	¿Me prestas diez **pesos**?
	Standard variant →	¿Me prestas diez **dólares**?

PICNIC (masc noun) = **loanword for "picnic" [US]**

- Interestingly, the term **picnic** appeared sporadically in the DRAE between 1927 and 1989 and has not been listed since—despite its confirmed use in standard Spanish.
- U.S Spanish adds a figurative connotation to its conventional meaning.

US usage

1. *picnic (event):*	*Yesterday we went on a picnic.*	Ayer nos fuimos **de picnic**.
	Standard variant →	Ayer nos fuimos **a comer en el campo**.
2. *picnic (meal):*	*She is preparing sandwiches for the picnic.*	Está preparando bocadillos para el **picnic**.
	Standard variant →	... para la **comida campestre**.
3. *picnic (fig.):*	*That meeting was no picnic.*	Aquella reunión no fue ningún **picnic**.
	Standard variant →	Aquella reunión no fue **muy agradable**.
4. *Selected expressions:*	*picnic basket* *picnic ground / site*	canasta de **picnic** lugar de **picnics**
	Standard variants →	canasta de **merienda** lugar **campestre / para comer al aire libre**

PIN (masc noun) = **loanword for "pin"** [DRAE 2001]

- The RAE and Moliner authorize the use of **pin** to mean "insignia."
- In U.S. Spanish, however, **pin** also occurs as the abbreviation for "personal identification number" and to refer to "safety pin."

Standard usage

1. *pin (=insignia):*	*I received a certificate and a pin from the honor society.*	Recibí un certificado y un pin de la sociedad de honor.
	Traditional variant →	Recibí un certificado y una insignia ...

Extended US usage

2. *PIN (=personal identification number):*	*The PIN will give you access to your account.*	El **PIN** te dará acceso a tu cuenta.
	Standard variant →	El **NPI** (número personal de identificación) te dará ...
3. *safety pin:*	*I'll fasten it with a safety pin.*	Lo voy a abrochar con un **pin de seguridad**.
	Standard variants →	Lo voy a abrochar con un **imperdible** / un **seguro**.

PLAN (masc noun) = **plan: scheme; idea, intention**
= **plan: diagram, map [US]**
= **outline; schedule [US]**

Standard usage

1. *plan (=scheme):*	*He drew up a development plan.*	Elaboró un plan de desarrollo.
2. *plan (=idea, intention):*	*What plans do you have for the summer vacation?*	¿Qué planes tienes para las vacaciones de verano?
	Traditional variants →	¿Qué proyectos tienes ...? ¿Qué tienes pensado ...?

Extended US usage

3. *plan (=diagram, map):*	*I would be interested in seeing a floor plan of the house.*	Me interesaría ver un **plan** de la casa.
	Standard variant →	Me interesaría ver un **plano** ...
4. *plan (=schedule):*	*What is the plan for today?*	¿Cuál es el **plan** de hoy?
	Standard variant →	¿Cuál es el **programa** de hoy?

PLANEAR (verb) = **to plan: organize, prepare, think ahead** [DRAE 1925]
= **to plan: intend [US]**

• **Planear** is a true cognate of "to plan" in standard Spanish—except when accompanied by another verb.

Standard usage

1. *to plan (=organize):*	*We're going to plan a party.*	Vamos a planear una fiesta.
	Traditional variant →	Vamos a organizar una fiesta.
2. *to plan (=think ahead):*	*You need to plan for the future.*	Hay que planear para el futuro.
	Traditional variants →	Hay que pensar en / preparar para el futuro.

Extended US usage

3. *to plan (=intend):*	*What do you plan to do this weekend?*	¿Qué **pleaneas** hacer este fin de semana?
	Standard variant →	¿Qué **piensas** hacer este fin de semana?

PLANTAR (verb)

= **to plant (a tree, flowers, crops)**
= **to plant: put, stick**
= **to stand someone up, dump, ditch**
= **to plant (seeds, a field) [US]**
= **to plant (a bomb, evidence) [US]**

- In most circumstances, **plantar** is a true cognate of the verb "to plant."
- Two common exceptions in standard Spanish are: **sembrar** for "planting seeds" and **colocar** for "planting a bomb" or "planting evidence."
- U.S. Spanish tends to use **plantar** in these situations as well.

Standard usage

1. *to plant (tree, flower):*	*They planted a tree in the garden.*	Plantaron un árbol en el jardín.
2. *to plant (=put, stick):*	*He planted a kiss on her cheek.*	Le plantó un beso en la mejilla.
3. *to stand someone up, give up, dump, ditch:*	*She dumped her boyfriend in front of everyone.*	Plantó a su novio delante de todos.

Extended US usage

4. *to plant (seeds, a field):*	*On this field they used to plant wheat.*	En este terreno se **plantaba** trigo.
	Standard variant →	En este terreno se **sembraba** trigo.
5. *to plant (bomb, evidence):*	*The terrorists planted a bomb under the car.*	Los terroristas **plantaron** una bomba debajo del carro.
	Standard variants →	Los terroristas **colocaron** / **pusieron** una bomba ...

PLAYBOY (masc noun) = **loanword for "playboy" [US]**

- Not sanctioned by the RAE, **playboy** occurs frequently in U.S. Spanish and is listed in many dictionaries (incl. Moliner).
- There are several traditional equivalents in standard Spanish.

US usage

1. *playboy:*	*That young man has a reputation as a playboy.*	Aquel joven tiene fama de **playboy**.
	Standard variants →	Aquel joven tiene fama de **libertino** / **mujeriego** / etc.

PODER

PODER (masc noun)
- = **power: control, charge; authority**
- = **power: capacity, capability [US]**
- = **power: powerful entity [US]**
- = **power: strength; forcefulness [US]**
- = **power (of engine, machine, etc.) [US]**
- = **power: source of energy [US]**
- = **power: mental faculty [US]**

- The word "power" renders a variety of translations in standard Spanish.
- **Poder** is "power" in the sense of "control over people" or "authority to act."
- **Fuerza** implies "strength, forcefulness" and has a more physical implication.
- **Potencia** is a combination of both, and tends to suggest "capability" or "powerful entity."
- **Energía** means "power" when the implication is "energy source."
- As would be expected, U.S. Spanish mimics English by using **poder** in very broad terms.

Standard usage		
1. power (=control, charge):	*There is a dictator in power.*	Hay un dictador en el poder.
2. power (=authority):	*He doesn't have the power to arrest anyone.*	No tiene el poder de detener a nadie.

Extended US usage		
3. power (=capacity):	*the power of concentration*	el **poder** de concentrarse
	Standard variant →	la **capacidad** de concentrarse
4. power (=capability):	*the military power of the U.S.*	el **poder** militar de los EEUU
	Standard variant →	la **potencia** militar de ...
5. power (=powerful entity):	*There will be a summit of the world powers.*	Habrá una conferencia de los **poderes** mundiales.
	Standard variant →	Habrá una conferencia de las **potencias** mundiales.
6. power (=physical strength):	*The weightlifter has incredible power.*	El levantador de pesas tiene un **poder** increíble.
	Standard variant →	... tiene **una fuerza** increíble.
7. power (=forcefulness):	*You need to say it with more power.*	Lo tienes que decir con más **poder**.
	Standard variant →	Lo tienes que decir con más **fuerza**.
8. power (of engine, machine, etc.):	*Did you feel the power of the engine?*	¿Sentiste el **poder** del motor?
	Standard variants →	¿Sentiste la **potencia** / la **fuerza** del motor?

9. power (=energy source):	nuclear power	**poder** nuclear
	Standard variant →	**energía** nuclear
10. powers (=mental faculty):	It looks like he's losing his (mental) powers.	Parece que está perdiendo sus **poderes**.
	Standard variant →	Parece que está perdiendo sus **facultades**.

PÓKER (masc noun)   see **PÓQUER**

POLIÉSTER (masc noun)   =   **loanword for "polyester"** [DRAE 1985]

- The popularity of this synthetic material has made it a universal term.

Standard/US usage		
1. polyester:	I don't like polyester pants.	No me gustan los pantalones de poliéster.

POMPA (fem noun)   =   **pomp, splendor, pageantry**
   =   **bubble**
   =   **pump, gasoline pump [US]**

- Aside from the distinct use of pompa in standard Spanish to refer to a "nautical pump," its traditional meaning is "pomp" (i.e., show, pageantry, glamorous display).
- U.S. Spanish prefers **pompa** to the more conventional **bomba** to refer to a "pump."

Standard usage		
1. pomp, splendor:	They celebrated the wedding with great pomp.	Celebraron la boda con mucha pompa.
2. bubble:	soap bubbles	pompas de jabón

Extended US usage		
3. pump:	water pump / air pump	**pompa** de agua / de aire
	Standard variant →	**bomba** de agua / de aire
4. gasoline pump:	This gas pump is not working.	Esta **pompa** de gasolina no funciona.
	Standard variant →	Este **surtidor** de gasolina no funciona.

PONCHAR (verb) = **adapted from "to puncture / to punch" [US]**

- Used widely in the United States, Mexico, and other parts of Latin America, this popular verb form is <u>not</u> listed in the DRAE. Moliner defines it as follows:

> **ponchar**. 1. (México). tr. y prnl. Pinchar[se] una rueda o un balón. 2. (Antill., México). tr. Picar un billete como señal de que ha sido utilizado. [Moliner]

US usage		
1. *to puncture:*	*I punctured my tire.*	Se me **ponchó** la llanta.
	Standard variant →	Se me **pinchó** la llanta.
2. *to punch (a ticket):*	*As you enter, they punch your ticket.*	Al entrar te **ponchan** el tique.
	Standard variant →	Al entrar te **pican** el tique.
3. *to punch (a hole):*	*Please punch three holes on each sheet.*	Favor de **ponchar** tres agujeros en cada hoja.
	Standard variant →	Favor de **hacer** tres agujeros en cada hoja.
4. *to punch (=hit)*	*He punched me on the shoulder.*	Me **ponchó** en el hombro.
	Standard variant →	Me **dio un puñetazo** en ...

PONCHAZO (masc noun) = **adapted from "puncture" or "punch"** [DRAE 1992]

- Unlisted in Moliner, the only use of **ponchazo** sanctioned by the RAE is regional, and not the primary connotation in U.S. Spanish:

> **ponchazo**. 1. m. Arg. Golpe dado con el poncho. [DRAE]

US usage		
1. *puncture:*	*The cause of the puncture was a very small nail.*	La causa del **ponchazo** fue un clavo muy pequeño.
	Standard variant →	La causa del **pinchazo** fue ...
2. *punch (=blow):*	*He knocked him out with one punch.*	Lo derribó con un **ponchazo**.
	Standard variant →	Lo derribó con un **puñetazo**.

PONCHE (masc noun)   =   **adapted from "punch" (drink)** [DRAE 1737]

ponche. (Del inglés *punch*, y éste del hindi *pãc*, cinco, número de sus ingredientes primitivos). 1. m. Bebida que se hace mezclando ron u otro licor espiritoso con agua, limón y azúcar. A veces se le añade té. [DRAE]

• **Ponche** was borrowed from English and standardized in 1737 (Corominas).

Standard/US usage		
1. punch (=mixed drink):	*a delicious fruit punch*	un sabroso **ponche** de frutas
	Traditional variant →	una sabrosa **bebida** de frutas

PONER (verb)   =   **to put: place, deposit, locate, set, etc.**
   =   **to put in, put out [US]**
   =   **to put: express [US]**
   =   **to put: invest, spend [US]**
   =   **to put the blame on [US]**

• In the vast majority of cases, **poner** coincides with "to put" and related forms in English.
• However, the literal translation of this verb has produced a significant number of nonstandard phrases in U.S. Spanish.

Extended US usage		
1. to put in:	*I put the money in the box.*	**Puse** el dinero en la caja.
	Standard variant →	**Metí** el dinero en la caja.
2. to put out:	*Please put the cat out.*	Favor de **poner** el gato afuera.
	Standard variant →	Favor de **sacar** el gato.
3. to put (=express):	*I wouldn't put it that way.*	Yo no lo **pondría** así.
	Standard variants →	Yo no lo **diría** de esa manera. Yo no lo **expresaría** así.
4. to put (=spend, invest):	*I have put too much money into this car.*	He **puesto** demasiado dinero en este carro.
	Standard variants →	He **gastado** / **invertido** demasiado dinero en este carro.
5. to put the blame:	*He always puts the blame on me.*	Siempre me **pone** la culpa a mí.
	Standard variant →	Siempre me **echa** la culpa ...

"Put" expressions in standard Spanish:	to put across (idea / message)	comunicar, transmitir
	to put aside (=save)	ahorrar, guardar, apartar
	to put away (in jail)	encerrar, meter en la cárcel
	to put back (=replace)	poner otra vez en su sitio
	to put behind (=forget)	olvidar
	to put down (=let go of)	dejar, soltar
	to put down (=supress)	reprimir, sofocar
	to put in (=work, devote)	trabajar, dedicar
	to put off (=postpone)	aplazar, posponer
	to put on weight	engordar, subir de peso
	to put through (=connect)	pasar, comunicar
	to put together (=assemble)	armar, montar, formar
	to put up (=erect, build)	construir, levantar

PONY (masc noun)   =   **loanword for "pony"** [DRAE 1984]

- Standard Spanish accepts two forms: **poni** and **póney**. The closest traditional equivalent would be **potro**, which simply means "young horse." U.S. Spanish prefers **pony**.

Standard/US usage		
1. pony:	He got on the pony and went for a ride.	Se montó sobre el **poni** / **pony** a dar una vuelta.
	Traditional variant →	Se montó sobre el **potro** ...

POP (adj)   =   **loanword for "pop"** (popular) [DRAE 1992]

pop. (Del inglés *pop*, y éste acortado de *popular*, popular). 1. adj. Se dice de un cierto tipo de música ligera y popular derivado de estilos musicales negros y de la música folclórica británica. 2. adj. Se dice de una corriente artística de origen norteamericano que se inspira en los aspectos más inmediatos de la sociedad de consumo. [DRAE]

Standard/US usage		
1. pop (artistic trend):	pop music / pop art	música **pop** / arte **pop**
2. pop (consumer-based):	Commercialization has created a pop culture.	La comercialización ha creado una cultura **pop**.
	Traditional variant →	La comercialización ha creado una cultura **de consumo**.

POBLACIÓN (fem noun) = loanword for "population" [US]

* **Populación** is a common variant in U.S. Spanish for the more conventional **población**.
* The corresponding adjective in standard practice is **demográfico**.

US usage		
1. *population (=inhabitants):*	*70% of the population lives in large cities.*	70% de la **populación** vive en ciudades grandes.
	Standard variant →	70% de la **población** vive ...
2. *population (expressions):*	*population growth* *population explosion*	**crecimiento demográfico** **explosión demográfica**

PÓQUER (masc noun) = loanword for "poker" [DRAE 1947]

* According to the RAE, **póquer** refers not only to the card game but also to a hand of four identical cards. Some dictionaries prefer **póker**.

Standard/US usage		
1. *poker:*	*He won $30 playing poker.*	Ganó 30 dólares jugando al **póquer**.
2. *four of a kind:*	*I have four queens.*	Tengo un **póquer** de reinas.
	Traditional variant →	Tengo **cuatro** reinas.
3. *Expressions:*	*poker face*	cara de **póquer**

verb + POR (prep) = common structure in U.S. Spanish

* There is a tendency in U.S. Spanish to translate the English preposition "for" with **por** in phrasal verbs such as "to look for" and "to wait for."
* Therefore, "I looked for you" may be rendered as **yo busqué por ti**, which could also be understood as "I searched instead of you" or "on your behalf."
* The use of standard forms often helps to avoid confusion of this sort.

US usage		
1. *to ask for (=request):*	*He asked me for money.*	Me **pidió por** dinero.
	Standard variant →	Me **pidió** dinero.
2. *to call for:*	*Did someone call for me?*	¿Alguien **llamó por** mí?
	Standard variant →	¿Alguien me **llamó**?
3. *to look for (=seek):*	*I'm looking for the key.*	Estoy **buscando por** la llave.
	Standard variant →	Estoy **buscando** la llave.
4. *to wait for:*	*He refused to wait for me.*	No quiso **esperar por** mí.
	Standard variant →	No quiso **esperar**me.

PORCHE (masc noun) = **portico, covered porch**
= **open porch [US]**

In standard usage, **porche** is a "covered portico" or "arcade" rather than a "porch."
In U.S. Spanish, **porche** refers primarily to an area (not necessarily covered) at the entrance of a house or building.

Standard usage		
1. portico:	*an Andalusian-style portico*	un porche de estilo andaluz
2. covered porch:	*I'll wait under the porch until the rain stops.*	Yo espero en el porche hasta que pare de llover.

Extended US usage		
3. open porch:	*We sat on the porch to get some fresh air.*	Nos sentamos en el **porche** a tomar un poco de aire.
	Standard variants →	Nos sentamos en el **portal** / en la **terraza** a tomar ...

PORTABLE (adj) = **loanword for "portable" [US]**

• Borrowed from English by U.S. Spanish speakers, this term is <u>not</u> approved by the RAE.
• The only acceptable equivalent in standard Spanish is **portátil**.

US usage		
1. portable:	*I need a portable TV set.*	Me hace falta un televisor **portable**.
	Standard variant →	Me hace falta un televisor **portátil**.

POSICIÓN (fem noun) = **position: location, posture**
= **position: social rank**
= **position: post, job [US]**
= **position: situation, circumstance [US]**
= **position: opinion [US]**

• **Posición** traditionally applies to "location, posture, or social rank."
• U.S. Spanish extends its usage to reflect the many applications of "position" in English, such as "job," "situation," "opinion," etc.

Standard usage		
1. position (=location):	*the position of the planets*	la posición de los planetas
2. position (=posture):	*They found the victim in a very strange position.*	Encontraron a la víctima en una posición muy rara.
3. position (=social rank):	*She is a woman of high social position.*	Es una mujer de alta posición social.

Extended US usage

4. *position (=post, job):*

I accepted the position of cashier.

Acepté la **posición** de cajera.

Standard variant →

Acepté el **puesto** de cajera.

5. *position (=situation, circumstance):*

We find ourselves in a very tough position.

Nos encontramos en una **posición** muy difícil.

Standard variant →

Nos encontramos en una **situación** muy difícil.

You are in no position to complain.

No estás en **posición** de quejarte.

Standard variant →

No estás en **condiciones** de quejarte.

6. *position (=opinion):*

What is your position on the subject of abortion?

¿Cuál es tu **posición** con respecto al aborto?

Standard variant →

¿Cuál es tu **postura** con respecto al aborto?

PÓSTER (masc noun)   =   **loanword for "poster"** [DRAE 1985]

> **póster.** (Del inglés "*poster*"). m. Cartel empleado parta decorar las paredes. [Moliner]

- In U S. Spanish, **póster** can also be a large sign—what in traditional Spanish would be called **letrero**.

Standard usage

1. *poster (decorative):*

My son has the walls covered with posters.

Mi hijo tiene las paredes cubiertas de pósters.

Traditional variants →

... cubiertas de **carteles** / de **afiches** (Lat Am).

Extended US usage

2. *poster (large sign):*

The sign says the hotel is two miles away.

El **póster** dice que el hotel está a dos millas.

Standard variant →

El **letrero** dice que ...

PRESCRIPCIÓN (fem noun)   =   **legal prescription**
   =   **medical prescription [US]**

- **Prescripción**, a term seldom used in standard Spanish, occurs mainly in legal circles to refer to a "claim of title to something by virtue of its use for a determined period of time."
- It occurs more frequently in U.S. Spanish to refer to a "medical prescription."

Standard usage		
1. prescription (legal):	*acquisitive prescription* *statute of limitations*	prescripción adquisitiva ley de prescripción
2. foreword, prologue:	*In the foreword, the author* *explains his motives.*	En la prescripción, el autor explica sus motivos.

Extended US usage		
3. prescription (medical):	*I gave the prescription to the* *pharmacist.*	Le di la **prescripción** al farmacéutico.
	Standard variant →	Le di la **receta** al farmacéutico.

PRESENTE (masc noun) = **present time**
= **present tense**
= **present: gift [US]**

- U.S. Spanish makes regular use of **presente** to mean "gift."
- Although this usage is sanctioned by the RAE, the more traditional term is **regalo**.

Standard/US usage		
1. present time:	*present, past, and future*	**presente**, pasado y futuro
2. present tense:	*Do you know how to conjugate* *"dormir" in the present?*	¿Sabes conjugar "dormir" en el **presente**?
3. present (=gift):	*My students gave me a very* *beautiful present.*	Mis estudiantes me dieron un **presente** muy bonito.
	Standard variant →	... un **regalo** muy bonito.

"Present" expressions **in standard Spanish**	*at present* *for the present* *to live for the present* *up to the present*	ahora / en este momento de momento / por lo pronto vivir el momento hasta ahora

PRESERVAR (verb) = **to preserve: protect, keep in existence**
= **to preserve: maintain [US]**
= **to preserve: keep from decay [US]**

preservar. (Del latín *praeservare*). 1. tr. Proteger, resguardar anticipadamente a una persona, animal o cosa, de algún daño o peligro. [DRAE]

- In academic Spanish, **preservar** essentially means "to protect."
- U.S. Spanish extends its meaning based on common English usage of "preserve."

Standard usage

1. *to preserve (=protect, keep in existence):*	*We want to preserve endangered species.*	Queremos preservar especies en peligro de extinción.

Extended US usage

2. *to preserve (=maintain):*	*Peace must be preserved.*	Hay que **preservar** la paz.
	Standard variant →	Hay que **mantener** la paz.
3. *to preserve (=perpetuate):*	*They want to preserve their traditions.*	Quieren **preservar** sus tradiciones.
	Standard variant →	Quieren **conservar** sus tradiciones.
4. *preserve (=keep from decay):*	*Olives are preserved in water and salt.*	Las aceitunas se **preservan** en agua y sal.
	Standard variant →	Las aceitunas se **conservan** en agua y sal.

PRESERVATIVO (masc noun) = **condom, contraceptive** [DRAE 1985]
= **preservative [US]**

- Since the late 1970s, **preservativo** primarily means "condom" in traditional Spanish.
- In the United States, it is more likely to mean "food preservative."

Standard usage

1. *condom:*	*Condoms can protect against venereal infection.*	El preservativo puede proteger contra la infección venérea.

Extended US usage

2. *preservative (in food):*	*These cookies do not contain preservatives.*	Estas galletas no contienen **preservativos**.
	Standard variant →	Estas galletas no contienen **conservantes**.
	Salt is a preservative.	La sal es un **preservativo**.
	Standard variant →	La sal es un **producto de conservación**.

PRESIONAR (verb)
- = **to press: exert physical pressure**
- = **to pressure: force, coerce**
- = **to press: push, touch [US]**
- = **to press: urge, insist [US]**

- The use of **presionar** in U.S. Spanish is merely an extension of standard usage ("to press"), the difference being one of degree or intensity.
- In all cases, there are traditional variants that convey the same idea.

Standard usage		
1. *to press* (=exert physical pressure):	*Does your stomach hurt when I press?*	¿Te duele el estómago cuando presiono?
	Traditional variant →	¿Te duele el estómago cuando aprieto?
2. *to pressure* (=force, coerce):	*They pressured me to accept the money.*	Me presionaron para que aceptara el dinero.
	Traditional variant →	Insistieron en que aceptara ...

Extended US usage		
3. *to press* (=push):	*You have to press the button.*	Hay que **presionar** el botón.
	Standard variants →	Hay que **apretar** / **tocar** / **oprimir** el botón.
4. *to press* (=urge, insist):	*People will press for him to resign.*	La gente **presionará para** que dimita.
	Standard variants →	La gente **exigirá** / **insistirá en** que dimita.

PRESUMIR (verb)
- = **to show off, be conceited**
- = **to presume: suppose [US]**

- **Presumir** is much more likely to mean "to show off" in standard Spanish.
- The traditional choice for "to presume, assume, suppose" is **suponer**.

Standard usage		
1. *to show off, to be conceited:*	*He likes to show off in front of his girlfriend.*	Le gusta presumir delante de su novia.

Extended US usage		
2. *to presume* (=suppose):	*I presume you are ready.*	**Presumo** que estás listo.
	Standard variant →	**Supongo** que estás listo.

PRETENDER (verb)
- = **to claim, contend**
- = **to aspire to, intend to**
- = **to pretend [US]**

Standard usage

1. *to claim, contend:*

She claims that nobody offered to help her.

Pretende que nadie le quiso ayudar.

2. *to aspire to, intend to:*

He intends to become a millionaire some day.

Pretende hacerse millonario algún día.

Extended US usage

3. *to pretend (=feign, fake, make believe):*

My little brother always pretends to be sick.

Mi hermanito siempre **pretende** estar enfermo.

Standard variant →

Mi hermanito siempre **se hace** el enfermo.

My son pretended not to know.

Mi hijo **pretendía** no saber.

Standard variant →

Mi hijo **fingía** no saber.

PRINCIPAL (adj & noun)
- = **main, principal, foremost**
- = **head, chief**
- = **principal: capital**
- = **school principal [US]**

- By influence of English, **principal** has come to mean "school principal" in U.S. Spanish as well as "chief" or "director" of a business or organization.

Standard usage

1. *main, principal (adj):*

This is the main road.

Ésta es la carretera principal.

2. *head, chief (noun):*

That man is the head of the company.

Ese señor es el principal de la empresa.

3. *principal (=capital):*

You will have to pay principal and interest.

Tendrás que pagar principal e intereses.

Extended US usage

4. *school principal:*

elementary school principal
high school principal

principal de escuela primaria
principal de escuela secundaria

Standard variants →

director de escuela primaria
director / **rector** de escuela secundaria

PRINTEAR (verb)   =   **adapted from "to print" [US]**

PRÍNTER (masc noun)   =   **loanword for "computer printer" [US]**

- These terms, unlikely to be listed in any standard dictionary, occur in U.S. Spanish primarily in the context of modern technology.
- Whereas **imprimir** is historically associated with a printing press, **printear** generally applies to a computer printer.

US usage		
1. *to print (text or photo):*	*Will you be able to print the documents?*	¿Vas a poder **printear** los documentos?
	Standard variant →	¿Vas a poder **imprimir** los documentos?
2. *to print (=write in block letters):*	*Please print your name.*	Favor de **printear** su nombre.
	Standard variant →	Favor de **escribir** su nombre **en letra de molde**.
3. *to print (money):*	*The government no longer prints two-dollar bills.*	El gobierno ya no **printea** billetes de dos dólares.
	Standard variant →	El gobierno ya no **emite** billetes de dos dólares.
4. *computer printer:*	*I bought a laser printer.*	Compré un **prínter** láser.
	Standard variant →	Compré una **impresora** láser.

PRIVACIDAD (fem noun)   =   **privacy (in general terms) [DRAE 2001]**
                             =   **privacy: intimacy [US]**
                             =   **privacy: seclusion, solitude [US]**

> **privacidad**. 1. f. Ámbito de la vida privada que se tiene derecho a proteger de cualquier intromisión. [DRAE]

- Recently sanctioned by the RAE, **privacidad** addresses "privacy" as a general concept.
- U.S. Spanish speakers make greater use of this term than allowed by standard definitions, motivated largely by the prevalence of the term "privacy" in English.

Standard usage		
1. *privacy (in general):*	*Privacy is the most controversial issue of our times.*	La privacidad es el tema más polémico de nuestra época.

Extended US usage

2. privacy (=intimacy):	*You can do what you want in the privacy of your home.*	Puedes hacer lo que quieras en la **privacidad** de tu casa.
	Standard variant →	Puedes hacer lo que quieras en la **intimidad** de tu hogar.
3. privacy (=seclusion, solitude):	*He left the big city to look for privacy.*	Se marchó de la ciudad a buscar **privacidad**.
	Standard variant →	... a buscar la **soledad**.

PRIVADO (adj) = **private: not public**
= **deprived**
= **private: personal, confidential [US]**
= **private: individual, one-on-one [US]**
= **private: reserved [US]**

• In standard practice, **privado** is essentially the opposite of **público**.

Standard usage

1. private (=not public):	*My private life is not anyone's business.*	Mi vida privada no es asunto de nadie.
	My nephew attends a private school.	Mi sobrino asiste a un colegio privado.
2. deprived:	*deprived of his rights*	privado de sus derechos

Extended US usage

3. private (=personal):	*That is my private opinion.*	Ésa es mi opinión **privada**.
	Standard variant →	Ésa es mi opinión **personal**.
4. private (=confidential):	*I tell this to you in private.*	Te lo digo en **privado**.
	Standard variant →	Te lo digo en **confianza**.
5. private (=individual, one-on-one):	*Do you give private lessons?*	¿Das lecciones **privadas**?
	Standard variant →	¿Das lecciones **particulares**?
6. private (=reserved):	*She is a very private person.*	Es una persona muy **privada**.
	Standard variant →	Es ... muy **reservada**.

"Private" expressions in standard Spanish	*keep something private*	no hablar de algo, guardárselo
	private and confidential	personal y confidencial
	private ceremony	ceremonia íntima
	private joke	chiste entre nosotros
	talk in private	hablar en privado / confianza

PROBAR (verb)

= **to taste, try**
= **to test, try out**
= **to try on (clothing)**
= **to prove: give proof of**
= **to prove: demonstrate; verify [US]**
= **to prove to be: turn out [US]**

Standard usage

1. *to taste, try:*	*Did you taste the paella?*	¿Probaste la paella?
2. *to test, try out:*	*Try it out to see if it works.*	Prúebalo a ver si funciona.
3. *to try on (clothing):*	*He didn't want to try on the shirt.*	No quiso probarse la camisa.
4. *to prove (=give proof of):*	*She couldn't prove that she was right.*	No pudo probar que tenía razón.

Extended US usage

5. *to prove (=demonstrate by action):*	*I'm going to prove to you how much I love you.*	Te voy a **probar** cuánto te quiero.
	Standard variant →	Te voy a **demostrar** cuánto te quiero.
6. *to prove (=verify):*	*They did the experiment to prove its effectiveness.*	Hicieron el experimento para **probar** su eficacia.
	Standard variant →	... para **comprobar** su eficacia.
7. *to prove (=turn out):*	*The book proved to be very useful.*	El libro **probó** ser muy útil.
	Standard variant →	El libro **resultó** ser muy útil.

PROPAGANDA (fem noun)

= **publicity, advertising**
= **leaflets, ads, junk mail**
= **propaganda**

• More often than not, **propaganda** simply means "publicity" in standard usage.

Standard/US usage

1. *publicity, advertising:*	*There was tremendous publicity for the movie.*	Le hicieron una tremenda propaganda a la película.
2. *leaflets, ads, junk mail:*	*I receive tons of junk mail every single day.*	Recibo gran cantidad de propaganda todos los días.
3. *propaganda (political, social, ideological...):*	*A dictator uses propaganda to maintain his authority.*	Un dictador usa la propaganda para mantener su autoridad.

PROSPECTO (masc noun) = **leaflet, prospectus**
= **directions for use**
= **prospect: candidate [US]**
= **prospect: possibility [US]**

• Prospecto refers to "prospectus" rather than "prospect" in standard Spanish.
• In U.S. Spanish it commonly refers to either.

Standard usage		
1. leaflet, prospectus:	The leaflets announced the inevitable strike.	Los prospectos anunciaban la destinada huelga.
2. directions for use, instructions:	Did you read the directions before taking the medication?	¿Leíste el prospecto antes de tomar el medicamento?

Extended US usage		
3. prospective candidate:	He is a good prospect for the dean's position.	Es un buen prospecto para el puesto de decano.
	Standard variant →	Es un buen candidato para el puesto de decano.
4. prospect (=possibility):	There was no prospect of winning the championship.	No había prospecto de ganar el campeonato.
	Standard variant →	No había posibilidad de ...

PROVEEDOR (masc noun) = **dealer, supplier**
= **provider: caretaker [US]**

proveedor, ra. 1. m. y f. Persona o empresa que provee o abastece de todo lo necesario para un fin a grandes grupos, asociaciones, comunidades, etc. [DRAE]

• In contrast to the rather limited standard definition, U.S. Spanish mirrors the many connotations of "provider" in English. Alternate forms are provedor and providor.

Standard usage		
1. dealer, supplier:	Who is the energy supplier for your region?	¿Quién es el proveedor de energía para tu región?

Extended US usage		
2. provider (=caretaker):	My brother is a good provider for his children.	Mi hermano es un buen provedor para sus hijos.
	Standard variant →	Mi hermano se ocupa bien de sus hijos.

PROVEER (verb) = **to provide: get ready, make available**
  = **to provide: supply food, money, materials...**
  = **to provide a service; an opportunity [US]**
  = **to provide for: stipulate [US]**

PROVIDEAR (verb) = **loanword for "to provide" [US]**

- *Providear*, which occurs occasionally in U.S. Spanish, does not exist in standard Spanish, while **proveer** indicates "to provide" in limited situations.
- Two of the most common standard variants are **proporcionar** and **brindar**.

Standard usage		
1. *to provide (=get ready, make available):*	*They will have to provide the basic necessities.*	Tendrán que proveer las necesidades básicas.
2. *to provide with (=supply with food, money, etc.):*	*We would like to provide all the children with clothing.*	Quisiéramos proveer de ropa a todos los niños.

Extended US usage		
3. *to provide, supply:*	*Who can provide us with the materials?*	¿Quién nos puede **providear** / **proveer** los materiales?
	Standard variant →	¿Quién nos puede **proporcionar** los materiales?
4. *to provide a service:*	*Do they provide health care?*	¿**Proveen** asistencia médica?
	Standard variant →	¿**Prestan** asistencia médica?
5. *to provide opportunity:*	*It provided me with an excellent opportunity.*	Me **provideó con** una excelente oportunidad.
	Standard variant →	Me **brindó** una excelente oportunidad.
6. *to provide for (=stipulate):*	*The law provides for your rights as a patient.*	La ley **provee por** tus derechos como paciente.
	Standard variants →	La ley **estipula** / **dispone que** **tienes** derechos ...

PUBLICADOR (noun) = **adapted from "publisher" [US]**

- Once used as a noun, **publicador** is primarily an adjective in standard Spanish.
- The noun form, as it occurs in U.S. Spanish, is simply an adaptation of "publisher."

US usage		
1. publisher (firm):	*Barron's is a publisher of educational books.*	Barron's es un **publicador** de libros educativos.
	Standard variant →	Barron's es una **casa editorial** de libros educativos.
2. publisher (person):	*He wants to be a magazine publisher.*	Quiere ser **publicador** de revistas.
	Standard variant →	Quiere ser **editor** de revistas.

PUDÍN (masc noun)   =   **loanword for "pudding"** [DRAE 1927]

• In standard Spanish, **budín** or **pudín** refers strictly to a type of "bread pudding," as opposed to the many varieties in U.S. Spanish.

Standard usage		
1. bread pudding:	*This bread pudding is delicious.*	Este pudín está muy sabroso.

Extended US usage		
2. flavored pudding:	*Would you like vanilla pudding or chocolate pudding?*	¿Desea **pudín** de vainilla o de chocolate?
	Standard variant →	¿Desea **natilla** de vainilla ...?
3. rice pudding:	*I like to add cinammon to my rice pudding.*	Me gusta ponerle canela al **pudín de arroz**.
	Standard variant →	... al **arroz con leche**.

PUZZLE (masc noun)   =   **loanword for "puzzle"** [DRAE 1985]

• According to Moliner and the DRAE, **puzzle** (also spelled **puzle**) is equivalent to **rompecabezas**, any game that qualifies as a "brain twister," such as a "jigsaw puzzle."
• In the U.S., it extends to other kinds of puzzles, and the English pronunciation prevails.

Standard usage		
1. jigsaw puzzle:	*My friend gave me a 500-piece puzzle.*	Mi amiga me regaló un puzzle de 500 piezas.

Extended US usage		
2. crossword puzzle:	*This crossword puzzle is very difficult.*	Este **puzzle de palabras** es muy difícil.
	Standard variant →	Este **crucigrama** es ...

RAQUETBOL (masc noun) = **loanword for "racketball" [US]**

- Standard Spanish has borrowed **béisbol**, **basquetbol**, and **voleibol** from English, but not **raquetbol**, a popular sport in the United States.

US usage		
1. *racketball:*	*Racketball is similar to tennis.*	El **raquetbol** es parecido al tenis.

RAQUETEAR (verb) = **adapted from "to racketeer" [US]**

RAQUETERO (masc noun) = **adapted from "racketeer" [US]**

- In standard Spanish, "racketeering," which entails "organized extortion," is generally known as **chantaje sistematizado**; and **raquetero** refers to one who makes rackets.
- U.S. Spanish uses both terms in the context of organized crime.

US usage		
1. *to racketeer:*	*For racketeering he served ten years in jail.*	Por **raquetear** cumplió diez años en la cárcel.
	Standard variant →	Por **hacer chantaje** cumplió diez años en la cárcel.
2. *racketeer:*	*They are known racketeers.*	Son **raqueteros** conocidos.
	Standard variant →	Son **estafadores** conocidos.

RARO (adj)
= **odd, strange**
= **rare item (book, stamp, etc.)**
= **rare plant / animal [US]**
= **rare: unique, exceptional [US]**
= **rare: infrequent [US]**
= **rare: undercooked [US]**

- The primary meanings of **raro** in standard Spanish are "strange" and "uncommon."
- In the U.S., it takes on additional meanings ("unique," "infrequent," "undercooked," etc.).

Standard usage		
1. *odd, strange:*	*What a strange person!*	¡Qué persona más rara!
2. *rare item (=uncommon):*	*She buys and sells rare books.*	Compra y vende libros raros.

Extended US usage

3. *rare plant/animal:*

The white tiger is a very rare animal.

El tigre blanco es un animal muy **raro**.

Standard variant →

El tigre blanco es un animal muy **poco común**.

4. *rare (=unique):*

You have a rare talent.

Tienes un talento **raro**.

Standard variant →

Tienes un talento **singular**.

5. *rare (=exceptional):*

a rare opportunity

una oportunidad **rara**

Standard variant →

una oportunidad **excepcional**

6. *rare (=infrequent):*

A total eclipse of the sun is a very rare occurrence.

Un eclipse total del sol es un acontecimiento muy **raro**.

Standard variant →

Un eclipse total ... es un acontecimiento **poco frecuente**.

7. *rare (=undercooked):*

He likes his meat very rare.

Le gusta la carne **muy rara**.

Standard variants →

Le gusta la carne **poco hecha** / **medio cruda**.

REALÍSTICO (adj) = loanword for "realistic" [US]

- **Realístico**, a product of U.S. Spanish, is used to indicate "lifelike," "reasonable," etc.
- The standard equivalent of "realistic" depends on the intended connotation in English.

US usage

1. *realistic (=pragmatic):*

realistic point of view

punto de vista **realístico**

Standard variant →

punto de vista **realista**

2. *realistic (=reasonable):*

That's not a realistic price.

No es un precio **realístico**.

Standard variant →

No es un precio **razonable**.

3. *realistic (=lifelike):*

The statue is so realistic!

¡Qué **realística** es la estatua!

Standard variants →

¡Qué **natural** es la estatua!
¡**Parece viva** la estatua!

REALIZAR(SE) (verb)

= **to come true, materialize, accomplish**
= **to carry out, complete**
= **to fulfill oneself, succeed**
= **to realize a financial gain**
= **to realize: learn, become aware of [US]**
= **to realize: know, comprehend [US]**

• The most common use of "to realize" (to become aware of) is often rendered in U.S. Spanish with the cognate **realizar**, in place of the more conventional **darse cuenta de**.

Standard usage

1. *to come true, materialize:*	*My dreams have come true.*	Mis sueños se han realizado.
2. *to carry out, complete:*	*The project was carried out in less than two months.*	El proyecto se realizó en menos de dos meses.
3. *to fulfill oneself, succeed:*	*She wants to succeed as a professor.*	Ella quiere realizarse como profesora.
4. *to realize financial gain:*	*We realized a profit of $1000.*	Realizamos una ganancia de mil dólares.

Extended US usage

5. *to realize (=learn, become aware of):*	*When did you realize that the class was cancelled?*	¿Cuándo **realizaste** que cancelaron la clase?
	Standard variant →	¿Cuándo **te diste cuenta de** que cancelaron la clase?
6. *to realize (=know, understand):*	*I realize you're looking for work, but I can't hire you.*	**Realizo** que buscas trabajo pero no te puedo contratar.
	Standard variant →	**Sé** que buscas trabajo pero ...

RECETA (fem noun)

= **recipe; medical prescription**
= **receipt [US]**

Standard usage

1. *recipe:*	*I have a great recipe for Valencian paella.*	Tengo una excelente receta para la paella valenciana.
2. *medical prescription:*	*You cannot get that medicine without a prescription.*	Ese medicamento no se puede conseguir sin receta médica.

Extended US usage

3. *receipt:*	*Keep the receipt in case you want to return it.*	Guarda la **receta** en caso de que lo quieras devolver.
	Standard variant →	Guarda el **recibo** en caso de que lo quieras devolver.

RECOLECCIÓN (fem noun) = **collection; harvesting**
= **recollection: memory [US]**

• **Recolección** and its corresponding verb form, **recolectar**, are considered false cognates of "recollection" and "to recollect" in standard academic Spanish.

Standard usage		
1. *collection:*	*garbage collection*	recolección de basura
2. *harvesting:*	*the harvesting of grapes*	la recolección de uvas

Extended US usage		
3. *recollection (=memory):*	*I have no recollection of what happened on that day.*	No tengo ninguna **recolección** de lo que pasó aquel día.
	Standard variant →	No tengo ningún **recuerdo** de lo que pasó aquel día.

RECOLECTAR (verb) = **to gather, collect**
= **to harvest**
= **to recollect: remember [US]**

recolectar. (Del latín *recollectum*, supino de *recolligere*, recoger). 1. tr. Juntar personas o cosas dispersas. 2. tr. Recoger la cosecha. [DRAE]

Standard usage		
1. *to gather, collect:*	*Please collect the papers from the table.*	Favor de recolectar los papeles de la mesa.
2. *to harvest:*	*We harvested a lot of corn this year.*	Se recolectó mucho maíz este año.

Extended US usage		
3. *to recollect (=remember):*	*Do you recollect the incident?*	¿Ud. **recolecta** el incidente?
	Standard variant →	¿Ud. **recuerda** el incidente?

RÉCORD (masc noun) = **loanword for "record" [DRAE 1927]**

• Fully standardized, **récord** occurs in traditional Spanish primarily in the context of sports.
• U.S. Spanish expands its use to other areas, such as business and entertainment.

Standard/US usage		
1. *record (noun):*	*The record has not been broken.*	No se ha batido el **récord**.
2. *record (adj):*	*He finished the race in record time.*	Terminó la carrera en tiempo **récord**.

RECORDAR (verb) = **to remember; remind**
= **to record [US]**

- In standard Spanish, **recordar** means "to remember" or "to remind" but not "to record."

Standard usage		
1. *to remember:*	*I don't remember the address.*	No recuerdo la dirección.
2. *to remind:*	*Let me remind you that you have an appointment at one.*	Te recuerdo que tienes cita a la una.

Extended US usage		
3. *to record (=in writing):*	*She recorded the experience in her diary.*	**Recordó** la experiencia en su diario.
	Standard variants →	**Documentó / Tomó nota de** la experiencia en su diario.
4. *to record (audio or video):*	*I would love to record the presentation.*	Me encantaría **recordar** la presentación.
	Standard variant →	Me encantaría **grabar** ...

REFUSAR (verb) = **loanword for "to refuse"**

- Popular in the early 1800s, **refusar** is no longer current in standard Spanish.
- The closest cognate of "to refuse" is **rehusar**, although there are several more common expressions: **rechazar**, **no querer**, **negarse a**, etc.
- By influence of English, **refusar** is used increasingly in U.S. Spanish.

US usage		
1. *to refuse (=decline):*	*They refused our offer.*	**Refusaron** nuestra oferta.
	Standard variants →	**Rechazaron / No aceptaron** nuestra oferta.
	I never refuse a good wine.	Nunca **refuso** un buen vino.
	Standard variant →	Nunca **digo que no a** un buen vino.
2. *to refuse (=not grant):*	*He was refused a student visa.*	Le **refusaron** un visado para estudiar.
	Standard variants →	Le **negaron / Denegaron** un visado para estudiar.
3. *to refuse to do:*	*She refused to answer me.*	**Refusó** contestarme.
	Standard variants →	**No quiso / Se negó a** contestarme.

REGISTRACIÓN (fem noun) = adapted from "registration"

- **Registración**, extremely widespread in U.S. Spanish, is not valid in standard usage.
- Traditional equivalents of "registration" vary greatly according to the context.

Context		
class, course:	*registration in a course*	inscripción en un curso
conference, workshop:	*registration for a workshop*	inscripción para un taller
enrolment process:	*registration of students*	matriculación de estudiantes
fees, charges:	*registration fees*	derechos de matrícula
form, application:	*registration form*	formulario de inscripción
plates (vehicle):	*registration plates*	placas de matrícula
property, trademark:	*registration of property*	registro de propiedad
vehicle:	*automobile registration*	matriculación de automóvil
voting:	*registration to vote*	inscripción para el voto

REGISTRAR (verb)

=	**to search, examine**
=	**to register: record, indicate**
=	**to check into hotel**
=	**to register: sign up for [US]**
=	**to register: enroll [US]**
=	**to register to vote [US]**
=	**to register mail [US]**
=	**to register luggage [US]**
=	**to register a complaint [US]**
=	**to register: show, indicate [US]**
=	**to register: be understood [US]**

- Of the many common applications of **registrar** in the United States, only a handful are considered appropriate in standard Spanish.

Standard usage

1. *to search, examine:*	*Didn't they search his luggage at customs?*	¿No le registraron el equipaje en la aduana?
2. *to register (=record):*	*Have you registered the birth of your child?*	¿Has registrado el nacimiento de tu hijo?
3. *to register (=indicate):*	*The earthquake registered 6.2 on the Richter scale.*	El terremoto registró un 6.2 en la escala Richter.
4. *to register (=check into):*	*We just checked into the hotel.*	Acabamos de registrarnos en el hotel.

Extended US usage

5. *to register (=sign up)*
[in school, program, etc.]:

I need to register my son in school.

Tengo que **registrar** a mi hijo en la escuela.

Standard variant →

Tengo que **inscribir** a mi hijo en la escuela.

6. *to register for a class:*

Will you be registering for the art class?

¿Te vas a **registrar** para la clase de arte?

Standard variants →

¿Te vas a **matricular** para / **inscribir** en la clase de arte?

7. *to register to vote:*

You need to register to be able to vote.

Te tienes que **registrar** para poder votar.

Standard variant →

Te tienes que **inscribir** para poder votar.

8. *to register mail:*

How much does it cost to register a letter?

¿Cuánto cuesta **registrar** una carta?

Standard variants →

¿Cuánto cuesta **certificar** / **recomendar** una carta?

9. *to register luggage:*

Have you registered your suitcases?

¿Has **registrado** las maletas?

Standard variant →

¿Has **facturado** las maletas?

10. *to register a complaint:*

The customers want to register a complaint.

Los clientes quieren **registrar** una queja.

Standard variant →

Los clientes quieren **presentar** una queja.

11. *to register (=show, indicate):*

The thermometer registered 100 degrees.

El termometro **registró** cien grados.

Standard variants →

El termometro **marcó** / **indicó** cien grados.

12. *to register (=be understood):*

He explained it to me but it did not register.

Me lo explicó pero no **registró**.

Standard variants →

Me lo explicó pero no **entendí** / no **caí en la cuenta**.

REGRESAR (verb)   see **VOLVER**

REGULACIÓN (fem noun)

= **regulation: control; reduction**
= **regulation: rule, norm [US]**

- In standard practice, **regulación** indicates "control" of some kind, or can be a euphemism for "reduction."
- In U.S. Spanish, it also suggests "rule" or "norm," as does its English cognate.

Standard usage

1. regulation (=control):	*the regulation of industry*	la regulación de la industria
	birth control	regulación de la natalidad
2. reduction, cut:	*reduction of prices*	regulación de precios

Extended US usage

3. regulation (=rule, law):	*a new state regulation*	una nueva **regulación** estatal
	Standard variants →	una nueva **ley** / un nuevo **reglamento** estatal
4. regulation (=norm):	*safety regulations*	**regulaciones** de seguridad
	Standard variant →	**normas** de seguridad

REGULAR (adj)

= **so-so, all right, not bad**
= **medium, average**
= **regular: scheduled, recurring**
= **regular: even, symmetrical**
= **regular: normal, ordinary [US]**
= **regular: usual, habitual [US]**
= **regular: frequent; permanent [US]**

- By influence of English, the adjective **regular** occurs frequently in U.S. Spanish in lieu of more standard variants such as **normal**, **corriente**, **habitual**.

Standard usage

1. so-so, all right:	*"How are you feeling?" "So-so."*	—¿Cómo te sientes?—Regular.
2. medium, average:	*I wear medium-sized clothing.*	Uso ropa de tamaño regular.
3. regular (=scheduled):	*There are three regular flights.*	Hay tres vuelos regulares.
4. regular (=even):	*I have very regular teeth.*	Tengo dientes muy regulares.
5. regular (=symmetrical):	*I use a regular pattern.*	Uso un patrón regular.

RELAJAR(SE)

Extended US usage

6. *regular (=normal):*	*What is your regular schedule?*	¿Cuál es tu horario **regular**?
	Standard variant →	¿Cuál es tu horario **normal**?
7. *regular (=ordinary):*	*My car uses regular gasoline.*	Mi carro usa gasolina **regular**.
	Standard variant →	... usa gasolina **corriente**.
8. *regular (=habitual):*	*She is a regular customer.*	Es una clienta **regular**.
	Standard variant →	Es una clienta **habitual**.
9. *regular (=usual):*	*He arrived at the regular time.*	Llegó a la hora **regular**.
	Standard variant →	... a la hora **acostumbrada**.
10. *regular (=frequent):*	*I take regular trips to Mexico.*	Hago viajes **regulares** a México.
	Standard variant →	Hago viajes **frecuentes** ...
11. *regular (=permanent):*	*Do you have a regular job?*	¿Tienes trabajo **regular**?
	Standard variant →	¿Tienes trabajo **permanente**?

RELAJAR(SE) (verb)

= **to relax** (trans): **loosen up**
= **to relax** (intrans): **unwind**
= **to relax: rest, lie down [US]**
= **to relax: calm down [US]**

• Moliner and the RAE sanction the loanword **relax** as well as the verb **relajarse**.
• Both are common in the U.S. along with anglicized forms such as **relaxar** and **relaxear**.

Standard usage

1. *to relax (=loosen up):*	*You need to relax those muscles.*	Tienes que relajar esos músculos.
2. *to relax (=unwind):*	*We're going to the beach to relax a bit.*	Vamos a la playa a relajarnos un poquito.

Extended US usage

3. *to relax (=rest):*	*Why don't you lie down on the sofa and relax for a while?*	¿Por qué no te echas sobre el sofá y **te relajas** un rato?
	Standard variant →	¿Por qué no te echas sobre el sofá y **descansas** un rato?
4. *to relax (=calm down):*	*Relax, don't worry!*	¡**Relájate**, no te preocupes!
	Standard variant →	¡**Cálmate**, no te preocupes!
5. *to relax (=stop worrying):*	*She relaxed when they said it wasn't serious.*	Se **relajó** cuando dijeron que no era grave.
	Standard variant →	Se **tranquilizó** cuando dijeron que no era grave.

RELATADO (adj) = **told, read, narrated**
                = **related, connected [US]**

RELATAR (verb) = **to tell, narrate, relate a story**
                = **to relate: have a connection [US]**
                = **to relate to: get along with [US]**
                = **to relate to: identify with [US]**
                = **to relate to: understand [US]**

• In standard practice, **relatar** can mean "to relate a story" but not "to relate to someone."

Standard usage		
1. to tell, narrate, relate:	*She told the story of her life.*	Relató la historia de su vida.
2. told, read, narrated:	*The passage was narrated by the author himself.*	El pasaje fue relatado por el autor mismo.

Extended US usage		
3. to be related (=have to do with, be connected):	*The ideas are not related to the main theme.*	Las ideas no están **relatadas** con el tema principal.
	Standard variant →	Las ideas no están **relacionadas** con el tema …
4. to relate (=connect with, get along with):	*The teacher relates well to her students.*	La maestra **relata** bien con sus alumnos.
	Standard variants →	La maestra **se lleva** bien / **tiene buenas relaciones** con sus alumnos.
5. to relate (=identify with):	*You will never be able to relate to my anguish.*	Nunca te podrás **relatar a** mi angustia.
	Standard variants →	Nunca te podrás **identificar con** / **sentir** mi angustia.
6. to relate (=understand):	*I relate to what you're saying.*	**Relato a** lo que dices.
	Standard variant →	**Entiendo** lo que dices.

RELATIVO (adj & noun) = **relative (adj): comparative**
                       = **relative (adj): grammatical term**
                       = **relating to, relevant to**
                       = **relative (noun): family member [US]**

• As an adjective, **relativo** coincides with "relative" in the majority of situations.
• However, as a noun meaning "family member," **relativo** occurs only in U.S. Spanish.

Standard usage		
1. *relative* (=comparative):	*They live in relative poverty.*	Viven en relativa pobreza.
2. *relative* (in grammar):	*The teacher taught us the relative pronouns.*	La maestra nos enseñó los pronombres relativos.
3. *relating to* (=relevant to):	*We discussed issues relating to health.*	Discutimos temas relativos a la salud.

Extended US usage		
4. *relative [noun]* (=family member):	*That young man is a distant relative of mine.*	Aquel joven es un **relativo distante**.
	Standard variant →	Aquel joven es un **pariente lejano**.
	I have many relatives in Puerto Rico.	Tengo muchos **relativos** en Puerto Rico.
	Standard variant →	Tengo muchos **familiares** en Puerto Rico.

RELAX (masc noun) = **loanword for "relax"** [DRAE 1985]

RELAXEO (masc noun) = **adapted from "relaxation" [US]**

relax. (Del inglés *relax*, derivado del latín *relaxare*, relajar). 1. m. Relajamiento físico o psíquico producido por ejercicios adecuados o por comodidad, bienestar o cualquier otra causa. [DRAE]

• Only **relax** is considered standard. **Relaxeo** is a product of U.S. Spanish.

Standard usage		
1. *relaxation:*	*The relaxation did me a lot of good.*	El relax me hizo mucho bien.

Extended US usage		
2. *relaxation* (=rest):	*A week of relaxation is what you need.*	Una semana de **relaxeo** es lo que te hace falta.
	Standard variant →	Una semana de **descanso** ...

RELAXEAR(SE) (verb) see **RELAJAR(SE)**

RELEVANTE (adj) = **outstanding, salient**
= **important, significant**
= **relevant (pertinent) [US]**

- The primary meanings of **relevante** in standard usage are "outstanding" and "important," although it is generally used in U.S. Spanish to mean "relevant."

Standard usage		
1. *outstanding, salient*:	*For outstanding work in the field of medicine, ...*	Por una labor relevante en el campo de la medicina, ...
2. *important, significant*:	*It is a significant piece of news.*	Es una relevante noticia.

Extended US usage		
3. *relevant (=pertinent)*:	*relevant information*	información **relevante**
	Standard variant →	información **pertinente**
4. *relevant to (=related to)*:	*It is not relevant to my case.*	No es **relevante** a mi caso.
	Standard variants →	No **está relacionado con** / No **tiene que ver con** mi caso.

REMARCA (fem noun) = **loanword for "remark" [US]**

REMARCABLE (adj) = **loanword for "remarkable" [US]**

REMARCAR (verb) = **to emphasize, underline**
= **to remark: say, point out [US]**
= **to remark: notice, observe [US]**

- The standard academic definition of **remarcar** is "**volver a marcar**" ("to mark again"). By extension, it can mean "to emphasize" or "underline."
- **Remarca** and **remarcable** (once approved as gallicisms by the RAE), have been removed from the standard Spanish lexicon, despite their continued use in parts of Latin America and, increasingly, in the United States.

Standard usage		
1. *to emphasize, underline*:	*They wanted to underline the importance of this case.*	Querían remarcar la importancia de este caso.

Extended US usage		
2. *remark (=comment):*	*He made an offensive remark.*	Hizo una **remarca** ofensiva.
	Standard variant →	Hizo un **comentario** ofensivo.
3. *to remark (=say, point out, declare):*	*She remarked that she didn't like the food.*	**Remarcó** que no le gustaba la comida.
	Standard variants →	**Comentó** / **Dijo** que no le gustaba la comida.
4. *to remark (=notice, observe):*	*I noticed that he had a flat tire.*	**Remarqué** que tenía una llanta desinflada.
	Standard variants →	**Observé** / **Noté** que tenía una llanta desinflada.
5. *remarkable (=notable):*	*She is a remarkable woman.*	Es una mujer **remarcable**.
	Standard variants →	Es una mujer **extraordinaria** / **excepcional** / **singular**.
6. *remarkable (=surprising):*	*It is remarkable how you have grown.*	Es **remarcable** cómo has crecido.
	Standard variants →	Es **increíble** / **sorprendente** cómo has crecido.

REMEMBRAR (verb) = **loanword for "to remember" [US]**

- **Remembrar**, an archaic term dating back to thirteenth century Spanish, appears in the most current editions of the Moliner and RAE dictionaries.
- Generally regarded as Spanglish, this verb and its variant form, **remembrear**, seem to coexist with conventional variants such as **recordar** and **acordarse**.

US usage		
1. *to remember:*	*I cannot remember all that information.*	Yo no puedo **remembrar** toda esa información.
	Standard variant →	Yo no puedo **recordar** ...

REMOVER (verb)
= **to move around** (trans)
= **to stir, shake, toss**
= **to agitate, stir up**
= **to remove [US]**

- **Remover** is not traditionally used to mean "remove," as is the case in U.S. Spanish.
- The standard equivalent of "to remove" is **quitar**.

Standard usage
1. *to move things around:*	*He decided to move around the furniture.*	Le dio por remover los muebles.
2. *to stir, shake, toss:*	*Stir before serving.*	Remover antes de servir.
3. *to agitate, stir up:*	*I'd rather not stir up the issue.*	Prefiero no remover el asunto.

Extended US usage
4. *to remove:*	*I couldn't remove the stain.*	No pude **remover** la mancha.
	Standard variant →	No pude **quitar** la mancha.
5. *to remove (=let go):*	*They removed him from his post.*	Lo **removieron** de su puesto.
	Standard variant →	Lo **despidieron** de su puesto.

RENTA (fem noun)
= **income, interest**
= **rent [US]**

RENTAR (verb)
= **to produce, yield**
= **to rent [US]**

- Most major dictionaries (including Moliner and DRAE) list four or five definitions of **renta**, none of which correspond to the customary use of "rent" in English.
- Both terms are widely used in the U.S. in reference to "renting" a house or apartment.

Standard usage
1. *interest:*	*He has so much money that he can live off his interest.*	Tiene tanto dinero que puede vivir de sus rentas.
2. *state income:*	*gross national income*	renta bruta nacional
3. *to produce, yield:*	*How much do these bonds yield?*	¿Cúanto rentan estos bonos?

Extended US usage
4. *rent (noun):*	*How much rent do you pay?*	¿Cuánto pagas de **renta**?
	Standard variant →	¿Cúanto pagas de **alquiler**?
5. *to rent (verb):*	*We would like to rent an apartment in the city.*	Quisiéramos **rentar** un apartamento en la ciudad.
	Standard variant →	Quisiéramos **alquilar** un apartamento en la ciudad.

REPORTAR (verb)

=	**to bring, create, produce**
=	**to report: inform (in the press)** [DRAE 1985]
=	**to report: state, inform, make known [US]**
=	**to report: be a reporter [US]**
=	**to report: notify the authorities [US]**
=	**to report: denounce [US]**
=	**to report: allege, rumor [US]**
=	**to report: present oneself, show up [US]**
=	**to report: be responsible to [US]**

REPORTEAR (verb) = **to photograph for the press** [DRAE 1985]

- The use of **reportar** to mean "communicate" or "transmit information" is sanctioned by the RAE as an Americanism.
- A variation of the verb, **reportear**, and the noun **reportero** ("reporter") are more closely linked in meaning to their English counterparts:

> **reportear**. 1. *Am.* Dicho de un periodista: Entrevistar a alguien para hacer un reportaje. 2. *Am.* Tomar fotografías para realizar un reportaje gráfico. [DRAE]

> **reportero, -a.** n. Periodista que se dedica a la recogida y redacción de noticias. [Moliner]

Standard usage

1. *to bring, create, produce:*	*This is going to create a lot of problems for us.*	Esto nos va a reportar un montón de problemas.

Latin American usage

2. *to report (in the press):*	*It was reported in all the papers.*	Lo **reportaron** en todos los periódicos.
3. *to photograph (for press):*	*They photographed the entire parade.*	**Reportearon** el desfile entero.

Extended US usage

4. *to report (=state, inform, make known):*	*They are reporting from Lima.*	Están **reportando** de Lima.
	Standard variant →	Están **informando** de Lima.
5. *to report (=be a reporter):*	*He reported for La Nación for many years.*	**Reportó para** La Nación por muchos años.
	Standard variant →	**Fue reportero** de La Nación por muchos años.
6. *to report (=notify the authorities):*	*to report an accident / a crime* *to report (someone) missing*	**reportar** un accidente / crimen **reportar** desaparecido (a uno)
	Standard variants →	**dar parte de** un accidente … **declarar** desaparecido (a uno)

7. to report (=denounce):	*He reported her to Immigration.*	La **reportó** a la Inmigración.
	Standard variant →	La **denunció** a la Inmigración.
8. to report (=allege, rumor):	*It is reported that she was sick.*	**Reportan** que estuvo enferma.
	Standard variant →	**Dicen** que estuvo enferma.
9. to report (=show up, turn up, present oneself):	*When will you be reporting to work?*	¿Cuándo vas a **reportar** al trabajo?
	Standard variant →	¿Cuándo vas a **presentarte** al trabajo?
10. to report to someone (=be responsible to):	*I report to the vice president.*	Yo **reporto** al vice presidente.
	Standard variant →	Yo **estoy bajo las órdenes** del vicepresidente.

REPORTE (masc noun)
- = **report: news story**
- = **report: gossip, rumor**
- = **report: school assignment [US]**
- = **report: piece of news [US]**
- = **report: bulletin, notification [US]**

- Standard academic Spanish permits the use of **reporte** to indicate "the report or account of a news item," although **reportaje** and **informe** are more traditional options.
- It also accepts "gossip" or "rumor" as a secondary meaning.
- Other applications, such as "book report" and "report card" are typical of U.S. usage.

Standard usage

1. report (=news story):	*They did a report on sexual abuse.*	Hicieron un reporte sobre el abuso sexual.
	Traditional variant →	Hicieron un reportaje sobre el abuso sexual.
2. report (=gossip, rumor):	*I have been hearing reports that you're getting married.*	Tengo oído reportes de que te vas a casar.
	Traditional variant →	Tengo oído rumores de que te vas a casar.

Extended US usage

3. *report (=school assignment):*

I wrote a report on the life of Cervantes.	Escribí un **reporte** sobre la vida de Cervantes.
Standard variants →	Escribí un **informe** / hice un **trabajo** sobre Cervantes.

4. *report (=piece of news):*

Did you hear the report (news)?	¿Oíste el **reporte**?
Standard variant →	¿Te enteraste de la **noticia**?

5. *report (=bulletin, notification):*

At what time do they give the weather report?	¿A qué hora se da el **reporte del tiempo**?
Standard variant →	¿A qué hora se da el **boletín meteorológico**?
My son just received his school report card.	Mi hijo acaba de recibir su **reporte escolar**.
Standard variant →	Mi hijo acaba de recibir su **boletín de notas**.

REPÓRTER (masc noun) = **loanword for "reporter"** [DRAE 1985]

- Listed by Moliner, **repórter** is a variant of the more traditional **reportero** (DRAE 1936).
- Both are used in U.S. Spanish to mean "journalist" as well as "radio / television reporter."

US usage

1. *reporter (press):*

Did you speak to the reporter from El Diario?	¿Hablaste con el **repórter** de El Diario?
Standard variants →	¿Hablaste con el **reportero** / el **periodista** de El Diario?

2. *reporter (radio, TV):*

I was interviewed by a reporter from Univision.	Me entrevistó un **repórter** de Univisión.
Standard variant →	Me entrevistó un **reportero** ...

REQUERIDO (adj) = **adapted from "required"** [US]

REQUERIR (verb) = **to require: call for, take**
  = **to require: need** [US]
  = **to require: demand, request** [US]

- Whereas **requerido** is an uncommon adjective in standard Spanish, **requerir** is a legitimate verb with close ties to its English cognate "to require."
- U.S. Spanish makes extensive use of both **requerir** and **requerido**.
- Some traditional equivalents of "to require" are: **hacer falta**, **necesitar**, **exigir**.

Standard usage

1. *to require (=call for, take):*	*That requires a lot of patience.*	Eso requiere mucha paciencia.

Extended US usage

2. *to require (=need):*	*Will you require any money?*	¿Vas a **requerir** dinero?
	Standard variants →	¿Vas a **necesitar** dinero? ¿**Te hará falta** dinero?
3. *required (=necessary):*	*I will call him if it's required.*	Lo llamaré si es **requerido**.
	Standard variant →	Lo llamaré si es **necesario**.
4. *to require (=demand, request):*	*They are going to require a deposit from you.*	Te van a **requerir** un depósito.
	Standard variant →	Te van a **exigir** un depósito.
5. *required (=obligatory, compulsory):*	*Is this course required?*	¿Es **requerido** este curso?
	Standard variant →	¿Es **obligatorio** este curso?
6. *required (=fixed, established):*	*within the required time*	dentro del **tiempo requerido**
	Standard variant →	dentro del **plazo establecido**

RESIGNACIÓN (fem noun) = **resignation: passivity, acceptance**
= **resignation: act of quitting [US]**

RESIGNAR(SE) (verb) = **to resign oneself: accept, comply**
= **to hand over (power, authority)**
= **to resign: quit (a job, etc.) [US]**

Standard usage

1. *resignation (=acceptance):*	*They received the sad news with resignation.*	Recibieron la triste noticia con resignación.
2. *to resign oneself (=accept):*	*They resigned themselves to accepting the truth.*	Se resignaron a aceptar la verdad.
3. *to hand over (authority):*	*The bishop will hand over authority next month.*	El obispo resignará el mando el mes que viene.

Extended US usage		
4. *resignation (=act of quitting):*	*He submitted his resignation yesterday.*	Sometió su **resignación** ayer.
	Standard variants →	Presentó la **dimisión** ayer. Declaró su **renuncia** ayer.
5. *to resign (=quit):*	*If they don't raise my salary, I resign.*	Si no me aumentan el sueldo, **resigno**.
	Standard variants →	Si no me aumentan el sueldo, **renuncio / dimito**.

RESPECTO (masc noun)

- = **respect: regard, reference**
- = **respect: admiration, esteem, consideration [US]**
- = **respect: point, detail, aspect [US]**
- = **respects: regards, greetings [US]**

- Influenced by English, U.S. Spanish uses **respecto** to mean "aspect" and "respect."
- Accordingly, it does not always distinguish between **respecto** and **respeto**.

Standard usage		
1. *respect (=regard, reference):*	*With respect to your question...*	Con **respecto** a tu pregunta...

Extended US usage		
2. *respect (=admiration):*	*He treats me with great respect.*	Me trata con mucho **respecto**.
	Standard variant →	Me trata con mucho **respeto**.
3. *respect (=consideration):*	*They have no respect for the law.*	No le tienen **respecto** a la ley.
	Standard variant →	No le tienen **respeto** a la ley.
4. *respect (=point, detail, aspect):*	*He is a gentleman in every respect.*	Es un caballero en todos los **respectos**.
	Standard variants →	Es un caballero en todos los **sentidos / aspectos**.
5. *respects (=greetings):*	*My wife sends her respects.*	Mi esposa manda **respectos**.
	Standard variants →	Mi esposa manda **saludos / recuerdos**.

RESUMEN (masc noun) = **summary, résumé**
                            = **résumé: curriculum vitae [US]**

Standard usage		
1. summary, résumé:	*Prepare a brief summary of the novel.*	Prepare un breve resumen de la novela.

Extended US usage		
2. résumé (=curriculum vitae):	*Please send your résumé along with the job application.*	Favor de mandar su **resumen** con la solicitud de empleo.
	Standard variants →	Favor de mandar su **hoja de vida** / su **currículum** ...

RETIRAR(SE) (verb) = **to withdraw: leave, take out**
                            = **to take away, remove**
                            = **to pull back, pull away**
                            = **to move back, move away**
                            = **to leave, go away**
                            = **to retire from work [US]**

• Although "retire from work" is one of the acceptable meanings of **retirarse** in standard practice, this usage is more typical of U.S. Spanish. The traditional variant is **jubilarse**.

Standard usage		
1. to withdraw (=leave):	*She withdrew from public life.*	Se retiró de la vida pública.
2. to withdraw (=take out):	*I need to withdraw a thousand dollars from my account.*	Tengo que retirar mil dólares de mi cuenta.
3. to take away, remove:	*Remove that toy from the table.*	Retira ese juguete de la mesa.
4. to pull back, pull away:	*When I went to shake his hand, he pulled away.*	Cuando fui a darle la mano, me la retiró.
5. to move back/away:	*Could you move back a little?*	¿Podrías retirarte un poquito?
6. to leave, go away:	*We had to leave the scene.*	Tuvimos que retirarnos de ahí.

Extended US usage		
7. to retire (=give up work):	*I'm planning to retire at sixty.*	Pienso **retirarme** a los sesenta años.
	Standard variant →	Pienso **jubilarme** a los sesenta años.

RETIRO (masc noun)

= **quiet place, secluded spot**
= **retirement pension**
= **withdrawal of money**
= **retirement: state of being retired**
= **retirement: act of retiring [US]**

• In standard practice, **retiro** denotes the "state of being retired, " whereas **jubilación** puts the stress on the "act of retirement" or the celebration associated with it.

Standard usage

1. *quiet, secluded spot:*	*I'm looking for a quiet place, far from the city.*	Busco un buen retiro, lejos de la ciudad.
2. *retirement pension:*	*My father lives off his pension.*	Mi padre vive de su retiro.
3. *withdrawal (of money):*	*I made a withdrawal of $500.*	Hice un retiro de 500 dólares.
4. *retirement (=state of being retired):*	*My grandfather enjoyed his years of retirement.*	Mi abuelo disfrutó de sus años de retiro.

Extended US usage

5. *retirement (=act of retiring):*	*Yesterday we celebrated our colleague's retirement.*	Ayer celebramos el **retiro** de nuestro colega.
	Standard variant →	Ayer celebramos la **jubilación** de nuestro colega.

REVISAR (verb)

= **to revise, update**
= **to check: look over, inspect**
= **to review: reexamine, reconsider**
= **to review: study, analyze [US]**
= **to review: critique [US]**
= **to review for an exam [US]**

• **Revisar** is used quite freely in U.S. Spanish to mean "review" as well as "revise."

Standard usage

1. *to revise, update:*	*They revised the first edition.*	Revisaron la primera edición.
2. *to check (=look over):*	*You had better look over your documents.*	Más vale que revises tus documentos.
3. *to check (=inspect):*	*Please check the oil.*	Favor de revisar el aceite.
4. *to review (=reexamine):*	*The judge will have to review the case.*	El juez tendrá que revisar el caso.

Extended US usage

5. to review (=study, analyze):	*They haven't reviewed the data.*	No han **revisado** los datos.
	Standard variants →	No han **estudiado** / **analizado** los datos.
6. to review (=critique):	*to review a film*	**revisar** una película
	Standard variant →	**reseñar** una película
7. to review (for an exam):	*We reviewed the last chapter.*	**Revisamos** el último capítulo.
	Standard variant →	**Repasamos** el último capítulo.

REVIVAL (masc noun) = **loanword for "revival" [US]**

• Cited by Moliner and listed in the DRAE between 1985 and 1992, this term (pronounced as in English) is in vogue in many parts of the Spanish-speaking world.

US usage

1. revival (of ideas, customs, values):	*There has been a revival of patriotism in this country.*	Ha habido un **revival** de patriotismo en este país.
	Standard variants →	Ha habido un **renacimiento** / **resurgimiento** de ...
2. revival (theater):	*I saw an excellent revival of an old play.*	Vi un excelente **revival** de una antigua obra teatral.
	Standard variant →	Vi una excelente **reposición** de una antigua obra teatral.

REVOLVER (verb) = **to stir, scramble; turn, toss**
= **to mix up, mess up**
= **to revolve [US]**

• Despite its traditional status as a false cognate, **revolver** is equated with "to revolve" in U.S. Spanish.

Standard usage

1. to stir, scramble:	*It's important to stir the paint before you use it.*	Es importante revolver la pintura antes de usarla.
2. stirred, scrambled:	*They served me scrambled eggs.*	Me sirvieron huevos revueltos.
3. to turn, toss:	*That food is going to turn your stomach.*	Esa comida te va a revolver el estómago.
4. to mix up, mess up:	*Don't mess up my papers.*	No me revuelvas los papeles.

Extended US usage

5. *to revolve (=rotate, spin):*	*The earth revolves around the sun.*	La tierra **revuelve** alrededor del sol.
	Standard variant →	La tierra **gira** alrededor del sol.
6. *to revolve around (=have to do with, relate to):*	*She thinks everything revolves around her.*	Piensa que todo **revuelve** alrededor de ella.
	Standard variant →	... todo **gira** en torno a ella.
7. *to revolve (=focus):*	*Our conversation revolved around politics.*	Nuestra conversación **revolvió alrededor de** la política.
	Standard variant →	Nuestra conversación **se centró en** la política.

REWIND (masc noun & verb)   =   **loanword for "rewind" [US]**

- Cited in the Vox Dictionary, **rewind** occurs both as a verb and a noun in U.S. Spanish, generally in reference to an audio or video cassette recording device.
- Usually pronounced as in English, it is also rendered phonetically in Spanish (re-güín).

US usage

1. *rewind button:*	*You need to press "rewind."*	Tienes que apretar el **rewind**.
	Standard variant →	Tienes que apretar el **botón de retroceso**.
2. *to rewind:*	*Please rewind the cassettes.*	Favor de **rewind** el casete.
	Standard variant →	Favor de **rebobinar** el casete.

ROBOT (masc noun)   =   **loanword for "robot"** [DRAE 1970]

- **Robot** (rendered phonetically in Spanish), along with **robótica** ("robotics") and **robotizar**, has been fully incorporated into standard academic Spanish.

Standard/US usage

1. *robot:*	*Robots are used to detonate explosives.*	Se usan **robots** para hacer detonar explosivos.
2. *robot (fig):*	*I am not a robot: I am quite capable of thinking for myself.*	No soy **robot**: soy muy capaz de pensar por mi cuenta.

ROL (masc noun)   =   **adapted from "role"** [DRAE 1985]

- **Rol** first came into standard usage within the context of theatre and film. It has since expanded to become a popular alternative to its traditional counterpart, **papel**.

Standard/US usage		
1. role (in theatre, film):	*Who will play the role of the villain?*	¿Quién hará el **rol** del malo?
	Traditional variant →	¿Quién hará el **papel** del malo?
2. role (in general):	*What is the role of the United Nations?*	¿Cuál es **rol** de las Naciones Unidas?
	Traditional variant →	¿Cuál es **papel** de las Naciones Unidas?

ROMPER (verb)   =   **to break: smash, shatter, fracture**

- = **to break: cease to function [US]**
- = **to break: violate, fail to observe [US]**
- = **to break a record, surpass [US]**
- = **to break: weaken, destroy [US]**
- = **to break: make change [US]**
- = **to break: become known [US]**
- = **to break: pause, take a break [US]**
- = **to break: end, cease [US]**

- The traditional meaning of **romper** is essentially "to fracture" or "to shatter."
- Its use is more widespread in the U.S. due to common word-for-word translations of the verb "to break."

Standard usage		
1. to break (=shatter):	*They broke the window to get into the house.*	Rompieron la ventana para entrar en la casa.
2. to break (=split, fracture):	*She broke her leg.*	Se rompió la pierna.

Extended US usage		
3. to break, break down (=cease to function):	*The vacuum cleaner just broke.*	La aspiradora se acaba de **romper**.
	Standard variants →	La aspiradora se acaba de **descomponer / estropear**.
4. to break a law/a rule (=violate, fail to observe):	*He has a tendency to break the rules.*	Tiene la tendencia de **romper** las reglas.
	Standard variants →	Tiene la tendencia de **violar / desobedecer** las reglas.

5. to break a record (=surpass, overcome):	He broke the swimming record.	**Rompió** el récord de natación.
	Standard variants ➔	**Batió / Superó** el récord ...
6. to break (=weaken, destroy):	They never succeeded in breaking his spirit.	No llegaron nunca a **romperle** el ánimo.
	Standard variants ➔	No llegaron nunca a **quebrantarle / quebrarle** el ánimo.
7. to break money (=make change):	Can you break a 50-dollar bill?	¿Me puedes **romper** un billete de 50 dólares?
	Standard variant ➔	¿Me puedes **cambiar** un billete de 50 dólares?
8. to break (=become known):	The news broke yesterday.	La noticia **rompió** ayer.
	Standard variant ➔	La noticia **se dio a conocer** ...
9. to break (=pause):	Let's break for lunch.	**Rompamos** para el almuerzo.
	Standard variant ➔	**Hagamos un descanso** para el almuerzo.
10. to break (=end, cease):	Finally, the heat broke.	Por fin **rompió** el calor.
	Standard variant ➔	Por fin **se terminó** el calor.
"Break" expressions in standard Spanish	to break a date	faltar a una cita
	to break a habit	quitar / perder una costumbre
	to break a promise	no cumplir con la palabra
	to break even	cubrir los gastos
	to break free	escaparse / soltarse / liberarse
	to break loose	desatarse / escaparse
	to break one's back	matarse
	to break someone's heart	partir el corazón (a alguien)

ROOKIE (masc noun) = loanword for "rookie" [US]

- **Rookie** (pronounced as in English) is not recognized in standard Spanish.
- Traditional variants include **bisoño, debutante, novato, principiante**.

US usage

1. rookie (in the police, armed forces):	The percentage of rookies on the police force is not high.	El porcentaje de **rookies** en el cuerpo de policía no es alto.
	Standard variants ➔	El porcentaje de **novatos / bisoños / principiantes** ...

2. *rookie (in sports):*	*It was a rookie who won the game.*	Fue un **rookie** quien ganó el partido.
	Standard variants →	Fue un **principiante** / un **debutante** quien ganó ...

ROSBIF (masc noun)   =   **adapted from "roast beef"** [DRAE 1984]

Standard/US usage

1. *roast beef:*	*Who ordered a roast beef sandwich?*	¿Quién pidió un sándwich de **rosbif**?

RÓSTER (masc noun)   =   **loanword for "roster"** [US]

- Whether it be "team roster" or "class roster," standard Spanish refers to a list of names as **lista** or **registro**, whereas U.S. Spanish often borrows the term **róster**.

US usage

1. *class roster:*	*How many students appear on the roster?*	¿Cuántos alumnos aparecen en el **róster**?
	Standard variant →	¿Cuántos alumnos aparecen en la **lista** (**de asistencia**)?
2. *team roster:*	*There are 25 players on the team's official roster.*	Hay 25 jugadores en el **róster** oficial del equipo.
	Standard variant →	Hay 25 jugadores en el **registro** oficial del equipo.

RUDO (adj)   =   **rough, coarse, unpolished**
        =   **simple, unsophisticated**
        =   **rude: impolite, indecent** [US]

- Although the DRAE lists " **descortés**, **áspero**, **grosero**" as a secondary definition, the use of **rudo** to mean "rude" is far more typical of U.S. Spanish.

Standard usage

1. *rough, unpolished:*	*This furniture is made with unpolished wood.*	Estos muebles están hechos de madera ruda.
2. *simple, unsophisticated:*	*They were simple people, poorly equipped to handle city life.*	Era gente ruda, mal preparada para la vida cosmopolita.

Extended US usage		
3. rude (=impolite):	*That man is very rude.*	Ese hombre es muy **rudo**.
	Standard variants →	Ese hombre es muy **grosero** / **maleducado**.
4. rude (=indecent):	*He made a rude comment.*	Hizo un comentario **rudo**.
	Standard variants →	Hizo un comentario **obsceno** / **grosero**.

SALARIO (masc noun)   =   **wage, wages**
=   **salary, compensation [US]**

• Often used interchangeably in the United States, **salario** and **sueldo** have slightly different connotations in academic Spanish. **Salario** refers primarily to "wages," whereas **sueldo** suggests "salary" or "compensation."

Standard usage		
1. wage, wages:	*They pay me minimum wage.*	Me pagan el salario mínimo.
	There will be a wage increase.	Va a haber un aumento de salarios.

Extended US usage		
2. salary, compensation:	*My dad earns a good salary.*	Mi papá gana un buen **salario**.
	Standard variant →	Mi papá gana un buen **sueldo**.

SALIR (verb)   =   **to leave: depart; go out of, come out of**
=   **to leave: check out, be discharged**
=   **to leave: go off, go astray**
=   **to go out (socially)**
=   **to come out: rise**
=   **to come out: be issued, published, released**
=   **to appear in the media**
=   **to leave: go away [US]**
=   **to leave: quit; abandon [US]**

• The verb **salir** has more than twenty uses in standard Spanish, the most common of which are "to depart," "to go out," and "to come out."
• The many applications of its closest English equivalent ("to leave") give rise to a handful of expressions in U.S. Spanish considered inappropriate in traditional usage.

Standard usage

1. *to leave (=depart):*	*The train leaves at ten o'clock.*	El tren sale a las diez.
2. *to leave (=go out of):*	*I left the house in a big hurry.*	Salí de casa con mucha prisa.
3. *to come out of:*	*He finally came out of his room.*	Salió por fin de su cuarto.
4. *to leave (=check out):*	*We checked out last night.*	Salimos del hotel anoche.
5. *to leave (=be discharged):*	*When did you leave the hospital?*	¿Cuándo saliste del hospital?
6. *to leave (=go off):*	*The car went off the road.*	El carro se salió del camino.
7. *to go out (socially):*	*Who are you going out with?*	¿Con quién vas a salir?
8. *to come out (=rise):*	*The sun rises at six tomorrow.*	El sol sale a las seis mañana.
9. *to come out (=be issued):*	*When is your book coming out?*	¿Cuándo sale tu libro?
10. *to appear (on TV):*	*We appeared on television.*	Salimos por televisión.

Extended US usage

11. *to leave (=go away):*	*They left yesterday.*	**Salieron** ayer.
	Standard variants →	**Se fueron / Se marcharon** ayer.
12. *to leave (=quit):*	*I had to leave my job.*	Tuve que **salirme** del trabajo.
	Standard variant →	Tuve que **dejar** el trabajo.
13. *to leave (=abandon):*	*He left his family and never came back.*	**Salió de** su familia y nunca regresó.
	Standard variant →	**Dejó / Abandonó a** su familia y nunca regresó.

"Leave" expressions in standard Spanish	*to leave (quit) school*	abandonar los estudios
	to leave the table	levantarse de la mesa
	to take leave (say good-bye)	despedirse

SALVAR (verb) = **to save: rescue**
= **to save: preserve, conserve [US]**
= **to save: keep, put aside [US]**
= **to save: not spend, not waste [US]**
= **to save: stop (in sports) [US]**
= **to save files (on computer) [US]**

• Whereas **salvar** primarily means "to rescue" in standard Spanish, its many uses in the United States stem from the multiple meanings of the English verb "to save."

Standard usage

1. *to save (=rescue):*	*This doctor saved my life.*	Este médico me salvó la vida.

Extended US usage

2. *to save (=conserve):*	*We must save energy.*	Hay que **salvar** energía.
	Standard variant →	Hay que **conservar** energía.
3. *to save (=keep, put aside):*	*Can you save it for me?*	¿Me lo puedes **salvar**?
	Standard variant →	¿Me lo puedes **guardar**?
4. *to save (=not spend):*	*We have saved $1000.*	Hemos **salvado** mil dólares.
	Standard variant →	Hemos **ahorrado** mil dólares.
5. *to save (=not waste):*	*You'll save a half hour if you go by bus.*	Te **salvas** media hora si vas en autobús.
	Standard variant →	Te **ahorras** media hora si vas en autobús.
6. *to save (=stop) in sports:*	*The goalie saved three shots.*	El portero **salvó** tres disparos.
	Standard variants →	El portero **paró** tres disparos. El portero **hizo** tres **paradas**.
7. *to save information (on a computer):*	*Did you save the document?*	¿**Salvaste** el documento?
	Standard variant →	¿**Archivaste** el documento?

SANGÍVIN / SANGUÍVIN (masc noun)   see **THANKSGIVING**

SANITACIÓN (fem noun)   =   **loanword for "sanitation" [US]**

• Non-existent in standard usage, **sanitación** is a creation of U.S. Spanish.

US usage

1. *sanitation (=hygiene):*	*We need to solve the sanitation problems.*	Tenemos que resolver los problemas de **sanitación**.
	Standard variant →	Tenemos que resolver los problemas de **higiene**.
2. *sanitation (=garbage collection, sewer service):*	*department of sanitation*	departamento de **sanitación**
	Standard variants →	departamento de **limpieza** / **de recogida de basuras** / servicio de **saneamiento**
	sanitation worker	**obrero de sanitación**
	Standard variant →	**basurero**

SANO (adj)
= **healthy, wholesome**
= **whole, intact**
= **sound, sensible**
= **sane [US]**

- Academic Spanish considers **sano** a false cognate of "sane," given that **sano** does not ordinarily apply to a person's "mental state," as does "sane" in English.
- U.S. Spanish makes less of a distinction.

Standard usage		
1. healthy, beneficial:	*A dry climate is healthier than a humid climate.*	Un clima seco es más sano que un clima húmedo.
2. hearty, wholesome:	*These natural products are very wholesome.*	Estos productos naturales son muy sanos.
3. intact, strong (w. estar):	*This rope is not very strong.*	Esta cuerda no está muy sana.
4. sound, sensible:	*It sounds like a very sound idea.*	Me parece una idea muy sana.

Extended US usage		
5. sane (person):	*It's hard to know who is crazy and who is sane.*	Es difícil saber quién es loco y quién es **sano**.
	Standard variant →	Es difícil saber quién es loco y quién es **cuerdo**.
6. sane (behavior, judgment, decision):	*As unstable as he might be, what he did was very sane.*	Por inestable que fuera, lo que hizo era muy **sano**.
	Standard variants →	... lo que hizo era muy **normal** / muy **sensato**.

SCOOTER (masc noun)   see **ESCÚTER**

SEDÁN (masc noun)   = **loanword for "sedan"** [DRAE 2001]

- Commonly employed in the U.S., **sedán** is now part of the standard Spanish lexicon.

   sedán. (Del inglés *sedan*). 1. m. Automóvil de turismo con cubierta fija. [DRAE]

Standard/US usage		
1. sedan:	*He was driving a blue four-door sedan.*	Manejaba un **sedán** azul de cuatro puertas.

SELECTAR (verb) = **adapted from "to select" [US]**

• Non-existent in standard Spanish, selectar is a U.S. Spanish variant of seleccionar.

US usage		
1. *to select (a person):*	*We are going to select two candidates as finalists.*	Vamos a selectar a dos solicitantes como finalistas.
	Standard variant →	Vamos a seleccionar a dos solicitantes como finalistas.
2. *to select (an item):*	*Which shoes will you select?*	¿Qué zapatos vas a selectar?
	Standard variant →	¿Qué zapatos vas a escoger?

SELF-SERVICE (masc noun) = **loanword for "self-service"** [DRAE 2001]

• Used widely throughout the Spanish-speaking world along with its more traditional variant, autoservicio, this borrowed term was recently authorized by the RAE.

Standard/US usage		
1. *self-service (noun):*	*We went to the self-service (restaurant) to have lunch.*	Fuimos al self-service a almorzar.
2. *self-service (adj):*	*This is a self-service gas station.*	Esta gasolinera es de self-service.
	Traditional variant →	Esta gasolinera es de autoservicio.

SENSIBLE (adj) = **sensitive**
= **sensible [US]**

• Often used to express "sensible" in the United States, sensible denotes "sensitive" in standard usage, and is therefore considered a false cognate.
• Traditional options for the English adjective "sensible," meaning "making or having good sense," are sensato, razonable, lógico.

Standard usage		
1. *sensitive (emotionally):*	*My daughter is more sensitive than I am.*	Mi hija es más sensible que yo.
2. *sensitive (physically):*	*I have very sensitive skin.*	Tengo la piel muy sensible.

Extended US usage		
3. *sensible (person):*	*Your father seems like a very sensible man.*	Tu padre parece ser un hombre muy sensible.
	Standard variants →	Tu padre parece ser un hombre muy sensato / juicioso / prudente.

4. *sensible (idea, decision, etc.):*	*That's a very sensible idea.*	Es una idea muy **sensible**.
	Standard variants →	Es una idea muy **sensata** / **lógica** / **razonable**.
5. *sensible (clothing, shoes):*	*He advised us to wear sensible clothing.*	Nos aconsejó llevar ropa **sensible**.
	Standard variant →	Nos aconsejó llevar ropa **práctica**.

SENSITIVO (adj) = **related to the senses**
= **sentient, capable of feeling**
= **sensitive: emotionally affected [US]**
= **sensitive: susceptible, touchy [US]**
= **sensitive: delicate, difficult [US]**
= **sensitive: secret, confidential [US]**
= **sensitive: sore, painful [US]**

• The widespread use of **sensitivo** in U.S. Spanish reflects the many connotations of "sensitive" in English. In standard Spanish, however, they are considered false cognates.

Extended US usage

1. *sensitive (=emotionally affected, responsive):*	*We are very sensitive to the tragedies of war.*	Somos muy **sensitivos** a las tragedias de la guerra.
	Standard variant →	Somos muy **sensibles** a las tragedias de la guerra.
2. *sensitive (=easily hurt, susceptible, touchy):*	*Are you sensitive to criticism?*	¿Eres **sensitivo** a las críticas?
	Standard variants →	¿Eres **susceptible** a / **te preocupan** las críticas?
3. *sensitive (=delicate, difficult to handle):*	*This is a very sensitive issue.* *Silk is a sensitive material.*	Es un asunto muy **sensitivo**. La seda es una tela **sensitiva**.
	Standard variants →	Es un asunto muy **delicado**. La seda es una tela **delicada**.
4. *sensitive (=confidential):*	*sensitive information*	información **sensitiva**
	Standard variant →	información **confidencial**
5. *sensitive (=sore, painful):*	*I'm looking for a toothpaste for sensitive teeth.*	Busco una pasta para dientes **sensitivos**.
	Standard variants →	Busco una pasta para dientes **sensibles** / **delicados**.

SENTENCIA (fem noun)
= **sentence: punishment, judgment**
= **maxim, saying**
= **sentence: group of words [US]**

• In academic Spanish, sentencia can refer to a "jail sentence" or to a "short philosophical statement" but not to a "grammatical sentence."

Standard usage		
1. sentence (punishment):	*The accused received a ten-year prison sentence.*	El acusado recibió una sentencia de diez años de cárcel.
2. maxim, saying:	*I read the sayings of Voltaire.*	Leí las sentencias de Voltaire.

Extended US usage		
3. sentence (=group of words, phrase):	*How many sentences did you manage to write?*	¿Cuántas sentencias llegaste a escribir?
	Standard variants →	¿Cuántas oraciones / frases llegaste a escribir?

"Sentence" expressions in standard Spanish	*death sentence*	pena de muerte
	life sentence	condena a cadena perpetua
	to serve a sentence	cumplir una condena

SERIAMENTE (adv)
= **seriously: solemnly, grimly**
= **seriously: in earnest [US]**
= **seriously: gravely, critically [US]**

SERIO (adj)
= **reliable, dedicated, professional, honest**
= **serious: solemn, grim**
= **serious: grave, critical, dangerous [US]**

• In standard Spanish, serio describes primarily a personality trait associated with reliability, dedication, honesty, professionalism, etc.
• Only secondarily does serio mean "solemn" or "grim."
• U.S. Spanish uses it to express "serious/seriously" in reference to an injury or illness.

Standard usage		
1. reliable, professional:	*It's a pleasure to work with reliable people.*	Es un placer trabajar con gente seria.
2. serious (=solemn, grim):	*You look very serious today. Is there anything wrong?*	Estás muy serio hoy. ¿Te pasa algo?
3. seriously (=solemnly):	*He spoke very seriously about his mother's death.*	Habló muy seriamente de la muerte de su madre.

Extended US usage

4. seriously (=in earnest):	*I don't take it seriously.*	Yo no lo tomo **seriamente**.
	Standard variant →	Yo no lo tomo **en serio**.
5. serious (=grave, critical, dangerous):	*The hostage situation is getting serious.*	La situación de los rehenes se está poniendo **seria**.
	Standard variant →	... se está poniendo **grave**.
6. seriously (=gravely):	*The driver is seriously hurt.*	El conductor está **seriamente** herido.
	Standard variant →	... está **gravemente** herido.
7. be serious (=be sincere, mean what one says):	*I was serious when I said I was leaving.*	Yo **estaba serio** cuando dije que me iba.
	Standard variant →	Yo **hablaba en serio** cuando dije que me iba.

SET (masc noun) = **loanword for "set"** [DRAE 1985]

> **set**. (Del inglés set). 1. m. Conjunto de elementos que comparten una propiedad o tienen un fin común. 2. m. En el tenis y otros deportes, parte o manga de un partido, con tanteo independiente. 3. m. Plató cinematográfico o televisivo. [DRAE]

• Most applications of **set** in U.S. Spanish are already sanctioned by the RAE.
• One of the few exceptions is "television set."
• Traditional alternatives include **juego**, **serie**, **equipo**, **conjunto**, **colección**.

Standard usage

1. set (=matching series):	*a new set of dishes*	un nuevo set de platos
	Traditional variant →	un nuevo **juego** de platos
2. set (=bundle, series):	*three sets of photocopies*	tres sets de fotocopias
	Traditional variant →	tres **series** de fotocopias
3. set (=stage, setting):	*They will build the set in one day.*	Van a montar el set en un día.
	Traditional variants →	Van a montar el **escenario** / el **plató** en un día.
4. set (in tennis):	*Who won the first set?*	¿Quién ganó el primer set?

Extended US usage

5. set (electrical):	*I bought a television set.*	Compré un set de televisión.
	Standard variants →	Compré un **aparato** de televisión / un **televisor**.

SEXY (adj & noun) = **loanword for "sexy"** [DRAE 1985]

• **Sexy** is approved in standard Spanish as an adjective and as a noun for "sex appeal."

Standard/US usage		
1. sexy (adj):	*You look very sexy in that dress.*	Te ves muy **sexy** en ese vestido.
2. sex appeal:	*He's a good actor but he lacks sex appeal.*	Es buen actor pero carece de **sexy**.

SHOCK (masc noun)   see **CHOQUE**

SHOPPING (masc noun) = **loanword for "shopping"** [US]

• Not approved in standard Spanish, this term is used with certain verbs in the United States to stress the recreational aspect of "shopping," along with the traditional **ir de compras**, which emphasizes "necessity" rather than "diversion."

US usage		
1. shopping:	*Let's leave the shopping for tomorrow.*	Dejemos el **shopping** para mañana.
	Standard variant →	Dejemos las **compras** para …
2. to go shopping:	*I love to go shopping in small stores.*	Me encanta **ir de shopping** en tiendas pequeñas.
	Standard variant →	Me encanta **ir de compras** …
3. shopping center:	*We spent five hours in the shopping center.*	Estuvimos cinco horas en el **shopping center**.
	Standard variant →	Estuvimos cinco horas en el **centro comercial**.

SHORT (masc noun) = **loanword for "shorts"** (short pants) [DRAE 1985]

• In standard Spanish, **short** is singular and primarily refers to "gym" or "team shorts."
• In U.S. Spanish, it tends to be plural and can indicate any kind of "short pants."

Standard usage		
1. shorts (sports):	*The Lakers are in yellow shorts.*	Los Lakers llevan short amarillo.
Extended US usage		
2. shorts (in general):	*During the day, you'll be more comfortable in shorts.*	Durante el día, estarás más cómodo en **shorts**.
	Standard variant →	… estarás más cómodo en **pantalones cortos**.

SHOW (masc noun) = **loanword for "show"** [DRAE 1985]

show. (Voz inglesa). 1. m. Espectáculo de variedades. 2. m. Acción o cosa realizada por motivo de exhibición. [DRAE]

- **Show** entered Spanish usage in the 1960s to refer to a certain type of "variety show." Since then, it has also taken on the meaning of "exposition" or "exhibition."
- Molner adds a more figurative meaning: "suceso extravagante que llama la atención."
- In the United States, it generally refers to a television or radio show.

Standard usage

1. *show (=spectacle):*	*We saw a spectacular show in Las Vegas.*	Vimos un show espectacular en Las Vegas.
	Traditional variant →	Vimos un gran espéctaculo...
2. *show (=exhibition):*	*Where does the automobile show take place this year?*	¿Dónde se da el show de automóviles este año?
	Traditional variants →	¿Dónde se da la exhibición / la exposición de autos ...?
3. *show, fuss (fig.):*	*The boy made a fuss and got what he wanted.*	El niño montó un show y consiguió lo que quería.
	Traditional variant →	El niño armó un lío y consiguió lo que quería.

Extended US usage

4. *show (TV, radio):*	*What is your favorite show?*	¿Cuál es tu **show** favorito?
	Standard variant →	¿Cuál es tu **programa** favorito?

SIGNATURA (fem noun) = **catalog number, press mark**
  = **person's signature [US]**

- **Signatura** does not traditionally refer to a "person's signature," but rather to a set of letters or numbers used to identify a book or document.
- In U.S. Spanish, it is used in place of **firma** to mean "signature," a viable option according to the Vox Dictionary ("acción de firmar un documento...importante").

Standard usage

1. *catalog number, item number, press mark:*	*The catalog number is PE-642.*	La signatura es PE-642.

Extended US usage

2. *person's signature:*	*Write your signature on the last line.*	Pon tu **signatura** en la última línea.
	Standard variant →	Pon tu **firma** en la última línea.

SIGNIFICANTE (adj & noun) = **significant**
= **signifier (ling)**
= **significant other: companion [US]**

- In both standard and U.S. Spanish, **significante** can be an adjective or a noun.
- It is more prevalent in the United States to refer to a "significant person."

Standard usage		
1. *significant (adj):*	*It has a significant value.*	Tiene un valor significante.
2. *signifier (linguistics):*	*A signifier is a set of phonemes with a particular meaning.*	Un significante es un conjunto de fonemas con significado.

Extended US usage		
3. *companion, spouse:*	*Don't forget to invite your significant other.*	No te olvides de invitar a tu **significante**.
	Standard variants →	No te olvides de invitar a tu **pareja** / **esposo** / **esposa**.

SIMILARIDAD (fem noun) = **loanword for "similarity" [US]**

- **Similaridad**, inappropriate in standard Spanish, is cited in Vox as an Americanism.
- Widely used in the U.S. along with traditional variants such as **semejanza** and **parecido**.

US usage		
1. *similarity (=resemblance):*	*There is no similarity between your situation and mine.*	No hay **similaridad** entre tu situación y la mía.
	Standard variants →	No hay **semejanza** / **parecido** entre tu situación y la mía.
2. *similarity (=common trait):*	*Those two paintings have many similarities.*	Aquellos dos cuadros tienen muchas **similaridades**.
	Standard variant →	Aquellos dos cuadros tienen muchos **rasgos comunes**.

SIMPATÍA (fem noun) = **liking, affection**
= **friendliness, friendly nature**
= **sympathy [US]**

- Despite their common origin, **simpatía** and "sympathy" are considered false cognates in standard Spanish. U.S. Spanish consolidates traditional definitions with English usage.

Standard usage		
1. *liking, affection:*	*I don't like him at all.*	No le tengo simpatía ninguna.
2. *friendly nature:*	*Her friendly nature has earned her many friends.*	Su simpatía le ha ganado muchas amistades.

Extended US usage

3. *sympathy (=compassion):*	*I feel great sympathy for our soldiers.*	Siento mucha **simpatía** por nuestros soldados.
	Standard variant →	Siento mucha **compasión** ...
4. *sympathy (=condolence):*	*We wanted to express our sympathies.*	Queríamos expresar nuestras **simpatías**.
	Standard variant →	Queríamos **dar el pésame**.
5. *sympathy (=agreement):*	*He needs a sympathy vote.*	Necesita un voto de **simpatía**.
	Standard variant →	... un voto de **solidaridad**.

SIMPLE (adj) = **simple: basic, elementary, easy**
= **simple-minded, foolish**
= **simple: mere, only**
= **simple: unpretentious, down to earth [US]**
= **simple: natural, plain, uncomplicated [US]**

Standard usage

1. *simple (=basic, easy):*	*The solution to this problem could not be simpler.*	La solución a este problema no podría ser más simple.
2. *simple-minded, foolish:*	*He is so simple-minded that he believes everything he hears.*	Es tan simple que todo lo que oye se lo cree.
3. *simple (=mere, only):*	*You can settle the matter with a simple apology.*	Puedes resolver el asunto con una simple disculpa.

Extended US usage

4. *simple (=unpretentious, down to earth):*	*My wife is a very simple person.*	Mi esposa es una persona muy **simple**.
	Standard variant →	Mi esposa es una persona muy **sencilla**.
5. *simple (=natural, plain, uncomplicated):*	*We live a simple life.*	Llevamos una vida **simple**.
	Standard variant →	Llevamos una vida **sencilla**.

SLOGAN (masc noun)   see **ESLOGAN**

SMOG (masc noun)   see **ESMOG**

SNACK (masc noun) = **loanword for "snack" [US]**

- The American concept of "snack" is not accurately conveyed with the traditional Spanish **merienda**. Hence, the popularity of **snack** or **esnac** in U.S. Spanish.
- Listed in the Vox Dictionary, this loanword is not sanctioned by the RAE.

US usage		
1. *snack:*	*When you give up snacks, you'll start to lose weight.*	Cuando dejes **los snacks**, empezarás a adelgazar.
	Standard variants →	Cuando dejes **la merienda** ... Cuando dejes **de picar** ...
2. *snack bar:*	*I went to the snack bar to have a sandwich.*	Fui al **snack** a comerme un sándwich.
	Standard variant →	Fui a la **cafetería** a comerme un sándwich.

SNÍQUERS (masc noun) = **adapted from "sneakers" [US]**

- Not listed in any major dictionary, **sníquers** (also spelled **sníkers**) seems to be gaining ground in U.S. Spanish over the traditional **zapatos de tenis**.

US usage		
1. *sneakers:*	*These sneakers are extremely comfortable.*	Estos **sníquers** son muy cómodos.
	Standard variants →	Estos **zapatos de tenis** / **de lona** son muy cómodos.

SNOB (adj & noun)   see **ESNOB**

SODA (fem noun) = **soda: chemicals containing sodium**
= **seltzer, club soda, carbonated water**
= **soda: soft drink [US]**

- None of the standard listings of **soda** define it as "flavored soft drink," despite its widespread use as such in the United States and parts of Latin America.

Standard usage		
1. *soda (chemical):*	*Sodium bicarbonate is sometimes called "soda."*	Al bicarbonato a veces se le dice "soda."
2. *seltzer, club soda:*	*Whisky with club soda, please.*	Un whisky con soda, por favor.

Extended US usage

3. *soda (=soft drink):*	*Would you like a soda with your sandwich?*	¿Te gustaría una **soda** con el sándwich?
	Standard variants →	¿Te gustaría una **gaseosa** / un **refresco** ...?

SOFTWARE (masc noun) = **loanword for "software"** [DRAE 2001]

software. (Voz inglesa). 1. m. Conjunto de programas, instrucciones y reglas informáticas para ejecutar ciertas tareas en una computadora. [DRAE]

• **Software** (pronounced as in English) is now fully integrated into standard Spanish.

Standard/US usage

1. *software program:*	*I have a software program for learning French.*	Tengo **software** para aprender francés.
	Standard variant →	Tengo **un programa** para aprender francés.
2. *software (=application, programming):*	*The problem is with the software, not the hardware.*	El problema proviene del **software**, no del hardware.
	Standard variant →	El problema proviene de la **programación** ...

SOLICITAR (verb)
= **to apply for a job, etc.**
= **to solicit: request, ask for**
= **to solicit: implore, beg for [US]**
= **to solicit: approach, proposition [US]**

• Traditionally, **solicitar** means "to ask" or "to apply," and rarely translates as "to solicit."

Standard usage

1. *to apply (for a job, etc.):*	*I applied for a job I saw advertised in the newspaper.*	Solicité un puesto que vi anunciado en el periódico.
2. *to solicit (=request):*	*We solicited funds to pay for the project.*	Solicitamos fondos para pagar el proyecto.

Extended US usage

3. *to solicit (=beg for):*	*They solicited everyone's help.*	**Solicitaron** ayuda de todos.
	Standard variant →	**Pidieron** ayuda a todos.
4. *to solicit (=approach, proposition):*	*I was solicited by a prostitute.*	Una prostituta me **solicitó**.
	Standard variant →	Una prostituta me **abordó**.

SOPORTAR (verb)

= **to support physically, hold up, withstand**
= **to bear, stand, endure, put up with**
= **to support financially [US]**
= **to support emotionally [US]**
= **to support: approve [US]**

• In standard usage, soportar implies physical rather than financial or emotional support.

Standard usage		
1. *to support (physically):*	*The shelf will not support the weight of the books.*	El estante no va a soportar el peso de los libros.
2. *to bear, stand, endure:*	*I put up with his complaints my entire life.*	He soportado sus quejas toda mi vida.
	I cannot stand this heat.	No soporto este calor.

Extended US usage		
3. *to support (financially):*	*One cannot support a family on this salary.*	No se puede soportar a una familia con este sueldo.
	Standard variants →	No se puede mantener / sostener a una familia …
	How do you support yourself?	¿Cómo te soportas?
	Standard variant →	¿Cómo te ganas la vida?
4. *to support (emotionally, ideologically):*	*Will you support your colleagues?*	¿Soportarás a tus colegas?
	Standard variant →	¿Apoyarás a tus colegas?
5. *to support (=approve):*	*I support his point of view.*	Soporto su punto de vista.
	Standard variant →	Apoyo su punto de vista.

SORORIDAD (fem noun) = **loanword for "sorority" [US]**

• Sororidad does not exist in standard Spanish, nor is there a precise translation for "college sorority." U.S. Spanish simply borrows the term from English.

US usage		
1. *sorority:*	*My daughter joined a college sorority.*	Mi hija se hizo socia de una sororidad universitaria.
	Standard variant →	Mi hija se hizo socia de una hermandad de mujeres.

SORTEAR (verb) = **to draw lots, raffle**
= **to toss, flip (a coin)**
= **to dodge, avoid skillfully**
= **to sort [US]**

- Sortear is related to **suerte** ("luck") in standard Spanish and, therefore, has no true connection to the English verb "to sort," from which **sortear** is derived in U.S. Spanish.

Standard usage		
1. to draw lots, raffle:	*The big prize will be drawn tonight.*	El premio gordo se sortea esta noche.
2. to toss, flip (a coin):	*Let's flip the coin to see who goes first.*	Vamos a sortear la moneda a ver quien va primero.
3. to dodge, avoid:	*The bullfighter dodged the bull numerous times.*	El torero sorteó al toro una cantidad de veces.

Extended US usage		
4. to sort (=classify):	*The books need to be sorted according to author.*	Hay que **sortear** los libros según el nombre del autor.
	Standard variant →	Hay que **clasificar** los libros ...
5. to sort (=arrange):	*This machine makes copies and then sorts them.*	Esta máquina saca copias y luego las **sortea**.
	Standard variant →	... y luego las **ordena**.
6. to sort (=separate):	*I asked her to sort the magazines from the newspapers.*	Le mandé **sortear** las revistas de los periódicos.
	Standard variant →	Le mandé **separar** las revistas de los periódicos.

SPANGLISH (masc noun)   see **ESPÁNGLISH**

SPEECH (masc noun)   =   **loanword for "speech"** [DRAE 2001]

- Recently sanctioned, **speech** (pronounced as in English) refers to a short address in U.S. Spanish, but without the pejorative connotation it tends to have in standard usage.

Standard usage		
1. speech (=brief, superficial address):	*He gave a speech completely lacking in sincerity.*	Hizo un speech totalmente falto de sinceridad.

Extended US usage		
2. *speech (=brief address):*	*The president gave a five-minute speech.*	El presidente hizo un **speech** de cinco minutos.
	Standard variant →	El presidente hizo un **pequeño discurso** de cinco minutos.

SPÓNSOR (masc noun)   see **"ESPÓNSOR"**

SPORT (masc noun)   =   **loanword for "sport"** [DRAE 1927]

(DE) SPORT (adj)   =   **loanword for "casual"** [DRAE 1985]

- Nowadays, **sport** is used primarily to characterize clothing ("casual, informal").
- U.S. Spanish also equates it with "sporty" in reference to items other than clothing.

Standard usage		
1. *casual, informal:*	*casual clothing*	ropa de sport
	to dress casually	vestir de sport
2. *sporty (clothing):*	*sports jacket*	chaqueta (de) sport
	sports shirt	camisa (de) sport

Extended US usage		
3. *sports, sporty:*	*She bought a sports car.*	Compró un carro **sport**.
	Standard variant →	Compró un carro **deportivo**.

SPRAY (masc noun)   see **ESPREY**

STAFF (masc noun)   =   **loanword for "staff"** [US]

staff. (Inglés). m. Equipo directivo de una empresa u organismo. [Moliner]

- Cited by Moliner, **staff** is not an entry in most standard Spanish dictionaries.

US usage		
1. *staff (=personnel):*	*the department staff*	el **staff** del departamento
	Standard variants →	el **personal** / los **empleados** del departamento
2. *staff (=teachers):*	*the teaching staff*	el **staff** de profesores
	Standard variants →	el **profesorado** / los **maestros**
3. *staff (military):*	*the military staff*	el **staff** militar
	Standard variant →	el **estado mayor**

"Staff" expressions in standard Spanish	staff association	asociación de personal
	staff meeting	reunión de personal
	staff training	formación de personal

STANDARD   see ESTÁNDAR

STARTER   see ESTÁRTER

STATUS   see ESTÁTUS

STEAM (masc noun)   =   **loanword for "steam (heat)" [US]**

• Nonexistent in standard usage, steam refers to the heating system of certain urban apartment buildings in the U.S. In most other situations, "steam" is translated as **vapor**.

US usage		
1. *steam heat:*	*It's going to be cold if they don't turn on the steam.*	Va a hacer frío si no ponen el **steam**.
	Standard variant →	Va a hacer frío si no ponen la **calefacción**.

STOCK (masc noun)   =   **loanword for "stock"** [DRAE 1985]

> **stock**. (Inglés). m. Cantidad de mercancías que se tienen en depósito. [Moliner]

• In standard practice, **stock** implies "inventory" or "supply."
• In U.S. Spanish, it may also refer to "security shares."

Standard usage		
1. *stock (=supply, inventory):*	*We don't have it in stock.*	No lo tenemos en stock.
	Traditional variant →	No lo tenemos en existencia.

Extended US usage		
2. *stock (=securities):*	*I invested $10,000 in stocks.*	Invertí diez mil dólares en **stocks**.
	Standard variant →	Invertí diez mil dólares en **acciones**.

"Stock" expressions in standard Spanish	a large stock (selection)	un amplio surtido
	the stock market	la bolsa / el mercado bursátil
	to be out of stock	estar agotado
	to keep a stock of	abastecerse de
	to take stock	hacer el inventario
	to take stock (fig)	evaluar la situación

STOP (masc noun) = **loanword for "stop" [US]**

• First listed in the DRAE in 1985, then removed in 1992, the noun **stop** appears in most current dictionaries (incl. Moliner and Vox). It occurs in the U.S. in a variety of contexts.

US usage		
1. stop sign:	When you get to the stop sign, you need to turn right.	Al llegar al **stop**, tienes que doblar a la derecha.
	Standard variant →	Al llegar al **señal de alto**, ...
2. stop (=station, terminal):	I get off at the first stop.	Yo me bajo en el primer **stop**.
	Standard variant →	... en la primera **parada**.
3. stop, stopover (air travel):	This flight makes a stop in Paris.	Este vuelo hace **stop** en Paris.
	Standard variant →	Este vuelo hace **escala** ...
4. stop button:	Did you press "stop?"	¿Le diste al **stop**?
	Standard variants →	¿Le diste al **botón de paro** / **botón de apagado**?

STRIPPER (masc & fem noun) = **loanword for "stripper" [US]**

STRIPTEASE (masc noun) = **loanword for "striptease"** [DRAE 2001]

• **Striptease** is now officially recognized as standard Spanish, but **stripper** is <u>not</u>.
• Both are common in U.S. Spanish.

Standard usage		
1. striptease:	We saw a striptease show in Las Vegas.	Vimos un espectáculo de striptease en La Vegas.
2. strip club:	You must be 18 years of age to enter a strip club.	Hay que tener 18 años para entrar en un striptease.

Extended US usage		
3. stripper:	She worked as a stripper in a New York club.	Trabajó de **stripper** en un club de Nueva York.
	Standard variant →	Trabajó de **persona que hace striptease** en un club ...

STROKE (masc noun)   see ESTROC

SUCEDER (verb)

=	**to happen, occur**
=	**to succeed: follow**
=	**to succeed in life, career, etc. [US]**
=	**to succeed: be able to [US]**
=	**to succeed: yield desired result [US]**

• Considered a false cognate of "to succeed" in standard academic Spanish, **suceder** traditionally means "to happen" or "to occur."

Standard usage

1. *to happen, occur:*	*What happened at the meeting?*	¿Qué sucedió en la reunión?
2. *to succeed (=follow):*	*Who will succeed you as department head?*	¿Quién te va a suceder como jefe de departamento?

Extended US usage

3. *to succeed (in life, career, studies):*	*This young man is going to succeed in life.*	Este joven va a **suceder** en la vida.
	Standard variants →	Este joven va a **tener éxito** / **triunfar** en la vida.
4. *to succeed (=be able to):*	*He tried to break the record but didn't succeed.*	Intentó batir el récord pero no **sucedió**.
	Standard variants →	Intentó batir el récord pero no **lo logró** / no **lo consiguió**.
5. *to succeed (=work, yield desired result):*	*The experiment did not succeed.*	El experimento no **sucedió**.
	Standard variants →	El experimento no **salió bien** / no **dio resultado**.

SUCESO (masc noun)

=	**event, occurrence**
=	**incident, accident**
=	**success [US]**

• As in the case of its corresponding verb, **suceder**, this traditional false cognate of "success" has the tendency to become a true cognate in U.S. usage.

Standard usage

1. *event, occurrence:*	*The demonstration was an unexpected event.*	La manifestación fue un suceso inesperado.
2. *incident, accident:*	*This morning's incident has made me very nervous.*	El suceso de esta mañana me tiene muy nervioso.

Extended US usage		
3. success:	*My brother has had great success as a dancer.*	Mi hermano ha tenido gran **suceso** como bailarín.
	Standard variant →	Mi hermano ha tenido gran **éxito** como bailarín.
	The movie was a box office success.	La película fue un **suceso** de taquilla.
	Standard variant →	La película fue un **éxito** de taquilla.

SUÉTER (masc noun) = loanword for "sweater" [DRAE 1970]

• Standard Spanish treats **suéter** as a synonym of **jersey**. U.S. Spanish makes a clearer distinction between the two: **suéter** tends to be warmer and heavier.

Standard/US usage		
1. sweater:	*I bought a sweater for the winter.*	Compré un **suéter** para el invierno.
	Traditional variants →	Compré un **jersey** / una **chompa** (Lat Am) ...

SUGESTIÓN (fem noun)
= **suggestion (psychological)**
= **suggestion: recommendation [US]**
= **suggestion: implication, insinuation [US]**
= **suggestion: indication, evidence [US]**

• "Suggestion" has at least four principal meanings in English, only one of which produces the cognate **sugestión** in standard Spanish.

Standard usage		
1. suggestion (psych):	*the power of suggestion*	el poder de la **sugestión**

Extended US usage		
2. suggestion (=recommendation):	*Do you have any suggestions?*	¿Tienes alguna **sugestión**?
	Standard variant →	¿Tienes alguna **sugerencia**?
3. suggestion (=implication, insinuation):	*The suggestion that I had lied was offensive to me.*	La **sugestión** de que yo había mentido me ofendió.
	Standard variant →	La **insinuación** de que ...
4. suggestion (=indication, evidence):	*There is no suggestion that it's going to rain this week.*	No hay **sugestión** de que vaya a llover esta semana.
	Standard variant →	No hay **indicación** / **prueba** de que vaya a llover ...

SUJETO (masc noun) = **subject of a sentence (grammar)**
= **individual, character**
= **subject: topic, theme [US]**
= **subject: matter, issue [US]**
= **academic subject [US]**
= **subject: subordinate [US]**

• The free translation of "subject" as **sujeto** makes this a widespread term in the U.S.

Standard usage		
1. *subject (in grammar):*	*What is the subject of this sentence?*	¿Cuál es el sujeto de esta oración?
2. *individual, character:*	*He is a rather strange individual.*	Es un sujeto algo extraño.

Extended US usage		
3. *subject (=topic, theme):*	*What is the subject of your presentation?*	¿Cuál es el **sujeto** de tu presentación?
	Standard variant →	¿Cuál es el **tema** de tu presentación?
4. *subject (=matter, issue):*	*This is a subject (matter) I cannot discuss.*	Es un **sujeto** que no puedo discutir.
	Standard variant →	Es un **asunto** que no puedo discutir.
5. *academic subject:*	*Biology is my favorite subject.*	La biología es mi **sujeto** preferido.
	Standard variants →	La biología es mi **asignatura** / **materia** preferida.
6. *subject (=subordinate):*	*The queen addressed her loyal subjects.*	La reina se dirigió a sus fieles **sujetos**.
	Standard variant →	... a sus fieles **súbditos**.

SUMARIO (masc noun) = **indictment, legal proceeding**
= **summary: contents, index**
= **summary: synopsis, brief description [US]**

SUMARIZAR (verb) = **loanword for "to summarize" [US]**

• **Sumario** is acceptable for "summary" in standard Spanish but not in the usual context of "brief outline" or "synopsis." The verb form **sumarizar** occurs only in U.S. Spanish.

Standard usage

1. *indictment:*	*The indictment of the suspect took place this morning.*	El sumario del acusado tuvo lugar esta mañana.
2. *summary (=index):*	*You'll find the article listed in the index.*	Encontrarás el artículo en el sumario.

Extended US usage

3. *summary (=synopsis, brief description):*	*We have to prepare a summary of what we read.*	Tenemos que preparar un **sumario** de lo que leímos.
	Standard variant →	Tenemos que preparar un **resumen** de lo que leímos.
4. *to summarize:*	*Could you summarize what he told you?*	¿Podrías **sumarizar** lo que te dijo?
	Standard variant →	¿Podrías **resumir** lo que te dijo?

SÚPER (masc noun) = **abbreviation for "supermarket"** [DRAE 2001]
= **building superintendent [US]**

SUPERMÁN (masc noun) = **loanword for "unusually strong man" [US]**

SUPERMUJER (fem noun) = **loan translation for "superwoman" [US]**

- **Super** is quite prevalent in standard and U.S. Spanish as an adjective (**gasolina súper**) and as a prefix (**supervisor**, **superdotado**, **superelegante**, etc.).
- In the United States, **súper** refers primarily to a "building superintendent" or "manager."
- **Superhombre**, the hispanicized form of **supermán**, is cited in all major dictionaries whereas **supermujer** is not.

Standard usage

1. *supermarket:*	*I'm going to the supermarket to buy milk and eggs.*	Voy al súper a comprar leche y huevos.

Extended US usage

2. *building superintendent:*	*Tell the super that there is no hot water.*	Dile al **súper** que no hay agua caliente.
	Standard variant →	Dile al **conserje** que no hay ...
3. *superman (=unusually strong / powerful):*	*The guy is a superman: he carried the furniture to the eighth floor.*	El tipo es un **supermán**: cargó los muebles al octavo piso.
	Standard variant →	El tipo es un **superhombre** ...
4. *superwoman (=able to handle many duties):*	*My mom is a superwoman: she has six kids and a career.*	Mi mamá es una **supermujer**: tiene seis hijos y una carrera.
	Standard variants →	Mi mamá es una **mujer** muy **capaz** / muy **especial** ...

SUPLIR (verb)
- = **to replace, substitute**
- = **to compensate, make up for**
- = **to supply: provide [US]**
- = **to supply: feed, carry [US]**

• **Suplir** does not usually translate as "to supply" in standard usage.

Standard usage

1. *to replace, substitute:*	*We are going to replace butter with margarine.*	Vamos a suplir mantequilla con margarina.
2. *to compensate for, make up for:*	*It is not easy to make up for two years of unemployment.*	No es fácil suplir dos años de desempleo.

Extended US usage

3. *to supply (=provide):*	*The Red Cross will be supplying food and medicine.*	La Cruz Roja va a **suplir** comestibles y medicina.
	Standard variants →	La Cruz Roja va a **facilitar** / **proporcionar** / **suministrar** comestibles y medicina.
4. *to supply (=carry, take):*	*The arteries supply blood to the heart.*	Las arterías **suplen** sangre al corazón.
	Standard variant →	Las arterías **llevan** sangre al corazón.

SUPUESTO (adj & noun)
- = **supposed: false, alleged**
- = **assumption**
- = **(to be) supposed to... [US]**

• **Supuesto** is used frequently in U.S. Spanish with the verb **estar** as an equivalent of the multifaceted English verbal phrase "to be supposed to."

Standard usage

1. *supposed (=false):*	*A number of patients sued the supposed doctor.*	Various pacientes demandaron al supuesto médico.
2. *supposed (=alleged):*	*The alleged crime took place in broad daylight.*	El supuesto delito tuvo lugar en pleno día.
3. *assumption (noun):*	*The assumption that it would rain discouraged us all.*	El supuesto de que iba a llover nos desanimó a todos.

Selected idioms

	assuming	supuesto que
	in the event of	supuesto que
	of course	por supuesto
	prior assumption	supuesto previo
	to take for granted	dar por supuesto

Extended US usage

4. *to be supposed to* (=be expected to):	*I'm supposed to be working on Saturdays.*	**Estoy supuesto** trabajar los sábados.
	Standard variants →	**Tengo que / Estoy obligado a** trabajar los sábados.
5. *to be supposed to* (=should, ought to):	*You are not supposed to talk that way.*	No **estás supuesto** hablar de ese modo.
	Standard variants →	No **deberías / debieras** hablar de ese modo.
6. *to be supposed to* (assumption):	*The concert is supposed to start at eight.*	El concierto **está supuesto** comenzar a las ocho.
	Standard variant →	**Se supone que** el concierto comienza a las ocho.

SWITCH (masc noun) = **loanword for "switch"** [DRAE 1985]

- **Switch** (spelled **suich** by Stavans) occurs frequently in U.S. Spanish both to refer to the electrical device and to mean "exchange."

US usage

1. *switch (electric device):*	*Where is the light switch?*	¿Dónde está el **switch** de la luz?
	Standard variant →	¿Dónde está el **interruptor** ...?
2. *switch (=exchange, substitution):*	*If it's not the class I need, I'll have to make a switch.*	Si no es la clase que necesito, tendré que hacer un **switch**.
	Standard variant →	... que hacer un **cambio**.

TAPE (masc noun) = **loanword for "tape"** [US]

- Exclusive to U.S. Spanish, **tape** (pronounced as in English) has a number of uses that reflect standard English applications, including adhesive, measuring, and recording tape.

US usage

1. *adhesive tape:*	*Please seal the envelope with tape.*	Favor de pegar el sobre con **tape**.
	Standard variant →	Favor de pegar el sobre con **cinta adhesiva**.
2. *measuring tape:*	*I need the tape to measure the desk.*	Necesito el **tape** para medir el escritorio.
	Standard variant →	Necesito la **cinta métrica** ...

| **3.** *recording tape:* | *There is a tape in the VCR.* | Hay un **tape** en el VCR. |
| | **Standard variants →** | Hay una **cinta** en el aparato de vídeo. |

"Tape" expressions in standard Spanish	*blank tape*	cinta / casete virgen
	on tape	grabado en cinta
	tape deck	tocacintas
	tape recorder	grabadora / magnetófono
	tape recording	grabación en cinta

TARDE (adv)
- **late: past a certain time**
- **(to arrive) late**
- **late: advanced [US]**
- **late: delayed [US]**
- **late: deceased [US]**
- **late in: in the final years [US]**
- **late within a time period [US]**

- In English, "late" functions as an adverb and an adjective. In standard Spanish, **tarde** can only be an adverb, and the adjective equivalents of "late" are specific to the context.

Standard usage

| **1.** *late (=past certain time):* | *It's too late to call.* | Es muy tarde para llamar. |
| **2.** *to be late, arrive late:* | *Yesterday I got home very late.* | Ayer llegué a casa muy tarde. |

Extended US usage

3. *late (=advanced):*	*It is already late in the illness.*	Ya es **tarde** en la enfermedad.
	Standard variant →	La enfermedad ya está **avanzada**.
4. *late (=delayed):*	*I am ten minutes late.*	**Estoy** diez minutos **tarde**.
	Standard variants →	**Me tardo** diez minutos / **Llevo** diez minutos **de retraso**.
5. *late (=deceased):*	*the late president Kennedy*	el **tarde** presidente Kennedy
	Standard variant →	el **difunto** presidente
6. *late (=in the final years):*	*She appeared in many movies late in her career.*	Salió en muchas películas **tarde en** su carrera.
	Standard variant →	Salió en muchas películas **al final de** su carrera.

7. *late (within a time period):*	*We do the evaluations late in the year.*	Hacemos las evaluaciones **tarde en el año**.
	Standard variant →	Hacemos las evaluaciones **a finales de año**.
	I found out late in the day.	Me enteré **tarde en el día**.
	Standard variant →	Me enteré **a última hora**.
	He continued to work late into the night.	Siguió trabajando **tarde en la noche**.
	Standard variant →	Siguió trabajando **bien entrada la noche**.

Expressions with "late" in standard Spanish	*as late as 1980*	aún en 1980
	in her late thirties	cerca de cuarenta años
	late / latest style	moda reciente / última moda
	sooner or later	tarde o temprano
	to sleep late	levantarse tarde
	to stay up late	acostarse tarde / trasnochar
	to work late	trabajar hasta tarde

TAX (fem noun) = **loanword for "tax" [US]**

- **Tax** and **income tax** have become an integral part of U.S. Spanish vocabulary, and seem to coexist with the more traditional **impuesto** and **tributo**.
- **Income tax** tends to be expressed in the masculine while **tax** is invariably feminine.

US usage		
1. *tax:*	*In certain states, you don't pay tax on clothing.*	En ciertos estados, no se paga **tax** sobre la ropa.
	Standard variant →	En ciertos estados, no se paga **impuesto** sobre la ropa.
2. *income tax:*	*I paid $5000 in income tax this year.*	Pagué 5.000 dólares de **income tax** este año.
	Standard variant →	Pagué 5.000 dólares de **impuesto sobre la renta** ...

Expressions with "tax" in standard Spanish	*luxury tax*	impuesto de lujo
	property tax	impuesto sobre la propiedad
	sales tax	impuesto de venta
	tax bracket	grupo impositivo
	tax collector	recaudador de impuestos
	tax cuts	reducciones en los impuestos
	tax evasion	evasión fiscal

tax exemption	exención de impuestos
tax incentive	aliciente fiscal
tax inspector	inspector de hacienda
tax rate	tasa impositiva
tax rebate	devolución de impuestos
tax return	declaración fiscal / de renta
tax year	año fiscal

TEENAGER (masc & fem noun) = **loanword for "teenager" [US]**

- Teenager (pronounced as in English) is quite common in the U.S.
- It is not sanctioned in standard Spanish.

US usage

1. teenager (=adolescent):

I was a teenager when I arrived in this country.

Yo era **un teenager** cuando llegué a este país.

Standard variant →

Yo era **adolescente** cuando …

2. teenagers (=youth):

A group of teenagers started to dance.

Una banda de **teenagers** se pusieron a bailar.

Standard variant →

Una banda de **jóvenes** …

TEMPORARIO (adj) = **loanword for "temporary" [US]**

TEMPORERO (adj) = **temporary: seasonal, migrant**

- Although **temporario** and **temporero** are both traditional terms, they are more typical of U.S. usage. Historically, **temporero** applies to a "seasonal" or "migrant" occupation.
- To express "temporary" in modern terms, standard Spanish favors variants such as **pasajero**, **provisional**, or **temporal**.

US usage

1. temporary (=with certain conditions/provisions):

First, they will give you a temporary license.

Primero te darán una licencia **temporaria / temporera**.

Standard variants →

Primero te darán una licencia **provisional / condicional**.

2. temporary (=not long-lasting):

a temporary pain

un dolor **temporario**

Standard variant →

un dolor **pasajero**

3. temporary (=seasonal):

Why don't you look for a temporary job?

¿Por qué no buscas un trabajo **temporario / temporero**?

Standard variant →

¿Por qué no buscas un trabajo **provisional**?

TEMPRANO (adj & adv)

= **early: before usual time**
= **(length of time) + early [US]**
= **early: soon within process [US]**
= **early: beginning of time period [US]**
= **early: first hours, days, weeks, etc. [US]**
= **early: first, primitive [US]**
= **early: with time to spare [US]**

- In Spanish as in English, **temprano** can be both an adverb and an adjective.
- The literal translation of "early" has created numerous uses of **temprano** in U.S. Spanish considered incorrect or inappropriate in standard Spanish.

Standard usage		
1. early [adv] (=before usual or appointed time):	I arrived to work early.	Llegué temprano al trabajo.
2. early [adj] (=before usual time):	My son began to walk at an early age.	Mi hijo empezó a andar a una edad temprana.
Extended US usage		
3. (length of time) + early:	You are early.	Estás temprano.
	Standard variant →	Llegaste temprano.
4. early (=soon, within a process):	It's much too early to have the results.	Es demasiado temprano para tener los resultados.
	Standard variant →	Es demasiado pronto para tener los resultados.
5. early (=beginning of time period):	The wedding will take place early in June.	La boda será temprano en junio.
	Standard variant →	La boda será a principios de junio.
6. early (=first hours, days, weeks, months, years, etc.):	in her early years	en sus años tempranos
	Standard variant →	en sus primeros años
	in the early afternoon	en la temprana tarde
	Standard variant →	a primera hora de la tarde
7. early (=first, primitive):	The Neolitihic is an early period.	La neolítica es una época temprana.
	Standard variant →	… una época primitiva.
8. early (=with time to spare):	You should reserve early.	Debes reservar temprano.
	Standard variants →	Debes reservar con tiempo / con anticipación.

Expressions with "early" **in standard Spanish**	*as early as possible*	lo más pronto posible
	as early as January	ya en enero
	early evening	media tarde, atardecer
	early flight	vuelo de primera hora
	early morning	a primera hora, madrugada
	early retirement	jubilación anticipada
	early riser	madrugador
	early stage / phase	etapa / fase inicial
	from an early age	desde pequeño
	have an early night	acostarse temprano
	marry early	casarse joven

TENIENTE (masc noun)
= **lieutenant, first lieutenant**
= **deputy, assistant**
= **tenant [US]**

- **Teniente** is used quite freely in U.S. Spanish to mean "tenant."
- It conforms to a subcategory of English loanwords, such as **bóiler** and **súper**, that could be classified as "urban U.S. Spanish."

Standard usage		
1. *lieutenant:*	*He was a lieutenant in the Spanish army.*	Era teniente en el ejército español.
2. *deputy, assistant:*	*deputy mayor*	teniente de alcalde

Extended US usage		
3. *tenant:*	*The tenants complained to the landlord.*	Los **tenientes** se quejaron al dueño.
	Standard variant →	Los **inquilinos** se quejaron ...

TEST (masc noun) = **loanword for "test"** [DRAE 1985]

- **Test** is a recognized term in standard academic Spanish.
- The RAE limits its use, however, to "multiple-choice test" and "psychological test."
- Moliner's definition, which encompasses all sorts of "tests," approximates U.S. Spanish.

Standard usage		
1. *multiple-choice test:*	*I never get good grades on multiple-choice tests.*	Nunca saco buena nota en los tests.
2. *psychological test:*	*The psychiatrist recommends a battery of tests.*	El siquiatra recomienda una batería de tests.

Extended US usage		
3. *test (=quiz, exam):*	*Our English teacher has given us three exams.*	La maestra de inglés nos ha dado tres **tests**.
	Standard variant →	La maestra de inglés nos ha dado tres **exámenes**.
4. *test (=trial, experiment):*	*pregnancy test* *nuclear tests*	**test** de embarazo **tests** nucleares
	Standard variants →	**prueba** de embarazo **pruebas** nucleares
5. *test (=study, analysis):*	*The doctor ordered a blood test.*	El médico mandó a pedir un **test** de sangre.
	Standard variant →	El médico mandó a pedir un **análisis** de sangre.
6. *test (=check, service):*	*eye test / hearing test*	**test** de los ojos / **test** del oído
	Standard variant →	**revisión** de la vista / del oído

"Test" expressions in standard Spanish	*comprehension test* *medical test* *test ban* *test drive* *test tube* *to put to the test*	prueba de comprensión examen médico prohibición de pruebas prueba en carretera / de rodaje tubo de ensayo someter a prueba

THANKSGIVING (masc noun) = loanword for "thanksgiving" [US]

- Despite a reasonable equivalent in standard Spanish (**acción de gracias**), this term is prevalent in the U.S., particularly in connection with the holiday of the same name.
- Stavans provides alternate transcriptions: **sanguívin, sanguibi, Sangívin**.

US usage		
1. *Thanksgiving holiday:*	*Happy Thanksgiving!*	¡Feliz Día de **Thanksgiving**!
	Standard variant →	¡Feliz Día de **Acción de Gracias**!

TIEMPO (masc noun)

= **time (general duration)**
= **time (coincidental)**
= **weather**
= **verb tense**
= **time: moment, instant [US]**
= **time: historical period [US]**
= **time: experience [US]**

	=	**time: occasion, occurrence [US]**
	=	**time of day; time of year [US]**
	=	**take time: delay [US]**

- The broad applications of the word "time" in English have had a clear impact on U.S. Spanish—to the extent that **tiempo** can replace a variety of time expressions such as **hora**, **momento**, **época**, **temporada**, etc.

Standard usage

1. *time (general):*	*It's incredible how time passes!*	¡Cómo pasa el tiempo!
	There is no time to lose.	No hay tiempo que perder.
2. *time (duration, length):*	*How long have you been here?*	¿Cuánto tiempo llevas aquí?
	I spent a lot of time in Italy.	Pasé mucho tiempo en Italia.
3. *time (coincidental):*	*You shouldn't eat and drink at the same time.*	No debieras comer y beber al mismo tiempo.
4. *weather:*	*What was the weather like in Seville?*	¿Qué tiempo hacía en Sevilla?
5. *verbal tense:*	*The present progressive is a compound tense.*	El presente progresivo es un tiempo compuesto.

Extended US usage

6. *time (=moment, instant):*	*This is the perfect time to ask questions.*	Éste es el **tiempo perfecto** de hacer preguntas.
	Standard variant →	Éste es el **momento oportuno** de hacer preguntas.
7. *time (=historical period):*	*the time of the Inquisition*	el **tiempo** de la Inquisición
	Standard variant →	la **época** de la Inquisición
8. *time (=experience):*	*Did you have a good time at the party?*	¿**Tuviste un buen tiempo** en la fiesta?
	Standard variants →	¿**Te divertiste / Lo pasaste bien** en la fiesta?
9. *time of day:*	*It's time to eat.*	Es **tiempo** de comer.
	Standard variant →	Es **hora** de comer.
10. *time of year, season:*	*It was Christmas time when we first met.*	Era **tiempo** de Navidad cuando nos conocimos.
	Standard variant →	Era **temporada** de Navidad ...
11. *to take time (=delay):*	*He took his time to answer.*	**Tomó su tiempo** en contestar.
	Standard variants →	**Tardó** en contestar.
		Se demoró en contestar.

"Time" expressions in standard Spanish		
	a long time ago	hace mucho (tiempo)
	a short time ago	hace poco (tiempo)
	ahead of time	temprano, con adelanto
	at all times	siempre, en todo momento
	at any time	en cualquier momento
	at that time (in history)	en aquella época
	for all time	para siempre
	for the time being	por ahora, de momento
	from time to time	de vez en cuando
	full-time (job)	(trabajo) de jornada completa
	it's about time	ya es hora
	part-time (job)	(trabajo) de jornada parcial
	spare time	ratos libres, horas libres
	take your time	tranquilo, con calma, sin prisa
	time after time	una vez y otra
	to be / arrive on time	ser puntual, llegar a la hora
	to have a bad time	pasarlo mal, no divertirse
	to have a good time	pasarlo bien, divertirse
	to have a hard time	tener dificultades, sufrir
	to keep up with the times	mantenerse al día
	to kill time	pasar el rato

TIPEAR (verb) = **adapted from "to type" [US]**

TIPO (masc noun) = **loanword for "typo" [US]**

- **Error tipográfico** abbreviates to **tipo** (usually pronounced "**taipo**") in U.S Spanish.
- Once listed in the DRAE (1985 & 1989), **tipear** is common in Latin America as well.
- Neither usage is currently sanctioned in standard academic Spanish.

US usage		
1. *to type:*	*I wrote the essay and now I have to type it.*	Escribí el ensayo y ahora lo tengo que **tipear**.
	Standard variant →	... y ahora lo tengo que **pasar a máquina**.
2. *typographical error:*	*I found twenty typos on the document you gave me.*	Descubrí veinte **taipos** en el documento que me diste.
	Standard variants →	Descubrí veinte **erratas** / **errores tipográficos** ...

TIQUE (masc noun) = **ticket (for transportation / event)** [DRAE 1985]
= **receipt stub, proof of purchase**
= **ticket: label, price tag** [US]
= **traffic ticket; lottery ticket** [US]

- Borrowed from English and widespread in the United States, usage of this term is approved by the RAE to express "ticket" or "receipt" in select situations.
- Alternate forms are **tíquet** (Vox) and **tiquete** (Moliner).

Standard/US usage

1. *ticket (bus or train):*   *I paid $60 for a round-trip ticket.*   Pagué 60 dólares por un **tique** de ida y vuelta.

    Traditional variants →   Pagué 60 dólares por un **boleto** / **billete** de ida y vuelta.

2. *ticket (ship or plane):*   *Don't forget your plane tickets.*   No olvides los **tiques**.

    Traditional variant →   No olvides los **pasajes**.

3. *ticket (theater, movie, concert, sports event):*   *How much did you pay for the (theatre) tickets?*   ¿Cuánto pagaste por los **tiques** (de teatro)?

    Traditional variant →   ¿Cuánto pagaste por las **entradas** (de teatro)?

4. *receipt stub:*   *Keep the receipt in case you want to return it.*   Guarda el **tique** en caso de que lo quieras devolver.

    Traditional variant →   Guarda el **recibo** ...

Extended US usage

5. *ticket (=label, price tag):*   *The price is on the ticket.*   El precio está en el **tique**.

    Standard variant →   El precio está en la **etiqueta**.

6. *lottery ticket:*   *How many lottery tickets are you going to buy?*   ¿Cuántos **tiques** de lotería vas a comprar?

    Standard variant →   ¿Cuántos **boletos** de lotería ...?

7. *traffic ticket:*   *He got a ticket because he was driving too fast.*   Le dieron un **tique** porque manejaba muy rápido.

    Standard variant →   Le dieron una **multa** porque manejaba muy rápido.

"Ticket" expressions in standard Spanish

round-trip ticket	billete / boleto de ida y vuelta
season ticket	abono; boleto de abono
ticket office	despacho de billetes; boletería
ticket window	ventanilla, taquilla

TISSUE (masc noun) = **loanword for "tissue" or "tissue paper" [US]**

- With no exact equivalent in standard Spanish, U.S. Spanish makes free use of loanwords such as **klínex** and **tissue**. Also spelled **tisú** (Vox) and **tishu** (Stavans).

US usage		
1. *tissue (=paper handkerchief):*	*I need two boxes of tissue.*	Necesito dos cajas de **tissue**.
	Standard variant →	Necesito dos cajas de **pañuelo de papel**.
2. *tissue (decorative):*	*She wrapped the gift in beautiful tissue paper.*	Envolvió el regalo en un lindo papel de **tisú**.
	Standard variant →	Envolvió el regalo en un lindo papel de **seda**.

TOCAR BASE (idiom) see **BASE**

TOILET (masc noun) = **loanword for "toilet" [US]**

- Moliner and Vox list **toilette**, of French derivation, as a Latin American variant.
- In U.S. Spanish, the prevalent forms are **toilet** (pronounced as in English) and **toile**.
- None of these terms are currently approved by the RAE.

US usage		
1. *toilet (=bathroom):*	*I need to use the toilet.*	Tengo que usar el **toilet**.
	Standard variants →	Tengo que usar el **baño** /el **servicio** / el **wáter**.
2. *toilet (fixture):*	*The toilet is backed up.*	El **toilet** está atascado.
	Standard variants →	El **retrete** / el **inodoro** /el **wáter** está atascado.
"Toilet" expressions in standard Spanish	*toilet (toiletry) bag*	neceser
	toilet bowl	taza de retrete
	toilet paper	papel higiénico
	toilet seat	asiento de retrete

TOMAR (verb) = **to take (in general)**
= **to drink, have, consume**
= **to take medicine**
= **to take, catch (bus, train, plane, etc.)**
= **to take: occupy, capture**
= **to take: remove; steal [US]**
= **to take: grab, seize [US]**
= **to take: select, buy [US]**
= **to take: carry, bring, transport [US]**
= **to take: accept [US]**
= **to take: have room for [US]**
= **to take: wear [US]**
= **to take: call for, require [US]**
= **to take: delay; last [US]**
= **to take: endure, put up with [US]**
= **to take for: assume to be [US]**
= **taken: occupied [US]**

- Distinguishing between standard and nonstandard usage can be problematic in the case of **tomar**, one of the most utilized verbs in Spanish.
- To the 39 uses stipulated by the RAE (we list the five most common), U.S. Spanish adds 19 of its own, mostly as a result of literal translations of the verb "to take."

Standard usage

1. *to take (general):*	*I took a sheet of paper and started to write.*	Tomé una hoja de papel y me puse a escribir.
2. *to drink, have, consume:*	*What will you have (to drink)?*	¿Qué vas a tomar?
	We don't drink beer.	No tomamos cerveza.
3. *to take medicine:*	*Why don't you take an aspirin?*	¿Por qué no te tomas una aspirina?
4. *to take (a bus, train, etc.):*	*I take the train every day.*	Tomo el tren todos los días.
5. *to take: occupy, capture:*	*They took the city in one day.*	Tomaron la ciudad en un día.

Extended US usage

6. *to take (=remove):*	*Who took my plate?*	¿Quién **tomó** mi plato?
	Standard variants →	¿Quién **se llevó** mi plato?
		¿Quién **me quitó** el plato?
7. *to take (=steal):*	*Someone took my purse.*	Alguien **tomó** mi bolso.
	Standard variants →	Alguien **se llevó** mi bolso.
		Me robaron el bolso.
8. *to take (=grab, seize):*	*They took him by the arm.*	Lo **tomaron por** el brazo.
	Standard variants →	Lo **cogieron** / Lo **agarraron** del brazo.

9. *to take (=select, buy):*	*I'll take the black scarf.*	**Tomaré** la bufanda negra.
	Standard variants →	**Me llevaré / Me llevo** la bufanda negra.
10. *to take (=carry, bring, transport):*	*Where did you take the garbage?*	¿Adónde **tomaste** la basura?
	Standard variant →	¿Adónde **llevaste** la basura?
11. *to take (=accept):*	*Would you take a check?*	¿**Tomarías** un cheque?
	Standard variant →	¿**Aceptarías** un cheque?
12. *to take (=have room for):*	*My car can take six people.*	Mi carro puede **tomar** seis personas.
	Standard variants →	Mi carro puede **llevar a** seis / En mi carro **caben** seis personas.
13. *to take (=wear):*	*What size dress do you take?*	¿Qué talla de vestido **tomas**?
	Standard variants →	¿Qué talla de vestido **usas / gastas**?
14. *to take (=require):*	*It takes patience to work with children.*	**Toma** paciencia trabajar con niños.
	Standard variants →	**Hace falta / Se necesita** paciencia para trabajar ...
15. *to take time (=delay):*	*It will only take ten minutes.*	Sólo va a **tomar** diez minutos.
	Standard variant →	Sólo va a **tardar** diez minutos.
16. *to take time (=last):*	*The movie took three hours.*	La película **tomó** tres horas.
	Standard variant →	La película **duró** tres horas.
17. *to take (=endure, put up with):*	*I can't take this heat.*	No **puedo tomar** este calor.
	Standard variants →	No **soporto / aguanto** este calor.
18. *to take for (=assume to be):*	*They took me for a student.*	Me **tomaron** por estudiante.
	Standard variants →	Me **tuvieron** por estudiante. **Creían que yo era** estudiante.
19. *taken (=occupied):*	*Is this seat taken?*	¿Está **tomado** este asiento?
	Standard variant →	¿Está **ocupado** este asiento?

Idioms with "to take" in standard Spanish	to take a bath	bañarse
	to take a beating	recibir una paliza
	to take a course	hacer / tomar un curso
	to take a photograph	sacar / tomar una fotografía
	to take a risk	arriesgarse
	to take a seat	sentarse, tomar asiento
	to take a step	dar un paso
	to take a trip	hacer un viaje
	to take a walk	dar un paseo
	to take a wife	casarse, contraer matrimonio
	to take action	hacer algo, tomar medidas
	to take advantage (of opportunity)	aprovechar
	to take advantage (of a person)	engañar, abusar
	to take advice	seguir un consejo
	to take after	parecerse a
	to take an exam	presentarse a un examen
	to take effect (drug)	surtir efecto
	to take effect (law)	entrar en vigor
	to take five / take ten	hacer una pausa, descansar
	to take hostage	tomar / agarrar como rehén
	to take it easy (=not rush)	ir despacio, no correr
	to take it easy (=not worry)	calmarse, no ponerse nervioso
	to take it easy (=rest)	descansar
	to take notes	anotar, tomar apuntes
	to take notice	hacer caso
	to take one's time	no correr, tomarse el tiempo
	to take pleasure	disfrutar, gozar
	to take responsibility	asumir la responsabilidad

TÓNER (masc noun) = **loanword for "toner"** [DRAE 2001]

- For lack of a precise equivalent, this term was recently integrated into standard Spanish to refer to the "ink toner" used in printers and photocopiers.

> **tóner**. (Del inglés *toner*). 1. m. Pigmento que utilizan ciertas fotocopiadoras e impresoras para reproducir letras e imágenes. [DRAE]

Standard usage *1. toner (ink):*	*The photocopy machine needs toner.*	Le hace falta tóner a la fotocopiadora.
Extended US usage *2. skin toner:*	*This toner helps darken the skin.*	Este **tóner** ayuda a broncear la piel.
	Standard variant →	Este **tonificante** ayuda a …

TÓPICO (masc noun & adj)

=	**cliché, commonplace**
=	**recurrent theme (in literature)**
=	**topical: external**
=	**medicine applied externally**
=	**topic: theme, subject [US]**
=	**topical: current [US]**

• Widely used in U.S. Spanish to mean "topic," this particular application of **tópico** is not officially recognized in standard Spanish.

Standard usage

1. *cliché, commonplace:*	*His description of New York was full of clichés.*	Su descripción de Nueva York estaba llena de tópicos.
2. *recurrent theme (in lit):*	Carpe Diem *is a common theme in Renaissance poetry.*	El *Carpe Diem* es un tópico de la poesía renacentista.
3. *topical, adj. (=external):*	*This cream is for external use.*	Esta crema es para uso tópico.
4. *skin ointment:*	*The doctor recommended an ointment for my sunburn.*	El médico me recomendó un tópico para la quemadura.

Extended US usage

5. *topic (=theme, subject):*	*What is the topic of your presentation?*	¿Cuál es el **tópico** de tu presentación?
	Standard variant →	¿Cuál es el **tema** de tu presentación?
6. *topic (=subject matter):*	*The movie deals with a very violent topic.*	La película trata de un **tópico** muy violento.
	Standard variant →	La película trata de un **asunto** muy violento.
7. *topical, adj. (=current):*	*The theme of the essay must be topical.*	El tema del ensayo tiene que ser **tópico**.
	Standard variant →	El tema del ensayo tiene que ser **actual** / **corriente**.

TRABAJAR (verb)

=	**to work (at a job)**
=	**to work: function [US]**
=	**to work: be effective [US]**
=	**to work: make someone work [US]**
=	**to work on: practice [US]**

• The verb "to work," regardless of its intended connotation, is often rendered as **trabajar** in U.S. Spanish.

Standard usage

1. to work (=perform a job):	*They work for the government.*	Trabajan para el gobierno.

Extended US usage

2. to work (=function):	*My computer is finally working.*	Ya **trabaja** mi computadora.
	Standard variant →	Ya **funciona** mi computadora.
3. to work (=be effective):	*Your remedy for a headache did not work.*	Tu remedio para el dolor de cabeza no **trabajó**.
	Standard variants →	Tu remedio ... no **fue eficaz** / no **dio resultado**.
4. to work (=operate):	*Do you know how to work this machine?*	¿Sabes **trabajar** esta máquina?
	Standard variants →	¿Sabes **manejar** / **operar** esta máquina?
5. to work (=make someone work):	*The boss works us hard.*	El jefe nos **trabaja** duro.
	Standard variant →	El jefe nos **hace trabajar** duro.
6. to work at / work on:	*I'm working on my English.*	Estoy **trabajando** en mi inglés.
	Standard variants →	Estoy **practicando** mi inglés. Le estoy **dando** al inglés.

TRÁNSFER (masc noun) = **loanword for "transfer" [US]**

- Unrecognized by the RAE, the choice of equivalent expressions in traditional Spanish (**traslado**, **transbordo**, **traspaso**, etc.) is dictated by the situation.
- According to Vox and Moliner, **tránsfer** refers strictly to the practice of "transfering soccer players" from one team to another.
- In U.S. Spanish, as in English, **tránsfer** occurs in a wide variety of contexts.

US usage

1. transfer (=move):	*Your transfer to the Los Angeles branch was approved.*	Aprobaron tu **tránsfer** a la sucursal de Los Ángeles.
	Standard variant →	Aprobaron tu **traslado** a ...
2. transfer (of money):	*Here is an application for the transfer of funds.*	Aquí está la solicitud para el **tránsfer** de fondos.
	Standard variant →	Aquí está la solicitud para la **transferencia** de fondos.

3. *transfer (of property):*	*You have to pay taxes for transfer of property.*	Hay que pagar impuestos para el **tránsfer** de propiedad.
	Standard variant →	Hay que pagar impuestos para el **traspaso** de propiedad.
4. *transfer (from one vehicle to another):*	*Because of the transfer, the flight was delayed.*	A causa del **tránsfer**, se demoró el vuelo.
	Standard variant →	A causa del **transbordo**, ...
5. *transfer stub (transp):*	*With a transfer stub you can connect to anohter bus.*	Con un **tránsfer** puedes hacer enlace con otro autobús.
	Standard variants →	Con un **boleto** / **tique de empalme** puedes ...

TRANSPORTACIÓN (fem noun) = **loanword for "transportation" [US]**

- **Transportación**, a valid word in standard Spanish, is more typical of U.S. usage.
- The more conventional term for "transportation" is **transporte**.

US usage		
1. *transportation:*	*I use public transportation.*	Uso **transportación** pública.
	Standard variant →	Uso **transporte** público.
2. *transport:*	*The transport of certain foods is prohibited.*	La **transportación** de ciertos comestibles está prohibida.
	Standard variant →	El **transporte** de ciertos comestibles está prohibido.

TRATAMIENTO (masc noun) = **treatment (of subject, idea)**
  = **medical treatment**
  = **processing**
  = **treatment of people [US]**
  = **dealings with people [US]**

Standard usage		
1. *treatment (of subject):*	*His treatment of the subject was very original.*	El tratamiento que le dio al tema fue muy original.
2. *medical treatment:*	*The patient did not respond to the treatment.*	El paciente no respondió al tratamiento.
3. *processing (of info):*	*His specialty is data processing.*	Su especialidad es tratamiento de datos.

Extended US usage

4. *treatment, handling (of people):*	*They criticize the treatment of prisoners.*	Critican el **tratamiento** de los presos.
	Standard variant →	Critican el **trato** que se les da a los presos.
5. *dealings, relationship:*	*We haven't had any dealings with them.*	No hemos tenido ningún **tratamiento** con ellos.
	Standard variant →	No hemos tenido ningún **trato** con ellos.

TRATAR (verb) = **to treat, handle (person, animal, object)**
= **to call, address (a person)**
= **to treat medically**
= **to deal with, be about**
= **to try / attempt to do something**
= **to have dealings with**
= **to try, attempt [US]**
= **to try out: sample, taste [US]**
= **to try: inquire, check, look [US]**
= **to try: put to the test [US]**
= **to try: prosecute, judge [US]**
= **to treat: invite, offer to pay [US]**

- There is a strong tendency in U.S. Spanish to render "to try" as **tratar** regardless of the situation or desired connotation. In standard practice, **tratar** primarily means "to treat."

Standard usage

1. *to treat (person, animal):*	*I treat my colleagues with respect.*	Yo trato a mis colegas con respeto.
2. *to treat, handle (object):*	*The figurines must be handled with great care.*	Hay que tratar las figurinas con mucho cuidado.
3. *to call, address (person):*	*How do you address a king?* *They called him crazy.*	¿Cómo se trata a un rey? Lo trataron de loco.
4. *to treat medically:*	*She is being treated with antibiotics.*	La están tratando con antibióticos.
5. *to deal with (=take up):*	*We will deal with this issue next week.*	Trataremos este asunto la semana que viene.
6. *to be about (=concern):*	*What is the movie about?*	¿De qué trata la película?
7. *to have dealings with:*	*Some countries have dealings with terrorists.*	Ciertos países tratan con terroristas.
8. *to try to do something:*	*I will try to arrive early.*	Trataré de llegar temprano.

Extended US usage

9. *to try, attempt:*	*How many times did you try?*	¿Cuántas veces **trataste**?
	Standard variant →	¿Cuántas veces **intentaste**?
10. *to try out (=sample, taste):*	*Did you try the tortilla I made?*	¿**Trataste** la tortilla que hice?
	Standard variant →	¿**Probaste** la tortilla que hice?
11. *to try (=inquire, check):*	*Why don't you try the bookstore?*	¿Por qué no **tratas** la librería?
	Standard variants →	¿Por qué no **preguntas** / **buscas en** la librería?
12. *to try (=put to the test):*	*They are going to try him in a new position.*	Lo van a **tratar** en un nuevo puesto.
	Standard variant →	Lo van a **poner a prueba** en un nuevo puesto.
13. *to try (=judge, prosecute):*	*She was tried and found guilty.*	La **trataron** y la declararon culpable.
	Standard variants →	La **procesaron** / **enjuiciaron** y la declararon culpable.
14. *to treat (=offer to pay):*	*Pass me the check, I'm treating.*	Pásame la cuenta, yo **trato**.
	Standard variant →	Pásame la cuenta, yo **invito**.

TWIST (masc noun) = loanword for "twist" [US]

• Sanctioned by the RAE in 1985, only to be rescinded in 1992, **twist** has two common applications in U.S. Spanish: the dance made popular in the 1960s, and a "squeeze" of lemon or lime. The latter appears in many dictionaries, including Vox and Moliner.

Standard/US usage

1. *twist (=dance):*	*I love to dance the twist.*	Me encanta bailar el **twist**.
2. *twist (=squeeze, small amount):*	*A twist of lemon, please.*	Un **twist** de limón, por favor.
	Standard variants →	Un **poquito** / Un **rizo** de limón, por favor.

ÚNICAMENTE (adv) = **only, solely**
= **uniquely [US]**

ÚNICO (adj) = **only, sole**
= **unique [US]**

• The traditonal meaning of **único** is not "unique" but rather "only" or "sole."

Standard usage

1. only, sole (adj):
Are you an only child?
Her only problem is her health.
¿Eres hijo único?
Su único problema es la salud.

2. only, solely (adv):
I'm referring only to her.
Me refiero únicamente a ella.

Extended US usage

3. unique (=original, unlike any other):
This latest fashion is unique.
Esta última moda es **única**.

Standard variant →
Esta última moda es **singular**.

4. unique (=exceptional):
My son has a unique talent for music.
Mi hijo tiene un talento **único** para la música.

Standard variants →
Mi hijo tiene un talento **sin igual / excepcional** ...

5. unique (=special):
Their relationship is very unique.
Su relación es muy **única**.

Standard variant →
Su relación es muy **especial**.

6. uniquely (=exclusively):
It's a uniquely Galician custom.
Es una costumbre **únicamente** gallega.

Standard variant →
... **exclusivamente** gallega.

7. uniquely (=exceptionally):
She is uniquely qualified to be a teacher.
Está **únicamente** capacitada para maestra.

Standard variant →
Está **excepcionalmente** capacitada para maestra.

UNIÓN (fem noun) = **union (in general; marriage; alliance, etc.)**
= **trade union [US]**
= **union: club, society [US]**

• To the many standard meanings of **unión**, U.S. Spanish adds two, borrowed from American English usage: "trade union" and "student union."

Extended US usage		
1. trade union:	*Are you a union member?*	¿Eres miembro de la **unión**?
	Standard variant →	¿Eres miembro del **sindicato**?
2. union (=club, society):	*student union center*	centro de **unión** estudiantil
	Standard variants →	centro de **sociedad** estudiantil centro de **clubes** estudiantiles

VACANCIA (fem noun) = **loanword for "vacancy" or "vacation" [US]**

- Although **vacancia** is RAE-approved, it is rarely used. Standard Spanish favors the use of adjectives such as **vacante**, **libre**, **disponible** to express the notion of **vacancy**.
- The traditional Spanish term for "vacation" is **vacaciones**.

US usage		
1. vacancy (=available job):	*Are there any vacancies in your company?*	¿Hay alguna **vacancia** en tu empresa?
	Standard variants →	¿Hay algún **puesto vacante** / **disponible** en tu empresa?
2. vacancy (=available room):	*We have no vacancies at this hotel.*	No tenemos **vacancia** en este hotel.
	Standard variant →	No tenemos **habitación libre** en este hotel.
3. vacation:	*Where are you spending your summer vacation?*	¿Dónde vas a pasar tu **vacancia** de verano?
	Standard variant →	¿Dónde vas a pasar tus **vacaciones** de verano?

VACUUM CLEANER (masc noun) = **loanword for "vacuum cleaner" [US]**

- The use of **vacuum cleaner** (pronounced as in English) and its abbreviated form, **vacuum**, is prevalent in U.S. Spanish along with its traditional counterpart, **aspiradora**.
- Stavans spells it **vacuncliner** and adds two verb forms: **vaquiumear** and **vacunear**.

US usage		
1. vacuum cleaner:	*You need a good vacuum cleaner.*	Te hace falta un buen **vacuum cleaner**.
	Standard variant →	Te hace falta una buena **aspiradora**.
2. to vacuum:	*I vacuumed the entire house.*	**Vaquimeé** toda la casa.
	Standard variant →	**Pasé la aspiradora por** toda la casa.

VALUABLE (adj & masc noun) = **loanword for "valuable" [US]**

- Whereas **valuar** is a legitimate verb form, **valuable** does not exist in standard Spanish.
- U.S. Spanish has borrowed it from English to use as both a noun and an adjective.

US usage

1. valuable (=in monetary terms) [adj]:	*This old desk is very valuable.*	Este viejo escritorio **es** muy **valuable**.
	Standard variants →	Este viejo escritorio **tiene** mucho **valor** / **vale** mucho.
2. valuable (=useful) [adj]:	*You gave me valuable advice.*	Me diste un **valuable** consejo.
	Standard variant →	Me diste un **valioso** consejo.
3. valuable [noun]:	*They lost many valuables in the fire.*	Perdieron muchos **valuables** en el incendio.
	Standard variant →	Perdieron muchos **objetos de valor** en el incendio.

VCR / VICIAR (masc noun) = **loanword for "VCR" [US]**

- What is generally known in standard practice as **aparato de vídeo** is commonly referred to as **VCR** among Spanish speakers in the United States.
- This three-letter acronym, pronounced as in English, is often seen rendered phonetically in Spanish language newspapers and magazines: **viciar**, **visiar**, **bisiar**, etc.

US usage

1. VCR (=video cassette player/recorder):	*The VCRs are on sale.*	Los **viciares** están de rebaja.
	Standard variants →	Los **aparatos de vídeo** / las **grabadoras de video** / los **videograbadores** (Lat Am) están de rebaja.

VEGETABLE (masc noun) = **adapted from "vegetable" [US]**

- **Vegetable** appears in the RAE and Moliner as an adjective, although it is rarely used.
- U.S. speakers borrow the noun form from English, adapt its pronunciation to Spanish, and employ it as a generic alternative to **legumbre**, **verdura**, **vegetal**, etc.

US usage

1. *vegetable (as opposed to animal or mineral):*	*We had to distinguish between vegetable and mineral.*	Teníamos que distinguir entre **vegetable** y mineral.
	Standard variant →	Teníamos que distinguir entre **vegetal** y mineral.
2. *vegetable (=food):*	*They served us a big plate of vegetables.*	Nos sirvieron un buen plato de **vegetables**.
	Standard variants →	Nos sirvieron un buen plato de **legumbres / hortalizas / verduras / vegetales** (PR)

"Vegetable" expressions in standard Spanish		
	vegetable dish	plato de verduras
	vegetable fat	grasa vegetal
	vegetable garden	huerta, huerto
	vegetable oil	aceite vegetal
	vegetable salad	ensalada verde
	vegetable soup	sopa de verduras

VENTAJA (fem noun)
= **advantage: benefit; headstart**
= **fringe benefits, extras, perks**
= **(to take) advantage [US]**

- The use of **ventaja** to mean "advantage" in the U.S. conforms to standard practice, with one exception: **tomar ventaja**, a loan translation of the verbal idiom "to take advantage."

Standard usage

1. *advantage (=benefit):*	*Being bilingual has many advantages.*	El ser bilingüe tiene muchas ventajas.
2. *headstart:*	*I gave him a ten-second headstart.*	Le di una ventaja de diez segundos.
3. *perks, fringe benefits:*	*They offered him many perks as part of the contract.*	Le ofrecieron muchas ventajas como parte del contrato.

Extended US usage

4. *to take advantage (of an opportunity):*	*Let's take advantage of the nice weather.*	**Tomemos ventaja** del buen tiempo.
	Standard variant →	**Aprovechemos** el buen tiempo.
5. *to take advantage (of someone):*	*They took advantage of you.*	**Tomaron ventaja** de ti.
	Standard variant →	**Se aprovecharon** de ti.
6. *to take advantage (sexually):*	*The man took advantage of the young woman.*	El hombre **tomó ventaja** de la joven.
	Standard variant →	El hombre **abusó de** la joven.

VENTANA (fem noun) = **window (general)**
= **window (computer)**
= **store window [US]**
= **service window [US]**
= **window (in envelope) [US]**

- Standard Spanish employs **ventana** to mean "window" in a general sense (opening to the outside world) as well as "computer window."
- U.S. Spanish extends its use to reflect other common English applications.

Standard usage

1. *window (general):*	*I will open the window and let some air in.*	Voy a abrir la ventana para que entre un poco de aire.
2. *window (computers):*	*You need to close the window to get to the application.*	Tienes que cerrar la ventana para llegar a la aplicación.

US usage

3. *store window:*	*She saw a beautiful dress in the (store) window.*	Vio un vestido muy lindo en la **ventana** (de la tienda).
	Standard variants →	Vio un vestido muy lindo en la **vitrina** / en el **escaparate**.
4. *service window:*	*He went to the window to pick up the tickets.*	Fue a la **ventana** a buscar las entradas.
	Standard variants →	Fue a la **ventanilla** / **taquilla** a buscar las entradas.
5. *envelope window:*	*The address must show through the window.*	Se tiene que ver la dirección por la **ventana**.
	Standard variant →	Se tiene que ver la dirección por la **ventanilla**.

VICIAR (masc noun)   see **VCR**

VIDEO / VÍDEO (masc noun) = **loanword for "video"** [DRAE 1984]

- **Vídeo** (Spain) and **video** (Lat Am) are common suffixes with words such as **cámara**, **club**, **conferencia**, **disco**, etc. In standard usage, **vídeo** can also be an abbreviation for "video system," "video recorder," and "video program."
- In U.S. Spanish, where **video** is the preferred form, it is also short for "videotape."

Standard usage

1. *video (=visual image):*	*The audio is fine but the video is distorted.*	El audio está bien pero el vídeo está distorsionado.
2. *video recorder:*	*Our VCR is not working.*	Nuestro vídeo no funciona.
3. *video (=film, recording):*	*Did you see her new music video?*	¿Viste su nuevo vídeo musical?

Extended US usage		
4. *videotape:*	*I bought three video cassettes for five dollars.*	Compré tres **videos** por cinco dólares.
	Standard variant →	Compré tres **videocintas** por cinco dólares.
5. *video store:*	*A new video store just opened.*	Acaba de abrir una nueva **tienda de videos**.
	Standard variant →	Acaba de abrir un nuevo **videoclub**.
6. *video library:*	*Our video library is extensive.*	Nuestra **librería de videos** es extensa.
	Standard variant →	Nuestra **videoteca** es extensa.

"Video" expressions in standard Spanish		
	video arcade	salón de videojuegos
	video camera	cámara de vídeo / videocámara
	video cassette	cinta de vídeo / videocinta
	video segment	videoclip
	video conference	videoconferencia
	video game console	videoconsola
	video disk	videodisco
	video film	película de vídeo
	video game	juego de vídeo / videojuego
	video library	videoteca
	video recorder	grabador(a) de vídeo
	video recording	videograbación
	video shop	videoclub

VIDEOTAPE (masc noun) = **loanword for "videotape" [US]**

- **Videocaset** and **videotape** (pronounced as in English) are more prevalent in U.S. Spanish than the standard **videocinta**. All three variants tend to be shortened to **video**.

US usage		
1. *videotape:*	*You can tape for two hours with this videotape.*	Puedes grabar dos horas con este **videotape**.
	Standard variant →	Puedes grabar dos horas con esta **cinta (de video)**.
2. *video cassette:*	*This video casette is defective.*	Este **videocaset** tiene defecto.
	Standard variant →	Este **casete (de video)** tiene defecto.

VIOLACIÓN (fem noun)
= **rape, sexual assault**
= **break-in, breach, infringement**
= **minor violation, traffic violation [US]**

• **Violación** and **violar** refer primarily to "rape" or "sexual assault" in standard Spanish.

Standard usage
1. *rape, sexual assault:* | The accused had committed a number of rapes. | El acusado había cometido una serie de violaciones.
2. *break-in, infringement:* | He was accused of breaking into a home. | Lo acusaron de violación de domicilio.

Extended US usage
3. *minor violation, traffic infraction:* | She got a ticket for a traffic violation. | Le echaron una multa por **violación** de tráfico.
| **Standard variant →** | Le echaron una multa por **infracción** de tráfico.

VIOLAR (verb)
= **to rape, assault sexually**
= **to violate: break, breach**
= **to violate trust; violate privacy [US]**

Standard usage
1. *to rape:* | The man who raped her is in jail. | El hombre que la violó está en la cárcel.
2. *to violate (=breach):* | At this point I cannot break the contract. | A estas alturas no puedo violar el contrato.

Extended US usage
3. *to violate (trust):* | You violated his trust. | **Violaste** su confianza.
| **Standard variant →** | **Abusaste de** su confianza.
4. *to violate (privacy, sanctity):* | They violated my family's privacy. | **Violaron la privacidad** de mi familia.
| **Standard variant →** | **Invadieron la intimidad** de mi familia.

VOLVER (verb)

= **to turn, turn over; rotate**
= **to turn: direct**
= **to turn: change, make, cause to be**
= **to return: put back, restore**
= **to return (intrans): go back, come back**
= **to (do) again**
= **to return (trans): give back [US]**
= **to return a call [US]**

- In the U.S. and many parts of Latin America, there is a tendency to use **volver** and **regresar** as transitive verbs meaning "to return" (an item to the store, for example).

Standard usage

1. *to turn, turn over:*	*Please turn to the next page.*	Favor de volver la página.
2. *to turn (=rotate):*	*He turned his head but did not answer.*	Volvió la cabeza pero no contestó.
3. *to turn (=direct):*	*She turned her thoughts toward the past.*	Volvió sus pensamientos hacia el pasado.
4. *to turn (=change):*	*The chlorine turned the shirt white.*	El cloro volvió blanca la camisa.
5. *to make (=cause to be):*	*Your indecision is making me me crazy.*	Tu indecisión me está volviendo loco.
6. *to return (=put back):*	*Did you put the books back in their place?*	¿Volviste los libros a su sitio?
7. *to return (=go back):*	*When will you be returning to work?*	¿Cuándo vas a volver al trabajo?
8. *to turn around (=come back):*	*There was a lot of traffic and we had to turn around.*	Había mucho tráfico y nos tuvimos que volver.
9. *to (do) again:*	*My brother got married again.*	Mi hermano volvió a casarse.

Extended US usage

10. *to return (=give back):*	*Thanks for the book; I'll return it to you tomorrow.*	Gracias por el libro; se lo **vuelvo / regreso** mañana.
	Standard variant →	... se lo **devuelvo** mañana.
11. *to return a call:*	*He didn't return my phone call.*	No me **volvió** la llamada.
	Standard variant →	No me **devolvió** la llamada.

WAFFLE (masc noun) = **loanword for "waffle" [US]**

- Although standard Spanish considers **gofre** a viable equivalent, U.S. Spanish speakers lean toward **waffle** (usually pronounced "guafle") to refer to the popular breakfast food.

US usage

1. *waffle:*	*How many waffles did you eat?*	¿Cuántos **waffles** te comiste?
	Standard variant →	¿Cuántos **gofres** te comiste?

WAX (masc noun)   =   **loanword for "wax" [US]**

WAXEAR (verb)   =   **adapted from "to wax" [US]**

- In the context of "polishing," **wax** and **waxear** are more common in U.S. Spanish than the traditional **cera** and **encerar**.

US usage		
1. wax:	*Which type of wax would you recommend for my car?*	¿Qué tipo de **wax** recomendarías para mi carro?
	Standard variant →	¿Qué tipo de **cera** recomendarías para mi carro?
2. to wax:	*The furniture needs to be waxed.*	Hay que **waxear** los muebles.
	Standard variant →	Hay que **encerar** los muebles.
3. wax paper:	*You should cover it with wax paper.*	Lo debes cubrir con papel **de wax**.
	Standard variant →	Lo debes cubrir con papel **encerado**.

WEB (fem noun)   =   **loanword for "World Wide Web"** [DRAE 2001]

WEBSITE (masc noun)   =   **loanword for "website" [US]**

> **web.** (Del inglés *web*, red, malla). 1. f. Inform. Red informática. [DRAE]

- Whereas **web** is sanctioned in standard Spanish in the realm of information technology, **website** is not. Both are prevalent in U.S. Spanish.

Standard usage		
1. Web (computers):	*The Web will help you find the information you need.*	El web te ayudará a encontrar la información que necesitas.

Extended US usage		
2. website:	*The application can be found on the university website.*	La solicitud se encuentra en el **website** de la universidad.
	Standard variant →	La solicitud se encuentra en la **página web** ...

WEEKEND (masc noun) = **loanword for "weekend" [US]**

- A universal expression, **weekend** is quite prevalent in U.S. Spanish and throughout the Spanish-speaking world. It is transcribed to **wikén** in certain parts of Latin America.
- **Weekend** appears as an entry in Vox and Moliner, but is not recognized by the RAE.

US usage		
1. weekend (noun):	*¿What are you planning to do this weekend?*	¿Qué piensas hacer este **weekend / wikén**?
	Standard variant →	¿Qué piensas hacer este **fin de semana**?
2. weekend (adj):	*We took a weekend trip.*	Hicimos un viaje de **wikén**.
	Standard variant →	Hicimos un viaje de **fin de semana**.

WELFARE (masc noun) = **loanword for "welfare" [US]**

- In U.S. Spanish, **welfare** (pronounced as in English) refers not to "well-being," which would be **bienestar**, but rather to the "social service agencies" managed by the state governments and the financial assistance they provide.
- This term is not approved by the RAE nor is it common in standard practice.

US usage		
1. welfare (=services):	*Are you on welfare?*	¿Recibes **welfare**?
	Standard variant →	¿Recibes **asistencia social**?
2. welfare (=funds):	*I didn't get my welfare check this month.*	No recibí el **welfare** este mes.
	Standard variant →	No recibí el **cheque de asistencia social** este mes.
3. welfare (=office):	*We went to the welfare office but it was closed.*	Fuimos al **welfare** pero estaba cerrado.
	Standard variant →	Fuimos a la **oficina de asistencia social** pero ...

WHISKY (masc noun) = **loanword for "whisky"** [DRAE 1984]

- Approved in standard Spanish, **whisky** is also spelled **whiskey** or **güisqui** in the United States and parts of Latin America.

Standard/US usage		
1. whisky:	*A whisky on the rocks, please.*	Un whisky con hielo, por favor.

WIKÉN (masc noun)   see **WEEKEND**

WORKSHOP (masc noun)   =   **loanword for "workshop" [US]**

• Popular in U.S. Spanish in professional circles along with its traditional variant, **taller**.

US usage		
1. workshop:	*We attended a computer workshop.*	Asistimos a un **workshop** de informática.
	Standard variant →	Asistimos a un **taller** de informática.

YANITOR (masc noun)   =   **loanword for "janitor" [US]**

• U.S. Spanish borrows **yanitor** from English to refer to the "resident repairman" of an office building or, less frequently, the "doorman" or "caretaker" of an apartment building.

US usage		
1. janitor (=building repairman):	*The janitor installed a fan in the office.*	El **yanitor** instaló un ventilador en la oficina.
	Standard variant →	El **conserje** instaló un ventilador en la oficina.
2. janitor (=doorman):	*The janitor has the keys to all the apartments.*	El **yanitor** tiene la llave de todos los apartamentos.
	Standard variants →	El **portero** / El **conserje** tiene la llave de …

YANQUI (adj & noun)   =   **loanword for "Yankee"** [DRAE 1899]

• Within the United States, Spanish speakers use **yanqui** to mean "northerner" as well as "American." The latter usage can be pejorative.

Standard usage		
1. Yankee (=American):	*There are many Americans in San Miguel.*	Hay muchos yanquis en San Miguel.

Extended US usage		
2. Yankee (=northerner):	*I'm going to Boston to visit my Yankee cousins.*	Voy a Boston a visitar a mis primos **yanquis**.
	Standard variant →	… a mis primos **norteños**.

YARDA (fem noun)   =   **yard: unit of measure**
=   **yard: garden [US]**
=   **yard: courtyard [US]**

- The RAE defines **yarda** strictly as "unit of measure."
- Other applications ("garden" or "courtyard") are indigenous to U.S. Spanish.

Standard usage		
1. *yard (=measure):*	*A yard is slightly shorter than a meter.*	Una yarda es poco menos que un metro.

Extended US usage		
2. *yard (=garden):*	*My mother is watering the flowers in the yard.*	Mi madre está rociando las flores en la **yarda**.
	Standard variant →	Mi madre está rociando las flores en el **jardín**.
3. *yard (=courtyard):*	*The kids can play in the yard.*	Los niños pueden jugar en la **yarda**.
	Standard variant →	Los niños pueden jugar en el **patio**.

YÉRSEY / YERSI (masc noun)   see **JERSEY**

YIP (masc noun)   see **JEEP**

YONQUI (masc / fem noun)   =   **loanword for "junkie" [US]**

> **yonqui**. (Del inglés *junkie*). m. Drogadicto. [Moliner]

- Once recognized by the RAE (1985–1992), U.S. Spanish takes **yonqui** beyond its standard usage as "drug addict" to refer to any kind of "addict," "lover," or "devoted fan."

Standard usage		
1. *junkie (=drug addict):*	*At night, the park fills up with junkies.*	Por la noche, el parque se llena de yonquis.
	Traditional variant →	Por la noche, el parque se llena de drogadictos.

Extended US usage		
2. *junkie (=addict, lover, devoted fan):*	*I am a chocolate junkie.*	Soy **yonqui** del chocolate.
	Standard variant →	Soy **adicto** al chocolate.

YÓQUEY, YOQUI (masc noun) = **loanwords for "jockey"** [DRAE 1970]

yóquey o **yoqui.** (Del inglés *jockey*). m. Jinete profesional de carreras de caballos. [DRAE] m. Formas castellanizadas de "jockey". [Moliner]

Standard/US usage

1. jockey:	*The jockey fell off the horse.*	El **yóquey** se cayó del caballo.
	Traditional variant →	El **jinete** se cayó del caballo.
2. jockey shorts:	*Do you wear jockey shorts?*	¿Usas **calzoncillos de yoqui**?
	Standard variant →	¿Usas **calzones cortos**?

ZOMBI (masc noun) = **loanword for "zombie"** [DRAE 1985]

• Both the literal and figurative meanings of "zombie" are recognized in standard Spanish.

zombi. (Voz de Haití, de origen africano occidental). 1. m. Persona que se supone muerta y que ha sido reanimada por arte de brujería, con el fin de dominar su voluntad. 2. adj. Atontado, que se comporta como un autómata. [DRAE]

Standard/US usage

1. zombie (=monster):	*We saw a horror movie about zombies.*	Vimos una película de terror en que aparecían **zombis**.
2. zombie, fig. (=tired, dazed, bewildered):	*Not having had a wink of sleep, I'm like a zombie.*	Por no haber pegado un ojo, estoy como un **zombi**.
	Traditional variant →	... estoy como **atontado**.

ZUM (masc noun) = **adapted from "zoom"** [DRAE 1992]

• Whether spelled **zum** (DRAE) or **zoom** (Vox, Moliner), this word has been fully incorporated into standard Spanish.

Standard/US usage

1. zoom lens:	*a high-quality zoom lens*	un **zum** de alta calidad
2. zoom (=action):	*I want a camera with a zoom function.*	Quiero una cámara con **zum**.

EXERCISES

I. FROM U.S. SPANISH TO STANDARD SPANISH

Replace the word(s) in parentheses with an appropriate equivalent in standard Spanish.

(1) U.S. Spanish words that start with A.

1. The price of admission was fifty dollars.
   El precio de (admisión) _____ era cincuenta dólares.
2. My brother collects ancient coins.
   Mi hermano colecciona monedas (ancianas) _____.
3. My five-year old son already knows how to add.
   Mi hijo de cinco años ya sabe (añadir) _____.
4. How could we access the information?
   ¿Cómo podríamos (accesar) _____ la información?
5. The Rockefellers are a very affluent family.
   Los Rockefeller son una familia muy (afluente) _____.
6. The woman acted very rudely in front of her guests.
   La señora (actuó) _____ muy mal delante de sus invitados.
7. Your mother treats everyone with affection.
   Tu mamá trata a todo el mundo con (afección) _____.
8. It was his first appearance in an American film.
   Fue su primera (apariencia) _____ en una película norteamericana.
9. Did you fill out the job application?
   ¿Llenaste (la aplicación) _____ de empleo?
10. These new regulations do not apply to me.
    Estos nuevos reglamentos no (se aplican) _____ a mí.
11. I cannot accept his apology.
    No puedo aceptar su (apología) _____.
12. There are always arguments at our meetings.
    Siempre hay (argumentos) _____ en nuestras reuniones.
13. He did not attend class because he was sick.
    No (atendió) _____ a clase porque estuvo enfermo.
14. I don't like the atmosphere in the cafeteria.
    No me gusta (la atmósfera) _____ en la cafetería.
15. My friend went to Spain as a student and never came back.
    Mi amiga fue a España de estudiante y nunca (vino para atrás) _____.
16. The members of the audience received gifts.
    Los miembros (de la audiencia) _____ recibieron regalos.
17. I need a C average to be able to graduate.
    Necesito un (average) _____ de C para poder graduarme.
18. My professor advised me to take this course.
    Mi profesor me (avisó) _____ que tomara este curso.

(2) U.S. Spanish words that start with B.

1. My mother takes care of the baby when I go to work.
   Mi madre cuida (al baby) _____ cuando voy al trabajo.
2. I would love to know the artist's cultural background.
   Me gustaría conocer (el background) _____ cultural del artista.
3. He bought a backpack for camping.
   Compró (un backpack) _____ para ir de camping.
4. The tightrope walker uses a beam to balance himself.
   El funambulista usa un astil para (balancearse) _____.
5. We went to the club to hear a jazz band.
   Fuimos al club a escuchar a (una banda) _____ de jazz.
6. This flashlight takes four batteries.
   Esta linterna lleva cuatro (baterías) _____.
7. Here is my beeper number just in case.
   Aquí está mi número de (bíper) _____ por si acaso.
8. What business does he have telling us to leave?
   ¿Qué (bisnes) _____ tiene él a mandarnos a salir?
9. Yesterday we saw a very bizarre film.
   Ayer vimos una película muy (bizarra) _____.
10. I live three blocks from the university.
    Yo vivo a tres (bloques) _____ de la universidad.
11. I bought a pair of bluejeans on sale.
    Compré un par de (bluyins) _____ a precio de rebaja.
12. You should ask your boss for a raise.
    Deberías pedirle un aumento a tu (boss) _____.
13. The professor gave us a ten-minute break.
    El profesor nos dio un (break) _____ de diez minutos.
14. The state is having budget problems.
    El estado está teniendo problemas de (budget) _____.

(3) U.S. Spanish words that start with C.

1. We couldn't ski because the weather was too warm.
   No pudimos esquiar porque (el tiempo estaba muy caliente) _____.
2. He didn't have the qualifications to be a doctor.
   No tenía (las calificaciones) _____ para ser médico.
3. I have always sent my children to summer camp.
   Siempre he mandado a mis hijos a (un campo) _____ de verano.
4. They canceled the game because of rain.
   (Cancelaron) _____ el juego a causa de la lluvia.
5. Don Quixote is the most famous character in Spanish literature.
   Don Quijote es (el carácter) _____ más famoso de la literatura española.
6. The carpet is covered with stains.
   (La carpeta) _____ está cubierta de manchas.
7. Which credit card do you have, Visa or Mastercard?
   ¿Qué (carta) _____ de crédito tienes, Visa o Mastercard?

8. I'm going to have to pay cash because I didn't bring a check.
   Voy a tener que pagar (cash) _____ porque no traje cheque.

9. Will you be dressing casually for the party tomorrow?
   ¿Vas a vestir (casualmente) _____ para la fiesta mañana?

10. My sister has a very close relationship with my mother.
    Mi hermana tiene una relación muy (cercana) _____ con mi mamá.

11. The teacher gave me another chance to take the exam.
    El maestro me dio otra (chance) _____ de tomar el examen.

12. I checked all over the house and I couldn't find it.
    (Chequeé) _____ por toda la casa y no lo encontré.

13. Our apartment has a closet in every room.
    Nuestro apartamento tiene (un clóset) _____ en cada habitación.

14. When I was a kid, I collected stamps from all over the world.
    Cuando era niño, yo (colectaba) _____ estampillas de todo el mundo.

15. My twenty-year-old son is attending college in Florida.
    Mi hijo de veinte años asiste a (un colegio) _____ en Florida.

16. If there is no compromise, it is almost certain that there will be a war.
    Si no hay (compromiso) _____, es casi seguro que habrá guerra.

17. Leonard Bernstein was a famous orchestra conductor.
    Leonard Bernstein fue un famoso (conductor) _____ de orquesta.

18. I am confident that I will pass the exam.
    Estoy (confidente) _____ de que aprobaré el examen.

19. This bed is not very comfortable.
    Esta cama no es muy (confortable) _____.

20. I will try to contact her by phone.
    Trataré de (contactarla) _____ por teléfono.

21. You were right; that chicken soup was awful.
    Tú (estabas correcto) _____; esa sopa de pollo estaba malísima.

22. They told him he was too short to play basketball.
    Le dijeron que era demasiado (corto) _____ para jugar al baloncesto.

23. Quality is more important than quantity.
    (La cualidad) _____ es más importante que la cantidad.

24. There are twenty questions on the first part of the text.
    Hay veinte (cuestiones) _____ en la primera parte del examen.

25. She did not qualify for the position.
    Ella no (cualificó) _____ para el puesto.

(4) U.S. Spanish words that start with D.

1. My son goes to the day care center three days a week.
   Mi hijo va (al daycare) _____ tres días por semana.

2. The sign says that you cannot make a left turn.
   El letrero (dice) _____ que no se puede doblar a la izquierda.

3. Who can tell how many people will come?
   ¿Quién (puede decir) _____ cúanta gente vendrá?

4. It is definite that there are no classes tomorrow.
   Es (definitivo) _____ que no hay clases mañana.

5. At what time did you leave the office?
   ¿A qué hora (dejaste) _____ la oficina?
6. When the package arrives, I'll let you know.
   Cuando llegue el paquete, yo te (dejaré saber) _____.
7. The judge demanded silence during the trial.
   El juez (demandó) _____ silencio durante el proceso.
8. There were more than 100,000 people at the demonstration.
   Había más de cien mil personas en (la demostración) _____.
9. Depending on what the president says, the strike may begin today.
   (Dependiendo de) _____ lo que diga el presidente, la huelga puede comenzar hoy.
10. You pay a lot in taxes because you have no dependents.
    Pagas mucho en impuestos porque no tienes (dependientes) _____.
11. The way he spoke to us was an absolute disgrace.
    La manera en que nos habló fue una absoluta (desgracia) _____.
12. They created a parking area for the disabled.
    Crearon una área de estacionamiento para los (deshabilitados) _____.
13. He devoted himself to finding a cure for cancer.
    (Se devotó) _____ a encontrar una cura para el cáncer.
14. Different people asked me the same question.
    (Diferentes) _____ personas me hicieron la misma pregunta.
15. We arrived on time because you gave us very good directions.
    Llegamos a tiempo porque nos diste muy buenas (direcciones) _____.
16. I was disgusted by the way he was eating.
    Me (disgustaba) _____ la manera en que comía.
17. The student dorms close during the summer.
    (Los dormitorios) _____ estudiantiles cierran durante el verano.
18. I need to go to the drugstore to buy aspirins.
    Tengo que ir a la (droguería) _____ a comprar aspirinas.

(5) U.S. Spanish words that start with E.

1. My brother works in the field of public education.
   Mi hermano trabaja en el campo de la (educación) _____ pública.
2. They are poorly educated but are familiar with their history.
   Son (mal educados) _____ pero conocen su historia.
3. This allergy medicine is very effective.
   Este medicamento para la alergia es muy (efectivo) _____.
4. That course is not required; it's an elective course.
   Ese curso no es obligatorio; es un curso (electivo) _____.
5. Did you receive the e-mail I sent you last week?
   ¿Recibiste el (e-mail) _____ que te mandé la semana pasada?
6. I felt very embarrassed that I didn't know her name.
   Me sentí muy (embarazado) _____ de que no sabía su nombre.
7. I just enrolled in a Master's program.
   Me acabo de (enrolar) _____ en un programa de Máster.

8. Don't get involved in other people's business.
   No te (envuelvas) _____ en los asuntos de otros.
9. Would you like to sponsor our annual dinner?
   ¿Quiere usted (esponsorizar) _____ nuestra cena annual?
10. This perfume is sold in the form of a spray.
    Este perfume se vende en forma de (spray) _____.
11. The standard treatment is plenty of rest and drinking lots of water.
    El tratamiento (estándar) _____ es un buen descanso y beber mucha agua.
12. This traffic is stressing me out.
    Este tráfico me está (estresando) _____.
13. The poor man suffered a stroke and became paralyzed.
    El pobre hombre sufrió (un estroc) _____ y quedó paralizado.
14. What is your marital status?
    ¿Cuál es tu (estatus de matrimonio) _____?
15. The estimate to paint the entire house is a thousand dollars.
    (El estimado) _____ para pintar toda la casa es mil dólares.
16. The detective did not find evidence of any crime.
    El detective no encontró (evidencia) _____ de ningún crimen.
17. The contestant got excited when she won the car.
    La concursante se (excitó) _____ cuando ganó el carro.
18. There are two exits on this floor.
    Hay dos (éxitos) _____ en este piso.
19. When does your credit card expire?
    ¿Cuándo (expira) _____ tu tarjeta de crédito?
20. The candidates will be discussing foreign policy.
    Los candidatos van a discutir la política (extranjera) _____.

(6) U.S. Spanish words that start with F.

1. There is a medical facility five minutes from here.
   Hay (una facilidad médica) _____ a cinco minutos de aquí.
2. My father used to work in a paper factory.
   Mi papá trabajaba en una (factoría) _____ de papel.
3. This university has an excellent faculty.
   Esta universidad tiene (una facultad) _____ excelente.
4. I don't want to fail my final exam.
   No quiero (fallar) _____ mi examen final.
5. It was nobody's fault.
   No era (falta) _____ de nadie.
6. I wasn't familiar with your situation.
   Yo no estaba (familiar con) _____ tu situación.
7. The feedback from those who attended the conference has been very positive.
   (El feedback) _____ de los que asistieron a la conferencia ha sido muy positiva.
8. There is a ferry that goes from Cancun to Cozumel.
   Hay (un ferry) _____ que va de Cancún hasta Cozumel.

9. He earns a six-figure salary.
   Él gana un sueldo de seis (figuras) _____.
10. I love films from the 1940s.
    Me encantan (los filmes) _____ de los años 40.
11. It's a good thing we had flashlights during the blackout.
    Menos mal que teníamos (flashlights) _____ durante el apagón.
12. He spent the afternoon flirting with the girls.
    Se pasó la tarde (flirteando) _____ con las niñas.
13. I made copies of the documents on a floppy disk.
    Hice copia de los documentos en un (floppy) _____.
14. Did you fill out the "change of grade" form?
    ¿Llenaste (la forma) _____ para el cambio de nota?
15. Do you plan to join a fraternity?
    ¿Piensas hacerte miembro de una (fraternidad) _____?
16. My wife just got a full-time job.
    Mi esposa acaba de conseguir un trabajo (full time) _____.

(7) U.S. Spanish words that start with G and H.

1. She gained almost fifty pounds during the pregnancy.
   (Ganó) _____ casi cincuenta libras durante el embarazo.
2. The gap between generations is getting wider.
   (El gap) _____ entre las generaciones está creciendo.
3. I spent an hour waiting for the bus.
   (Gasté) _____ una hora esperando el autobús.
4. Don't waste the little money you have.
   No (gastes) _____ el poco dinero que tienes.
5. Our goal is to raise 100,000 dollars for the hurricane victims.
   (Nuestro gol) _____ es recaudar 100.000 dólares para las víctimas del huracán.
6. I'm not happy with the grade I received in math.
   No estoy contenta con (el grado) _____ que me dieron en matemáticas.
7. We're going to cook chicken and steak on the grill.
   Vamos a preparar pollo y biftec (al grill) _____.
8. My mother went to the grocery store to buy milk.
   Mi madre fue a la (grocería) _____ a comprar leche.
9. He has a habit of talking very loudly.
   Tiene (el hábito) _____ de hablar en voz alta.
10. We need to make a decision immediately.
    Tenemos que (hacer) _____ una decisión inmediatamente.
11. I used to make a lot of money when I worked as a cab driver.
    Yo (hacía) _____ mucho dinero cuando trabajaba de taxista.
12. Her handicap won't prevent her from participating in the game.
    Su (hándicap) _____ no le impedirá que participe en el partido.
13. Can you get light bulbs in a hardware store?
    ¿Puedes conseguir bombillas en una (tienda de hardware) _____?

14. You shouldn't hesitate to call a doctor.
    No debieras (hesitar) _____ en llamar a un médico.
15. Collecting toy trains is an interesting hobby.
    La colección de trenes de juguete es un (hobby) _____ muy interesante.

(8) U.S. Spanish words that start with I and J.

1. What happens when you turn off the ignition?
   ¿Qué pasa cuando apagas (la ignición) _____?
2. When he starts to talk that way, it's better to ignore him.
   Cuando se pone a hablar de esa manera, es mejor (ignorarlo) _____.
3. Everyone congratulated me, including the president of the company.
   Todo el mundo me felicitó, (incluyendo) _____ el presidente de la empresa.
4. You could hear the infants cry all night long.
   Se oía llorar a (los infantes) _____ toda la noche.
5. I am not going to be influenced by anyone.
   Yo no me voy a dejar (influenciar) _____ por nadie.
6. The cyclist suffered many injuries when he fell off his motorcycle.
   El ciclista sufrio varias (injurias) _____ al caerse de la moto.
7. We are very interested in input from our students.
   Nos interesa mucho (el input) _____ de nuestros alumnos.
8. He has been insensitive to his family's problems.
   Ha sido (insensitivo) _____ a los problemas de su familia.
9. I intend to file a complaint against the policeman.
   (Intento) _____ presentar una queja contra el policía.
10. I have an interview tomorrow at nine o'clock.
    Tengo (una interviú) _____ mañana a las nueve.
11. He left the party completely intoxicated.
    Se fue de la fiesta completamente (intoxicado) _____.
12. My wife introduced me to the school principal.
    Mi esposa me (introdujo) _____ al director de la escuela.
13. I am disoriented because of the six-hour jet lag.
    Estoy desorientado por el (jet lag) _____ de seis horas.
14. We embarked on a journey around the world.
    Emprendimos (una jornada) _____ alrededor del mundo.
15. Let's buy tickets for tonight's game.
    Vamos a comprar entradas para el (juego) _____ de esta noche.
16. Do you know how to play the trumpet?
    ¿Sabes (jugar) _____ la trompeta?

(9) U.S. Spanish words that start with K and L.

1. I needed so many tools that I decided to buy the whole kit.
   Me hacían falta tantas herramientas que decidí comprar el (kit) _____ entero.
2. I am going to call the landlord and ask for a new lease.
   Voy a llamar al (landlord) _____ y pedirle un nuevo contrato.

3. My husband was laid off from work without being given a reason.
A mi esposo (le dieron layoff) _____ sin darle razones.
4. Why don't you sign a two-year lease?
¿Por qué no firmas un (lease) _____ de dos años?
5. The professor will be giving a lecture on Lope de Vega.
El profesor va a dar una (lectura) _____ sobre Lope de Vega.
6. Russian continues to be an official language of the United Nations.
El ruso sigue siendo (un lenguaje) _____ oficial de las Naciones Unidas.
7. We live across the street from the county library.
Vivimos en frente de la (librería) _____ del condado.
8. The president met with various Latin American leaders.
El presidente se reunió con varios (líderes) _____ de Latinoamérica.
9. You better get on line if you want service.
Más vale que (te pongas en línea) _____ si quieres que te atiendan.
10. There is a link to the departments on the university website.
Hay un (link) _____ a los departamentos en la página web de la universidad.
11. What brand of lipstick do you use?
¿Qué marca de (lipstick) _____ usas?
12. I ate too much; I am full.
He comido demasiado; (estoy lleno) _____.
13. We found a house in an excellent location.
Encontramos una casa en (una locación) _____ excelente.
14. We had lunch in a Mexican restaurant.
(Lonchamos) _____ en un restaurante mexicano.
15. It looks like the (traffic) light is not working.
Parece que (la luz) _____ no funciona.

(10) U.S. Spanish words that start with M.

1. The pants and shoes don't match.
Los pantalones y zapatos no (machean) _____.
2. What magazine are you reading?
¿Qué (magacín) _____ estás leyendo?
3. I want to declare a major in Spanish.
Quiero declarar (un major) _____ en español.
4. Every Sunday, she goes to the mall to do her shopping.
Todos los domingos va al (mall) _____ a hacer compras.
5. Good manners are learned in the home.
(Las buenas maneras) _____ se aprenden en casa.
6. I have been looking for a map of New York City.
He estado buscando un (mapa) _____ de la ciudad de Nueva York.
7. There is a big market (demand) for cell phones.
Hay (una marqueta grande) _____ para teléfonos celulares.
8. I am doing a Masters in education.
Estoy haciendo un (máster) _____ en pedagogía.
9. Wool is a good material for winter suits.
La lana es (buen material) _____ para trajes de invierno.

10. I know someone who had a minor role in a famous movie.
    Conozco a alguien que tuvo un papel (menor) _____ en una película famosa.
11. She has been miserable since her boyfriend left her.
    Ha estado (miserable) _____ desde que su novio la dejó.
12. My colleagues arrived late to the department meeting.
    Mis colegas llegaron tarde (al mitin) _____ del departamento.
13. He was fired for having molested one of his students.
    Lo despidieron por haber (molestado a) _____ uno de sus alumnos.
14. I had to pay with a money order because they didn't accept checks.
    Tuve que pagar con (money order) _____ porque no aceptaban cheques.
15. My computer mouse is not working very well.
    El (maus) _____ de mi computadora no funciona muy bien.
16. They moved to California last month.
    Se (movieron) _____ a California el mes pasado.
17. Every morning I have a muffin with my coffee.
    Todas las mañanas me como una (mofin) _____ con el café.

(11) U.S. Spanish words that start with N and O.

1. We are studying the native cultures of the Andean region.
   Estudiamos las culturas (nativas) _____ de la región andina.
2. Every weekend, they go out dancing in the nightclubs.
   Todos los fines de semana, salen a (los nightclubs) _____ a bailar.
3. I can't remember the exact name of the book.
   No recuerdo el (nombre) _____ exacto del libro.
4. Please write your last name on the list.
   Favor de escribir su (último nombre) _____ en la lista.
5. For this type of operation they won't need to knock you out (anesthesize you).
   Para este tipo de operation no te tienen que (noquear) _____.
6. The nurse that takes care of me is wonderful.
   La (norsa) _____ que se ocupa de mí es estupenda.
7. Do you take notes in philosophy class?
   ¿Tomas (notas) _____ en la clase de filosofía?
8. I will send out a notice about tomorrow's lecture.
   Mandaré (una noticia) _____ acerca de la conferencia de mañana.
9. The parties concerned decided to nullify the agreement.
   Los interesados decidieron (nulificar) _____ el acuerdo.
10. I'm sorry to tell you that your friend was obnoxious in my opinion.
    Siento decirte que tu amigo me resultó (obnoxio) _____.
11. Lying to the authorities is a very serious offense.
    El mentir a las autoridades es (una ofensa) _____ muy grave.
12. Did you hear what happened to my brother?
    ¿(Oíste) _____ lo que le pasó a mi hermano?
13. I haven't heard from her since she got married.
    No he (oído) _____ de ella desde que se casó.
14. The class was OK, neither very interesting nor very boring.
    La clase estuvo (okey) _____, ni muy interesante ni muy aburrida.

15. This semester I will be taking two courses on line.
    Este semestre voy a tomar dos cursos (on line) _____.
16. My son always seems to do the opposite of what I ask of him.
    Mi hijo parece siempre hacer lo (opósito) _____ de lo que le pido.
17. Are you all ready to order?
    ¿Están ustedes listos a (ordenar) _____?

(12) U.S. Spanish words that start with P.

1. It's important not to panic in an emergency.
   Es importante no (paniquearse) _____ en una emergencia.
2. If you buy five or more panties, you get a discount.
   Si compras un mínimo de cinco (pantis) _____, te dan un descuento.
3. The professor liked the paper I wrote for his course.
   Al profesor le gustó (el papel) _____ que escribí para su curso.
4. Teachers and parents must work together.
   Maestros y (parientes) _____ tienen que colaborar.
5. You are not allowed to park on this street.
   No se puede (parquear) _____ en esta calle.
6. If I find a part-time job, I'll be able to pay my tuition.
   Si encuentro un trabajo (part-time) _____, podré pagar la matrícula.
7. Do you think you passed the test?
   ¿Crees que (pasaste) _____ el examen?
8. If you don't do some kind of exercise, you won't lose weight.
   Si no haces algún ejercicio, no vas a (perder peso) _____.
9. The students are going to perform the opera *Carmen*.
   Los estudiantes van a (performar) _____ la ópera *Carmen*.
10. Do you plan to invite all your friends?
    ¿(Planeas) _____ invitar a todos tus amigos?
11. My mother is planting tomatoes in the yard.
    Mi madre está (plantando) _____ tomates en el jardín.
12. There isn't even one gas pump available.
    No hay ni (una pompa) _____ de gasolina que esté libre.
13. They forgot to punch our tickets when we came in.
    Se olvidaron de (ponchar) _____ los tiques cuando entramos.
14. What is the current population of Spain?
    ¿Cuál es la (populación) _____ actual de España?
15. I prefer to use a portable projector.
    Prefiero usar un proyector (portable) _____.
16. The position of manager is still available.
    (La posición) _____ de gerente todavía está disponible.
17. I have a Beatles poster from 1964.
    Tengo un (póster) _____ de los Beatles de 1964.
18. This cheese contains many preservatives.
    Este queso contiene muchos (preservativos) _____.
19. He pretended to be sick in order to miss work.
    (Pretendió) _____ estar enfermo para no ir al trabajo.

20. Were you able to connect the printer to the computer?
    ¿Llegaste a conectar (el prínter) _____ a la computadora?
21. You're going to pay a lot of money for private lessons.
    Vas a pagar mucho dinero por lecciones (privadas) _____.
22. This organization provides funds for certain projects.
    Esta organización (providea) _____ fondos para ciertos proyectos.

(13) U.S. Spanish words that start with R.

1. I had to give back my steak because it was too rare.
   Tuve que devolver el biftec porque estaba (demasiado raro) _____.
2. This video game is very realistic.
   Este juego de video es muy (realístico) _____.
3. He didn't realize that I was a student in his class.
   No (realizó) _____ que yo era estudiante en su clase.
4. The suspect said he had no recollection of the incident.
   El acusado dijo que no tenía (recolección) _____ del incidente.
5. I begged her to wait for me but she refused.
   Le supliqué que me esperara pero (refusó) _____.
6. What courses are you registering for?
   ¿Para qué cursos te vas a (registrar) _____?
7. I don't understand the new parking regulations.
   No entiendo (las nuevas regulaciones) _____ de estacionamiento.
8. She went to spend some time with relatives in Puerto Rico.
   Fue a pasar un tiempo con (relativos) _____ en Puerto Rico.
9. What I need is a month of relaxation.
   Lo que me hace falta es un mes de (relaxeo) _____.
10. Unfortunately, the information we found is not relevant to the case.
    Desgraciadamente, la información que encontramos no (es relevante)
    _____.
11. The way that little boy plays the piano is remarkable.
    La manera en que ese niño toca el piano es (remarcable) _____.
12. I tried to remove the nails but I couldn't.
    Intenté (remover) _____ los clavos pero no pude.
13. If he doesn't leave me alone, I'm going to report him to the police.
    Si no me deja tranquila, lo voy a (reportar) _____ a la policía.
14. The teacher asked me to write a report on Argentina.
    La maestra me mandó escribir un (reporte) _____ sobre la Argentina.
15. What are the required courses?
    ¿Cuáles son los cursos (requeridos) _____?
16. The resignation of the dean was a complete surprise.
    La (resignación) _____ del decano fue una absoluta sorpresa.
17. It looks like there is revival of 1940s music.
    Parece que hay un (revival) _____ de la música de los años 40.
18. Not everything revolves around your needs.
    No todo (revuelve) _____ alrededor de tus necesidades.

19. The role of women has changed a great deal in the last decades.
    El (rol) _____ de la mujer ha cambiado mucho en las últimas décadas.
20. Some people like to break the rules from time to time.
    A ciertas personas les gusta (romper) _____ las reglas de vez en cuando.
21. The roster indicates that there are thirty students in this class.
    (El róster) _____ indica que hay treinta estudiantes en este clase.
22. The secretary spoke to me in a very rude manner.
    La secretaria me habló de una manera muy (ruda) _____.

(14) U.S. Spanish words that start with S.

1. They offered me a good salary but no benefits.
   Me ofrecieron un buen (salario) _____ pero ningún beneficio.
2. We have to save electricity.
   Tenemos que (salvar) _____ electricidad.
3. I forgot to save the document (on a computer).
   Se me olvidó (salvar) _____ el documento.
4. That was a very sane decision on your part.
   Fue una decisión muy (sana) _____ de tu parte.
5. It's difficult to select when there are so many options.
   Es difícil (selectar) _____ cuando hay tantas opciones.
6. I have very sensitive skin.
   Tengo la piel muy (sensitiva) _____.
7. You should write shorter sentences.
   Deberías escribir (sentencias) _____ más cortas.
8. He says he has a million dollars but I don't think he's serious.
   Dice que tiene un millón de dólares pero no creo que (está serio) _____.
9. I have an enormous amount of shopping to do.
   Tengo cantidad de (shopping) _____ que hacer.
10. They gave me back the form because the signature was missing.
    Me devolvieron la hoja porque le faltaba la (signatura) _____.
11. We're going to give our sympathies to the family of the deceased.
    Vamos a dar (nuestras simpatías) _____ a la familia del fallecido.
12. She bought the latest style in sneakers.
    Se compró la última moda de (sníquers) _____.
13. I don't know how he supports his family with what he earns.
    No sé cómo (soporta) _____ a su familia con lo que gana.
14. Would you mind sorting these papers for me?
    ¿Me haces el favor de (sortear) _____ estos papeles?
15. The e-mail message was sent to the entire staff.
    El correo electrónico se mandó a (todo el staff) _____.
16. You need to get off at the last stop.
    Te tienes que bajar en (el último stop) _____.
17. Julio Iglesias has had international success.
    Julio Iglesias ha tenido un (suceso) _____ internacional.
18. It seems like an excellent suggestion to me.
    A mí me parece una excelente (sugestión) _____.

19. I cannot speak about that subject.
    No puedo hablar de ese (sujeto) _____.
20. We are going to have to make a switch.
    Vamos a tener que hacer un (switch) _____.

(15) U.S. Spanish words that start with T.

1. I need strong tape to wrap this box.
   Necesito (un tape) _____ bien fuerte para envolver esta caja.
2. He called to say he was late.
   Llamó para decir que (estaba tarde) _____.
3. They charged me a 10% sales tax.
   Me cobraron (una tax) _____ de venta de 10%.
4. I was a teenager when I arrived in this country.
   Yo era (teenager) _____ cuando llegué a este país.
5. Our living situation is temporary.
   Nuestra situacion de vivienda es (temporaria) _____.
6. The tenants refuse to sign the new lease.
   Los (tenientes) _____ se negaron a firmar el nuevo contrato.
7. The teacher gave us back our tests.
   La maestra nos devolvió (los tests) _____.
8. I hope you have a good time at the wedding.
   Espero que (tengas un buen tiempo) _____ en la fiesta de bodas.
9. Does the essay need to be typed?
   ¿Hace falta (tipear) _____ el ensayo?
10. Did you buy the tickets for the concert?
    ¿Compraste (los tiques) _____ para el concierto?
11. He took my book and never returned it.
    (Tomó) _____ mi libro y nunca me lo devolvió.
12. This is going to take at least an hour.
    Esto va a (tomar) _____ por lo menos una hora.
13. The professor gave us a list of topics to choose from.
    El profesor nos dio una lista de (tópicos) _____ para que podamos escoger.
14. This tape recorder doesn't work well.
    Esta grabadora no (trabaja) _____ bien.
15. Ask the bus driver to give you a transfer ticket.
    Pídele un (tránsfer) _____ al conductor.

(16) U.S. Spanish words that start with U, V, W, Y, and Z.

1. This is a very unique situation.
   Es una situación muy (única) _____.
2. All the workers are members of the union.
   Todos los obreros son miembros (de la unión) _____.
3. I had to buy a new vacuum cleaner.
   Tuve que comprar (un nuevo vacuum cleaner) _____.

4. You should eat lots of vegetables.
   Debes comer cantidad de (vegetables) _____.
5. He took advantage of my innocence.
   (Tomó ventaja) _____ de mi inocencia.
6. I saw a beautiful dress in the store window.
   Vi un lindo vestido en (la ventana de la tienda) _____.
7. How many videotapes do you need?
   ¿Cuántos (videotapes) _____ necesitas?
8. After the third violation, they take away your driver's license.
   A partir de la tercera (violación) _____ te quitan el permiso de conducir.
9. My son loves waffles with strawberry jam.
   A mi hijo le encantan los (waffles) _____ con mermelada de fresa.
10. The furniture needs to be waxed.
    Hace falta (waxear) _____ los muebles.
11. I found an interesting website about classical art.
    Encontré (un website) _____ interesante sobre el arte clásico.
12. Last weekend we celebrated our tenth anniversary.
    El (weekend) _____ pasado celebramos nuestro décimo aniversario.
13. I plan to conduct a workshop about online courses.
    Pienso dirigir un (workshop) _____ sobre cursos en la red.
14. The kids are playing in the yard.
    Los niños están jugando en (la yarda) _____.
15. After not having slept two nights in a row, I'm like a zombie.
    Después de no dormir dos noches seguidas, estoy como (zombi) _____.

ANSWER KEY (Exercise 1)

1. entrada
2. antiguas
3. sumar
4. conseguir
5. rica / adinerada
6. se comportó
7. amor / cariño
8. actuación / aparición
9. solicitud
10. me afectan
11. disculpa / excusa
12. discusiones
13. asistió
14. el ambiente
15. volvió / regresó
16. del público
17. promedio
18. aconsejó

ANSWER KEY (Exercise 2)

1. al nene / a la criatura
2. el trasfondo / la formación
3. una mochila
4. equilibrarse
5. conjunto / grupo
6. pilas
7. localizador
8. derecho
9. extraña
10. cuadras / manzanas
11. vaqueros
12. jefe / jefa
13. descanso
14. presupuesto

EXERCISES

ANSWER KEY (Exercise 3)

1. hacía mucho calor
2. los requisitos
3. una colonia
4. Suspendieron
5. el personaje
6. La alfombra
7. tarjeta
8. en efectivo / al contado
9. informalmente / de sport
10. íntima
11. oportunidad
12. Busqué
13. un armario / un ropero
14. coleccionaba
15. una universidad
16. arreglo / acuerdo
17. director
18. seguro
19. cómoda
20. comunicarme con ella
21. tenías razón
22. bajo
23. La calidad
24. preguntas
25. cumplió con los requisitos

ANSWER KEY (Exercise 4)

1. a la guardería
2. indica
3. sabe
4. seguro
5. saliste de
6. avisaré
7. exigió / pidió
8. la manifestación
9. Según / De acuerdo a
10. hijos / personas a tu cargo
11. vergüenza / deshonra
12. incapacitados / discapacitados
13. Se dedicó
14. Varias
15. señas / instrucciones
16. repugnaba / daba asco
17. Las residencias
18. farmacia

ANSWER KEY (Exercise 5)

1. enseñanza / instrucción
2. incultos / de poca instrucción
3. eficaz
4. optativo / facultativo
5. correo electrónico
6. avergonzado
7. inscribir
8. metas
9. patrocinar / respaldar
10. atomizador
11. habitual / normal
12. agitando / afectando los nervios
13. un derrame cerebral
14. estado civil
15. El presupuesto / El coste aproximado
16. pruebas / indicios
17. entusiasmó / puso contenta
18. salidas
19. caduca / se vence
20. exterior

ANSWER KEY (Exercise 6)

1. un centro médico
2. fábrica
3. un profesorado
4. suspender
5. culpa
6. enterado de
7. La reacción
8. un transbordador
9. cifras
10. las películas
11. linternas
12. coqueteando
13. un disquete /un disco flexible
14. la hoja / el formulario
15. hermandad
16. a tiempo completo

ANSWER KEY (Exercise 7)

1. Engordó
2. La diferencia / La distancia
3. Pasé
4. malgastes / derroches
5. Nuestra meta
6. la nota / la calificación
7. a la parrilla
8. tienda de comestibles
9. la costumbre
10. tomar
11. ganaba
12. discapacidad / minusvalía
13. ferretería
14. vacilar
15. pasatiempo

ANSWER KEY (Exercise 8)

1. el motor / el arranque
2. no hacerle caso
3. incluso
4. las criaturas / los bebés
5. influir
6. heridas / lesiones
7. el consejo / la opinión
8. insensible
9. Pienso / Tengo la intención de
10. una entrevista
11. borracho / ebrio
12. presentó
13. desfase (horario)
14. un viaje
15. partido
16. tocar

ANSWER KEY (Exercise 9)

1. juego
2. dueño / propietario
3. lo despidieron
4. contrato de arrendamiento
5. conferencia
6. una lengua / un idioma
7. biblioteca
8. jefes de estado
9. hagas cola
10. enlace
11. lápiz de labios
12. estoy harto / no puedo más
13. un lugar
14. Almorzamos
15. el semáforo

ANSWER KEY (Exercise 10)

1. hacen juego / combinan bien
2. revista
3. una especializacion / una concentración
4. centro comercial
5. Los buenos modales
6. plano
7. mucha demanda
8. programa de maestría
9. buen tejido / buena tela
10. secundario
11. triste / deprimida
12. a la reunión
13. abusado de
14. giro bancario
15. ratón
16. mudaron
17. magdalena

EXERCISES

ANSWER KEY (Exercise 11)

1. indígenas
2. las discotecas / los clubes nocturnos
3. título
4. apellido
5. anestesiar / dormir
6. enfermera
7. apuntes
8. un aviso / un anuncio
9. anular / invalidar
10. desagradable / ofensivo
11. un delito
12. Te enteraste de
13. terrido noticias
14. regular / así así
15. por la red
16. contrario / opuesto
17. pedir

ANSWER KEY (Exercise 12)

1. dejarse llevar por el pánico
2. bragas / calzones
3. el ensayo / la monografía
4. padres
5. estacionar / aparcar
6. a tiempo parcial / de medio tiempo
7. aprobaste
8. adelgazar
9. representar
10. Piensas
11. sembrando
12. un surtidor
13. picar
14. población
15. portátil
16. El puesto
17. cartel
18. conservantes
19. Fingió
20. la impresora
21. particulares
22. proporciona

ANSWER KEY (Exercise 13)

1. medio crudo / muy poco hecho
2. realista / verosímil
3. se dio cuenta de
4. recuerdo
5. no quiso
6. matricular / inscribir
7. los nuevos reglamentos
8. parientes / familia
9. descanso
10. es pertinente / viene al caso
11. increíble / extraordinaria
12. quitar / arrancar
13. denunciar
14. trabajo / informe
15. obligatorios
16. dimisión / renuncia
17. renacimiento / resurgimiento
18. gira
19. papel
20. violar / desobedecer
21. La lista de asistencia / El registro
22. grosera / descortés

ANSWER KEY (Exercise 14)

1. sueldo
2. conservar
3. archivar
4. sensata / buena
5. seleccionar / escoger
6. delicada
7. oraciones
8. habla en serio
9. compras
10. firma
11. el pésame
12. tenis / zapatos de tenis
13. mantiene / sostiene
14. ordenar / arreglar
15. todo el personal / todos los empleados
16. la ultima parada / estación
17. éxito
18. sugerencia
19. asunto / tema
20. cambio / intercambio

ANSWER KEY (Exercise 15)

1. una cinta adhesiva
2. estaba atrasado / llegaba tarde
3. un impuesto
4. adolescente
5. provisional
6. los inquilinos
7. los exámenes / las pruebas
8. te diviertas / lo pases bien
9. pasar a máquina
10. las entradas / los boletos
11. Se llevó
12. tardar / durar
13. temas
14. funciona
15. boleto / tique de empalme

ANSWER KEY (Exercise 16)

1. singular / excepcional
2. del sindicato
3. una nueva aspiradora
4. vegetales / verduras / legumbres
5. Se aprovechó
6. el escaparate / la vitrina
7. casetes de video
8. infracción
9. gofres
10. encerar
11. una página web
12. fin de semana
13. taller
14. el patio / el jardín
15. atontado

II. FROM STANDARD SPANISH TO U.S. SPANISH

Replace the word(s) in parentheses with a corresponding expression likely to be used in U.S. Spanish

Hint: Think of a common English equivalent, then adapt it to Spanish or translate it literally. Very often, U.S. Spanish simply uses a borrowed word.

(17) Responses that start with A

1. Estaré ocupado toda la mañana pero tengo la tarde (disponible) _____.
2. El pasajero se salvó gracias a (la bolsa de aire) _____.
3. Mi novia va a (solicitar) _____ para el puesto de maestra.
4. Te mandaré los documentos por (archivo adjunto) _____.
5. En este curso, la (asistencia) _____ a clase es muy importante.

(18) Responses that start with B

1. Dejamos al niño con (una niñera) _____.
2. El alcalde no ha podido (nivelar) _____ el presupuesto.
3. Una vez a la semana, jugamos al (baloncesto) _____.
4. Para el desayuno, me comí dos huevos con (panceta ahumada) _____.
5. Los niños están jugando en el (sótano) _____.
6. No hay agua caliente porque no funciona (la caldera) _____.

(19) Responses that start with C

1. Los sábados, mi hijo mira los (dibujos animados) _____ en la televisión.
2. Una vez al año me hago un (reconocimiento) _____ médico.
3. Cuando estaba en París, me gustaba ir a (las discotecas) _____.
4. El partido (conservador) _____ ganó las últimas elecciones.
5. Tuve que ir al doctor porque estuve (estreñido) _____ toda una semana.
6. La pena capital es un asunto muy (polémico) _____ en este país.
7. Si no te paga lo que te debe, llévalo (al tribunal) _____.

(20) Responses that start with D

1. Los bomberos (manifestaron) _____ delante de la alcaldía.
2. La esposa de mi amigo es una mujer muy (hogareña) _____.
3. No me dio tiempo (descargar) _____ la información del internet.
4. El (farmacéutico) _____ me dio unas píldoras para el dolor.

(21) Responses that start with E

1. ¿Quién tiene la responsabilidad de (enseñar) _____ a nuestros hijos?
2. Parece que el (ascensor) _____ no funciona.
3. El coche no arranca porque se dañó el (motor de arranque) _____.
4. Después de tres horas en tráfico, estoy completamente (agobiado) _____.
5. Estuvo muy (emocionado) _____ de volver a estar con su familia.

(22) Responses that start with F and G

1. Guardamos los documentos importantes en (una carpeta) _____.
2. Quisiera una (salchicha) _____ con mostaza, por favor.
3. Resulta que el joven que arrestaron es miembro de (una pandilla) _____.
4. Si no encontramos una (gasolinera) _____ nos vamos en quedar sin gasolina.
5. El 18 de junio es el día de (entrega de títulos) _____ en mi universidad.

(23) Responses that start with H, I, and J

1. Almorcé una (hamburguesa) _____ con papas fritas.
2. Muchas canciones de Julio Iglesias han sido (éxitos) _____ internacionales.
3. Me (revisaron) _____ todas las maletas cuando pasé por la aduana.
4. Encontrarás mucha información sobre viajes a Europa en (la red) _____.
5. Mi hijo de quince años lleva (vaqueros) _____ todos los días.
6. ¿Sabes cuánto pagué por (una camisa) _____ de los Yankees?

(24) Responses that start with L

1. Mi hermano acaba de comprarse (una computadora portátil) _____.
2. ¿Quieres una cerveza regular o una cerveza (baja en calorías) _____?
3. Hay mucha gente en (la planta baja) _____ que espera el ascensor.
4. Es importante comer un buen (almuerzo) _____ todos los días.

(25) Responses that start with M

1. ¿Quién es el (gerente) _____ de esta tienda?
2. Mi mamá fue (al mercado) _____ a comprar pescado y legumbres.
3. Muchos usan el (horno microondas) _____ sólo para calentar la comida.
4. Estoy buscando (el trapeador) _____ para limpiar el piso.
5. El carro hace tanto ruido porque le falta un nuevo (silenciador) _____.

(26) Responses that start with N, O, and P

1. Los (centros nocturnos) _____ de Las Vegas son famosos.
2. Decidimos (encargar) _____ pizza porque nadie quería cocinar.
3. Estuve una hora buscando (estacionamiento) _____.
4. El niño se comió tres (salchichas) _____ en el partido de béisbol.
5. Ese joven tiene fama de (mujeriego) _____.
6. El médico me dio una (prescripción) _____ para un antibiótico.
7. Mañana tenemos que hablar con el (director) _____ de la escuela.

(27) Responses that start with R

1. La (matriculación) _____ de estudiantes comienza el lunes.
2. Me han aumentado (el alquiler) _____ un veinte por ciento.
3. Mi hermano va a (jubilarse) _____ a los cincuenta años.
4. Tienes que apretar el (botón de retroceso) _____.

EXERCISES

(28) Responses that start with S

1. Vamos a necesitar cuatro (juegos) _____ de cada libro de texto.
2. A mi madre le gustaba mucho el (programa) _____ de Cristina.
3. Cómete (una merienda) _____ mientras esperamos la cena.
4. Mis hijos beben demasiada (gaseosa) _____.
5. El diccionario que busco no lo tienen en (existencia) _____.
6. El (conserje) _____ es el único que tiene la llave de todos los apartamentos.

(29) Responses that start with T

1. Espero con ansiedad los resultados de mi (análisis) _____ de sangre.
2. Me pusieron (una multa) _____ por haber estacionado enfrente de una iglesia.
3. Le di un (pañuelo de papel) _____ para que se limpiara las lágrimas.
4. (Intenté) _____ comunicarme con ella pero no pude.
5. Tengo cita mañana para hacerme (una revisión) _____ del oído.

ANSWER KEY (Exercise 17)

1. abierta
2. el airbag
3. aplicar
4. attachment / atachmen
5. atendencia

ANSWER KEY (Exercise 18)

1. un baby-sitter
2. balancear
3. básquetbol
4. beicon / bacón
5. basement / béismen
6. el bóiler

ANSWER KEY (Exercise 19)

1. cartunes
2. chequeo
3. clubes
4. conservativo
5. constipado
6. controversial
7. a la corte

ANSWER KEY (Exercise 20)

1. demostraron
2. doméstica
3. hacer download de
4. droguista

ANSWER KEY (Exercise 21)

1. educar
2. elevador
3. estárter / starter
4. estresado
5. excitado

ANSWER KEY (Exercise 22)

1. un fólder / un file / un fail
2. frankfurter / franfura
3. una ganga / un gang
4. gasetería
5. graduación

ANSWER KEY (Exercise 23)

1. hamburger / jambergue
2. hits / jits
3. inspectaron
4. el internet
5. jeans / yins
6. un jersey / un yersi

ANSWER KEY (Exercise 24)

1. un laptop
2. light / lait
3. el lobby
4. lonche / lunch

ANSWER KEY (Exercise 25)

1. mánager / mánayer
2. a la marqueta
3. microwave / maicrogüey
4. la mopa
5. muffler / mofle

ANSWER KEY (Exercise 26)

1. nightclubs / naitclubes
2. ordenar
3. párking / parqueo
4. perros calientes
5. playboy
6. receta
7. principal

ANSWER KEY (Exercise 27)

1. registración
2. la renta
3. retirarse
4. rewind

ANSWER KEY (Exercise 28)

1. seta
2. el show
3. un snack / un esnac
4. soda
5. stock / estoc
6. súper

ANSWER KEY (Exercise 29)

1. test
2. un tique
3. tissue / tisú
4. traté de
5. un test

ENGLISH–SPANISH GLOSSARY AND INDEX

This list covers words and expressions that have U.S. Spanish variants that differ from standard academic Spanish. Each entry contains a representative selection of standard Spanish equivalents illustrated in this book, including common United States variants. All adjectives are given in the masculine form. An asterisk (*) indicates U.S. usage that is sanctioned by the *Real Academia Española*.

access v. *(on computer)* conseguir acceso, accesar (US) **1**

act v. *(=perform)* hacer teatro, hacer cine; *(=pretend)* fingir; *(=take action)* tomar medidas; **act as** *(=take the place of)* hacer de; actuar (US) **2**

actual adj. *(=real)* real, verdadero, actual (US) **2**

actually adv. en realidad, realmente, actualmente (US) **2**

add v. *(=calculate)* sumar, adicionar, añadir (US) **8**

additional adj. *(people)* más, de más; *(=supplementary)* suplementario, de más; adicional (US) **3**

admission n. *(confession)* confesión, *(entry)* entrada; admisión (US) **4**

admit v. *(to a program, school, etc.)* aceptar, admitir (US); **be admitted** *(to school, hospital, etc.)* ingresar, ser admitido (US) **4**

advantage n. provecho, ventaja (US); **to take advantage** *(of an opportunity)* aprovechar, *(of a person)* aprovecharse de, *(sexually)* abusar de; tomar ventaja de (US) **282**

advice n. consejo, aviso (US) **18**

advise v. aconsejar, avisar (US) **17**

affection n. *(=esteem)* afecto; *(fondness, love)* cariño, amor; afección (US) **5**

affluent adj. *(rich)* rico, adinerado, afluente (US) **5**

ago adv. hace, atrás* (US) **15**

airbag n. bolsa de aire, airbag* (US) **6**

ambition n. *(=longing, desire)* anhelo, deseo, ambición (US) **7**

ambitious adj. *(=eager, industrious)* ávido, trabajador, ambicioso (US) **7**

ancient adj. *(=classical, of old)* antiguo, anciano (US) **7**

apology n. *(=excuse)* excusa; *(expression of regret)* disculpa, apología (US) **11**

appear v. *(=seem)* parecer; *(in public, on TV)* salir; *(in court)* comparecer; *(=be published)* salir, publicarse; aparecer (US) **8**

appearance n. *(=aspect, look)* aspecto; *(=presence)* presencia; *(=coming into view)* aparición; *(on TV, film, theater)* actuación, aparición; *(in court)* comparecencia; apariencia (US) **9**

application n. *(=request)* solicitud; *(form)* formulario, aplicación (US) **10**

apply for v. *(=request)* pedir, solicitar, aplicar para (US) **11**

apply to v. *(=be relevant)* tener que ver con; *(=affect)* afectarle a uno; aplicar, aplicarse a (US) **11**

appreciate v. *(=give thanks for)* agradecer; *(=understand)* entender; apreciar (US) **12**

argument n. *(=debate)* polémica; *(=disagreement)* discusión, discordia; *(=quarrel)* discusión; *(=fight)* pelea, disputa; argumento (US) **12**

around adv/prep. *(=near, next to)* cerca de; *(=everywhere)* por todas partes; *(=through)* por; alrededor de (US) **6**

ask for v. *(=request)* pedir, pedir por (US) **197**

assistant n. *(=associate)* agregado, *(=helper)* ayudante; *(=subordinate)* sub-; asistente (US) **13**

atmosphere n. *(=ambience)* ambiente, atmósfera (US) **15**

attachment n. *(=computer file)* archivo adjunto, atachmen (US) **14**

attend v. *(=be present)* asistir, atender (US) **13, 14**

attendance n. *(=presence)* presencia; *(number of people)* asistencia; atendencia (US) **14**

audience n. *(of people)* público; *(viewing ~)* espectadores; *(listening ~)* oyentes; audiencia (US) **16**

average adj. medio, average (US) **17**

average n. promedio, average (US) **17**

baby n. *(=infant)* bebé, criatura, nene; *(=creation, fig.)* obra, creación; baby (US) **18**

babysitter n. canguro (Sp), niñera (LatAm), baby-sitter* (US) **19**

back n. *(=reverse side)* dorso, revés, atrás (US) **15**

background n. *(=away from limelight)* en segundo plano; *(=education)* formación, preparación; *(=experience)* experiencia; *(=preceding events)* antecedentes, trasfondo; *(spatial)* fondo; background / bagraun (US) **19**

backpack n. mochila, backpack (US) **20**

bacon n. panceta ahumada, tocino, bacón* / beicon* (US) **26**

bagel n. rosco, bagel / beigol (US) **21**

baggage n. *(=luggage)* equipaje, bagaje (US) **20**

balance n. *(=equilibrium)* equilibrio; *(=harmony)* armonía, equilibrio; *(=remainder)* saldo; *(=scale)* balanza; balance (US) **21**

balance v. *(=place in equilibrium)* mantener en equilibrio; *(=compare)* comparar, compensar; *(to ~ a budget, an account)* nivelar, hacer cuadrar; **balance oneself** equilibrarse; balancear, balancearse (US) **22**

balanced adj. *(meal, viewpoint, etc.)* equilibrado, balanceado (US) **22**

band n. *(=orchestra)* orquesta; *(ensemble)* conjunto; banda (US) **23**

barbecue n. *(food)* parrillada; *(grill)* parrilla; *(party)* parrillada, barbacoa; barbecue (US) **23**

bartender n. camarero, barman*, bartender (US) **24**

base n. [used figuratively] *(first base)* primera meta, primer paso, primera base (US); *(to touch base)* ponerse en contacto, tocar base (US); *(to cover all bases)* abarcar todo, cubrir todas las bases (US); *(to be off base)* estar totalmente equivocado, estar fuera de base (US) **24**

basement n. sótano, béisment (US) **26**

basket n. *(in basketball)* canasta, básquet* (US) **25**

basketball n. *(sport)* baloncesto, básquetbol* (US); *(ball)* pelota de baloncesto, basketball (US) **25**

battery n. *(=dry cell)* pila; *(=assault)* asalto; *(=series)* serie; batería (US) **25**

beep v. *(=make a sound)* [trans] tocar; *(=make a sound)* [intrans] sonar; *(=call on a beeper)* llamar, localizar; bipear (US) **27**

beeper n. localizador, bíper (US) **27**

best-seller n. éxito de ventas, best seller* (US) **26**

bizarre adj. extraño, raro, bizar / bizarro (US) **29**

blame v. echar la culpa, culpar (US); **put the blame on** echar la culpa a, poner la culpa a (US) **195**

blister n. *(on skin)* ampolla; *(on paintwork)* burbuja; blíster (US) **29**

block n. *(of buildings, city block)* cuadra, manzana; *(section)* sección; *(series)* grupo, serie; bloque (US) **31**

blue jeans n. see **jeans**

bluff v. *(=deceive)* engañar; *(=pretend, make believe)* hacer creer, fingir; blofear (US) **30**

boiler n. *(for heating)* caldera, bóiler (US); **boiler room** sala de calderas, bóiler (US) **32**

boom n. *(=noise)* retumbo, estruendo; *(of microphone)* jirafa, boom (US) **32**

boss n. *(=employer)* jefe / jefa, patrón / patrona; *(=manager)* gerente; *(=owner)* dueño; *(=one whom decides)* quien manda, quien decide; boss (US) **33**

boss around v. dar órdenes, mandar, bosear (US) **33**

boycott n. boicoteo* / boicot* (US) **31**

break n. *(=pause, rest)* descanso; *(=chance, opportunity)* oportunidad; *(=discount)* descuento; break (US) **33**

break v. *(=pause)* hacer un descanso; *(=weaken, destroy)* quebrantar, quebrar; *(=end, cease)* terminarse, acabarse; *(=become known)* darse a conocer; *(~ a rule, ~ the law)* desobedecer; *(~ a record)* superar, batir; *(~ money)* cambiar; romper (US) **233**

break down v. *(=cease to function)* descomponerse, estropearse, romperse (US) **233**

budget n. presupuesto, budget (US) **34**

business n. *(field of study)* comercio; *(=enterprise)* negocio; *(=firm)* empresa; *(=occupation)* oficio; *(=clients)* clientela; *(=profit)* dinero, ganancia; *(=duty, responsibility)* responsabilidad; *(=matter, issue)* asunto, cuestión; *(=right)* derecho; bisnes* (US) **27**

byte n. octeto, byte* (US) **34**

call for v. llamar, llamar por (US) **197**

camp n. *(activity)* colonia de vacaciones; *(campground)* campamento; *(political party)* bando; campo (US) **37**

camping n. *(activity)* acampada; *(site)* campamento, cámping* (US) **36**

cancel v. *(plans, event)* suspender; *(contract, reservation)* anular; *(trip, flight)* suspender; *(subscription)* anular; cancelar (US) **37**

card n. *(ID, credit, greeting)* tarjeta; *(business ~)* tarjeta de visita; *(membership ~)* carné; *(index ~)* ficha; carta (US) **39**

care for v. *(=love)* querer, cuidar de (US) **63**

carpet n. alfombra, carpeta (US) **38**

cartoon n. *(=animated film)* dibujo animado; *(=comic strip)* historieta, viñeta; cartoon / cartún (US) **40**

cash n. *(means of payment)* al contado; *(=with bills and coins)* en efectivo; cash (US) **40**

cassette n. *(=audio tape)* casete; *(=video tape)* casete de video; **cassette player** *(audio)* magnetófono; casete* / caset (US) **40, 284**

casual adj. *(=informal)* informal; *(=nonchalant)* despreocupado; casual (US) **41**

casually adv. *(=informally)* informalmente; *(=occasionally)* de vez en cuando; casualmente (US) **41**

catsup n. see **ketchup**

CD n. *(=compact disk)* disco compacto, CD* (US) **41**

chance n. *(=coincidence)* casualidad; *(=hazard, fate)* azar, destino; *(=hope)* esperanza; *(=opportunity)* oportunidad; *(=possibility)* posibilidad; *(=risk)* riesgo; chance (US) **43**

character n. *(fictitious)* personaje; *(=role)* papel, rol; *(=individual)* tipo; carácter (US) **38**

chat v. *(online)* charlar, chatear (US) **43**

check n. *(=mark, symbol)* marca, señal; *(restraint, security ~)* control; chequeo (US) **45**

check v. *(=examine)* examinar; *(=look over, look through)* revisar; *(=flag, mark)* señalar, marcar; *(=register)*

315

facturar; *(=test, taste)* probar; *(=verify)* comprobar; *(=look around)* buscar; *(=look at)* mirar, ver, fijarse; *(=contain, stop)* detener, frenar; *(=consult)* consultar; chequear (US) **44**

checkup n. *(medical)* examen, reconocimiento; *(mechanical)* inspección, revisión; chequeo* (US) **45**

chips n. *(snack)* fritas de bolsa, chips (US) **46**

clip n. *(=film clip, video clip)* secuencia; *(=paper clip)* presilla, sujetapapeles; clip* (US) **47**

close adj. *(=intimate)* íntimo, cercano (US) **42**

close adv. *(emotionally)* unido, cerca (US) **42**

closet n. armario, ropero, clóset* (US) **48**

clown n. payaso, clown* (US) **48**

club n. *(=association)* sociedad; *(=nightclub)* discoteca; *(=building, center)* centro, club (US) **49**

collect v. *(~ as a hobby)* coleccionar; *(=gather)* acumular; *(=pick up)* recoger; *(=take, get)* ir por, venir por; *(~ money)* hacer una colecta; *(=get paid)* pagarle a uno; colectar (US) **49**

college n. *(=university)* universidad, colegio (US) **50**

come back v. regresar, volver, venir para atrás (US) **15**

comfort n. *(=well-being)* bienestar; *(=convenience)* comodidad; *(=solace, consolation)* consuelo; confort* (US) **54**

comfortable adj. cómodo, a gusto, confortable* (US) **55**

competition n. *(=contest)* concurso; *(=rivalry)* competencia; *(=rival)* competidor; competición (US) **50**

complexion n. *(=skin tone)* piel, tez; *(=skin texture)* cutis; *(=facet)* faceta, aspecto; complexión (US) **50**

compromise n. *(=agreement, settlement)* arreglo; *(=giving in)* transigencia; compromiso (US) **51**

conductor n. *(music)* director, conductor (US) **52**

conference n. *(=convention)* congreso; *(=assembly)* asamblea; *(=meeting)* reunión; conferencia (US) **53**

confidence n. *(=trust, secrecy)* confianza; confidencia (US) **53**

confident adj. *(=secure, certain)* seguro, confiado, confidente (US) **53**

connection n. *(train, bus, plane)* enlace, correspondencia, conexión (US) **52**

conservative adj. *(=traditional)* tradicional, conservador; *(=classic)* clásico, elegante; *(=cautious)* prudente, cauteloso; *(political party)* conservador; conservativo (US) **55**

constipated adj. estreñido, constipado (US) **56**

contact v. *(=get in touch)* ponerse en contacto; *(=find)* encontrar, localizar; *(by phone)* comunicarse con; contactar (US) **56**

contest v. *(=protest)* rebatir, rechazar; *(=compete)* disputarse; contestar (US) **57**

controversial adj. *(=much debated)* discutido, polémico; *(=antagonistic)* controvertido, controversial* (US) **57**

correct adj. *(=exact)* exacto, correcto (US); **be correct** *(=be right)* tener razón, estar correcto (US); *(=do the right thing)* hacer bien, ser correcto (US) **58**

court n. *(of law)* tribunal; *(tennis)* cancha; corte (US) **59**

courtyard n. patio, corte (US) **59**

cowboy n. *(profession)* vaquero; *(in the movies)* americano; cowboy (US) **60**

current adj. *(=present)* actual, presente, corriente (US) **59**

day care n. guardería, daycare (US) **63**

deceived adj. engañado, decepcionado (US) **64**

deception n. engaño, decepción (US) **64**

definite adj. *(=certain, sure)* seguro; *(=clear)* claro; *(=firm)* firme; definitivo (US) **65**

demand v. *(=request)* exigir, pedir; *(=insist on)* insistir en; *(=require)* requerir, exigir; *(=claim)* reclamar; demandar (US) **66**

demanding adj. exigente, demandante (US) **66**

demonstrate v. *(=protest)* manifestar; *(=display)* expresar; demostrar (US) **67**

demonstration n. *(=protest)* manifestación; *(=model, demo)* muestra, modelo; demostración (US) **67**

dependent n. *(child, etc.)* hijo, persona a cargo, dependiente (US) **68**

depending on adv. según, de acuerdo a, dependiendo de (US) **68**

devote v. *(=dedicate)* dedicar; *(=assign, earmark)* asignar; devotar (US) **70**

different adj. *(=various)* varios; *(=another)* otro; *(=changed)* cambiado; diferente (US) **70**

directions n. *(for use)* instrucciones, modo de empleo; *(to a place)* señas; direcciones (US) **71**

disabled adj. discapacitado, minusválido, deshabilitado (US) **69**

disgrace n. *(=shame)* deshonra, desgracia (US) **69**

disgraced adj. deshonrado, desgraciado (US) **69**

disgust n. *(=repugnance)* repugnancia, asco, disgusto (US); **in disgust** adj. *(=in anger)* indignado, ofendido, en disgusto (US) **72**

disgust v. *(=be repugnant)* repugnar, dar asco; *(=offend)* ofender, indignar; disgustar (US) **72**

diskette n. *(computer)* disquete* / disket* (US) **73**

dollar n. dólar, peso (US) **188**

domestic adj. *(=homebody)* hogareño, casero; *(=national)* nacional; *(=internal)* interno; doméstico (US) **73**

donut n. see **doughnut**

dormitory n. *(=student residence)* residencia estudiantil, dormitorio (US) **74**

doughnut n. buñuelo, dona / dónut (US) **73**

download n. descarga, download (US) **74**

download v. descargar, hacer download (US) **74**

driver n. *(paid)* chófer, conductor (US) **52**

druggist n. *(=pharmacist)* farmacéutico, droguista (US) **75**

drugstore n. *(=pharmacy)* farmacia; *(=convenience store)* tienda de comestibles y medicamentos; droguería (US) **74**

dumping n. *(=spillage of wastes)* vertido; dumping (US) **75**

early adj. *(=soon)* pronto; *(=with time to spare)* con tiempo; *(=first, primitive)* primero, primitivo; *(=in the first stages)* a principios de; temprano (US); **be / arrive early** v. llegar temprano; estar temprano (US) **264**

earn v. *(money)* ganar dinero, hacer dinero (US) **122**

editing n. *(text ~)* redacción, tarea editorial (US) **76**

editor n. *(chief ~)* director; *(text ~)* redactor; editor (US) **76**

educate v. *(=teach, provide instruction)* enseñar, instruir, educar* (US) **79**

educated adj. *(=academically prepared)* instruído; *(=cultured, refined)* culto, refinado; educado (US) **78**

education n. *(=schooling, training)* estudios, formación; *(=knowledge)* conocimientos; *(=teaching)* enseñanza; *(=pedagogy)* pedagogía; educación (US) **77**

educational adj. *(=academic)* académico; *(for school use)* escolar; *(related to teaching)* de enseñanza; *(role, function)* docente; *(theory)* pedagógico; educacional (US) **77**

effective adj. *(=competent)* capaz, eficiente, competente; *(yields positive results)* eficaz; *(=striking)* logrado; efectivo (US) **79**

elaborate v. *(=develop)* desarrollar; *(=provide details)* dar detalles; *(=explain)* explicar; elaborar (US) **80**

elective adj. *(=optional)* optativo, facultativo, opcional, electivo (US) **80**

elevator n. *(passenger)* ascensor; *(freight)* montacargas, ascensor; elevador* (US) **81**

e-mail n. *(system)* correo electrónico; *(message)* mensaje electrónico; e-mail / emilio (US) **81**

embarrass v. avergonzar, hacer pasar verguenza, embarazar (US) **82**

embarrassed adj. avergonzado, comprometido, embarazado (US) **82**

enforce v. *(=carry out)* ejecutar; *(=impose)* imponer; *(=insist on)* insistir en; *(=make effective)* hacer cumplir; enforzar (US) **82**

enroll v. *(in school, in a course)* inscribir(se), matricular(se), enrolar(se) (US) **83**

enter v. *(=be admitted to)* ingresar en; *(=join)* incorporarse a; *(~ a field or profession)* meterse en; *(~ a contest)* inscribir(se) en, participar en; entrar en (US) **84**

enter button n. *(on keyboard)* tecla de retorno, énter (US) **83**

estimate n. *(=approximate calculation)* cálculo aproximativo; *(=approximate cost)* presupuesto; estimado (US) **92**

estimate v. *(=calculate)* calcular, *(=do a budget)* hacer el presupuesto, estimar (US) **93**

evaluation n. *(=calculation)* cálculo; *(=appraisal of value)* valoración, valorización; evaluación (US) **94**

evidence n. *(=proof)* prueba; *(=signs)* indicios; *(=example)* muestra, ejemplo; evidencia (US) **95**

excited adj. *(=enthusiastic)* muy contento, entusiasmado; **get excited** *(=become emotional)* emocionarse; *(=become happy)* entusiasmarse, ponerse contento; *(=become ner-*

vous) ponerse nervioso; excitarse (US) **96**

exciting adj. *(=emotional)* emocionante; *(=passionate)* apasionante; *(=fascinating)* fascinante; excitante (US) **96**

excuse v. *(=pardon)* disculpar, excusar (US); **excuse me** *(when asking permission)* con permiso; *(to get someone's attention)* por favor; excúseme (US) **97**

exit n. salida, éxito (US) **98**

experience v. *(~ problems)* tener, pasar por; *(~ pain, loss, hardship)* sentir, sufrir, pasar; experimentar (US) **98**

expire v. *(=end, conclude)* terminar; *(=lapse)* caducarse, vencerse; expirar / expirarse (US) **99**

express adj. *(=fast)* rápido; *(=urgent)* urgente; express / exprés* (US) **99**

fabric n. *(=cloth)* tela, tejido, fábrica (US) **100**

facilities n. *(=services)* servicios, facilidades (US) **101**

facility n. *(=building, center)* centro; *(=equipment)* equipo; *(=plant)* planta; *(=prison)* prisión, cárcel; *(for sports, recreation)* instalación; facilidad (US) **101**

factory n. fábrica, factoría* (US) **101**

faculty n. *(=teaching staff)* profesorado, facultad (US) **102**

fail v. *(~ exam, course)* suspender; *(=not succeed, fall apart)* fracasar; *(fail to fulfill obligation)* no cumplir con, faltar a; *(fail to do something)* dejar de; fallar (US) **102**

familiar adj. *(with facts)* enterado; *(=well-known)* conocido; familiar (US) **104**

fault n. *(=blame)* culpa; *(=weakness)* defecto; falta (US) **103**

fault v. *(=blame, criticize)* echar la culpa, criticar, faltar (US) **104**

fax v. enviar / mandar por fax; faxear* (US) **105**

feedback n. *(=reaction)* reacción; *(=information)* información; feedback (US) **105**

ferry n. transbordador, ferry* (US) **106**

fifty-fifty adj. (=doubtful, uncertain) incierto, inseguro, inestable; (=split, even, shared) compartido, a medias; (=fifty per cent) a cincuenta por ciento; fifty-fifty (US) **106**

figure n. (=number) cifra; (=statistic) estadística, dato; (physique) tipo, físico; figura (US) **106**

file n. (=folder) carpeta; (=dossier, records) expediente; (computer file) fichero, archivo; file / fail (US) **107**

film n. (=movie) película, filme* (US) **108**

film v. (=photograph) fotografiar; (film a movie) rodar; filmar (US) **108**

flash n. (camera) flash; (flash of light) destello de luz; (news flash) noticia de última hora; flash* (US) **108**

flashback n. (in film or narrative) flashback; (=memory of past event) recuerdo; flashback* (US) **108**

flashlight n linterna, flashlight (US) **109**

flip out v. (under the effect of drugs) drogarse; (=lose one's temper) ponerse furioso; (=lose one's mind) volverse loco; fliparse* / flipearse (US) **109**

flirt v. (=behave amorously) coquetear; (=challenge) jugar con; (=consider, think about) acariciar, jugar con; flirtear* (US) **110**

flirtation n. coqueteo, flirteo* (US) **110**

floppy disk n. disco flexible, disquete* / floppy (US) **110**

folder n. carpeta, fólder* (US) **111**

foreign adj. (=external, international) exterior, internacional, extranjero (US) **100**

forgive v. (=pardon) perdonar, excusar (US) **97**

form n. (=document) documento; (form to be filled) hoja, formulario, planilla; forma (US) **111**

formal adj. (dress, event) de etiqueta, de gala; (=official) oficial; (=in writing) por escrito; formal (US) **112**

format v. (text, disk) darle forma, formatear* (US) **112**

frankfurter n. salchicha, perro caliente* / frankfurter (US) **113**, **188**

fraternity n. (student association) círculo estudiantil; (union, organization) hermandad; fraternidad (US) **113**

freeze v. [trans] congelar; [intrans] morirse de frío, congelarse; frisar / frisarse (US) **113**

freezer n. congelador, fríser (US) **113**

full adj. (from eating) harto; (=entire) entero; lleno (US) **146**

full house id. (sold out performance) estar completo, estar lleno (US) **147**

full-time adj. a tiempo completo, full time* (US) **114**

furniture n. mueble, furnitura (US) **114**

gain v. (=increase) aumentar, subir; (=benefit) beneficiar, sacar provecho; ganar (US); **gain friends** hacerse amigos, ganarse amigos (US); **gain weight** engordar, aumentar de peso, ganar peso (US) **115**

game n. (=sport) deporte; (=match) partido; (=card game, round) partida; juego (US) **137**

gang n. banda, pandilla, gang* / ganga (US) **23**, **115**

gap n. (=distance, separation) distancia, separación; (=vaccum) hueco, vacío; gap* (US) **116**

gas station n. gasolinera, gasetería (US) **117**

gay adj/n. (homosexual) homosexual, gay* (US) **118**

give back v. devolver, dar para atrás (US) **15**

go back v. regresar, volver, ir para atrás (US) **15**

goal n. (=aim, objective) meta, objetivo, gol (US) **118**

grade n. (=mark, score) calificación, nota; (=school year) año, curso; (=quality) calidad; grado (US) **118**

graduate v. (from school) recibir el título / diploma, graduarse* (US) **120**

graduation n. (ceremony) entrega de títulos, graduación (US) **119**

grill n. (utensil) parrilla; (restaurant) restaurante; grill* (US) **120**

grocery n. (food) comestible; (grocery store) tienda de comestibles; bodega / grocería (US) **120**

grow v. (=cultivate) cultivar; (grow hair, beard) dejarse crecer el pelo, la barba; crecer / crecerse (US) **61**

habit n. (=customary behavior) costumbre, hábito* (US) **121**

hallway n. pasillo, corredor, hall (US) **123**

hamburger n. hamburguesa* / hamburger (US) **123**

handicap n. (=physical incapacity) discapacidad, minusvalía, (=disadvantage) desventaja, hándicap*; hándicap (US) **124**

handicapped adj. discapacitado, minusválido, deshabilitado (US) **69**

hardware n. (=tools and supplies) herramienta; (computer) hardware*; **hardware store** ferretería; hardware / tienda de hardware (US) **124**

hear v. (=find out) oír decir, enterarse de; (=receive news) tener noticias, saber; (=understand) entender; oír (US) **173**

help v. [+ verb] (~ to do something) ayudar a, asistir a (US) **13**

hesitate v. (=be apprehensive) vacilar; (=think, ponder) pensarlo; (=pause, stutter) titubear; hesitar (US) **125**

hit n. (=blow, stroke) golpe; (=success) éxito; hit / jit (US) **125**

hobby n. pasatiempo, afición, hobby* (US) **125**

hot adj. (=spicy) picante, caliente (US); **be / feel hot** (weather) hacer calor, tener calor, estar caliente (US) **34**

hot dog n. salchicha, perro caliente* / hot dog / frankfurter (US) **113**, **188**

humorous adj. *(person)* gracioso, chistoso; *(story, joke, movie)* cómico, divertido; humorístico (US) **126**

idiom n *(=phrase, expression)* giro, modismo; *(=lingo)* lenguaje, habla; idioma (US) **126**

ignition n. *(automobile)* arranque, encendido, ignición (US) **127**

ignore v. *(=disregard)* no hacer caso; *(=omit, forget)* omitir, olvidar; ignorar (US) **127**

including prep. *(=together with)* incluido; *(=as well as, even)* incluso; *(=inclusive)* inclusive, incluyendo (US) **128**

income tax n. impuesto sobre la renta, income tax (US) **262**

infant adj. infantil, de infantes (US) **128**

infant n. *(=baby)* criatura, bebé, *(=newborn)* recién nacido; *(=small child)* nene, niño; infante (US) **128**

influence v. *(action, decision)* influir, influenciar (US) **129**

informal adj. *(=friendly)* de confianza; *(=unofficial)* no oficial; *(=colloquial)* familiar, coloquial; informal (US) **129**

initialize v. *(computer disk)* inicializar* (US) **130**

injury n. *(physical)* golpe, herida; *(emotional)* ofensa, agravio; injuria* (US) **130**

input n. *(=advice, help, opinion)* ayuda, consejo; *(=electrical connection)* enchufe, entrada; input (US) **130**

insensitive adj. *(person)* insensible; *(action, behavior)* falto de sensibilidad; insensitivo (US) **131**

inspect v. *(=examine)* examinar; *(=look over, look through)* revisar; *(inspect vehicle, building)* inspeccionar, inspectar (US) **131**

insulated adj. *(=protected)* protegido, insulado (US) **132**

intend to v. *(=mean to)* querer, tener la intención de; *(=plan to)* pensar; intentar (US) **132**

intended for adj. para, destinado a, intentado para (US) **132**

interface n. *(computer)* interfaz*, interface (US) **132**

interface v. *(computer)* conectar, interfacer (US) **132**

internet n. red, internet (US) **133**

interview n. entrevista / interviú* (US) **133**

interview v. entrevistar / interviuvar* (US) **133**

intoxicated adj. *(=drunk)* borracho, ebrio, intoxicado (US) **134**

introduce v. *(person to person)* presentar(se), introducir(se) (US) **134**

involve v. *(=implicate)* implicar, meter, involucrar; *(=concern)* concernir, tener que ver con; *(=entail, imply)* suponer; *(=require)* requerir; envolver (US) **85**

involved adj. *(=implicated)* implicado, involucrado, metido; *(=absorbed)* absorto; *(=complicated)* complicado; envuelto (US); **get involved** v. meterse, involucrarse, envolverse (US); **people involved** n. interesados involucrados, envueltos (US) **85, 86**

irrelevant adj. sin relación;. irrelevante (US); **be irrelevant** no venir al caso, ser irrelevante (US) **135**

isolated adj. aislado, insulado (US) **132**

janitor n. *(=repairman, caretaker)* conserje; *(=doorman)* portero; yanitor (US) **289**

jeans n. vaqueros, jeans / bluyins (US) **31, 135**

jeep n. vehículo todo terreno, jeep / yip (US) **135**

jersey n. *(=team shirt)* camisa, jersey* / yersi (US) **136**

jet lag n. desfase horario, jet lag (US) **136**

jockey n. jinete, yóquey* / yoqui* (US) **291**

jockey shorts n. calzones cortos, calzoncillos de yoqui (US) **291**

journey n. *(=trip)* viaje; *(=trajectory)* trayecto; jornada (US) **136**

jungle adj. selvático, de la jungla (US) **138**

jungle n. selva, jungla* (US) **138**

junkie n. *(=drug addict)* drogadicto; *(=lover, devoted fan)* adicto, fanático; yonqui (US) **290**

ketchup n. salsa de tomate, ketchup* (US) **139**

kit n. bolso, bolsa, juego, kit (US) **139**

knock out v. *(in boxing)* echar fuera de combate, noquear*; *(=render unconscious)* dejar sin sentido; *(=sedate, anesthesize)* drogar, anestesiar; noquear (US) **168**

knocked out adj. *(in boxing)* fuera de combate, noqueado* (US) **168**

landlord n. *(=property owner)* dueño, propietario; *(=manager)* encargado, gerente; landlord (US) **140**

language n. *(national)* idioma, lengua, lenguaje (US) **142**

laptop n. *(computer)* ordenador portátil, computadora portátil, laptop (US) **140**

laser n. rayo, láser* (US) **141**

late adj. *(=delayed)* atrasado, de retraso; *(=advanced)* avanzado; *(=deceased)* difunto; *(=in the final years)* al final; *(=late within a time period)* a última hora, a finales de; tarde (US) **261**

layoff n. *(act)* despido; *(period)* paro, baja; layoff / leyó (US) **141**

leader n. *(=head of state)* jefe de estado; *(=head of team)* jefe de equipo; *(=first, best)* primero, mejor; líder* (US) **143**

lease n. contrato, lease (US) **141**

leasing n. *(=option to buy)* arrendamiento, leasing* (US) **141**

leave v. *(=go away)* irse, marcharse; *(leave a place)* salir de, *(=abandon)* abandonar; *(=quit)* dejar, renunciar; dejar / salir (de) (US) **66, 236**

lecture n. *(=class)* clase; *(=formal presentation)* conferencia; *(=informal presentation)* charla, discusión; *(=sermon, lesson)* sermón, lección; lectura (US) **142**

let v. *(=allow)* permitir, dejar (US); **let someone know** *(idiom)* avisar, hacer saber, dejar saber (US) **66**

library n. bilbioteca, librería (US) **143**

light adj. (=soft) suave, ligero; (low-calorie) bajo en calorías; (low-tar) de bajo contenido en alquitrán; light* (US) **144**

light n. (=traffic light) semáforo; (for cigarette) fuego; luz (US) **149**

lighting n. iluminación, luz (US) **149**

line n. (=drawn line, underline) raya; (=family, heritage) familia, linaje; (=row of people) cola, fila; (=row of objects) fila; (=wrinkle) arruga; línea (US); **wait on line** hacer cola; esperar en línea (US) **144**

link n. (=association) lazo, vínculo; (to website) enlace; link (US) **145**

lipstick n. lápiz de labios, lipstick (US); **put on lipstick** pintarse los labios, ponerse lipstick (US) **146**

living room n. sala, sala de estar, living* / living room (US) **146**

lobby n. (=ground floor) planta baja, primer piso; (=vestibule, foyer) vestíbulo; hall* / lobby* (US) **123, 147**

locating n. (act of finding) localización, locación (US) **148**

location n. (=place, site) lugar, sitio; (=placement) ubicación; (=position) posición; locación (US) **148**

look n. (=appearance) aspecto, aire; (=fashion, style) moda, estilo, look* (US) **149**

look for v. buscar, buscar por (US) **197**

lose v. perder; (=confuse) confundir, perder (US); **lose weight** adelgazar, bajar de peso, perder peso (US) **185**

lost adj. perdido; **be lost** (=be missing) estar perdido, faltar (US) **104**

lottery n. lotería, lotto (US); (lottery ticket) boleto / billete de lotería, tique de lotto (US) **269**

luggage n. equipaje, bagaje (US) **20**

lunch n. (food, meal) almuerzo, lunch* / lonche (US); **eat lunch** almorzar, lonchar / comer lunch (US) **148**

luncheon n. almuerzo, lunch* / lonche (US) **148**

luncheonette n. café, mostrador, lonchería (US) **148**

macho adj. (=chauvinist) machista, macho (US) **151**

magazine n. (publication) revista, magacín* (US); (TV program format) programa de temas diversos, de tipo magacín* (US) **151**

major adj. (=very important) de mayor importancia, fundamental; (=main, principal) principal, de mayor interés; mayor (US); **major league** (in sports) grande liga, liga mayor (US) **156**

major n. (=main academic discipline) concentración, especialización; (=student who specializes) estudiante del programa; major (US) **151**

major v. (=specialize in a subject) especializarse, hacer el major (US) **151**

make v. hacer, causar, crear, etc.; (make a decision) tomar una decisión, hacer una decisión (US); (make a mistake) equivocarse, hacer una falta (US); (make trouble) causar problemas, hacer problemas (US); (make a difference) influir, tener impacto, hacer una diferencia (US) **122**

mall n. (=shopping mall) centro comercial; (=pedestrian mall) calle peatonal; mall / mol (US) **152**

manager n. (of firm, bank) director; (of hotel, sales) gerente; (of restaurant, store) encargado; (of finances) administrador; (=performer's agent) representante; mánager (US) **152**

manners n. (=behavior) modales, maneras* (US) **153**

map n. (world, country) mapa; (street, city, subway map) plano, mapa (US) **153**

market n. (=food store) mercado; (stock market) bolsa de valores; (=demand) demanda; marqueta (US) **154**

marketing n. (=selling, advertising) venta, comercialización; (academic subject) mercadotecnia; márketing* (US) **154**

mascara n. rímel, máscara de pestañas*, mascara (US) **154**

master n. (=master copy, original) original, máster (US); **Master** (academic program) programa de maestría, programa de máster* (US); (degree) título de maestría, máster* (US) **155**

match v. (=correspond) corresponder, coincidir; (=equal) igualar; (=find pairs) emparejar; (=go together) hacer juego, combinar bien, machear (US) **150**

material n. (=cloth) tela, tejido; (=potential) madera; (raw material) materia prima; material (US) **155**

mayor n. alcalde, mayor (US) **156**

meeting n. (business ~) reunión; (arranged ~) cita, compromiso; (accidental ~) encuentro; (=session) sesión; mítin* (US) **160**

microwave n. (oven) horno microondas, microwave (US) **157**

minor adj. (=not serious) leve, poco grave; (=unimportant) insignificante, de poca importancia; (=secondary) secundario; menor (US) **157**

minor n. (secondary academic subject) concentración secundaria, menor / minor (US) **157**

minority n. (=small portion) minoría; (=ethnic group) minoría étnica; minoridad (US) **158**

miserable adj. (=very sad) muy triste, deprimido, abatido; (=troublesome, difficult) infeliz, desdichado, deprimente; (=unpleasant) desagradable, muy malo, fatal; (=wretched, squalid) mísero, en la miseria; (=complete, fig) rotundo, completo, total; miserable (US) **158**

miss n. (=young woman) señorita, miss (US) **159**

miss v. (=feel the absence of) extrañar, echar de menos, faltar (US) **104**

missing adj. perdido; **be missing** (=be lost) estar perdido, faltar (US) **104**

modem n. módem* (US) **160**

molest v. *(sexually)* abusar de, molestar (US) **161**

money n. dinero, plata / chavos (coloc) / moneda (US) **161**

money order n. giro bancario, giro postal, money order (US) **161**

mop n. fregona, trapeador (LatAm), mopa* (US) **162**

mop v. fregar, trapear (LatAm), mopear (US) **162**

mouse n. *(computer)* ratón, mouse / maus (US) **162**

move n. *(in a game)* jugada; *(=turn)* turno; *(=step, action)* paso; *(decision)* decisión; *(=job relocation)* traslado; movimiento (US) **164**

move v. *(=transport)* transportar, trasladar; *(=relocate)* mudar(se); *(=convince)* convencer; *(=propose)* proponer; *(=affect emotionally)* conmover, emocionar; *(~ to tears)* hacer llorar; *(=sell merchandise)* vender, liquidar; *(=travel, flow)* ir, circular; *(=take steps)* tomar medidas; mover / moverse (US) **163**

moving n. *(=relocation)* mudanza, movimiento (US) **164**

muffin n. magdalena, muffin / mofin (US) **165**

muffler n. *(automobile)* silenciador, mufler / mofle (US) **165**

multimedia adj. multimedia* (US) **166**

name n. *(=last name)* apellido; *(=title)* título; nombre (US); **my name is...** me llamo, mi nombre es... (US) **167**

native adj. *(native country, soil)* patria, país natal, país nativo (US); *(native language)* lengua materna, lengua nativa (US); *(native of)* natural de, nacido en, nativo de (US) **166**

nightclub n. discoteca, club nocturno, nightclub (US) **167**

note n. *(=musical note)* nota; *(=key on an instrument)* tecla; *(=banknote)* billete; **notes** *(=written information)* apuntes; nota / notas (US) **169**

notice n. *(=announcement)* anuncio; *(=warning)* aviso; *(=sign, poster)* letrero, cartel; *(=intention to quit)* renuncia; *(=intention to dismiss)* despedida; noticia (US) **170**

nullify v. anular, invalidar, nulificar (US) **171**

nurse n. *(medical)* enfermera, norsa (US) **169**

nylon n. nailon* / nilón* (US) **166**

obnoxious adj. *(=annoying, unpleasant)* desagradable; *(=offensive)* ofensivo; *(=repulsive)* repugnante; obnoxio (US) **171**

occult n. ocultismo, oculto (US) **172**

offense n. *(=crime, infraction)* delito; *(in sports)* falta; ofensa (US) **172**

OK adj/excl. *(=fine, all right, yes)* sí, vale, está bien; *(=well)* bueno, pues; *(=stop, that's enough)* ya, basta, está bien; *(=in good health)* bien; *(=not bad, acceptable)* regular; *(=no harm done)* tranquilo, ningún problema; okey (US) **174**

okay adj/excl. see **OK**

online adj. *(=long-distance)* a distancia; *(=connected)* conectado; en línea / online (US) **175**

online adv. por la red, por internet / online (US) **175**

open adj. *(=available, vacant)* vacante, abierto (US) **1**

opposite adj/adv/prep. *(=contrary)* contrario; *(=opposing)* opuesto; *(=facing)* enfrente; opósito (US) **175**

order v. *(=request)* pedir, encargar; *(=have made)* mandar a hacer; ordenar (US) **176**

ordinary adj. *(=average, unremarkable)* común y corriente; *(=normal, usual)* normal, corriente; ordinario (US) **176**

output n. *(=production)* producción; *(=processed information)* datos, información; output* (US) **177**

overbooking n. exceso de reservas, overbooking* (US) **177**

pancake n. tortita, panqueque / panquei (US) **178**

panic v. [trans] asustar, provocar el pánico; [intrans] asustarse, dejarse llevar por el pánico; paniquear / paniquearse (US) **177**

panties n. bragas (Sp), calzones (Lat Am), pantis (US) **178**

paper n. *(=newspaper)* periódico, diario; *(=essay)* ensayo; *(=article)* artículo; *(=term paper)* monografía; papel (US) **178**

paperback n. edición rústica, paperback (US) **179**

parent adj. *(=central)* central, matriz, pariente (US); n. *(=mother or father)* madre, padre, pariente **179**

park v. *(~ vehicle)* estacionar, aparcar, parquear* (US); *(=place, sit)* colocar(se), instalar(se), parquear(se) (US) **180**

parking n. estacionamiento, aparcamiento, párking / parqueo* (US); **parking lot** playa de estacionamiento; párking / parqueo* (US) **180**

part n. *(mechanical)* pieza; *(=role)* papel, rol*; *(in hair)* raya; parte (US); *(the best ~)* lo mejor, la mejor parte (US); *(the worst ~)* lo peor, la peor parte (US) **181**

part v. *(=separate)* separar(se), partir (US); *(=open)* abrir(se), partir(se) (US); **part with** *(=let go of)* soltar, desprenderse de, partir con (US) **182**

part-time adj. a tiempo parcial, de jornada reducida, part-time (US) **183**

party n. *(=celebration)* fiesta, party (US) **183**

pass v. *(course, exam, law)* aprobar, pasar **183**

patron n. *(=sponsor, benefactor)* patrocinador; *(=customer)* cliente; patrón (US) **184**

penalty n. *(=additional charge)* recargo; *(=fine)* multa, penalti (US) **184**

perform v. *(=put on a play, show)* representar; *(=act in play or movie)* actuar; *(=sing, dance)* interpretar;

(=carry out) realizar, llevar a cabo; performar (US) **186**

performance n. *(=show, presentation)* función, representación; *(=acting, singing, etc.)* actuación, interpretación; *(=outcome, result)* resultado; *(of vehicle)* rendimiento; performance (US) **185**

permission n. permiso, permisión (US) **187**

picnic n. comida campestre, picnic (US) **189**

pin n. *(=insignia)* insignia, pin* (US); *(=safety pin)* imperdible, seguro, pin de seguridad (US); **PIN** *(personal ID number)* NPI, número personal de identificación, PIN (US) **189**

plan n. *(=diagram, map)* plano; *(=schedule, itinerary)* programa, itinerario; plan (US) **190**

plan v. *(=organize)* organizar; *(=think ahead, intend)* pensar, preparar; planear* (US) **190**

plant v. *(seeds, a field)* sembrar; *(=bomb, evidence)* poner, colocar; plantar* (US) **191**

play v. *(an instrument)* tocar; *(=show)* dar, pasar; *(=sound)* sonar, jugar (US); *(=pretend to be)* hacerse el, jugar a (US); *(play a role)* hacer el papel, jugar el rol (US) **138**

playboy n. libertino, mujeriego, playboy (US) **191**

poker n. póquer* / póker (US) **197**

polyester n. poliéster* (US) **193**

pony n. potro, pony* / poni (US) **196**

pop adj. *(artistic trend)* popular; *(consumer-based)* de consumo; pop* (US) **196**

population n. población, población (US); adj. demográfico, de población (US) **197**

porch n. *(=open porch)* portal, terraza, porche (US) **198**

portable adj. portátil, portable (US) **198**

position n. *(=post, job)* puesto; *(=circumstance, situation)* condición, situación; *(=opinion)* postura; posición (US) **198**

poster n. *(decorative)* cartel, afiche; *(=large sign)* letrero; póster* (US) **199**

power n. *(=capacity, ability)* capacidad; *(=physical strength, forcefulness)* fuerza; *(=powerful entity)* potencia; *(of engine, machine)* potencia, fuerza; *(=energy source)* energía; *(=mental faculty)* facultad; poder (US) **192**

prescription n. *(medical)* receta, prescripción (US) **199**

present n. *(=gift)* regalo, presente* (US) **200**

preservative n. *(in food)* conservante, preservativo (US) **201**

preserve v. *(=maintain)* mantener; *(=perpetuate)* conservar; *(=keep from decay)* conservar; preservar (US) **200**

press v. *(=exert physical pressure)* apretar; *(=push)* apretar, tocar; *(=urge, insist)* exigir, insistir en; presionar* (US) **202**

pressure v. *(=force, coerce)* insistir en, presionar (US) **202**

presume v. *(=suppose)* suponer, presumir (US) **202**

pretend v. *(=feign, make believe)* fingir, hacerse, pretender (US) **203**

principal n. *(school director)* director, rector, principal (US) **203**

print v. *(text, photo)* imprimir; *(money)* emitir; *(=write in block letters)* escribir en letra de molde; printear (US) **204**

printer n. *(computer)* impresora, prínter (US) **204**

privacy n. *(=intimacy)* intimidad; *(=solitude, seclusion)* soledad, privacidad (US) **204**

private adj. *(=personal, one-on-one)* personal; *(=confidential)* particular; *(=reserved)* reservado; privado (US) **205**

prospect n. *(=candidate)* candidato; *(=possibility)* posibilidad; prospecto (US) **207**

prove v. *(=demonstrate)* demostrar; *(=verify)* comprobar; *(=turn out)* resultar; probar (US) **206**

provide v. *(=supply)* proporcionar; *(a service)* prestar; *(an opportunity)* brindar; *(=stipulate)* estipular, disponer; proveer* / providear (US) **208**

provider n. *(=caretaker)* que se ocupa, providor / proveedor (US) **207**

publisher n. *(firm)* casa editorial; *(person)* editor; publicador (US) **208**

pudding n. *(flavored)* natilla, pudín (US); *(rice pudding)* arroz con leche; pudín de arroz (US) **209**

pump n. *(air, water)* bomba; *(gas)* surtidor; pompa (US) **193**

punch n. *(=blow, hit)* puñetazo, ponchazo (US); *(=mixed drink)* bebida, jugo, ponche* (US) **194, 195**

punch v. *(a ticket)* picar; *(holes)* hacer agujeros; *(=hit with fist)* dar un puñetazo, ponchar (US) **194**

puncture n. pinchazo, ponchazo (US) **194**

puncture v. pinchar, ponchar (US) **194**

put v. *(=express)* expresar, poner (US); **put in** meter, poner dentro (US); **put into** *(=spend, invest)* invertir, gastar, poner (US); **put outside** sacar, poner fuera (US); **put the blame** echar la culpa, poner la culpa (US) **195**

puzzle n. rompecabezas, puzzle* (US) **209**

qualification n. *(=ability)* capacidad, aptitud; *(=requisite)* requisito; *(=title, diploma)* diploma, título; calificación (US) **35**

qualify v. *(=possess ability)* tener capacidades; *(=meet requirements, criteria)* satisfacer / cumplir con los requisitos; *(=have the credentials)* tener título / licencia; *(=be eligible)* tener derecho a; *(=be considered)* considerarse; *(=count as)* contar; calificar / cualificar (US) **36, 62**

quality n. *(=condition, standard)* calidad; *(=merit, worth)* calidad; cualidad (US) **61**

question n. *(=inquiry)* pregunta; *(=doubt)* duda; cuestión (US) **62**

racketeer n. estafador, raquetero (US) **210**

racketeer v. hacer chantaje, raquetear (US) **210**

rare adj. *(=uncommon)* poco común; *(=infrequent)* infrecuente; *(=unique)* singular; *(=exceptional)* excepcional; *(=undercooked)* medio crudo, poco hecho; raro (US) **210**

realistic adj. *(=pragmatic)* realista; *(=reasonable)* razonable; *(=lifelike)* natural, vivo; realístico (US) **211**

realize v. *(=become aware of)* darse cuenta de; *(=know, understand)* saber; realizar (US) **212**

receipt n. recibo, receta / tique* (US) **212, 269**

recollect v. *(=remember)* recordar, recolectar (US) **213**

recollection n. *(=memory)* recuerdo, recolección (US) **213**

record n. *(in sports)* récord* (US) **213**

record v. *(=document)* documentar; *(=tape)* grabar; recordar (US) **214**

refuse v. *(=decline)* rechazar, no aceptar; *(=not grant)* negar, denegar; *(=refuse to do)* no querer, negarse a; refusar (US) **214**

register v. *(=sign up, enroll in a class)* inscribir(se), matricular(se); *(to vote)* inscribirse; *(mail)* certificar, recomendar; *(luggage)* facturar; *(=indicate, show)* marcar, indicar; *(=be understood)* entenderse; *(~ a complaint)* presentar una queja; registrar, registrarse (US) **215**

registration n. *(for school, to vote)* inscripción; *(=enrollment)* matrícula; *(automobile)* matriculación; registración (US) **215**

regular adj. *(=normal)* normal; *(=ordinary)* corriente; *(=habitual)* habitual; *(=usual)* acostumbrado; *(=frequent)* frecuente; *(=permanent)* permanente; regular (US) **217**

regulation n. *(=rule, law)* reglamento, ley; adj. *(=normal, usual)* norma; regulación (US) **217**

relate v. *(=get along with)* llevarse bien con; *(=identify with)* identificarse con, sentir; *(=understand)* entender; relatar a / con (US) **219**

related adj. *(=having to do with)* relacionado, relatado (US) **219**

relative n. *(=family member)* pariente, familiar, relativo (US) **219**

relax adj. *(=rest)* descansar; *(=calm down)* calmarse; *(=stop worrying)* tranquilizarse; relajar(se) (US) **218**

relaxation n. *(=rest)* descanso, relajamiento* / relax* / relaxeo (US) **220**

relevant adj. *(=pertinent)* pertinente; *(=related)* relacionado; relevante (US) **221**

remark n. *(=comment)* comentario, remarca (US) **221**

remark v. *(=say, point out)* comentar, decir; *(=notice, observe)* observar, notar; remarcar (US) **221**

remarkable adj. *(=notable)* extraordinario; excepcional; *(=surprising)* sorprendente, increíble; remarcable (US) **221**

remember v. recordar, remembrar (US) **222**

remove v. quitar; *(=fire, dismiss)* despedir; remover (US) **223**

rent n. alquiler, renta (US) **223**

rent v. alquilar, rentar (US) **223**

report n. *(=news story)* reportaje; *(=piece of news)* noticia; *(=gossip, rumor)* rumor; *(=school assignment)* informe; *(=bulletin, notification)* boletín; reporte (US) **225**

report v. *(=inform, make known)* informar; *(=be a reporter)* ser reportero; *(=notify authorities)* declarar, dar parte de; *(=denounce)* denunciar; *(=allege, rumor)* decir, contar; *(=show up, turn up)* presentarse; *(=be responsible to)* estar bajo el mando de; reportar (US) **224**

reporter n. *(on radio, TV)* reportero; *(newspaper)* periodista, reportero; repórter* / reportero* (US) **226**

require v. *(=demand, request)* exigir; *(=need)* necesitar; requerir (US) **226**

required adj. *(=necessary)* necesario; *(=obligatory, compulsory)* obligatorio; *(=fixed, established)* establecido; requerido (US) **226**

resign v. *(=quit)* renunciar, dimitir, resignar (US) **227**

resignation n. *(=act of quitting)* renuncia, dimisión, resignación (US) **227**

respect n. *(=admiration, consideration)* respeto; *(=detail, aspect)* sentido, aspecto; **respects** *(=greetings)* saludos, recuerdos, respeto(s) (US) **228**

resumé n. *(=curriculum vitae)* hoja de vida, currículum, resumen (US) **229**

retire v. *(from work)* jubilarse, retirarse (US) **229**

retirement n. jubilación, retiro (US) **230**

return v. *(=give / bring back)* devolver, volver / regresar (US) **286**

review v. *(=study, analyze)* estudiar, analizar; *(=critique book or film)* reseñar; *(for an exam)* repasar, estudiar; revisar (US) **230**

revival n. *(=of ideas, values, customs)* renacimiento, resurgimiento; *(theater)* reposición; revival (US) **231**

revolve v. *(=rotate, spin)* girar; *(=have to do with, focus on)* centrarse en, girar en torno a; revolver (US) **231**

rewind v. rebobinar, rewind (US); **rewind button** botón de retroceso; rewind (US) **232**

roast beef n. carne asada, rosbif* (US) **235**

robot n. máquina, robot* (US) **232**

role n. papel, rol* (US) **233**

rookie n. *(in sports)* principiante, debutante; *(police, armed forces)* novato, bisoño, principiante; rookie (US) **234**

roster n. *(=class list)* lista de asistencia; *(=team players)* registro oficial; róster (US) **235**

rude adj. *(=impolite)* maleducado, descortés; *(=indecent)* obsceno, grosero; rudo (US) **235**

rug n. alfombra, carpeta (US); *(area rug)* tapete, moquera, carpeta (US) **38**

salary n. sueldo, salario (US) **236**

sane adj. *(person)* cuerdo, racional; *(behavior)* sensato, normal, racional; sano (US) **239**

sanitation n. *(=hygiene)* higiene; *(=garbage collection)* recogida de basuras, saneamiento; sanitación (US) **238**

save v. *(=conserve)* conservar; *(=keep, put aside)* guardar; *(=not spend, not waste)* ahorrar; *(=make a stop)* parar; *(save data on computer)* archivar; salvar (US) **237**

say v. *(=indicate, represent)* indicar, representar, decir (US) **64**

scanner n. escáner* / scanner (US) **87**

scooter n. escúter* / scooter (US) **87**

sedan n. sedán* (US) **239**

select v. seleccionar, escoger, selectar (US) **240**

self-service adj. autoservicio, self-service* (US) **240**

sensible adj. *(person)* sensato, prudente, juicioso; *(idea, decision)* razonable, lógico, *(=practical)* práctico; sensible (US) **240**

sensitive adj. *(=emotional)* sensible; *(=delicate, fragile)* delicado; *(=susceptible, easily hurt)* susceptible; *(=confidential)* confidencial; *(=sore, painful)* sensible, delicado; sensitivo (US) **241**

sentence n. *(=group of words)* oración, frase, sentencia (US) **242**

serious adj. *(=grave, critical)* grave; *(=sincere)* sincero; serio (US); **be serious** *(be sincere)* hablar en serio, estar serio (US) **242**

seriously adv. *(=gravely)* gravemente; *(=in earnest)* en serio; seriamente (US) **242**

set n. *(=matching series)* juego; *(=bundle, series)* serie; *(=stage, setting)* escenario, plató; set * (US); *(TV set)* televisor; set de televisión (US) **243**

sexy adj. sexy* (US) **244**

shock n. *(=surprise)* sorpresa; *(=scare, fright)* susto; *(=strong impression)* impresión; *(medical condition)* postración nerviosa; *(=electrical discharge)* descarga, calambre; choque / shock (US) **47**

shoot v. *(a film)* rodar, filmar* (US) **108**

shopping n. compras, shopping (US); *(go shopping)* ir de compras, hacer shopping (US); **shopping center** centro comercial; shopping center (US) **244**

short adj. *(in height)* bajo; *(in quantity)* falto, escaso; corto (US); *(short memory)* mala memoria, memoria corta (US); *(short for)* abreviado, corto para (US) **60**

shorts n. pantalones cortos, shorts* (US); *(jockey shorts)* calzones cortos, calzoncillos de yoqui (US) **244, 291**

show n. *(=spectacle)* espectáculo; *(=exhibition)* exhibición, exposición; *(=TV, radio program)* programa; show* (US) **245**

signature n. firma, signatura (US) **245**

significant adj. importante, significante (US); **significant other** n. pareja, significante (US) **246**

similarity n. *(=resemblance)* semejanza, parecido; *(=common trait)* rasgo común; similaridad (US) **246**

simple adj. sencillo, simple (US) **247**

slogan n. eslogan* / slogan (US) **87**

snack n. merienda, snack / esnac (US) **248**

sneakers n. zapatos de tenis, zapatos de lona, sníquers (US) **248**

snob adj./n. elitista, presumido, esnob* / snob (US) **88**

soda n. *(=soft drink)* refresco, gaseosa, soda (US) **248**

software n. *(computer)* programa, programación, software* (US) **249**

solicit v. *(=ask for, beg for)* pedir ayuda; *(=approach, proposition)* abordar; solicitar (US) **249**

sorority n. hermandad de mujeres, sororidad (US) **250**

sort v. *(=classify)* clasificar; *(=arrange)* ordenar; *(=separate)* separar; sortear (US) **251**

Spanglish n. espanglish / espanglés / spanglish (US) **88**

speech n. *(=brief address)* discurso, speech* (US) **251**

spend v. pasar, gastar, dedicar, etc. *(spend time)* pasar tiempo, gastar tiempo (US) **117**

sponsor n. patrocinador, espónsor* / sponsor (US) **89**

sponsor v. *(=support)* respaldar, apoyar; *(=fund)* patrocinar; *(=propose)* proponer; esponsorizar (US) **89**

sports, sporty adj. deportivo, de sport* (US) **252**

spray n. atomizador, spray* / esprey (US) **89**

spray v. rociar, espreyar (US) **89**

staff n. *(=personnel)* personal, empleados, *(of teachers)* maestros, profesorado; *(military)* estado mayor; staff (US) **252**

standard adj. normal, normativo, oficial, estándar* / standard (US) **90**

starter n. *(motor)* motor de arranque, estárter* / starter (US) **91**

state-of-the-art adj. moderno, de vanguardia, estado de arte (US) **90**

status n. *(=rank, prestige)* rango, importancia, estatus (US); *(legal status)* estado legal, estatus legal (US) **91**

steam n. *(=steam heat)* calefacción, steam / estim (US) **253**

stock n. *(=company share, security)* acción; *(=supply, inventory)* existencia; stock* (US); **stock market** bolsa de valores; marqueta (US) **154, 253**

stop n. *(=station, terminal)* parada; *(=stop button)* botón de apagado; *(stop sign)* señal de alto; *(=stopover)* escala; stop (US) **254**

stranger n. *(=unknown person)* desconocido; *(from another area)* forastero; extranjero (US) **100**

stress n. nervios, estrés* / stress (US) **93**

stress out v. [trans] poner a uno nervioso, estresar* a uno (US) **94**

stressed adj. agobiado, estresado* (US) **93**

stressful adj. agitado, estresante* (US) **93**

stripper n. persona que hace striptease, stripper (US) **254**

striptease n. baile al desnudo, striptease* (US) **254**

stroke n. (=hit, swing) golpe; (medical condition) derrame cerebral; estroc / estroque (US) **94**

stub n. (=transfer ticket) boleto / tique de empalme; tránsfer (US) **276**

subject n. (=topic, theme) tema; (=matter, issue) asunto; (=academic subject) materia, asignatura; (=subordinate) súbdito; sujeto (US) **257**

succeed v. (in general, life, career) tener éxito, triunfar; (=be able to) lograr, alcanzar, conseguir; (=yield desired result) salir bien, dar buen resultado; suceder (US) **255**

success n. éxito, suceso (US) **255**

suggestion n. (=recommendation) sugerencia; (=implication, insinuation) insinuación; (=indication, evidence) indicación, prueba; sugestión (US) **256**

summarize v. resumir, sumarizar (US) **257**

summary n. resumen, sumario (US) **257**

superintendent n. (=building caretaker) conserje, súper (US) **258**

superman n. superhombre / supermán (US) **258**

supermarket n. supermercado, supermarqueta (US) **154**

superwoman n. mujer muy capaz, supermujer (US) **258**

supply v. (=provide) proporcionar, facilitar, suministrar; (=carry, transport) llevar; suplir (US) **259**

support v. (financially) mantener, sostener; (emotionally, ideologically) apoyar; soportar (US) **250**

supposed to adj./v. (=expected to) obligado a; (per suggestion) deber; (by assumption) suponerse que; (estar) supuesto (US) **259**

sweater n. jersey, chompa (LatAm), suéter* (US) **256**

switch n. (=exchange, substitution) cambio; (electrical) interruptor; switch* (US) **260**

sympathy n. (=compassion) compasión, (=agreement, solidarity) solidaridad; (=condolence) pésame, condolencia; simpatía (US) **246**

take v. (=remove) llevarse, quitar; (=steal) llevarse, robar; (=grab, seize) coger, agarrar; (=select, buy) llevarse; (=carry, transport) llevar; (=accept) aceptar; (=have room for) llevar, caber; (=wear) usar, gastar; (=require) hacer falta, necesitar; (=delay) tardar, demorar; (=last) durar; (=endure) soportar, aguantar; (=assume to be) tener por; tomar (US) **271**

taken adj. (occupied) ocupado, tomado (US) **272**

tape n. cinta, tape (US); (adhesive) cinta adhesiva; (measuring) cinta métrica; (recording) casete, cinta de video; tape (US) **260, 284**

tax n. impuesto, tax (US) **262**

taxi driver n. taxista, conductor de taxi (US) **52**

teenager n. joven, adolescente, teenager (US) **263**

tell v. (=narrate, reveal) contar, decir (US); (can tell) saber, poder decir (US); (=distinguish) distinguir, decir la diferencia (US) **64**

temporary adj. condicional, provisional, pasajero, temporero* / temporario (US) **263**

tenant n. inquilino, teniente (US) **265**

test n. (=quiz, exam) examen; (=trial, experiment) prueba; (=analysis, study) análisis; test (US) **265**

thanksgiving n. acción de gracias, thanksgiving / sanguivin (US) **266**

ticket n. (for bus, train) boleto, billete; (for ship, plane) pasaje; (to an event) entrada; (=label, price tag) etiqueta; (lottery ticket) boleto / billete de lotería; (traffic ticket) infracción, multa; tique* (US) **269**

time n. (=moment, instant) momento; (=historical period) época; (=time of day) hora; (=time of year) temporada; tiempo (US); **take time** (=delay) tardar, demorarse, tomar tiempo (US); **have a good time** (=have fun) divertirse, pasarlo bien, tener un buen tiempo (US) **266**

tissue n. (=handkerchief) pañuelo de papel; (=decorative tissue) papel de seda; tissue / tisú (US) **270**

toilet n. (bathroom) baño, servicio, wáter; (fixture) retrete, inodoro; toilet (US) **270**

toner n. (for the skin) tonificante; (=ink) tinta; tóner =* (US) **273**

topic n. (=theme) tema; (=subject matter) asunto; tópico (US) **274**

topical adj. (=current) actual, corriente, tópico (US) **274**

touch base id. ponerse en contacto, tocar base (US) **24**

traffic light n. semáforo, luz de tráfico (US) **149**

train v. (=educate, develop) desarrollar, educar (US) **79**

transfer n. (=move, relocation) traslado; (~ of money) transferencia; (~ of property) traspaso; (from one vehicle to another) transbordo; (=transfer stub) boleto / tique de empalme; tránsfer (US) **275**

transportation n. transporte, transportación (US) **276**

treat v. (=offer to pay) invitar; tratar (US) **277**

treatment n. (of people) trato, tratamiento (US) **276**

truck driver n. camionero, conductor de camión (US) **52**

try v. (=attempt) intentar; (=sample, taste) probar; (=check, inquire) buscar en; (=put to the test) poner a prueba; (=prosecute, judge) procesar, enjuiciar; tratar (US) **277**

twist n. (=squeeze, small amount) un poquito, rizo (de limón), twist (US) **278**

type v. pasar / escribir a máquina, tipear / taipear (US) **268**

typographical error n. error tipográfico, errata, tipo / taipo (US) **268**

uneducated adj. *(=unschooled, uncultured)* inculto, mal educado (US) **78**

union n. *(=trade union)* sindicato; *(=club, society)* club, sociedad; unión (US) **279**

unique adj. *(=original)* singular, original; *(=exceptional)* excepcional, sin igual; *(=special)* especial; único (US) **279**

uniquely adv. *(=exclusively)* exclusivamente; *(=exceptionally)* excepcionalmente; únicamente (US) **279**

vacancy n. *(=available lodging)* habitación libre; *(=available job)* puesto vacante; vacancia (US) **280**

vacation n. vacaciones, vacancia / vacación (US) **280**

vacuum v. pasar la aspiradora, vaquiumear / vacunear (US) **280**

vacuum cleaner n. aspiradora, vacuum cleaner (US) **280**

valuable adj. *(=in monetary terms)* que tiene valor, que vale mucho; *(=useful)* valioso; valuable (US) **281**

valuable n. objeto de valor, valuable (US) **281**

VCR n. *(=video cassette recorder)* grabadora de video, videograbador, viciar / VCR (US) **281**

vegetable n. legumbre, verdura, vegetable / vegetal* (US) **281**

video n. vídeo (Sp), video (LatAm, US); **video cassette** casete de video, videocaset (US); **video library** videoteca (Sp), librería de videos (US); **video store** videoclub (Sp), tienda de videos (US); **videotape** cinta de video, videotape (US) **284**

violate v. *(trust)* abusar de; *(privacy, sanctity)* invadir; violar (US) **285**

violation n. *(traffic)* infracción, violación (US) **285**

waffle n. gofre, waffle (US) **286**

wait for v. esperar, esperar por (US) **197**

warm adj. *(=climate)* cálido, caliente (US); *(=affectionate)* cariñoso, caluroso (US); **to be warm** id. *(weather)* hacer calor, tener calor, estar caliente (US) **34**

waste v. *(time)* perder; *(money)* malgastar, derrochar; *(=food)* desperdiciar; *(talent, opportunity)* desaprovechar; gastar (US) **117**

wax n. cera, wax (US); *(wax paper)* papel encerado, papel de wax (US) **287**

wax v. encerar, waxear (US) **287**

way n. *(=style)* estilo; *(=aspect, respect)* sentido, aspecto; manera (US); *(have a way with)* saber manejar, llevarse bien, tener maneras con (US) **153**

website n. página web, website (US) **287**

weekend n. fin de semana, weekend / wikén (US) **288**

weight n. peso; **lose weight** adelgazar, bajar de peso, perder peso (US) **185**

welfare n. *(=services)* asistencia social; *(=funds)* cheque de asistencia social; *(=office)* oficina de asistencia social; welfare (US) **288**

whisky n. whisky* (US) **288**

window n. *(store window)* escaparate, vitrina; *(service window)* ventanilla, taquilla; *(in envelope)* ventanilla; ventana (US) **283**

work v. *(=function)* funcionar; *(=be effective)* dar resultado; *(=operate)* manejar, operar; *(=make someone work)* hacer trabajar; trabajar (US); **work on** *(=practice, study)* practicar; trabajar en (US) **274**

workshop n. taller, workshop (US) **289**

wrong adj. *(incorrect answer)* incorrecto, equivocado; **be morally wrong** estar mal, hacer mal, ser equivocado (US) **86**

Yankee adj./n. *(=American, US citizen)* norteamericano; *(=northerner)* norteño, yanqui* (US) **289**

yard n. *(=garden)* jardín; *(=courtyard)* patio; yarda (US) **290**

zombie n. *(=tired, bewildered)* atontado, zombi* (US) **291**

zoom n. *(=lens, action)* zum* / zoom (US) **291**